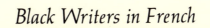

Black Writers in French

LILYAN KESTELOOT

Black Writers in French

A Literary History of Negritude

Translated by Ellen Conroy Kennedy

HOWARD UNIVERSITY PRESS
Washington, D.C.
1991

First published as *Les écrivains noirs de langue française: Naissance d'une littérature,* copyright 1963 by Editions de l'Institut de Sociologie de l'Université Libre de Bruxelles

First English translation edition © 1974 by Temple University Press

Howard University Press, Washington, D.C. 20008

Copyright © 1991 by Ellen Conroy Kennedy and Lilyan Kesteloot

International Standard Book Number: 0–88258–066–3

Manufactured in the United States of America

This book is printed on acid-free paper.

10   9   8   7   6   5   4   3   2   1

Library of Congress Cataloging-in-Publication Data

Kesteloot, Lilyan.
  [Ecrivains noirs de langue française. English]
Black writers in French : a literary history of negritude / Lilyan
  Kesteloot : translated by Ellen Conroy Kennedy.
p. cm.
  Translation of : Les écrivains noirs de langue française.
Reprint, with new pref. and supplementary bibliography. Originally
published: Philadelphia : Temple University Press, 1974.
  Includes bibliographical references and index.
ISBN 0-88258-066-3 (pbk.) : $19.95
1. French literature — Black authors — History and criticism.
2. Negritude (Literary movement) 3. Blacks in literature.
I. Title.
PQ3897.K3913   1991
840.9′896 — dc20   91-14178
                                                                CIP

ATHENEUM PUBLISHERS, INC.: Quotations from "A l'appel de la race de Saba," "Que m'accompagnent kôras et balafongs," "Le retour de l'enfant prodigue," "Le totem," "Nuit de Sine," "Femme noire," "Au Gouverneur Eboué," "Neige sur Paris," "Désespoir d'un volontaire libre," "Ndessé ou Blues," "Camp 1940," "Aux tirailleurs sénégalais morts pour la France," and "Prière aux masques," by Léopold Sédar Senghor are translated by special permission of Atheneum Publishers, Inc.

THE THIRD PRESS-JOSEPH OKPAKU PUBLISHING CO., INC.: Quotations from "Le message," "Joal," "Vacances," "Lettre à un prisonnier," "Au guelowar," "Prière de paix," "Tyaroye," and "Le Kaya-Magan," from *Poèmes* by L. S. Senghor, copyright © 1964 by Editions du Seuil, are translated by special permission of The Third Press-Joseph Okpaku Publishing Co., Inc., who hold an English translation copyright © 1974.
  Quotations from *Les armes miraculeuses* by Aimé Césaire, copyright © 1970 by Editions Gallimard, are translated by special permission of The Third Press-Joseph Okpaku Publishing Co., Inc., who hold an English translation copyright © 1974.
  Quotations from "Corps perdu" in *Cadastre* by Aimé Césaire, copyright © 1961 by Editions du Seuil, appear in English translation from "Disembodied," copyright © 1973 by The Third Press-Joseph Okpaku Publishing Co., Inc., by permission.

EDITIONS GALLIMARD: Quotations in French from *Les armes miraculeuses* by Aimé Césaire, © 1946 by Editions Gallimard, are reprinted and translated by permission of the publisher.

GEORGES BORCHARDT, INC.: Quotations in French from *Poèmes* by L. S. Senghor (Paris: Editions du Seuil, 1964) are reprinted by permission of Georges Borchardt, Inc.

Quotations in French from "Corps perdu" in *Cadastre* (Paris: Editions du Seuil, 1961) and from "Vampire liminaire" in *Ferrements* (Paris: Editions du Seuil, 1960), both by Aimé Césaire, are also reprinted by permission of Georges Borchardt, Inc.

PRESENCE AFRICAINE: Extracts from Aimé Césaire's *Cahier d'un retour au pays natal*, published by Présence Africaine (Paris) in 1956, are reprinted and translated by permission of the publisher.

Quotations in French from the édition définitive of L. G. Damas's *Pigments*, published by Présence Africaine (Paris) in 1962, are reprinted by permission. "Trêve," "Rappel," "S.O.S.," "Pour sûr," Savoir-vivre," Sur une carte postale," "Des billes pour la roulette," "Bientôt," "En file indienne," "Regard," and "Un clochard m'a demandé dix sous" from *Pigments* are translated by permission.

ELLEN CONROY KENNEDY: English translations of portions of sixteen other poems from Léon Damas's *Pigments*, "Obsession," "There Are Nights," "Sellout," "Hiccups," "Reality," "Blues," "The Black Man's Lament," "Whitewash," "If Often," "Shine," "Their Thing," "Et Cetera," "Position," "Like the Legend," "They Came That Night," and "Sleepless Night," copyright © 1972 by Ellen Conroy Kennedy, appear by permission of the translator.

LEON DAMAS: The excerpt from *Black-Label* (Paris: Gallimard, 1956) by Léon Damas is reprinted and translated by permission of the author.

ALFRED A. KNOPF, INC.: "I, Too," copyright 1926 by Alfred A. Knopf, Inc., and renewed 1954 by Langston Hughes, is reprinted from *Selected Poems* by Langston Hughes by permission of the publisher.

Lines from "Our Land" and from "Poem—For the Portrait of an African Boy," copyright 1926 by Alfred A. Knopf, Inc., and renewed 1954 by Langston Hughes, are reprinted from *The Weary Blues* by Langston Hughes by permission of the publisher.

HARCOURT BRACE JOVANOVICH, INC.: Excerpts from *Banjo* by Claude McKay are reprinted by permission of Harcourt Brace Jovanovich, Inc., copyright 1929 by Harper and Brothers, copyright 1967 by Hope McKay Virtue.

TWAYNE PUBLISHERS, INC.: Lines from "If We Must Die" and "The White House" in *Selected Poems of Claude McKay*, copyright 1953 by Bookman Associates, are reprinted with the permission of Twayne Publishers, Inc.

FARRAR, STRAUS & GIROUX, INC.: Passages from *The Big Sea* by Langston Hughes, copyright 1940 by Langston Hughes, are reprinted with the permission of Farrar, Straus & Giroux, Inc.

HARPER & ROW, PUBLISHERS, INC.: The poem "Incident" and lines from "Heritage," both copyright 1925 by Harper & Row, Publishers, Inc., renewed 1953 by Ida M. Cullen; and lines from "From the Dark Tower," copyright 1927 by Harper & Row, Publishers, Inc., renewed 1955 by Ida M. Cullen, are from *On These I Stand* by Countee Cullen and are reprinted by permission of the publisher.

Contents

Illustrations

Translator's Preface

In an enthusiastic review I contributed some years ago to *Comparative Literature Studies,* then published at the University of Maryland, I suggested the English-language edition of this book. The project appealed to a certain university press editor, who shepherded it through negotiations with the original publisher, and eventually commissioned me to undertake the translation.

Preparing an English-language edition, however, involved more than straight translation. The scholarly detective work it called for, in addition, turned out to be rewarding and engrossing in itself. The book could only be of maximum use to new readers, I felt, if it provided English-language sources for the documentation whenever possible. For chapters 4 and 5 this meant tracing the clues in Kesteloot's footnotes to their original American sources. It led to a fascinating day at the Library of Congress, first in the Archive of Folk Song and later searching through microfilms of little magazines of the 1930s. It also meant tracking down and matching passages from French translations (for example, of Claude McKay's novel *Banjo*) with their English originals, or identifying fragments, in their French translations, of Harlem Renaissance poetry and replacing them with the original English texts. Similarly, when quotations from, and references to, French works were available in English (the writings of Frantz Fanon, for instance), I sought them out and have included their publication facts and sources here. However remote or isolated our readers may be, they will now have ample tools for the further exploration of these literatures and of their manifold international cross-fertilization.

Readers with a more purely literary interest in the material, or interest in a particular poet, will be glad to know that, for aesthetic and stylistic reasons, all citations of the poetry in French are retained with my translations following only in brackets. Those well acquainted with French are thus left the pleasure of the original text and the possibility of dialogue with the translations. With the Parnassian-inspired poetry that illustrates chapter 2, a rather literal rendering of prose seemed advisable. On the other hand, with the poetry of Damas, Césaire, and Senghor, quoted in abundance throughout the rest of the volume, I attempted more—to re-create the verse in English. Many of these translations are included in more complete versions in *The Negritude Poets,* an anthology in translation I have edited for Viking Press and its paperback arm, Compass Books (New York, 1974).

For this new edition of Kesteloot's now classic study, minor editorial changes have been made in the chapter titles and chapter arrangements. Some cumbersome tables have been omitted from chapters 21 and 22, and an assortment of photographs has been added in their place. Omitted, too, are a preface by Professor Luc de Heusch of the Université Libre de Bruxelles and Madame Kesteloot's bibliography, both dated by a decade. They are replaced by my "Translator's Introduction" and by a "Selected Bibliography" compiled by Janet Mac-Gaffey. Kesteloot's related essay, "Problems of the Literary Critic in Africa," has been included as an appendix, to make it available to a wider audience than that of the Cameroonian cultural review, *Abbia,* where it appeared in an earlier version in 1965.

At a time when I was overwhelmed with other commitments, Madame Alice Jugie of Paris kindly undertook a draft translation of prose portions of the manuscript, which considerably shortened the preparation time and for which I am extremely grateful. Olwen Price, too, deserves many thanks for the intelligence and care with which she deciphered, typed, and retyped revisions of the manuscript. For their always generous and resourceful response to my numerous telephone calls, the reference librarians of the Moorland-Spingarn Research Center at Howard University and the Library of Congress in Washington, D.C., as well as Enoch Pratt Library in Baltimore, deserve the warmest applause.

Last but not least, the English-language edition of this work would not have come to fruition without a special grant to the translator from the Africa Section of the Ford Foundation.

E.C.K.

Columbia, Maryland

Translator's Introduction

In 1963 a small university press in Belgium published the original edition of *Black Writers in French: A Literary History of Negritude.* Between its unimpressive, mustard-brown paper covers, *Les écrivains noirs de langue française: naissance d'une littérature* was an exciting and pioneering piece of scholarship, the first history and criticism of a new literature and the international ethnic awareness closely identified with it, "negritude." Lilyan Kesteloot's highly respected book is still the indispensable background study of this important twentieth-century cultural and intellectual movement, and of the poetry through which it first found expression. It is a great pleasure and satisfaction to introduce so basic and useful a work to a new and rapidly growing audience of English-language readers.

In the United States in 1963, the phrases "black power" and "black studies" had not yet been uttered, though Malcolm X had begun to make Americans aware of "black rage." It was the year of the first march on Washington, one glowing day in an era of courageous civil-rights struggle punctuated intermittently with violence. August 1963 was nonetheless a time of exhilaration and hope. The next two years would bring a legal end to Jim Crow (racial discrimination in public places) and strong federal protection of minority voting rights. The social changes implied were revolutionary, but the moral power of organized, peaceful demonstrations (sit-ins at lunch counters, pray-ins on "public" library steps, marches on state capitals, voter-registration and literacy drives) had come home to the American public in the morning papers and on the nightly TV news. Americans were confronting racism in their society, and it seemed to be changing for the better. We had not yet had riots in the urban ghettos; the assassinations of the Kennedys, Malcolm X, and Martin Luther King; the deeper troubles erupting in 1968 over the controversial issue of the Viet Nam War.

In 1963, the relationship of black America to Africa and African independence still seemed remote. During that integration-oriented era in America, to call attention to racial differences was somewhat disturbing; one's goal was to ignore differences by treating everyone alike. During that year, when an American expressed interest in Léopold Senghor of Senegal—thinking he was a French poet—an African friend sent her to Kesteloot for enlightenment. What a revelation it was to discover so much in Kesteloot's pages! Despite the barriers of language, history, and geography, here was evidence of an ethnic literature, international in scope (occurring in three European languages) and united by common themes, to a more limited extent by style, but above all by those common moral, psychological, and political concerns that Ralph Ellison has called "an identity of passions."[1] To meet this new literature and its ideas was a shock, tremendously exciting, eventually very nourishing, but at the time not easily absorbed.

Contemporary African literature in French, one finds, is closely linked to the work of certain black poets and thinkers of the French-speaking Caribbean (Haiti, Martinique, Guadeloupe, Guiana). To understand Senghor and the negritude he spoke of, one also has to know Aimé Césaire and Léon Damas, who along with Senghor shaped it, and Alioune Diop, who, as editor-creator of the magazine *Présence Africaine* and founder of the Société Africaine de Culture, has been the movement's chief ambassador since 1960. To understand these important French-speaking intellectuals, moreover, one has to take account of their long and deep interest in black America. While students in France during the thirties, in their own quest for identity and direction, these future "poets of negritude" were markedly influenced—through the poetry and novels of Claude McKay, Langston Hughes, James Weldon Johnson, and Sterling Brown—by the Harlem Renaissance. What Alain Locke had presented in his 1925 anthology, *The New Negro: An Interpretation* (New York: Boni), already articulated the main themes of the self-awareness that the small group of French-language blacks would later develop into negritude.

The negritude poets had received notable attention from French critics outside their group before Kesteloot, of course. Robert Desnos had prefaced Léon Damas's poems, *Pigments,* in 1937. In 1944 André Breton, the father of French surrealism, had written high praise of Aimé Césaire, "A Great Black Poet," in the French magazine *Fontaine.* Later, this article prefaced the first complete edition of Césaire's early and still best-known work, *Cahier d'un retour au pays natal.* Lastly Jean-Paul Sartre's stunning essay, "Orphée noir," had prefaced selections from the group poetry for Senghor's 1948 landmark, *Anthologie de la nouvelle poésie nègre et malgache.*

Individually, as well as through their anthologies (Damas had pro-

---

1. *Shadow and Act* (New York: New American Library, Signet, 1964), p. 255: "It is not culture which binds the peoples who are of partially African origin now scattered throughout the world, but an identity of passions."

duced one, too, in 1947[2]), the three elder poets (Damas, Senghor, Césaire) continued to attract attention as they published in France through the 1950s. Although the African novel in French was also developing significantly toward the close of the decade, poetry had become so popular a medium that every francophone black (see note 10 below) seemed to try his hand at it. Many, particularly students, published verse in the traditionally short-lived student reviews or in *Présence Africaine;* some achieved the flattering distinction of having their verse gathered in individual paperbound volumes. Among these newer poets, some composed a few good poems; a handful had real talent. Others turned out heartfelt verses, and their respectful emulation of their elders was sometimes signalled by a dedication line, "to L.S.S.," "for L.D.," "A.C.," or perhaps "J.R." (Jacques Roumain). Usually the themes, vocabulary, and imagery alone were familiar enough to make their inspiration apparent. The literary value of much of this derivative verse was nil. But its consciousness-raising value was great. However hotly debated it was in French-speaking African and West Indian circles, "negritude" became an umbrella concept, a banner of black identity. It was never without political ramifications, yet its adherents encompassed a spectrum of political persuasions. One of its two principal exponents, Aimé Césaire, was a member of the French Communist Party until the ill-fated Hungarian Revolution; the other, Léopold Sédar Senghor, though long an advocate of African independence, politically has always stood close to the conservative Gaullists.

European literary critics from Desnos to Sartre were aware of the moral and political, as well as the psychological, implications of the new black poetry in French. However, the German critic Janheinz Jahn, in *Muntu: An Outline of Neo-African Culture* (Düsseldorf, 1958), rhapsodized—in a fascinating but probably misleading manner—on certain pan-African mystical, philosophical properties that he felt black poetry in French shared with nearly every other kind of "African" writing.

In contrast, *Les écrivains noirs de langue française,* appearing several years later, was refreshingly unpretentious and straightforward. Rather than hazard sweeping philosophical conclusions, Kesteloot's modest goal was to trace the history of an idea and survey the school of poetry and essays that expressed it. She combined the sound discipline and research methods of history and sociology, as well as traditional French literary criticism. While she too was European and European-educated, Kesteloot had been raised in the former Belgian Congo, and was the first European critic to combine a good grounding in the recent cultural history of France with lengthy, firsthand, not merely textbook, experience of Africa.

2. *Poètes d'expression française* (Paris: Seuil, 1947).

Kesteloot's study required extensive background reading, often under the guidance of Damas, Césaire, and Senghor, whom she came to know well through correspondence and personal interviews; examination of all the historical documents to which she could gain access (the little magazines, letters, manuscripts in personal collections, and so forth); and careful, sensitive considerations of the three leading poets whose early work she analyzes in depth in three of the most valuable chapters of her book. Part III of *Black Writers in French* "situates," to use the French phrase, each author and his work in terms of his personal history. Selected poems are then illuminated by classical "explication de texte," a French tradition that goes back to Sainte-Beuve and Hippolyte Taine.

A generation before Frantz Fanon's now celebrated analysis, *Peau noire, masques blancs* (1952), Kesteloot points out, the short-lived, Martiniquan student magazine in Paris, *Légitime Défense* (1932), had exposed the discomfort and alienation felt by bourgeois blacks who dared not be themselves yet rejected the "borrowed personality" being foisted on them by the French. For the black colonial elite in the early 1930s, West Indian cultural life was summarized by what Damas called its "tracing paper poetry," exclusively concerned with the picturesque—echoing uncritically the values of metropolitan France. Art lacked vitality and originality because nowhere were the deeper realities of the people's lives portrayed. Etienne Léro and the other student editors of the radical *Légitime Défense* prescribed surrealism as the necessary antidote, the only route to an authentic, unfettered African self buried in the black unconscious. Communism, or rather the ideals the communist movement expressed during the early 1930s, appeared similarly to promise not only the eradication of racism and the promotion of individual dignity, but also relief from social and economic oppression. Lynchings, Jim Crow, and the rampant injustice and severely restricted conditions of life for the black masses in the West Indies and America were matters of real concern to these privileged black students. René Maran's rollicking *Batouala: véritable roman nègre*, Prix Goncourt winner in 1921, had exposed even harsher realities of the French colonial administration in Africa—and not incidentally ended its Martiniquan author's career in the French colonial service. Black students in France were beginning to realize there were less savory aspects to the West and its colonialism than the benevolent paternalism they had been raised upon.

Meanwhile, American jazz, the blues, and Negro dancing, reaching Paris via recordings and the cinema as well as in the nightclubs where expatriate American blacks performed, were testimony to the cultural vitality of black America. During these same years American anthropologist Melville Herskovits was gathering evidence from his field work of the roots of this vitality in the African heritage.[3] Black American writers visited Paris, and some met the black students there through the American graduate student Mercer Cook and the Martiniquan Mlle Paulette Nardal, an editor of *La Revue du Monde Noir*, another small but influential literary magazine. The realism and unashamed self-acceptance of "The New Negro," typified in the poetry and novels of Langston Hughes and Claude McKay, provided a background for what later crystallized as "negritude," the French version of black self-awareness. Through the literary documents themselves Kesteloot traces the stages by which these ideas developed, from one knot of black students to another, over the next several years.

By 1934, a new group led by Damas, Senghor, and Césaire brought African and Caribbean students together. Temporarily they shelved Western-oriented party politics (wisely, too, since *Légitime Défense*'s single issue had been officially suppressed) in favor of seeking "original solutions" to the unique situation of the black man. Realizing the limitations of European ideologies as well as European civilization where the black man is concerned, they were in search of *a single mystique for the entire black race.* This was a major and daring step forward. Surrealism was an influence they would permit, not a doctrine they would subscribe to *in toto.* Perhaps the little-known "African patrimony" held an answer for them. Senghor had participated in a rich, traditional Serer life (in Senegal) until coming to France in his twenties, and as Frenchified as many felt he was, Senghor knew the value of his own roots. Césaire and Damas plunged into a study of the new European ethnology of Africa. The German Leo Frobenius's *Historie de la civilisation africaine*—though it was ethnology still in a very preliminary and insufficient stage—had at least begun a trend reversing the "givens" of colonialism (that all Negro Africans are backward, savage people needing to be "raised" to the level of a "higher" Western, industrial, Christian civilization). Frobenius was the first to insist on the richness and sophistication of past African civilizations. Later, more careful and objective historical research by Delafosse disproved the race-supremacist theories of Gobineau that had been accepted in France for a century.

3. See Melville Herskovits, *The Myth of the Negro Past* (Boston: Beacon Press, 1941, 1964); and *The New World Negro* (Bloomington: Indiana University Press, 1966). The late American cultural anthropologist was a pioneer in the field study of advanced West African cultures and of their survival in the Caribbean, Central and South America as well as in the United States. His work did much to dispel myths and erroneous assumptions of earlier lay observers, establishing that New World Negroes *do* have a rich and valuable African past.

The new group was greatly interested by the inspiration Picasso, Braque, and other European artists had found in African art, and by Georges Hardy's study, *L'art nègre* (Paris: Laurens, 1927), calling attention to the originality, the aesthetic and social values of African sculpture, music, and oral literary forms. They held discussions and, as a medium for debating and disseminating their ideas, founded another student journal, *L'Etudiant Noir.* Not only the work of earlier scholars like the German Frobenius but, even more, the interest and encouragement of the French ethnologists who were teaching, researching, and writing from the 1930s onward, lent objectivity and scientific authority to their beliefs.

Years later, the *Etudiant Noir* group came to call the complex of feelings behind their search for identity and direction "negritude." The word was invented by Aimé Césaire and apparently first appeared in print in his poem *Cahier d'un retour au pays natal* in 1939. Senghor has defined negritude many times, perhaps most basically as "the cultural patrimony, the values and above all the spirit of Negro African civilization." Far from turning their backs on these qualities of "black soul" formerly dismissed as primitive and backward, the *Etudiant Noir* trio recognized and insisted on them. They noted many points of contrast between white European civilization—dominated by Reason, the Technical, Christianity, Individualism—and African cultures—typified by group solidarity in tribal life, rhythm and symbol in art and religion, participation in cosmic forces, different forms of logic. They insisted on the capacity of African culture to *give* to the West (as it already had with art) and not merely to *receive.* This growing awareness of their cultural difference from white Europeans proved in time to be an "effective instrument of liberation" (Senghor). At the same time these three men gave negritude a historical dimension: Césaire has described it as "the awareness of being black, the simple acknowledgement of a fact that implies the acceptance of it, a taking charge of one's destiny as a black man, of one's history and culture."

Part II of Mme Kesteloot's book continues to trace and define the route by which the negritude poets explored and elaborated their ideas. Contrasting the Césaire and Senghor definitions of negritude with Jean-Paul Sartre's, in his essay "Orphée noir," Kesteloot points out the latter's deficiency: Sartre's amalgamation of class and race. The goal of the negritude writers was never, Kesteloot strongly points out, what Sartre understood it to be, "a society without race." *It was not race, but "racism" they wished to see eliminated.* They fully expected differences of pigment, culture, and life-style to remain and be enriched, not disappear.

The densest part of Kesteloot's study, and the most literary, is Part III, mentioned earlier, with its close textual analysis and commentary on the early poetry of each of the three founding fathers. Here the personalities and backgrounds of Damas, Césaire, and Senghor are compared and contrasted. Kesteloot examines the form, rhythm, images, vocabulary, and style of each of these highly individual but nonetheless closely related poets. In so doing, I find that she underlines, perhaps inadvertently, the extent to which the poets *differ* in style, form, and temperament, despite the fact that they draw on group themes. Kesteloot seems to disprove Senghor's oft-repeated assertion that "the negritude in poetry is more a matter of style than of theme."

In Part IV, Kesteloot returns to a narrative account of the extrapoetical activities through which each of the three leaders continued to develop and promulgate their ideas. In 1938, on his return to Paris from field work he had supervised for the Musée d'Ethnographie (now the Musée de l'Homme), Léon Damas published *Retour de Guyane*. The book was an indictment of France for having permitted his colonial homeland, largely because of its infamous penal colony, to become a "septic tank for the mother country." Damas attacked the French cultural-assimilation policy for alienating the Guianese elite from their responsibility to the masses. But despite its careful documentation, the work was received as a polemic. Damas's candor was years ahead of its time.

In 1939, not long after Damas's *Retour de Guyane*, Senghor was asked to contribute to a church-sponsored volume, *L'homme de couleur*, characterized by its idealistic and paternalistic view of France's colonizing mission, a view still prevalent outside the black group. The courteous, tactful tone of Senghor's article, "Ce que l'homme noir apporte" ("What the black man brings"), offered subtle but potent argument against "the state of intellectual degradation and moral depravity" then presumed characteristic of African peoples generally. To a European audience on the eve of World War II—threatened by the aggression of police states practicing race genocide and in a time of industrialization where workers were beginning to feel like machines— Senghor wrote of harmonious and peaceful African civilizations with "moral values where love, charity, and clan solidarity are preeminent," of respect for the elders and ancestors, of democratic government by *palavers,* the working of the soil, the beauty and usefulness of African art. The African will choose to assimilate what he wishes from the West, but do not expect him to assimilate it *in toto*, Senghor advised. The societies created by blacks, he implies, are every bit as good as those the West wishes to impose, and in them the black man can attain his full stature. As the war drew closer, ideas the group had debated for several years, explored in their student journal *L'Etudiant Noir,* and in their more intimate writings, began to reach out to a wider audience, whether through poetry or prose.

Just as Damas, Senghor, and Césaire each proved to be a different kind of poet, despite the many views they held in common, so each had a different style in prose and in life of acting upon those beliefs and communicating them to others. Césaire returned to Martinique to teach and shape a new generation of black students through yet another small magazine, *Tropiques*. Several of the poems later collected in Césaire's *Les armes miraculeuses* first appeared in *Tropiques,* and these, too, receive Mme Kesteloot's critical attention. For three years under the Vichy regime, *Tropiques* subtly promulgated the new ideas under the guise of "folklore." Understand "the African fact," regain a deepened sense of self by understanding your past, heed the example of black American poets, respect the African-derived folklore that is the Martiniquan heritage, employ surrealism as "a miraculous weapon" in the rediscovery of your authentic self—these were among the spiritual messages the magazine, edited by lycée professors Aimé and Suzanne Césaire, attempted to convey. In so doing, *Tropiques* helped shape a generation that included a Frantz Fanon, an Edouard Glissant.

Senghor and Damas, on the other hand, remained in France during the war years. Other stranded colonials in Paris joined their group of black intellectuals, which included Senegalese philosophy professor Alioune Diop, who gradually began to play a leading role. In those years under German occupation, the leaders confess, there was perhaps an excessively romantic bent to their discussions of negritude. But the tendency seemed to correct itself after the war. The creation of the French Union in 1946 granted some colonies political representation in the French parliament for the first time and increased the representation of others. Many of the negritude intellectuals (Senghor and Alioune Diop of Senegal, Césaire and Damas from the West Indies, and Jacques Rabemananjara of Madagascar) took on new roles as elected representatives. Alioune Diop soon withdrew from politics to devote himself to the creation of *Présence Africaine,* an independent and modestly produced magazine which soon became the principal voice of the black world in France.

Today, in its twenty-fifth continuous year of publication, *Présence Africaine* is known the world round. Through it and Diop's twin creation, the Société Africaine de Culture, he has played a quiet, consistent, and impressive role as catalyst bringing artists, intellectuals, social scientists, and scholars of the black world together. One need but point to his leading role in organizing the first and second international congresses of black writers and artists (Paris, 1956, and Rome, 1959), and the First World Festival of Negro Arts in Dakar (1966). Diop also has a leading role in organizing the Second World Festival, to be held in Lagos, Nigeria, in 1975. Although "negritude" has never been a popular word with English-speaking Africans, the fact that a world festival will take place for the first time outside the francophone sphere, under the sponsorship of the Nigerian government, appears to demonstrate that negritude's central premise, the existence of a cultural relationship among peoples of the black world, is increasingly viable and relevant.

The last two sections of Kesteloot's volume, parts V and VI, are no longer current, yet they are no less interesting when viewed as recent history. Part V is Kesteloot's analysis of her 1960 survey of some forty black writers in French, representing two generations, from Africa, the Caribbean, and Madagascar. French colonization was at an end. Guinea was already independent; Senegal, Mali, Dahomey, Cameroon, Ivory Coast, and others were soon to follow. Decolonization was already a much-discussed word in anticipation of the spiritual and intellectual change that would follow the end to political colonization.

By personal interviews and a detailed questionnaire, Kesteloot attempted to get a collective picture of the goals and motives of these forty intellectuals; the literary and ideological influences on their work; their degree of commitment or lack of commitment to the writer's role as a mediator in the decolonization process. She was particularly interested in the younger writers' reaction to "negritude." Many were uncomfortable with the term, which they perceived as a label for certain outmoded attitudes of an older generation. They preferred to speak of "African personality"—a-rose-by-any-other-name which appeared to mean much the same thing.

At the same time Kesteloot found an astonishing homogeneity of themes in their writings (the suffering of the slave past, resentment of the evils of colonization—poverty, hunger, forced labor, the exploitation of great masses, nostalgia for the traditional life) and a continuing emphasis on group or mass themes, however personal their expression, whether in poetry (from Damas's *Pigments*, 1937, and Jacques Roumain's *Bois d'ébène*, 1945, to David Diop's *Coups de Pilon*, 1956, and René Depestre's *Minerai noir*, 1956); the essay (particularly Fanon's *Peau noire, masques blancs*, 1952); or novels (such as Mongo Beti's *Mission terminée*, 1957, Ferdinand Oyono's *Une vie de boy*, 1956, or Ousmane Sembene's *Les bouts de bois de Dieu*, 1960). There were exceptions, of course, but even when the writer spoke for himself alone, or for a particular small group or place, there was an overtone of the whole—the black man in general.

In the francophone world, the literary explosion of the fifteen years just prior to African independence has not been matched. Since 1960, the older, established poets have continued to create, but at a less intense pace, and without the same impact. In literature at least, others have remained silent (Birago Diop, Jacques Rabemananjara, Paul Niger, Guy Tirolien). Among the younger poets, David Diop was lost at age thirty-three in a tragic plane crash near Dakar. Tchicaya U Tam'si, born in Congo/Brazzaville, and Edouard Maunick, an emigrant from the Indian Ocean island Mauritius are writing fine poetry that continues and expands negritude themes, but they do so from Paris, where both live and work. The 1950s and early 1960s brought a number of noteworthy novels in French by West Indians and West Africans (Cheikh Hamidou Kane's *L'aventure ambiguë*, Camara Laye's *L'enfant noir*, Edouard Glissant's *La lézarde*). Not all have continued to publish. Ousmane Sembene now devotes his major attention to creating films. One or two new novelists and poets appeared in the late sixties (Yambo Ouologuem and Ahmadou Kourouma, for example), but no recovery seems in sight from the slowdown in literary activity since independence.

Although the future direction of black writing in French remains unclear, black literature in French retains its rich past, the product of two generations of intellectual ferment—from René Maran *(Batouala)* through the negritude poets of Africa and the Caribbean who wrote during the 1930s and 1940s and the novelists and essayists who joined them in the 1950s. This literature is still being retrieved and reevaluated in light of the new and still-changing perspective through which the black man in the world, his past, present, and future are being viewed. Many early works are now in print once more, and have become classics that continue to be read and to influence the young. With translation, of course, their influence extends beyond the francophone audiences.

Despite the still high illiteracy rates in the West Indies and continental Africa, the forty writers questioned in 1960 were convinced that within twenty years instead of Europeans blacks would be the principal audience for their books. The rapidly expanding educational systems in Africa, together with the Africanization of much of the primary- and secondary-school and university curricula seem to be making this a reality in the 1970s. Probably it is also the case in the Caribbean.

Surprisingly, neither Kesteloot nor the forty young writers she interviewed in 1960 seem to have imagined their writings might have a future in the United States. Who could have foreseen the vastly altered perspective the next decade would bring? A new black ethnic awareness rising from the American civil-rights struggles of the 1960s was accompanied not only by a drive for "black power" and a reaffirmation of black identity, but by a veritable hunger for "black studies," avenues of knowing and sharing the experience of others of African descent the world over. Who could have foreseen that one of these forty writers, Frantz Fanon, would become a posthumous prophet of the black American revolution? Yet the English translation of Frantz Fanon's *Les damnés de la terre* (1961) quickly catapulted him to that status. Today, among black writings in the United States, *The Wretched of the Earth* sells second only to *The Autobiography of Malcolm X* and ranks among the sacred writings in black American militant circles. Kesteloot knew Fanon as an essayist and thinker for *Peau noire, masques blancs* and from his contributions to *Présence Africaine* and the black writers' conferences in Paris and Rome, but *Les damnés de la terre* appeared after Kesteloot's pioneering study was in production.

Fanon was very much an heir of the negritude generation: He was shaped at the outset by its thought, and only now is this beginning to be appreciated in the United States.[4] *Black Skin, White Masks*, striking in its analysis of the colonized personality, is permeated with the Césaire of *Cahier d'un retour au pays natal* and punctuated throughout with quotations from the poetry and prose of Césaire, Damas, Jacques Roumain, Senghor, Alioune and David Diop. It is the violent spirit of Césaire's Rebel, from his disturbing and prophetic play *Et les chiens se taisaient* ("And the dogs fell silent"), on the other hand, that dominates Fanon's final testament, *The Wretched of the Earth*. This last work appears to endorse violence, or at the very least struggle, as necessary to the decolonization process, as the only method by which oppressed peoples can be restored to a full sense of their authentic selves.[5]

In part VI of *Black Writers in French* Kesteloot attempts to summarize what the leading writers saw as their contribution to a larger humanism. In expressing themselves they have also spoken for others. They have attempted to use the "decolonization" of Africans and West Indians as a starting point from which the cultural contributions of blacks the world over will be seen in relation to one another, and fully accepted and appreciated "at the universal table." The latter image is Senghor's. He reminds us that the goal toward which mankind strives in this last quarter of the twentieth century, if we survive it, will not be complete if it excludes a single people, a single culture. What we must seek, in his view, is a universal civilization that will legitimize the Negro's place at that table, welcoming his unique contributions so long undervalued. "What all these writers cry out for is therefore not to reject what the West brought them, not a return to the Africa of pre-colonial times, closed in upon itself; nor is it to be able to construct their own world totally separate from the white. What they want is precisely the opposite: to contribute to the formation of a universal

4. See these recent biographies: *Fanon: The Revolutionary as Prophet*, by Peter Geismar (New York: Grove, 1971); *Frantz Fanon*, by David Caute (New York: Viking, 1970); and *Frantz Fanon: A Critical Study*, by Irene L. Gendzier (New York: Pantheon, 1973).

5. This position grew out of Fanon's experience in the long, bloody Algerian Revolution, which he first witnessed as a psychiatrist in a French colonial hospital; later, after resigning his medical position, he served the Algerian cause in various capacities until his untimely death in 1961, at age thirty-six of leukemia.

humanism, in collaboration with all races."[6] As Alioune Diop has put it: "The gifts of the West to the formation of our personality remain precious. Yet we claim the freedom to enrich them, and in our turn, to give. And not only to receive . . . in order to recreate with all men a world brotherly with peace and mutual understanding."[7]

Kesteloot's brief and more recent essay, *Negritude et situation coloniale*, has been translated with a new and somewhat overstated title (see note 6 below). Originally this essay was conceived as part of the present volume, but Kesteloot was advised to drop it from her original draft of *Les écrivains noirs* because the Congo situation in the early sixties made direct reference to the revolutionary implications of this literature too controversial. The material was left unpolished and unfinished until its publication in 1968 in Cameroon, when Kesteloot was at last free to write concisely and forcefully, with the benefit of further hindsight, what is only subtly and diffusely illustrated in this volume —that the black poets' revolt was always more than literary and more than a simple protest against cultural assimilation by the French. It had political, psychological, and social overtones for which poetry, merely for a time, was the major and only possible vehicle. From the mid-1930s, Kesteloot shows, black writers in French evoked in their poems the passion of the whole race, put the white man on trial for the hypocrisy of his colonization, cried out their revolt in poems "red with blood." Since effective, direct action was then impossible, they sang their nostalgia for the precolonial past; studied and sought to deepen their awareness of it and of their present situation. Did the black poets exaggerate? No more, suggests Kesteloot, than any literature of protest. If European hypocrisy insisted on painting only one side of the colonial coin, the "rosy" side, what the negritude poets did was to reveal the other. What were the negritude writers seeking, Kesteloot asks in the final pages of this little book. Not the pure and simple return to an outmoded past, she states, reiterating the conclusions of her *Les écrivains noirs*. Quite simply, in the confusion of a rapidly changing world, they were searching for the emotional security and spiritual nourishment of traditional life.

Appended to *Black Writers in French* is "Problems of the Literary Critic in Africa," a related essay which appeared in the Cameroonian journal *Abbia* in 1965. The version printed here was amended by Kesteloot in 1971. After surveying modern literature in all of continen-

6. Kesteloot, *Intellectual Origins of the African Revolution* (Washington, D.C.: Black Orpheus Press, 1972), p. 113.

7. Opening speech at the Second Conference of Black Writers and Artists, p. 44, quoted in ibid.

tal Africa, she broadened her commentary to include English-language, as well as French-speaking, African writers, bringing us rapidly up-to-date on the situation since independence. Except for Edouard Maunick and Tchicaya U Tam'si, she finds, in the French-speaking zone of Africa, no major new poetic talents who either continue or react against the influence of the preceding generation. There has been development in the novel and the essay, and in literary criticism, but it has been less impressive in the French-speaking zone than the veritable literary explosion since independence among writers in English from Nigeria, Ghana, and East Africa, as well as among black South African writers in exile.

At the time of the *Abbia* article, as a result of several years of living and teaching in Africa, Kesteloot was becoming more and more impressed with the "living, flourishing, generous" oral literary heritage of Africa. For vast numbers of Africans, she points out, it is the *only* literature, and still the most important. Kesteloot speaks of the *mvet* singers in Cameroon, where she had been teaching. She notes the diversity and complexity of African oral literary genres. Performance is vital in the oral literatures of Africa, transmitted since antiquity only by rote, to be danced, drummed, acted, accompanied, sung and improvised from performer to performer, generation to generation, often with the spectators taking part. Western critics, or indeed any foreign critic, are baffled by these literatures, and not only because of linguistics. To transcribe these ancient, yet vigorously contemporary, literary forms into writing, and/or to translate them into European languages, as well as to attempt an informed criticism, is almost by definition a job primarily for African specialists, since only they are participants in the cultures from which these literary forms spring.[8] Ethnological and linguistic training, very different from the European literary and historical background of specialists (such as Mme Kesteloot herself) in the new written literatures, is required to accomplish useful study in the traditional field. Since the *Abbia* article, however, Kesteloot has collaborated with several noted African scholars to collect, transcribe, edit, and translate into French traditional oral works, making them available not only to a non-African audience in French,

8. Important work has, of course, also been published in this field by non-Africans. Among ground-breaking works which analyze, transcribe, and translate vernacular, oral African literary forms into English are: *Tzibongo: Zulu Praise Poems*, by Trevor Cope (1968), and *Somali Poetry: An Introduction*, by the linguist-anthropologist team, B. W. Andrzejewski and T. M. Lewis (1964), both in the Oxford Library of African Literature, London; *Dahomean Narrative: A Cross-Cultural Analysis*, by Melville J. and Frances S. Herskovits (Evanston, Ill.: Northwestern University Press, 1958); and *A Recitation of Ifa, Oracle of the Yoruba*, by Judith Gleason (New York: Grossman, 1973).

but to Africans of other vernacular languages as well.[9]

Kesteloot, one of the first specialists in black literature in French, returned to West Africa from Europe to teach in the early 1960s. She has been among the few Europeans to play a role, along with young African scholars like Abiola Irele of Nigeria and Mohamadou Kane of Senegal, in adding black literature to the once exclusively English- or French-oriented primary, secondary, and university curricula. As a literary scholar and critic, she has also pioneered in bringing black writing to the rest of the world. Her introduction to *Aimé Césaire*, in the popular Seghers paperback series Les Poètes d'Aujourd'hui, came out in 1962, slightly in advance of *Les écrivains noirs*. She edited a small collection, *Neuf poètes camerounais*, published in Yaoundé in 1965. Research on the origins of negritude had acquainted her with the worldwide scope of black writing. Indeed, it is part of what she has taught at the Ecoles Normales Superieures in the Cameroon, Mali, and the Ivory Coast, and most recently at the University of Dakar. To fill the need for teaching materials in a convenient form, Kesteloot put together a paperback, *Anthologie négro-africaine*, in 1967. This anthology of twentieth-century black writers offers samplings of prose and poetry by a total of eighty-eight authors, from all over Africa, the Caribbean, and the U.S.A. Some of the selections were written in French, others translated from English or Portuguese. While Kesteloot is less deeply read in English-language African literature and American black literature, her grasp of the breadth of these contemporary literatures and their thematic relationship is impressive and authoritative. Even more than *Les écrivains noirs,* this 1967 anthology outlines a new field of comparative literary scholarship still in its infancy.

At mid-career, Lilyan Kesteloot's achievements as teacher, scholar, and critic are already impressive. From my vantage point as an American colleague, I see her (if the comparison is not excessively parochial) as the Germaine Brée or the Margaret Mead of black literary studies. In *Les écrivains noirs,* her first and still most important scholarly work, Kesteloot demonstrated by sound research and well-focused criticism that since the 1930s black authors in French have expressed a collective, not merely an individual, search for identity and direction; an ethnic, not merely individual, cultural awareness. Poetry and essays

9. Among these are *Kaydara, récit initiatique peul* ("Kaydara, Peuhl initiation story") in collaboration with Amadou Hampate Ba (Paris: Julliard, 1969); *La poésie traditionelle* and *L'épopée traditionelle* (Paris: Fernand Nathan, 1971); *Da monzon de Ségou, épopée bambara,* with J. B. Traoré, Amadou Traoré, and A. Hampate Ba (Paris: Fernand Nathan and Cahier de l'Homme, 1972); *L'éclat de l'étoile, récit initiatique peul,* with Amadou Hampate Ba, Classiques Africains (Paris: Armand Colin, 1973); and *La prise de Dkonkoloni, épisode bilingue de l'épopée bambara,* with Gerard Dumestre and Jean Baptiste Traoré, Classiques Africains (Paris: Armand Colin, 1973).

from the Caribbean and Africa were forming a new literature, which, though indebted to the mainstream of French writing, needed to be seen as a separate entity, as well as in relationship to other black literatures (the Harlem Renaissance, for example) which had influenced it and which it, in turn, would influence. This critical work was a major and valuable contribution to black literary studies, which Kesteloot certainly helped launch, to comparative literature, to modern intellectual history, and to what the French have recently begun to promote as *francophonie*.[10]

Black writings in French are already receiving serious attention in Europe, Africa, the Caribbean, and Japan, as well as in the United States. And as black literary studies continue to develop, we can look forward to more English translations of the leading writers in French (as well as to keeping existing translations in print) and to supportive critical work from a growing cadre of international scholars. In addition to critiques on genre,[11] there will undoubtedly be searching studies of individual writers, perhaps investigations of such longstanding literary and intellectual relationships as the near forty-year friendship of Césaire and Senghor, two men of intriguingly different personalities and political persuasions. Eventually there will be biographies, perhaps published correspondence, collections from magazines such as *Présence Africaine* and others. It is ironic (publication being the haphazard process that it is) that *Whispers from a Continent* (1969), Wilfred Cartey's sensitive and highly lyrical appreciation of contemporary black writing, with its abundant allusions to poets and novelists who wrote in French, was published *before* works of most of those poets and writers appeared in English, and several years before so helpful an auxiliary guide as the present Kesteloot volume was available as background.

Aimé Césaire proclaimed some thirty-five years ago in *Cahier d'un retour au pays natal* that it is "bon et beau et légitime d'être nègre" ("good and beautiful and legitimate to be black"). Public acceptance

10. The French-speaking Université Laval in Quebec has established a study center and a magazine to further *francophonie*. Theoretically, and viewed from the most inoffensive perspective, this is the principle by which the French, acknowledging the cultural originality of various peoples of former French dominions, seek to encourage their cultural ties to one another, rather than with the metropole alone, by means of their common language. French Canadians, West Indians, Africans, Madagascans, Mauritians, Southeast Asians, and North Africans fall within their scope of interest. Having had Césaire, Damas, and Kesteloot as visiting lecturers, l'Université Laval, not surprisingly, has shown a marked interest in the literature of negritude.

11. At this writing, in the United States we have had three book-length studies of the African novel, by Gleason, Tucker, and Larson (see bibliography) and no less than four anthologies devoted exclusively to black poetry in French, by editors Shapiro, Collins, Jones, and Kennedy (see bibliography).

of the "legitimacy" of blackness, however, is still very new. Early in the sixties, one New York publisher told me, "No one will be interested in a black poet from some corner of the Caribbean. But poets from Africa, that's a different story!" The "newly emergent" continent evoked a certain glamour that the common situation of blackness then did not. As recently as 1967, the director of a small American foundation, when approached for support to translate this volume on the grounds of its contemporary relevance in the humanities, replied disdainfully (and without even asking to examine the book) that he found "the entire negritude movement and all its writers" not only "utterly boring" but guilty of an "ethno-mysticism" that was "backward-looking," "frothing with jungly black blood," and in short, "a literary abortion of the first order." (I summarize two single-spaced pages of invective.) In the same letter, this academician (since resigned from a post in which he had shown such poor judgment) spoke favorably of the English-speaking African poets in Ibadan, whom he described as "working toward literary and intellectual values." His implication was clear: the "ethnic and would-be mystical values" that negritude writers brought into discussion were suspect, if not downright repulsive, while the tidy, comfortable, neutral, and apparently assimilationist "literary and intellectual" goals of the young Nigerians were deserving only of praise. We regret such utter lack of understanding.

Several years later, in our correspondence about an appropriate title for this volume in English (the translation project having found support from a Ford Foundation grant and a publisher in the Temple University Press), Mme Kesteloot warned that the term "negritude" also provokes "allergic reactions" among some Africans, not necessarily only in the English-speaking zones. In the United States, of course, we have some understanding of the semantics at play because of the revolution since the late sixties in our own race terminology. Overseas readers of this volume may or may not know that "Negro" or "colored" used to be the respectful way whites referred to blacks and blacks of various hues described themselves, while "black" was avoided: for example, the National Association for the Advancement of Colored People, the National Council of Negro Women. Yet in speaking of "the New Negro" (the concept embodied in the title of Alain Locke's 1925 landmark anthology on black American writers) at Federal City College in Washington, D.C., in 1970, Léon Damas was baffled by his students' first reaction to his use of the word "Negro" as an "Uncle-Tomism."[12] At this writing in the United States, white

---

12. Popular feeling on this issue has grown so strong that the venerable Association for the Study of Negro Life and History (founded in 1915) recently changed "Negro" in its name to "Afro-American."

with a small *w* and black with a small *b* seem the generally accepted terms. "Afro-American" is another current term, less universal than "black" in that it confines itself to Western hemisphere blacks, leaving out Africans. The official posters from the 1966 festival in Dakar read, in their English edition, "First World Festival of Negro Arts." On the other hand, the advance notices of the second festival, scheduled for Lagos in 1975—with Alioune Diop and one or two other "high priests of negritude" serving on its sponsoring committees—speak of "The Second World Festival of Black Art and Culture."

This volume, we concluded, cannot and should not shun the term. To avoid whatever confusion the word "negritude" may evoke, let me point out that Mme Kesteloot's book neither endorses nor rejects an ethno-mysticism the word may suggest. She has simply sought to present a set of ideas and trace their origins, and she does so by means of an admirably objective historical study and sensitive literary analysis. Quite apart from whether one accepts, rejects, or remains indifferent to negritude as a mystique, Kesteloot introduces three important poets whose works have their own social and aesthetic values, and she alludes to other writers she was not able to treat in similar depth. By examining the situation of French-speaking Africans and black West Indians toward the end of the colonial era, by describing the ferment of their university years and early adulthood, *Black Writers in French* illuminates an exciting cultural and intellectual movement. The events of the late 1930s and World War II provided the impetus for a new group literature, launched by a handful of poets and through which a new international self-awareness and race-awareness, the dynamic and useful complex of ideas they eventually called "negritude," was born.

Preface

Thirty years have passed since the early heady days of African independence when this study was undertaken in faith and hope. A new world was beginning from which racism and tribalism, along with injustice and inequality, oppression and repression, would be banished.

Today we recognize, as Césaire wrote, that, "deliriously, expansively happy, we had our knees where our brains should be."[1]

But, you'll say, what about black African literature? What has become of that? African literature is flourishing. It may be the only thing in Africa that is flourishing.

The negritude movement blossomed like a great flower, nourishing two generations of writers who counted themselves in the Senghor/Césaire problematic right up to 1968. The novelists were the first to break the euphoria of that splendid period when Africa was entering the UN, UNESCO, the Food and Agriculture Organization, opening embassies, establishing republican governments, building universities, creating publishing houses, literary magazines, and theaters.

From 1968 on, artists and intellectuals, those always sensitive observers, began to perceive the less savory effects of independence. A great surge of work arose criticizing the mores of the new African governments, dramatizing the conflicts of social change, of village versus city life, of traditional versus modern; treating issues of religious syncretism, educational systems, the emancipation of women.

A new generation of writers with new names — Amadou Kourouma, William Sassine, Alioum Fantouré, Henri Lopes, Valentin Yves Mudimbe — sounded the knell of too facile hope and denounced the drift of political systems already under attack by the termites of corruption. *Termites* was in fact the title of a play on the subject written by the Ivory Coast/West Indian Eugène Dervain in the 1970s, while Bernard Dadié's *Monsieur Togognini*, prototype of the corrupt and unscrupulous African politician, was a hit in Abidjan.

At the same time, a historical drama still very much inspired by negritude continued to develop in West Africa (Guinea, Mali, Senegal) where the memory of ancient empires offered noble subjects. Cheik Aliou Ndao, Djibril Tamsir Niane, Massa Makan Diabaté, Jean Pliya, and

---

1. Tr.: that is, we were carried away by unrealistic hopes.

Bernard Z. Zadi drew upon them for exciting plays of a more or less didactic nature, following the example of Aimé Césaire's *The Tragedy of King Henri-Christophe*, written in 1962. This way great heroes of the past were brought to life again: Da Monzon of Segou, Chaka, BaBemba of Sikasso, King Glele of Dahomey, the Sofas of Samori, Albouri Ndiaye, king of Djolof, Abra Pokou of the Baoules. Could examples from the precolonial past prove inspiring to those in power today? Through them the writers set forth lessons in honor, courage, and integrity. Even today a tradition of historical theater is carried on in the national languages and is still very popular with the African masses.

The themes of negritude persist in African poetry from Charles Nokan and Edouard Maunick to Fernando d'Almeida, Noël Ebony, and Marouba Fall. Poets have hope in their bones and are not likely to give up their dreams. With the 1980s, however, the novel and short story take a new turn that results in more and more tragic works in which horror leads to madness, nightmare, hallucination, or biting satire. One could describe this as oneiric neorealism, or as an African novel of the absurd. From the great talents of Ibrahima Ly, Boris Diop, Tierno Monenembo, Laurent Owondo, or Yodi Carone to the still clumsy writings of Véronique Tadjo, Séverin Cécile Abéga, Maurice Bandaman; with the Congolese Sony Labou Tansi leading the pack as much by his plays as through his novels, their work has wide repercussions in the European media. The novels and plays of Tansi's countryman Tchicaya U Tam'si follow the same tendency toward an "African absurd," more and more involving caricature, if not metaphysics.

Novels like *l'Anté-peuple* (by S. L. Tansi), *Tamango* (by Boris Diop), *Les écailles du ciel* (by T. Monenembo), like *Toile d'araignée*, and *Noctuelles* (by Ibrahima Ly), seem to touch the bottom of the abyss of African destiny, where there is no way out but madness or death. These novels are the spiritual children of Ayi Kwei Armah and Ngugi wa Thiong'o, whose cruel lucidity precedes them by several years. One cannot speak of influences, but rather of analogous social and political conditions in the different African countries where things are breaking down, and which therefore give rise among these writers to analogous works filled with nausea, despondency, with fantastic quests for improbable salvation, with stunned resignation, or sarcastic despair.

Translating the stagnation of underdevelopment into symbolic fables is more or less what this fourth generation of intellectuals has undertaken as its task. A lucid examination of the continent's present reality leads them to conclude that its future will be chaotic.

Long past today are the debates over negritude and the African personality that once separated those in Senghor's camp from those in Soyinka's. Long past also are more recent jousts over national literatures versus a continental black African literature; or even speculations about the cultural identity of this group or that. The novelists of today's Africa no longer ask the old questions: where do we come from, who are we, but where are we going and how painfully? For what with famine in Ethiopia; refugees from Nambia, Sudan, and Mauritania; trouble in Zaire and Rwanda; crime and drugs in the capital cities; juvenile delinquents and a hundred thousand beggars in Dakar; recurring drought and epidemics, the wars that have torn Nigeria, Chad, and Angola; military coups d'état, the decay of hospitals, the corruption of civil servants, the scorn for law and the law of the strong man; Africa is losing its eternal smile.

Africa is very ill, and its writers are truthtelling and unhappy witnesses. Some of them evade the unbearable by writing detective novels or fantasy like the very beautiful *Upside Down Life* by Patrice Etoundi Mballa, or the marvelous autobiography by Wole Soyinka, *Aké: The Years of Childhood,* in which one nostalgically rediscovers a universe full of poetry and meaning. It's not for nothing that he got a Nobel Prize!

One must therefore confirm the vitality of African literature today. The voice of Africa, even when it is tragic, will never again be silent. More than ever, the moral conscience of Africa is concentrated in its writers, who dare — while awaiting the tidal wave of future revolutions — to name the unnameable, or, as Césaire has written, "to stave off the amorphous with words."

Certainly, that consciousness, that moral sense may last, may even prevail! But for the impatient, who feel that the world is moving faster and that Africa has brakes on, accentuating the extent to which it lags behind, I would advise a plunge into Maryse Condé's beautiful fresco, *Ségou: les murailles de pierres.*[2] In this novel, appearing during these final disorderly years at the end of the century, an Afro-Caribbean writer has measured that immense African patience, that complex and superhuman patience that transcends time and the continents, a patience founded on a profound strength, still intact, which once again will seek out the good men who are yet to come and make them succeed.

For, at the moment, as the novel by Kwei Armah of Ghana puts it: "The Beautyful Ones Are Not Yet Born."

LILYAN KESTELOOT

Dakar, 1989

---

2. Tr.: Condé's novel "Ségou: the Walls of Stone," has been published in translation as *Segu.* Trans. Barbara Bray (New York: Penguin, 1987; Ballantine, 1988).

Black Writers in French

ils ont prévalu leurs yeux intacts au plus fragile
de l'image impardonnée
de la vision mémorable du monde à bâtir
de la fraternité qui ne saurait manquer de venir,
quoique malhabile

[they prevailed their unsullied eyes
upon that most fragile
upon that unforgiven image
upon that memorable vision of the world to build
out of the fraternity that could not help but come,
however clumsy]

Aimé Césaire, "Vampire liminaire,"
from *Ferrements*

Preface to First Edition

This study was written between 1958 and 1961. It has never been revised, and, since it was the first study synthesizing the history of the negritude movement, one will notice in it today a certain number of inaccuracies and oversights. I should like to point these out myself, as well as to call attention to the work of colleagues who since then have made important clarifications. In fifteen years, moreover, the literature has been enriched by new and not lesser writers and has taken the new directions outlined in my *Anthologie négro-africaine* (Brussels: Editions Marabout, 1967). Numerous colleagues have written articles and essays that are of capital importance in assessing the present status of black literature.

Let me begin with a few corrections of my own work. Well-informed readers have kindly pointed out some errors. Before it appeared in Haiti, the magazine *Lucioles* had been created in Fort-de-France by a group of Martiniquan writers, among them Gilbert Gratiant. The *Cahier d'un retour au pays natal* appears to have been conceived after a return trip Césaire made to his country in about 1936. My interpretation of the passage that begins "Partir!" ["To leave!"], ending the description of the West Indies, is therefore open to discussion. Does the passage concern a departure from the West Indies for Europe, as I then understood it, or, on the other hand, a departure from France for Martinique, corresponding to the return visit Césaire had recently made? It is in this latter sense that Georges Ngal has interpreted the passage in his thesis at the University of Geneva, "L'évolution psychologique et intellectuelle d'Aimé Césaire."

I have been reproached a number of times for not giving more attention to *La Revue du Monde Noir*, which preceded *Légitime Défense* by two years. It is true that I ought to have examined more closely the activity and influence of this little magazine, of which there were six issues. Messrs Okechukwu Mezu, Georges Ngal, and Tidjani Serpos (the latter in his 1973 thesis at Vincennes, "L'idéologie de la négritude chez Senghor") have since accomplished this remarkably well. However, with me it was less an oversight (for I do mention the review directed by Mlle Paulette Nardal and Dr. Léo Sajous) than a mistake in judgment. With further research I would have seen that *Légitime Défense*, despite its ideological opposition to *La Revue du Monde Noir*, was not so distant from it; that Etienne Léro, by participating in *La Revue*, had become acquainted with the Negro Renaissance writers among whom he counted himself; that despite its middle-class and assimilationist orientation, *La Revue du Monde Noir* nonetheless launched two of the major themes of negritude: the ennoblement of the Negro race and the revaluation of African civilizations.

Another misjudgment in my study was the slight importance I accorded Jacques Roumain and the Cuban writer, Nicolas Guillén. Even though they did not participate personally in the current of ideas that centered about *L'Etudiant Noir*, their works and their activities strongly influenced several of the negritude writers. There are very recognizable traces of Roumain in Césaire and Senghor, in David Diop's *Coups de pilon*, in J. F. Brierre's *Black Soul*, in the poems of René Belance, and even among the new generation, in the Haitian Gérard Chenet's *Zombis nègres* and in the Congolese Tchicaya U Tam'si's *Epitomé*.

I think, too, that I underestimated writers like André Gide and Albert Londres, whose works, like those of René Maran, bore lucid and courageous witness to the price of colonization. Léon Fanoud Siefer's *L'Image du noir dans la littérature française* (Paris: Klincksieck, 1968) and J.-M. Abanda Ndengue's *De la négritude au négrisme* (Yaoundé: Editions C.L.E., 1970) have given these writers their true place in the history of negritude, just as J. P. Goldenberg's thesis on Blaise Cendrars at the University of Paris has demonstrated Cendrars's fascination with African civilization.

Lastly, this book suffers from the faults common to works that break new ground: errors of perspective. One looks backward, often simplifying and idealizing, and is likely to do the same looking forward toward the future. Re-reading my concluding chapter I am struck by its naïve optimism. I scarcely foresaw the problems of Africa today, nor, consequently, the impasses and difficulties black writers now encounter.

Also, on the political, social, and economic levels, one must re-read the works of Frantz Fanon, particularly *The Wretched of the Earth* and *Toward the African Revolution*. Important, too, are René Dumont's *L'Afrique est mal partie*, Albert Meister's *East Africa: The Past in Chains, the Future in Pawn* (New York: Walker, 1968), Yves Bénot's *Les idéologies africaines*, Mahjemout Diop's *Histoire des classes sociales dans l'Afrique de l'Ouest*, all of Samir Amin's work, and Guy L. Hazoumé's recent study *Idéologies tribalistes et nations en Afrique* (Paris: Présence Africaine, 1972).

The range in African critical thinking on literature and ideology in recent years is illustrated by Marcien Towa's *Essai sur la problématique* *philosophique dans l'Afrique actuelle* (Éditions C.L.E.), Memel Fote's *Les institutions politiques chez les Adjoukrou* (Institut Ethnologique d'Abidjan), Pathé Diagne's *Micro-états et intégration économique* (Anthropos), Stanis-las Adoteir's *Négritude et négrologues,* and in Tidjani Serpos's work, as well as in the writings of Joseph Ki Zerbo, Thomas Melone, Jean-Pierre Ndiaye, Barthelemy Kotchy, Mohamadou Kane, Henri Lopez, Bernard Fonlon, Clément Mbom, Georges Ngal, and Vincent Mudimbe, to mention only the French-speaking scholars. To these one can add studies written in French by the English-speaking Africans Okechukwu Mezu, Abiola Irele, and Sunday O. Anozie. Among European and American intellectuals, the late Janheinz Jahn, Vincent Thomas, Michel Fabre, Bernard Mouralis, Rodney Harris, Gerald Moore, Alain Ricard, Mineke Schipper de Leeuw, and Sylvia Washington Ba have made notable contributions to the recognition of Negro and African creative writing.*

Black and white critics alike have thus been verifying the extent to which the negritude movement has been rich and fertile. Today, whether it seeks to justify, to contest, or to go beyond the movement, the new generation of African intellectuals, by defining itself in rela-tionship to its elders, still uses negritude as a departure point for its thinking. Whatever the present attempts to revive the movement in neocolonialism, no one can forget that negritude was, at its origins, an awareness of and reaction to racial oppression, an affirmation of hu-man dignity, a struggle against injustice, a revolutionary act.

LILYAN KESTELOOT

Paris
November 1973

*Translator's note: Mme Kesteloot's preface reached us after most of this volume had gone to press. Since several of the new critics and scholars to whom she calls attention are not included in our bibliography, I will mention here some of their works: *The Unfinished Quest of Richard Wright* by Michel Fabre, translated by Isabel Barzun (New York: Morrow, 1973); *Théâtre et nationalisme: Wole Soyinka et Leroi Jones* by Alain Ricard (Paris: Présence Africaine, 1972); *Individualité et collectivité dans le roman négro-africain d'expression française* by Bernard Mouralis (Editions de l'Université d'Abidjan, 1969); *L'humanisme dans le théâtre d'Aimé Césaire* by Rodney Harris (Sherbrooke, Quebec: Editions Antoine Naamen, 1973); and *The Concept of Negritude in the Poetry of Léopold Sédar Senghor* by Sylvia Washington Ba (Princeton University Press, 1973).

Introduction

With the awakening of the African continent, demanding its freedom, it is time to recognize that black writers of the French language form a comprehensive and authentic literary movement. As early as 1948, "Black Orpheus," Jean-Paul Sartre's brilliant preface to L. S. Senghor's *Anthologie de la nouvelle poésie nègre et malgache de langue française* ("Anthology of the new Negro and Malagasy poetry in French") saluted the accession of the poets of "negritude." Today, everything about this poetry, its abundance and quality, its diversity of style and form, its incontestable originality, prompts us to consider these neo-African authors as creators of an authentic literary school. It is obvious that an important phenomenon has occurred in creative writing in the French language, and that it must not be underestimated.

Purely and simply to integrate black writers into French literature would be to ignore the fact that they represent a cultural renaissance which is neither French nor even Western. They have only made use of French in order to express the resurrection of their race. All their writings reflect this single inspirational impulse. These black writers must not be considered one by one, nor should they, in spite of themselves, be considered part of our literature. One would belong to the surrealist school, another would be a disciple of Claudel or of Saint-John Perse, still another would fit into a lingering line of naturalists—just so many vain attempts to contain them artificially! Why avoid examining their true significance? Why choose to be blind? Plainly, they all speak the same language, they express themselves not in relation to the literature or the society of France, but in relation to colonized Negro societies. Finally, they all convey the same obsessive message.

If we wish to understand the meaning and scope of today's neo-Negro literature, we must trace it back to the soil from which it sprang, where it took root and sap—the newly recovered dynamic of colored peoples.

If it is true that literature is one of the most important signs of culture, we may, along with Aimé Césaire,[1] look upon the appearance of literary works in the colonies as a symptom of their rebirth, and as proof that colonial peoples are capable of taking the initiative and reexamining their concept of a world thrown into confusion by colonization. Is it not above all the task of writers and artists—those whom Césaire calls "men of culture"—to bring order from this chaos? It is they who catalyze the aspirations of the masses, helping them to regain their place in history, strengthening their national feeling—in other words, preparing them for freedom. This major role of élites was described with considerable foresight by Césaire in 1959 at the black writers' congress in Rome.

In our present situation we are propagators of souls, multipliers of souls, and almost inventors of souls.

And I say too that it is the mission of the man of black culture to prepare a good decolonization, not just any kind of decolonization.

For even in the midst of colonial society, it is the man of culture who must shorten his people's apprenticeship in liberty. And the man of culture, whether writer, poet, or artist, achieves this for his people because, within the colonial situation itself, the creative cultural activity which precedes the concrete collective experience is already an apprenticeship.[2]

The West began to be interested in Negro culture almost fifty years ago. Both Vlaminck and Apollinaire are credited with "discovering" Negro art in France. Vlaminck fell in love with a statuette Derain had bought for practically nothing, and showed it to Picasso, for whom it was a revelation. We know what this led to in Picasso's work and, more generally, that it inspired cubism. As for Apollinaire, "weary of this ancient world," he turned for inspiration to the fetishes of Guinea and the South Sea Islands.[3] After World War I, black American jazz and the blues revolutionized European music. With the work of Leo Frobenius and Maurice Delafosse in the new field of ethnology, serious attention was given to the black peoples of Africa, who until then had been considered as completely lacking in civilization. In 1921, a collection of African legends edited and classified according to subject by Blaise Cendrars met with considerable success.

The same year, René Maran's *Batouala: véritable roman nègre* won the Prix Goncourt but created a scandal. Ethnology might show that the black race had a more glorious past than imagined—well and good! That blacks had proved themselves great artists was also acceptable. Exotic art, moreover, was a fine form of escapism for the French from

1. A. Césaire, "L'homme de culture et ses responsabilités," *Présence Africaine*, February–May 1959.
2. Ibid., pp. 118–20.
3. As stated in his poem "Zone."

the disquieting political and psychological climate of the day. *Batouala,* however, dealt with neither art nor science but with colonial realities. French public opinion could not accept a Negro who dared to question European superiority or the right to colonize. The few Negroes who attempted to go beyond aesthetics rapidly came to grief. *La Revue du Monde Noir*[4] lasted only six issues and *Le Cri des Nègres* (definitely communist) was banned.

Yet Paris was a favorable milieu for the spiritual revolution of young blacks who came there for their higher education. This was true despite the dilettantism which Paris pays as tribute for its reputation as the "crossroads of the Western World." Particularly between 1928 and 1940, West Indian and African students who came to Paris found themselves in extraordinary intellectual and political ferment. From the beginning of the century, philosophy, art, and literature had questioned the cultural foundations of French society. Measure, Reason, Progress, Absolute Truth, all the pillars upon which previous centuries had rested, could no longer be written with capital letters. They were threatened by a mighty wave which was sweeping away all shackles of mind and spirit. The most spectacular manifestation of this ferment was surrealism.

A similar eruption was taking place in politics, where the bourgeois democratic ideas that had nourished the nineteenth century were on the wane. Furthered by the economic crisis of 1930, Marxism pursued its international conquest in France. By 1936, the Popular Front had been formed with a social-democratic majority, serving as a barrier to the disquieting growth of fascist ideologies in Germany, Italy, and Spain.

Fascism, often accompanied by racism, was particularly alarming to young Negroes, who, rightly or wrongly, saw a personal threat in the persecution of Jews and in the Ethiopian war. A number of French intellectuals reacted similarly; the great voices of Malraux, Bernanos, Mounier, and many others are not forgotten.

The rise of the European fascist movements, which finally led to World War II, certainly turned the black university students toward socialism. But there were still other reasons. As early as 1922, Lenin had dreamed of extending "proletarianism" to all colonized peoples, and the Communist Party was greatly interested in the lot of black Americans. There is no doubt that these ideological battles greatly encouraged black students to criticize the West.

During the same period, the nationalism of colored peoples was

4. Important personalities of color such as René Maran, Dr. Jean Price-Mars, Claude McKay, Dr. Sajous, Mlle Paulette Nardal, and the Achille brothers contributed to this essentially cultural little magazine.

beginning to awaken. Gandhi already enjoyed considerable prestige between 1930 and 1935, when the first flutterings of political independence became apparent in North Africa. By the time Kwame Nkrumah entered Lincoln University in 1934, "black African nationalism was being molded in English and American universities, thanks to the influence of Asiatic students."[5]

But it was to Paris that others came to be educated, Bourguiba, Césaire, Senghor, Apithy, and several of today's Moroccan cabinet ministers, all of whom would rapidly become leaders of former French colonies. It was also in Paris that African and West Indian blacks first met the revolutionary American Negro writers.

For all these reasons, the French capital seems to have been the crucible in which the ideas of a black elite were forged. This elite would later not only furnish the trained personnel and managerial cadres of the new African states, but also sow the seeds of authentic cultural movements quite distinct from those of the capital, even though they were expressed in the French language. One example is the remarkable renaissance of North African literature, of which Henri Kréa, Jean Amrouche, Mohamed Dib, Albert Memmi, and particularly Kateb Yacine are the best-known writers in France today. In a parallel manner, and also from the fertile soil of the French capital, sprang what Senghor calls both "the New Negro movement" and the literature "of negritude," whose power and originality lies precisely in its commitment.

This is the literature we propose to study. We have therefore eliminated a number of black authors who were not formed in the Parisian crucible. Though the works of these authors often have merit, they are not strong enough to attract an important audience by artistic excellence alone. A single exception is the great Madagascan poet Rabearivelo. However, he is an Indonesian and, although he also suffered from colonization, he nevertheless has no experience of antiblack prejudice and has taken no part in African culture. We could therefore not include him in the Negro movement.

Nor will we speak of black writers prior to the *Légitime Défense* manifesto. We mention here, only as a reminder, the Senegalese infantryman Bakary Diallo, whose novel *Force-Bonté*, published in 1926, was merely a naïve panegyric of France. The learned works of Paul Hazoumé, Maximilien Quenum, and Dim Delobson, most interesting in themselves, are likewise not sufficiently literary to be included in our study.

We have limited ourselves to tracing those writers and intellectuals

5. Nkrumah, as quoted by L. S. Senghor, "African Nationalism," 1958 conference, multiple-copied section, p. 9.

who seem to have influenced the young black authors of 1960. Each group was represented at each stage of the movement's development by a newspaper or a review. We shall first study the reactions of the *Légitime Défense* group to traditional West Indian literature, to American Negro writers, to communism, and to surrealism. We shall then show what Senghor, Césaire, and Damas thought of their elders, how they laid the foundations of today's negritude, propagated their ideas in the newspaper *L'Etudiant Noir,* and created the first works of the new Negro literature. We shall also show how the action begun in Paris was carried on by Césaire, upon his return to Martinique, in the little magazine *Tropiques.*

Our study will therefore be both a history and an analysis: a history of the Negro cultural movement born about 1932 in a Parisian university milieu and flourishing today among a multitude of original writers; an analysis of the influences which nourished the movement, its dominant themes, the interaction of personalities, of the magazines and writings by means of which black writers formed an ideology and a style synthesizing the double culture—French and African—of which they are the heirs. Finally, this study is an analysis of the continuity between contemporary literature of the *Présence Africaine* school and the first Negro intellectuals who laid its foundations when colonialism was at its zenith.

We hope to demonstrate that black writers became truly original only after they had committed themselves. A French West Indian literature had existed for more than a century—a literature devoid of value because it was created in a state of complete subjugation to the mother country's prestigious culture. The present movement produces masterpieces in French only when the black writer, having discovered his own identity, gives free rein to his sensibility and his vision of the world, and does not try to imitate the European classics. It is in this that he commits himself. It is not only himself that he expresses but all Negro peoples in all parts of the world. He expresses an African soul which before had found *written* expression only in certain ethnological works such as those by Frobenius, Bauman, or Griaule.

From the moment they realized and accepted their "Negro" condition, black writers—stirred by an immense desire to express this condition and lead their peoples to freedom—were able to create a literature with its own characteristics whose ultimate appeal lies in the universality of its values.

I   THE BEGINNINGS

1 / *Légitime Défense:* A Manifesto

The first of June, 1932: on the bright red cover of a slender booklet, large black letters spell out *"Légitime Défense"* ("Rightful vindication" or "Legitimate defense"). The admonitions of the first few pages look very much like a manifesto. Declaring themselves "suffocated by this capitalistic, Christian, bourgeois world," a few young colored natives of Martinique, students in Paris, aged twenty to twenty-three, are determined no longer "to compromise with the disgrace surrounding them." To attain this end, they propose to use the new arms that the West itself is offering: communism and surrealism. Choosing as masters Marx, Freud, Rimbaud, and Breton, they declare war on that "abominable system of coercion and restrictions which destroys love and delimits dreams, generally known as Western civilization." Above all, they vehemently attack the bourgeoisie of the West Indies, who seem to them a stiff, unnatural, and ridiculous reflection of the impugned Western values. In their vocabulary of student polemic, abuse is intermingled with professions of faith. "Of all the filthy bourgeois conventions, we particularly despise humanitarian hypocrisy, the stinking emanation of Christian decay. We hate pity. Sentiment means nothing to us," the young rebels declare, and, utterly rejecting the "borrowed personality" worn by blacks and mulattoes of the West Indian bourgeoisie, these students take the "infernal road of absolute sincerity." "We refuse to be ashamed of what we feel."

In short, and this is the important thing, these young people realize that, despite their education, they are different from the Europeans with whom their fathers tried so hard to be assimilated. They see racial and cultural differences not as a deficiency but rather as a fruitful promise. Their words are addressed to all black West Indians, they claim, rather than merely to the bourgeois mulattoes: "We consider

15

that they especially suffer from capitalism, and because their ethics are materially determined that they seem to offer a generally greater potential for revolt and joy."

In the West Indies of 1932, this manifesto proposed the absolute reversal of a solidly established hierarchy of values, a system which was still causing pain in countries already independent, like Haiti. In the preceding century, Victor Schoelcher had written with lucidity: "No man with African blood in his veins can ever do enough to rehabilitate the name of Negro, which slavery has shamed. One might call it a filial duty. The day when mulatto men and particularly mulatto women call themselves black will mark the disappearance of that discrimination contrary to the laws of fraternity and fraught with future misfortunes. Let us face this and never forget it, dear fellow citizens and friends. This is the virus which is now destroying the people of Haiti and leading them to ruin."[1]

It is remarkable that this reversal of values—the first step toward the recognition of negritude—should have been accomplished by young, idealistic intellectuals[2] who were themselves the product of a bourgeois background based on color discrimination and the exploitation of the masses. With the exception of Etienne Léro, all the young contributors to *Légitime Défense* were mulattoes and belonged "under protest" to the very bourgeoisie they so bitterly criticized. Holders of government scholarships or sons of well-to-do officials, they risked losing their means of support, for the periodical had caused a tremendous scandal in the West Indies, outraging their families and friends. This violent reaction, however, proved to the authors that they had touched the heart of the matter.

Of far greater importance to us, however, was the influence of *Légitime Défense* on black students in Paris. It went far beyond the West Indian circle and reached the Africans.[3] Already the little periodical presented completely and coherently all the ideas which would grow into the French-speaking black cultural renaissance: a critique of rationalism, the need to regain an original personality, the rejection of an art subservient to European standards, revolt against colonial capitalism.

The principal founders of this renaissance—Césaire, Senghor and Léon Damas—were directly influenced by these themes. Senghor, who was older than the others and had lived longer in Paris, was in close

1. Victor Schoelcher, *Esclavage et colonisation* ("Slavery and colonization"), ed. F. Tersen (Paris: PUF, 1948), p. 197. Schoelcher's prestige with the generation which immediately preceded the poets of negritude cannot be overestimated.
2. The signers of the manifesto were: Etienne and Thélus Léro, Jules Monnerot, René Ménil, Maurice-Sabat Quitman, Michel Pilotin, Simone Yoyotte.
3. This was confirmed in a letter by L. S. Senghor in February 1960.

contact with the group. Léon Damas devoted three pages of his anthology to the work and personality of Etienne Léro, whom he knew well and admired.[4] Senghor confirms Aimé Césaire's interest in the young manifesto: "When Jules Monnerot, Etienne Léro and René Ménil hurled the manifesto *Légitime Défense* at the West Indian bourgeoisie, Aimé Césaire, then a 'Khagne' student at the lycée Louis-le-Grand, was the first to hear it and to listen to it. Realizing that this message must be thoroughly studied, he turned, on the one hand, to French sources, Rimbaud and Lautréamont, and, on the other hand, to his own sources, to his 'Bambara ancestors,' to Negro African poetry."[5] Senghor acknowledges the importance of Etienne Léro's group:[6] "More than a magazine, more than a cultural group, *Légitime Défense* was a cultural movement. Starting with a Marxist analysis of Island society, he revealed the West Indian as the descendant of Negro African slaves, held for three centuries in the stupefying condition of a proletariat. Surrealism alone, he declared, could liberate him from his taboos and allow him complete expression. We were a long way from *Lucioles.*"[7]

Nevertheless, although the authors of *Légitime Défense* had paved the way for a cultural rebirth, they did not themselves produce any literary works. It is still not quite clear why. René Ménil and Jules Monnerot were obviously more gifted as critics than as writers. After rejecting communism and negritude,[8] Monnerot became famous for his essay *La poésie moderne et le sacré* ("Modern poetry and the sacred").[9] Ménil returned to Martinique and became a professor of philosophy at the lycée in Fort-de-France. He participated actively in the creation of Aimé and Suzanne Césaire's periodical *Tropiques,*[10] but published only articles. Today, he is still an ardent communist. Etienne Léro, who really was a poet, died in 1939 at the age of thirty, while preparing his doctorate in philosophy.

4. Léon Damas, *Poètes d'expression française* (Paris: Seuil, Editions Pierres Vives, 1947).

5. L. S. Senghor, *Anthologie de la nouvelle poésie nègre et malgache de langue française* (Paris: PUF, 1948), p. 55. It was normal that A. Césaire, also from Martinique, should feel and rebel in the same manner as the authors of *Légitime Défense.* As regards his ties with surrealism and later with communism, they came too late to be laid to the influence of the periodical. They can be explained more logically by the character of the writer and his Martinique environment.

6. Ibid., p. 49.

7. *Lucioles* was a small periodical founded in 1927 by the Haitian Léon Laleau, in favor of a more national poetry.

8. J. Monnerot, the only one of the team who remained in Paris, replied very curtly to our request for information, saying that "he wished to have no dealings with these people and had nothing to say!" J. Monnerot now professes extreme right opinions.

9. Paris: Gallimard, 1945, 5th reprint.

10. See part III below, entirely devoted to the periodical *Tropiques.*

The role of the group was essentially to launch and discuss ideas which were only brought to literary fruition later on by Césaire, Senghor, and Damas—a team to which the *Légitime Défense* group, after several years of refining its position, finally yielded its place. After *Légitime Défense,* there was no longer any question that West Indian literature in French was stagnant, and that both more authentic art and more authentic social behavior were called for.

With *Légitime Défense* the New Negro movement in French letters was officially inaugurated. This is why we believe it will be useful to analyze both its content and its sources.

2/ West Indian Literature in French: "A Tracing Paper Poetry"

The violence with which *Légitime Défense* attacked French West Indian literature deserves our attention. It was the sign of a sorely wounded conscience.

Above all these young men censured their elders' writings for "exceptional mediocrity, closely bound to the existing social order." Etienne Léro ruthlessly denounced the conformity in themes and style, "the refusal to adopt any poetic rule unless it is approved by white experience of a hundred years standing."[1]

Why such mediocrity? "The West Indian writer, stuffed to bursting with white morality, white culture, white education, white prejudice, fills his little books with a swollen image of himself. Merely to be a good imitation of the white man fulfills both his social and his poetic requirements. He cannot be too modest or too sedate. Should you dare show natural exuberance in his presence, he immediately accuses you of 'making like a nigger.' So naturally, he does not want 'to make like a nigger' in his poems. It is a point of honor with him that a white person could read his entire book without ever guessing the author's pigmentation."

This was sheer insanity. Léro believed the West Indian's inferiority complex was the cause of this literary servility. "He will stifle his originality in order to be considered 'civilized.' Because of this borrowed personality, his poetry is hardly better than pastiche," declared Léro, aware nonetheless that the "caricature poets" were not entirely responsible for their lot: "Some indigestible mix of French *esprit* and

1. Unless otherwise indicated, all the quotations at the beginning of this chapter are taken from *Légitime Défense*. For René Ménil: "Généralités sur l'écrivain de couleur antillais," pp. 7–9. For Etienne Léro: "Misère d'une poésie," pp. 10–12.

19

classical humanities has produced these babblers and the soothing syrup of their poetry."

Nor did Léro spare his contemporaries, who delighted "in the antiquated prosody and bric-a-brac of the last 150 years: golden wings, transparency, swans, moons, and flutterings." On these grounds he denounced two poets much admired in their own country: Emmanuel Flavia-Léopold and Gilbert Gratiant. "Their age, thirty years, their concern for respectability, their impenitent conformity, their greco-latin university background, their addiction to the past and the trite, make them worthy successors to their pretentious elders."

Léro also rebelled against the poverty of subject matter: landscapes, paintings, conventional historical plots, and idylls in the Parnassian style. "A stranger would search this literature in vain for a profound or an original thought, for the sensuous and colorful imagination of the black man, for an echo of the hates and dreams of an oppressed people. Daniel Thaly, one of the pundits of this class poetry, has celebrated the death of the Caribbean Isles (which is immaterial to us, since, to the last one, they have been exterminated), but remains silent on the revolt of a slave torn from his soil and his family."

René Ménil was even harsher. While Léro, a surrealist poet, was particularly sensitive to the poverty of his compatriots' poetry, Ménil attacked the profound deficiencies of this literature more directly, charging that it systematically avoided the expression of his people's fundamental feelings or needs, which were "condemned" as subject matter "only because they are not mentioned in European literature."[2]

Ménil listed the themes banned by these writers who refuse to accept their race: "the feelings of a cane cutter facing the relentless growth of the factory; the loneliness of the black man all over the world; revolt against the injustices he suffers, particularly in his own country; his love of love; his love of drunken dreams; his love of inspired dancing; his love of life and joy, etc., etc."

Black North American writers such as Langston Hughes and Claude McKay, in contrast, dealt openly with these aspects of the Negro soul. Léro mentions them enthusiastically: "These two revolutionary black poets have brought us . . . the African love of life, African joy, and the African dream of death." "Our distinguished writers never touch these subjects" adds Ménil, "although they could touch the emotions of blacks, yellows, and whites just as poems by American Negroes have moved the whole world. . . . This abstract and hypocritically 'objective'

2. In 1932, West Indian poets were still patterning themselves on the French Parnassian school and had not followed the evolution of poetry toward realism, naturalism, and symbolism.

literature is of no interest to anyone—because it is a poor imitation of dated French writings."

Why are our authors so mediocre? René Ménil asks. Because they have effaced their personality for the benefit of foreign masters, but also because these masters were Banville, Samain, Hérédia, de Régnier, "who could face neither life nor dreams." The Parnassian indifference, formalism, lack of commitment have proved a most efficient means of blinding West Indian blacks to their condition. Ménil concludes his "case" by pointing out the two positive roads which West Indian writers should take to rise out of this psittacism. Either they must accept the world and its problems through a literature seeking to modify life and addressed to those suffering the same passions; or else they must study themselves, explore their egos, rich in turbid and dynamic originality, and by this route rediscover the ancient African depths.

To reply to such a severe indictment, it is well to consult both black and white historians of West Indian literature in French. Also, a few examples will give us a better understanding of the way the young *Légitime Défense* team reacted.

First of all, the judgment passed on the imitative style of West Indian authors is confirmed both by Auguste Viatte and by Dr. Price-Mars.[3] The latter attributes this bondage and lack of authenticity to social causes. Colonized since the sixteenth century, the West Indies and, more particularly, Haiti had and still have a population that is 90 percent illiterate, speaking only Creole. They obviously form a proletarian class. The remaining 10 percent are both educated and French-speaking. They know Creole but despise it. Under these conditions, a written literature had to be in French if it were to reach anyone. Even after Haiti's independence in 1802, to please this "tiny, narrow, boneless" elite, entirely dominated by the cultural prestige of France, poets, novelists, and critics "applied themselves with greater or lesser success to the imitation of French models." Their highest ambition was to become an integral part of the stream of French literature. Any Haitian writer who was favorably received in Paris was sure to find favor with his countrymen. As a result, "his one ambition was to be a success in France. Therefore, in both choice of subject and manner of treating it, he would do his best to imitate those writers who carried weight on the banks of the Seine. Consequently, for a long time our writings were but a pale reflection of the literature of France. . . . The various phases of French literary schools—classic, neoclassic, roman-

3. Dr. Jean Price-Mars, *De Saint-Domingue à Haïti*, an essay on culture, arts, and literature (Paris: Présence Africaine, 1959).

tic, etc.—each had their repercussion in the literature of Haiti."[4] In 1804, when Haiti was proclaimed independent, France remained the center of attraction for Haitian writers, particularly as the revolutionary situation in both countries tended to foster the same kind of creative stimulus. With a marked preference for eloquence and epic or historic forms, Haitian poets closely followed French romanticism and blindly copied its masters, Victor Hugo and Alexandre Dumas. In the West Indies as in France, romanticism provided the same liberation from cramped, lifeless neoclassical forms. It gave free rein to a lyricism which might, according to Brunetière, have become "the expression of the poet's personal feelings, translated into rhythms similar to the nature of his emotions." But, alas! for our West Indian poets, to be lyrical was only a new way to be like French poets. They took little advantage of the opportunity to develop their own originality of temperament.

Yet they did not lack talent. Oswald Durand, for example, a local celebrity, imitated Victor Hugo's style so perfectly that his poem "Idalina" might well have been written by the author of "Sara la baigneuse."

> Je m'en allais, triste et sombre,
>   Cherchant l'ombre
> Propice aux amants jaloux,
> Ecoutant la blanche lame
>   Qui se pame
> En mourant sur les cailloux.
>
> Mais tout à coup sur la rive
>   Elle arrive
> La gentille Idalina
> La brune fille des grèves
>   Qu'en mes rêves
> Le ciel souvent m'amena.
>
> J'étais caché sous les branches,
>   Ses dents blanches
> Mordaient le raisin des mers,
> Elle restait, l'ingénue,
>   Jambe nue
> Jouant dans les flots amers.
>
> [I went my way, sad and somber,
>   Seeking the shadow
> As befits a jealous lover,
> Listening to the white waves break
> And wave upon the pebbled shore.

---

4. Ibid., p. 91.

But suddenly upon the bank
　　She came
The gentle Idalina
Brown maiden of the sands
Whom heaven oft had sent to haunt my dreams.

Hidden in the branches I glimpsed
　　Those white teeth
Nibbling sea-grapes,
How artlessly she sat
　　Bare limbed
Playing 'mongst the briny waves.]　　　　　　　(O. Durand)

Sara, belle indolence,
　　Se balance
Dans un hamac, au-dessus
Du bassin d'une fontaine
　　Toute pleine
D'eau puisée à l'Illyssus.

Elle bat d'un pied timide
　　L'onde humide
Où tremble un mouvant tableau.
Fait rougir son pied d'albâtre
　　Et, folâtre,
Rit de la fraîcheur de l'eau.

Reste ici caché, demeure.
　　Dans une heure
D'un œil ardent tu verras
Sortir du bain l'ingénue
　　Toute nue
Croisant ses mains sur son bras.

[Indolently lovely Sara
　　Swings
In a hammock above
A pool of running water
Water drawn from the Illyssus.

With timid foot she strokes
　　The damp below
In which a morning picture trembles.
Her alabaster foot turns red
　　And playfully
She laughs at the water's coldness.

Stay hidden here! Remain!
　　Within the hour
Your ardent eye will see

> The artless one emerging from her bath
>> Quite nude
> Hands crossed upon her breast.]   (V. Hugo)

Oswald Durand can hardly be criticized for writing like Victor Hugo before André Breton was born. He can, however, be criticized for aping a fashionable French author without adding any personal touch of his own. What is deplorable is that critics should have judged his merits only according to the degree of his "depersonalization."

As faithfully as they had followed the romantic school, West Indian writers next imitated the Parnassian. Leconte de Lisle, François Coppée, Sully Prudhomme, and, at best, Baudelaire were the undisputed masters for so long that as late as 1945 Hérald L. C. Roy was able to write the following verses:

> Le soleil me surprit chez ces vieilles catins
> Ou le Rappel déjà basculait son tocsin
> Réveillant quelque enfant très belle mais trop fière
> Glacée à mon desir comme une fleur de pierre.[5]

> [The sun surprised me among these old whores
> As memory already was striking its chord
> Awakening some very beautiful but too proud child
> As cold to my desire as a flower made of stone.]

Let us now see what Auguste Viatte, the author of a very thorough literary history of Haiti and the Lesser Antilles, has to say. The excerpts we have given prove that this literature is definitely in the French style and without originality. However, far from branding these bonds with his country as "alienating," Mr. Viatte happily collects Haitian intellectuals' statements praising "the glorious destiny of Canada and the French West Indies to preserve the traditions and the language of France."[6] "The greatest country of the black man is France . . . for it must be repeated that the first time a man of the black race was a citizen, he was a French citizen; the first time a man of our race was an officer, he was a French officer. And where is our birth certificate? Is it not in France, in the Declaration of the Rights of Man?"[7] Or again: "Anything which can serve to strengthen French influence, harmless politically, seems to us worth encouraging."[8]

Mr. Viatte is also very lenient toward authors such as Daniel Thaly

5. Hérald L. C. Roy, *Les variations tropicales* (Port-au-Prince, 1945), p. 51.
6. Auguste Viatte, *Histoire littéraire de l'Amérique française, des origines à 1950* (Paris: PUF, 1954), p. 440.
7. Ibid., p. 429.
8. Ibid., p. 451.

or Ida Faubert who in 1939 published the following platitudinous lines:

> Ne plus penser, ne plus sentir
> Laisser son coeur à la dérive
> Sans lourd chagrin, sans peine vive
> N'être plus rien, s'anéantir.
>
> Mais ce bonheur, je n'en veux pas
> Il est pour moi trop incolore
> Je veux voir les jasmins éclore
> Et sentir l'odeur des lilas.
>
> Je veux garder dans ma poitrine
> Un cœur palpitant de désir;
> Qu'importe si je dois mourir
> De joie et d'extase de vivre.[9]

> [To think no more, to feel no more,
> To set one's heart adrift,
> Relieved of heavy cares, of living grief
> To be nothing any more, to die.
>
> But this happiness I do not wish,
> For me it is too dull
> I want to see the jasmines bloom
> And smell the scent of lilac.
>
> Within my heart I want to keep
> A heart that trembles with desire;
> What matter if I die of joy
> And the ecstasy of living?]

Gilbert Gratiant of Martinique, who was so violently attacked by *Légitime Défense*, was rehabilitated by Viatte, doubtless because he wrote, "This is my climate, the atmosphere of France"* and because he "thanks France for the extravagance and openess of the love she shows for other races." Gratiant also "invites his fellow blacks the world over . . . to return much to France in a mystical coalescing which will expand West Indian destiny to a universal dimension." Forgiven for his lack of imagination, the poet is urged to achieve "a synthesis beyond racism" by "freeing his personality from servility and from violence."[10]

It is perfectly understandable that Gilbert Gratiant was no partisan of negritude and laid claim to his French culture instead. He was

9. Ida Faubert, *Cœur des Iles* (Paris, 1939). Quoted in A. Viatte's study, p. 453.

* Translator's note: *la présence française*, as distinct, for example, from *la présence africaine*.

10. Auguste Viatte, *Histoire littéraire*, pp. 498–99.

educated almost entirely in France and was a very light mulatto. To forgive him his naïve faith in an idyllic vision of colonial France, despite reality, is one thing. But to place him on the same level as Aimé Césaire can only be explained by a patriotism to which Mr. Viatte seems unconsciously to fall victim. Whatever the occasional pearl one may find in it, Gilbert Gratiant's work never rises above the mediocre. If Gratiant has one merit worth underscoring, it is to have acknowledged without shame the few drops of black blood that flow in his veins. He is one of the few before the negritude[11] generation who dared do this.

Our research brings us to the conclusion that prior to *Légitime Défense* there was no originality in West Indian literature in French.

Yet the case of Haiti, which anticipates that of the neighboring islands, must be considered separately. Paradoxically, the American occupation in 1915 provoked a sort of identity crisis among Haitian intellectuals and prepared them for a literary renewal. Out of patriotism and a spirit of resistance, they became interested in folklore and native traditions. They passionately studied habits, beliefs, folk legends, and found all of them intact and alive among the Haitian peasants. The intellectuals were amazed. Their national culture, so long unappreciated, now seemed worth studying. It was raw material for research in ethnology, psychology, and art. Little magazines such as the *Nouvelle Ronde*, the *Revue Indigène*, the *Revue des Griots*[12] expressed this new trend.

Carl Brouard, editor of the *Revue des Griots*, described the aim of his magazine as follows: "We Haitian Griots must sing the splendor of our landscapes . . . the beauty of our women, the achievements of our ancestors. We must study our folklore with passion and remember that to 'change religions is to venture into an unknown desert,' that to ignore one's history is to risk the loss of racial genius and traditions. The wise man does not abandon these; he tries to understand them."[13]

Let us now consider the determining influence of Jean Price-Mars,

---

11. We shall examine the word *negritude* in chap. 9.

12. *Griots*, common through West Africa, are both troubadors and historians. In certain tribes they form a hereditary caste, exactly like other artisan groups. Some of them, from father to son, have been in the service of a prince or noble family. At important ceremonies (religious or secular festivals, war commemorations, funerals, etc.) they celebrate family exploits; they also serve as historians and counselors, and transmit verbally the mighty deeds of their overlords. Others are public story tellers, musicians, poets. They go from village to village and enliven the social evenings or, in the cities, hire their services to rich families on a temporary basis.

For more information on the *griots*, see Roland Colin's interesting study in *Les contes de l'Ouest africain* (Paris: Présence Africaine, 1957).

13. Quoted in J. Price-Mars's study, *De Saint-Dominque à Haïti*, p. 52.

the Haitian physician and diplomat. He actively encouraged the new current of ideas through his lectures, books, and articles, and by founding the Ethnological Institute of Haiti. Later, he became a deputy, a plenipotentiary minister, president of the Haitian delegation to the United Nations, and rector of the University of Haiti. All these important functions strengthened his intellectual authority and influence still further. Price-Mars was the first to expose the literary deficiencies of his compatriots, who did not dare to think of themselves as Negroes. "By dint of seeing ourselves as 'colored' Frenchmen," said Price-Mars, "we had forgotten to be simply Haitians, namely, men born under specific historical conditions."[14] Price-Mars considered Haitian folklore, Creole dialect, and the voodoo religion as the essential bedrock upon which "the race could rebuild the inmost feelings of its genius and the certainty of its indestructible vitality."[15] Pursuing the inner logic of this line of thought, as he reevaluated his race and culture, Price-Mars concluded by recognizing his African origins. "Our only chance to be ourselves is to repudiate no part of our ancestral heritage. For eight-tenths of us this heritage is a gift from Africa."[16]

So influential was Price-Mars that the Americans who occupied Haiti obtained but one victory, which they hardly expected: "What they had unwittingly aroused was a return to Africa."[17]

Dr. Price-Mars nevertheless met considerable resistance. If younger Haitians were enthusiastically in favor of these new ideas, the scholars of his own generation poked fun at an Africanism that dared to compete with French culture—a culture still profoundly influential. Ten years later, when the new ideas had made their impact and Haitians were more aware of their origins, it was still in classical French form that Léon Laleau expressed longing for his lost African heritage:

> Ce cœur obsédant qui ne correspond
> Pas avec mon langage et mes costumes
> Et sur leguel mordent, comme un crampon,
> Des sentiments d'emprunt et des coutumes
> D'Europe, sentez-vous cette souffrance
> Et ce désespoir à nul autre égal
> D'apprivoiser, avec des mots de France,
> Ce cœur qui m'est venu du Sénégal?[18]

14. J. Price-Mars, *Ainsi parla l'oncle*, an essay on ethnography (Compiègne: Bibliothèque Haïtienne, 1928), p. 11.

15. Ibid., p. 20.

16. Ibid., p. 210.

17. Auguste Viatte, *Histoire littéraire*, p. 439.

18. Léon Laleau's poem "Trahison," in *Musique nègre* (Port-au-Prince, 1931). In 1927, assisted by G. Gratiant, L. Laleau had founded a journal called *Lucioles*, which lasted but a short time but already demonstrated the cultural originality of the West Indies.

[This haunted heart that does not fit
My language or the clothes I wear
Chafes within the grip of
Borrowed feelings, European ways.
Do you feel my pain
This anguish like none other
From taming with the words of France
This heart that came to me from Senegal?]

Actually the influence of Price-Mars and the *Revue des Griots* bore important literary fruit only after 1930, with Léon Laleau's *Le choc* ("The impact," 1932), in which he describes the consequences of the American occupation; with the peasant novels of Jean-Baptiste Cinéas (1936) or Jacques Roumain (1934), which deeply affected the entire younger generation of his country.[19]

If the negritude movement found a fairly well-prepared soil in Haiti, the situation was considerably different in the Lesser Antilles. In 1925, Emmanuel Flavia-Léopold had appreciated and translated the black American poets Langston Hughes and Claude McKay. In 1951 Gilbert Gratiant sang:

Le chant primordial de la vie
L'enchaîné des cadences,
L'envoûte des riches palabres,
L'insatiable mangeur d'amour
Et le fumeur de songeries
   le Nègre
Si grand par le service et si haut par le don.[20]

[The primordial song of life
The linked sequence of rhythms,
The magic of rich words—
Insatiable consumer of love
And spinner of day-dreams
   The Negro
So great in his service and so lofty in his gifts.]

But apart from these, there was nothing further.

In 1937, the Guadeloupian Gilbert de Chambertrand published a whole collection of poems still in the pure Parnassian style, which

19. Jacques Roumain is only known in France for one novel, *Gouverneurs de la rosée*, written in 1944, published in 1946 by the Editeurs Français Reunis, Paris. [Translator's note: published in English as *Masters of the Dew* (1947; reprinted 1971), trans. Langston Hughes and Mercer Cook.] A contemporary Haitian writer, Jacques Stéphen Alexis, continues the tradition of the peasant novel.

20. Gilbert Gratiant, *Poèmes en vers faux* (Paris, 1931), p. 76.

might easily have been signed almost a century earlier by Leconte de Lisle:

> Midi ! L'air qui flamboie, et brûle, et se consume,
> Verse à nos faibles yeux l'implacable clarté.
> Tout vibre dans l'espace et sur l'immensité;
> L'azur est sans nuage et l'horizon sans brume.
>
> Là-bas, sur les récifs lointains frangés d'écume,
> Dans un grondement sourd par l'écho répété,
> La mer éclate et gicle au chaud soleil d'été,
> Et sur le flot mouvant chaque crête s'allume.
>
> Parfois, au bord du ciel et de l'océan bleu,
> On croit apercevoir sous l'atmosphère en feu
> Le contour d'une voile immobile et brillante . . .
>
> Et sur la plage d'or, les sveltes cocotiers,
> Dressant leurs fûts étroits dans l'heure étincelante,
> Ont toute une ombre épaisse écrasée à leur pieds.[21]

> [Noon! The air is flame, and burns, and is consumed,
> Pours out to our weak eyes its implacable brilliance.
> In space, in the immensity everything vibrates;
> The blue is without cloud, the horizon is clear.
>
> Out there, on the distant reefs, all fringed with foam,
> Its booming muffled by the constant echo,
> The sea bursts and splashes in hot summer sun
> And every crest is lit atop the moving flood.
>
> Sometimes, at the meeting of blue sky and water
> One thinks one sees beneath the fiery air
> The contour of a reef shining and immobile . . .
>
> And on the golden beach, the cocoa palms
> Raising slender trunks at this dazzling hour
> Leave great thick shadows crumpled at their feet.]

A whole poetry of the exotic was developing along parallel lines. Excellent examples were included in the literary exhibition organized in Paris by the Ministry of Colonies in 1945. It had a significant title, "The happy Antilles," "in honor of all those who have dreamed of the Islands with a poet's heart."[22] The exhibition brought together a number of authors who had written about the West Indies, from Madame de Maintenon to Gilbert Gratiant, including Hérédia, Loti, de Régnier, Francis Jammes, René Maran, and Saint-John Perse.

---

21. Gilbert de Chambertrand, *Images guadeloupéennes,* a collection of poetry quoted in Léon Damas's anthology *Poètes d'expression française* (Paris, 1947), p. 43.
22. *Les Antilles heureuses* (Paris: Ministry of Colonies, June–July 1945).

(The name of Aimé Césaire was only mentioned.)

It seems worthwhile to quote liberally here from these Frenchmen, some of whom never actually saw the West Indies close up. Already in that period, and even earlier as indicated by the dates of the poems, we find that Frenchmen in France had a charming, idyllic, and exclusively external vision of the Islands, and cared not at all about real conditions there. That blindness was maintained by the organizers of the exhibition, with their insistence on the "happy life" of the West Indies. The preface to their catalogue gave notice that "the mission of a colonizer must not be limited to progress and prosperity. More than any other colonies, Martinique and Guadeloupe have remained faithful to the décor, attitudes, and rhythms of centuries past. The world as it is now developing must not sacrifice poetry to economic problems."

Here are some excerpts:

Mme Desbordes-Valmore (1786–1859):

> Qui me consolera?—Nous, m'ont dit les voyages
> Laisse-nous t'emporter vers de lointaines fleurs.
> ....
> Viens sous les bananiers, nous trouverons l'ombrage
> Les oiseaux vont chanter en voyant notre amour
> Vos longs soleils, votre ombre et vos vertes fraîcheurs.

> [Who will console me?—We shall, travel told me
> Let us carry you toward distant flowers
> ....
> Come 'neath the banana trees, we shall find the shady places
> Birds will sing to see our love,
> Your long sunshine, your shade and your verdant coolness.]

Hérédia (1842–1905):

> Là-bas où les Antilles bleues
> Se pâment sous l'ardeur de l'astre occidental.

> [There where the blue Antilles
> Swoon beneath the ardour of the western star.]

Saint-John Perse (1887–1975):

> Un monde balance entre des eaux brillantes
> Connaissant le mât lisse des fûts, la
> hune sous les feuilles, les haubans de
> liane, ou trop longues, les fleurs jaunes
> s'achevaient en cris de perruches.

> [A world at anchor on the shining waters

Familiar with the smooth masts of tree trunks
mainsails among their leaves, creeping vines like shrouds
and those too long yellow flowers
with screaming parakeets above.]

René Maran (1887–1960):

Ah! toute la douceur de ma petite enfance
Ces languissantes nuits du port de Fort-de-France
Paradis végétaux
Enchantez-moi longtemps du jeu de vos prestiges.

[Ah! all the sweetness of my early childhood
Those languid nights in the port of Fort-de-France
A vegetable paradise
Long do you enchant me with your captivating play.]

René Chalupt (1885–19--):

Je songe à mon aïeul qui était médecin
Il avait sa maison sise à Pointe-à-Pitre.
Le soir on se réunissait entre voisins
Quand des insectes d'or volaient contre les vitres
Une négresse souple avec un pagne clair
Dont le pas nu rythmait le silence en sourdine
Apportait au jardin sur la table de fer
De l'eau et des confitures de barbadines
. . . Iles où mes parents connurent le bonheur
De longs jours coulés à l'abri d'un climat tendre.

[I recall my doctor relative
And his house at Point-à-Pitre,
His garden where the neighbors used to gather in the evenings
As golden insects flew against the panes
A supple black girl brightly dressed would come
With Barbado sweets and drinks on a small wrought iron table
Her bare feet made mute rhythm in the silence
. . . Islands where my folk knew happiness
Long flowing days in the comfort of a tender clime.]

John-Antoine Nau (1860–1918):

La houle molle des cocotiers sur les Açores
La rythmique floraison
Dans la brise des madras multicolores
Sur les tiges des corps balancés.

[The soft crowd of cocoa palms along the Azores
The rhythmic blooming

> In the breeze of multicolored madras
> About the shapes of swaying bodies.]

Léonard (1744–93):

> Quels beaux jours j'ai goûtés sur vos rives lointaines
> Lieux chéris que mon cœur ne saurait oublier
> Antille merveilleuse où le baume des plaines
> Va jusqu'au sein des mers, saisir le nautonier.

> [Such lovely days I've savored upon your distant shores
> Cherished scenes my heart will not forget
> Marvellous Antilles, the sweet scent of your fields
> Reaches out to seize the mariner at sea.]

Elsewhere it is said that Paul Gauguin and Charles Naval spent happy days in this paradise, "eating fish and fruit, painting palm and banana trees and, above all, the natives!"* The transformation of men (the natives) into things is perfectly expressed in that sentence.

This whole literature is filled with Creole nonchalance, the sweetness of living, and evocations of paradise as false and naïve as Gilbert Gratiant's description of France:

> Terre de sécurité, d'accueil et salvatrice
> . . . Pays sans injustice
> . . . Pays de mille merveilles
> Pays de pralines, de pruneaux, de dragées
> Pays de joujoux multicolores
> ....
> Pays où les torts se redressent
> Pays des maladies guéries
> ....
> Pays d'où viennent, polis et lisses
> Précis et merveilleux
> Miracle du fini
> Les objets compliqués qui sortent des fabriques
> Pays des trains, des gares, des monuments vus au stéréoscope
> Pays de la neige tombant sur des manchons de loutre.[23]

> [Land of security, of welcome and salvation
> . . . Land without injustice
> . . . Land of a thousand marvels
> Country of pralines, and prunes, of sugared almonds
> Land of multicolored playthings
> ....

---

*Translator's note: Gauguin spent 1887 in Martinique, several years before his first visit to Tahiti.

23. Gilbert Gratiant, *Credo des sang-mêlé, ou Je veux chanter la France* (Fort-de-France, 1950).

Land where wrongs are turned to right
Land where illnesses are cured
....
Land from which come things
All smooth and polished
All marvellous precise
Miracle of the finite—
The complicated objects
That emerge from factories
Land of trains, of stations, monuments seen through stereoscopes
Land of falling snow on muffs of otter fur.]

It may be permissible for a stranger to see only the picturesque in a country, as Gratiant does intentionally here. But the problem becomes serious when a native describes his own land the same way. This is exactly what happened in the West Indies. Read these excerpts from an unpublished poem by Gilbert Gratiant, "Martinique totale," written in 1957:

Coffre à baisers
Colibri du tourisme
Bijou géographique
....
Cher jardin des petits cadeaux
Sol pour les démarches souples
Et l'ample enjambée des femmes de couleur
Petit cirque des corridors du cœur
Familière boîte à surprise
....
Jet d'eau de menus mots d'amour
Cage de femmes au langage d'oiseaux parleurs
Cascatelle chantante de syllabes-caresses
Chaude patrie des beaux yeux
Des longues mains et des gorges assurées . . .[24]

[Coffer of kisses
Hummingbird to tourists
Geographic gem
....
Dear garden of small gifts
Ground for the supple footsteps
And ample stride of colored women
Small circus of the hallway of the heart

24. Gilbert Gratiant, from an unpublished poem also containing more realistic evocations than in the excerpt given above (Negro strikers, social injustice, and exploitation). Note, however, in spite of his many years standing as a Communist Party member—and the literary themes this necessarily entailed—Gratiant could not refrain from spontaneously returning to his original exotic style.

> Familiar Jack-in-the-box
> ....
> Fountain of fine words of love
> Cage to women who speak like talking birds
> Singing waterfall of syllable caresses
> Warm land of lovely eyes,
> Long hands, firm breasts . . .]

Having made it a habit to be towed along by the French, West Indian writers were unaware that they had placed themselves in an unreal situation. The end effect was that they too began to look at their country through foreign eyes, no longer seeing anything but its exotic aspects.

An article by René Ménil analyzes this phenomenon with great lucidity.[25] The natural tendency of exoticism, he says, is to miss the seriousness and authenticity of a foreign country's drama, and to see only the décor, the external picturesque, and man as part of this décor. But can one imagine a man having this exotic vision of himself? For him to describe himself and his people "remotely, externally, superficially, without personal drama"? Yet there are the texts. René Ménil, who has had the time to reflect upon his youthful rebellion, explains the paradox this way: "The phenomenon of cultural oppression inseparable from colonialism will, in each colonized country, result in the suppression of the national spirit (history, religion, customs) in order to introduce what we shall call "the soul-of-the-other-mother-country." The result is depersonalization and estrangement. I see myself as a stranger, as exotic. Why? I am "exotic-to-myself" because my way of looking at myself has become, after three centuries of colonial conditioning, the white man's way."

The exoticism in literature, we must add, is only one aspect of color prejudice in the West Indies. The black West Indian's scale of values is a copy of the white man's. That is the cause of his fundamental alienation, as we shall see in chapter 4.

Depersonalization was greater in the Lesser Antilles than in Haiti because the political situation was different.[26] It is significant that the *Légitime Défense* group was composed entirely of students from Martinique. This explains the extremity of their revolt, its bitterness of tone and violent causticism that are perceptible even today. It also explains why Léon Damas, a native of French Guiana educated in Martinique, was so harshly critical of the "tracing paper poets."[27] It

25. René Ménil, "Sur l'exotisme colonial," in the *Nouvelle Critique*, May 1959, p. 139.

26. Haiti won its independence in 1804, whereas Martinique and Guadeloupe are to this day French states, in which slavery was abolished only in 1848.

27. Léon Damas, *Poètes d'expression française*, p. 9.

also explains Suzanne Césaire's youthful ferocity, as late as 1941, as she tore into a "typical" Martiniquan writer, John-Antoine Nau:[28]

> Les Martiniquais ne l'ont pas oublié.
> Nul n'a décrit plus amoureusement nos paysages
> Nul n'a plus sincèrement chanté les «charmes» de la vie créole.
> Langueur, douceur, mièvrerie aussi. Saint-Pierre . . . le volcan . . .
> «les matins de satin bleu» . . . «les soirs mauves» . . .
>
> «Le ciel net et floral, conscient de ravir
> Dôme en cristal vermeil qui tinte au chant des cloches
> Miroite lumineux et doux: au pied des roches
> Des noirs plongent au flot rosé qui va bleuir.»
> «Dans les tamariniers des franges de frémir
> De clairs gosiers d'oiseaux perlent de triples-croches.»
>
> Des pamoisons, du bleu, des ors, du rose. C'est gentil. C'est léché. De la littérature? Oui. Littérature de hamac. Littérature de sucre et de vanille. Tourisme littéraire . . . Allons, la vraie poésie est ailleurs. Loin des rimes, des complaintes, des alizés, des perroquets. Bambous, nous décrétons la mort de la littérature doudou. Et zut à l'hibiscus, à la frangipane, aux bougainvilliers. La poésie martiniquaise sera cannibale ou ne sera pas.

> [Martiniquans have not forgotten him.
> No-one has described our landscapes more amorously
> No-one has sung more sincerely of the "charm" of Creole life.
> Languor, sweetness—affectations too—Saint-Pierre, the volcano,
> "mornings like blue satin," "lavender evenings."
>
> "The clear and floral sky, aware that it is ravishing,
> vault of silver crystal tinkling at the ringing of the bells,
> the luminous sweet shimmer: the rocks—
> the blacks plunging into rosy waters which are turning blue,"
> "Fronds quiver in the tamarind trees,
> as clear throated birds let peal their triple-warbles."
>
> Swoonings, blues, golds, pinks. How nice! How overdone! Literature? Yes. Literature from the hammock, made of sugar and vanilla. Tourist literature . . . Come now! Real poetry is somewhere else. Far from shyness, laments, soft breezes, parrotings. We decree the death of *frou frou* literature. And to hell with hibiscus, the scent of jasmine, and bougainvillea. Either the poetry of Martinique will be done with them or there will be no poetry in Martinique!]

The attack on West Indian literature opens the attack on all "acquired" culture. René Ménil begins it: "We have read other people's

---

28. Suzanne Césaire, *"Misère d'une poésie:* John-Antoine Nau," in *Tropiques* (Fort-de-France), no. 4, 1941.

culture. . . . The mechanical recitation of the past, the childish hobby of collecting picture postcards, the repetition of words invented by others, have turned the best of us into political sorcerers, stage comedians, vaticinating with less conviction and beauty than Australian rainmakers. Culture is elsewhere. So is life. . . . All our cultural manifestations so far have been nothing but copies . . . useless mirror images."[29] And Aimé Césaire punctuates Ménil with this remark: "We have had no art. No poetry. Rather, a hideous leprosy of counterfeits."[30]

West Indian literature had indeed not much aesthetic value. One might find a few good lines or even a few moving poems. This did not, however, relieve the overall mediocrity. One can understand the iconoclastic rage that drove the young West Indians to reject this poetry as soon as they had understood that there is no art without authenticity. They found no trace of their own feelings or of real problems in this literature. It lacked life and, in search of some Western mirage, had been cut off from its real sources. The group were painfully aware of the efforts and contortions their compatriots underwent in an effort to resemble the French. If they reacted with such violence, it was because they realized this literary imitation was the expression of a cultural servility which had in turn social, political, and racial roots. In spirit and at heart, West Indians were still enslaved.

Césaire describes his countrymen in *Cahier d'un retour au pays natal:*

Et dans cette ville inerte, cette foule criarde si étonnamment passée à côté de son cri . . . sans inquiétude, à côté de son vrai cri, le seul qu'on eut voulu l'entendre crier parce qu'on le sent sien, lui seul . . . dans cette ville inerte, cette foule à côté de son cri de faim, de misère, de révolte, de haine, cette foule si étrangement bavarde et muette.[31]

[And within the inert city, the noisy crowd so surprisingly missing the point of its noise . . . making insouciant detours from its true cry, the only one one would want to hear cried because one feels it *is* this town's belonging to it alone . . . within this inert city, within this crowd that overlooks its cries of hunger, misery, revolt and hate, this crowd so strangely talkative and mute.]

Such were West Indian poets, "strangely talkative and mute," failing to hear their own cry, singing instead of "an old life, deceptively smiling."[32]

29. René Ménil, "Naissance de notre art," in *Tropiques*, no. 1, April 1944.
30. Aimé Césaire, Introduction to issue no. 1 of *Tropiques.*
31. Paris: Présence Africaine, 1956, p. 27.
32. Ibid., p. 26.

3/ Surrealism and Criticism of the West

As an antidote to the dated, mediocre, inauthentic Caribbean literature in French, *Légitime Défense* brandished a new literary credo.

"We accept surrealism without reservation and—today in 1932—we pledge our future development to it. Our readers are referred to André Breton's two 'Manifestos' and to the work of Louis Aragon, André Breton, René Crevel, Salvador Dali, Paul Eluard, Benjamin Péret, Tristan Tzara. It is the shame of our time that they are so little known among French-speaking peoples."[1]

The West Indian students of *Légitime Défense* thus openly declared themselves disciples of the French surrealist school. The very title of their journal was taken from a small book by André Breton, published in 1926, which favored communism but disapproved of the French Communist Party for manifesting "veiled hostility" to its surrealist members.[2]

"Surrealism was both school and teacher to *Légitime Défense*'s contributors, to whom the movement had the universal value of discovery. . . . Monnerot and his friends were closely connected with the surrealist poets," writes Senghor.[3] Breton, too, recalls the young West Indian

1. *Légitime Défense*, "Avertissement," p. 1.

2. André Breton, *Légitime Défense* (Paris: Editions Surréalistes, September 1926). At the request of the Communist Party, the author later withdrew this manifesto from publication. He left the party a few years later. The following is an excerpt from the booklet, which shows its general tone: "I do not know why I should abstain any longer from saying that *L'Humanité*—puerile, declamatory, needlessly moronic—is an unreadable newspaper, unworthy of its supposed role of educating the proletariat" (p. 7). When we quote *Légitime Défense*, it is always in reference to the West Indian periodical.

3. L. S. Senghor, letter of 8 February 1960.

group as a parallel movement to his own.[4] The epigones of surrealism were numerous at the time. In addition to the front-rank team, of which Roger Vailland was a member, there were also the adherents of simultaneism, vorticism, zenithism, imaginism, and constructivism, who made a great deal of noise without any aim except to shock.[5]

This undoubtedly explains the lack of reaction in French intellectual milieus when the explosive little magazine was published. *Légitime Défense*, whose violent tone is still surprising, went almost unnoticed amid the many scandals occasioned by the surrealists: insulting letters to Paul Claudel and university rectors, burlesque processions at the funeral of Anatole France, and other unwonted abuse.[6]

Although the magazine explained at length why it rejected West Indian literature, it gave no reasons for its adherence to surrealism. In the light of later articles by René Ménil, and with a little thought, it is easy to discover these reasons.

First, there were literary reasons. It was normal for these young students, graduates of a lycée in Martinique who had only been given Parnassian models or local imitations thereof, to be dazzled by surrealism in France. Surrealism was protesting against practically everything that irritated them about their own bourgeois literature and art. R. M. Alberès describes with feeling what had happened to French poetry and painting and what useful work of destruction the surrealists were doing. "For centuries, feelings had been refined to the point of insipidness, until poetry had become mere psittacism. Ever since the Renaissance, man's vision of things had been perfecting a realism originally introduced for the purpose of perspectives and optical illusions. Imagination turned round and round within the same circle of conventional ideas. From the constant effort to improve skills, always along the same lines, art became little more than a collection of recipes. A poem was constructed according to certain associations of ideas, calling invariably upon certain established rhythms and clichés. The beauty of nature was inevitably involved—the passage of clouds and the song of birds. A painting showed objects in perspective and in three-dimensional Euclidian space. These conventions, which eye and memory had registered since school days, had now become Truth and Beauty. In written texts it was considered a crime not to precede the word 'poppy' with the adjective 'red,' and in a painting, not to reduce objects in proportion to their distance.

"Surrealism set dynamite under these conventions and blew them

---

4. Interview with André Breton, January 1960.
5. Cf. R. M. Alberès, *L'aventure intellectuelle du XXe siècle* (Paris: Albin Michel, 1959).
6. Cf. R. M. Alberès, *L'aventure*, and Roger Vailland, *Le surréalisme contre la révolution* (Paris: Editions Sociales, 1948).

up. New foliage grew in the ruined palaces of sentiment and rhetoric. A jungle of wild plants, their roots drawing strength from the unconscious and their strange shapes breaking all known rules of botany, fertilized the fields of rubble—the ruins of the ever heavier constructions of a civilization which, from a surfeit of rational humanism, had drowned in the habitual.

"Thought, sensitivity, imagination, had fashioned themselves into veritable laws which at last proved suffocating. The surrealists made a clean sweep of these laws in order to return to sincerity."[7]

Literary revolution, the freeing of style and the imagination, the debunking aspect of a movement then at its zenith, would inevitably attract those young people disgusted by the "rigidity and datedness," to quote Etienne Léro, of their islands. Léro declared that a poem ought to be "a ribbon of dynamite." "It is surrealism's glory and strength ever more deeply to have fused poetry and its purpose." He explained his idea with a metaphor: "Until she saw her father naked, a little girl had always confused him with the clothing he wore. Suddenly, naked, he became dark and incomprehensible. This is also true of prudes with surrealist poetry."[8]

To renew sensibilities and imaginations impoverished by rationalism, the surrealists turned to the theories of Freud. Freud's vision of a world of children and primitive people seemed specially significant. Indeed, this vision, not yet cut off from the living strengths of the unconscious, seemed naturally poetic, piercing straight through appearances and the pragmatic. André Breton confirmed this appraisal again in 1946:

In the twentieth century, the European artist, swept along by the reasonable and the useful, can guard against the drying up of his sources of inspiration only by returning to a so-called primitive vision, the synthesis of sensorial perception and mental image. Black sculpture has already been put to brilliant use. Today it is particularly the plastic arts of the red race that give us access to a new method of knowledge and correspondence. In his *La poésie moderne et le sacré* ("Modern poetry and the sacred"), Monnerot has skillfully demonstrated the affinity between surrealist poetry and Indian poetry which, I affirm, is still as alive and as creative as ever.[9]

This reevaluation of primitive peoples and their arts did not pass unnoticed among representatives of races still considered inferior because of their nonrational cultures. Senghor well understood that, since surrealism, it was no longer pejorative to write that "Negroes had

7. R. M. Alberès, *L'aventure*, p. 168.
8. Etienne Léro, "Misère d'une poésie," in *Légitime Défense*, p. 12.
9. Jean Duche, "André Breton nous parle," in *Figaro*'s literary supplement, 5 October 1946.

not left the Kingdom of Childhood."[10] Values had, in effect, been reversed; it was now the most "civilized" man who was the most "naked," the least pure.

Surrealism thus provided an excellent brake to cultural assimilation and furnished new weapons against the academic style of traditional French West Indian art. Surrealism had the added advantage of shocking bourgeois society and stimulating social revolution. In France as well, Breton and his disciples used surrealism—expressed at the time in humorous or vulgar gestures, words, or actions—to declare their rejection of the "narrow, miserable world that is inflicted on us."[11]

In addition to the literary reasons we have mentioned, surrealism was adopted by West Indian students in France for its revolutionary spirit, its "permanent rebellion against art, morals, society."[12]

Nothing better illustrates this characteristic than Dada's manifesto, which borders on nihilism:

No more painters, no more men of letters, no more musicians, no more sculptors, no more religions, no more republicans, no more royalists, no more imperialists, no more anarchists, no more socialists, no more bolsheviks, no more politics, no more proletarians, no more democrats, no more bourgeois, no more aristocrats, no more army, no more police, no more countries, but enough of these stupidities, no more anything, anything, NOTHING, NOTHING, NOTHING.[13]

Surrealism was only drawing conclusions from the more general case being brought by all European writers against the very foundations of their civilization. The first of these conclusions acknowledged the failure of Universal Reason.

The ruling classes, which for two centuries had based their culture on free rational examination, were now refusing to follow this rationalism. They declared it arid and outdated. Literature promptly sought new sources of life. Pragmatic philosophy was the signal for this change which was to lead to Bergson and to existentialism.

Since Bacon de Verulam, there had been hope that . . . human intelligence left to its own designs would attain total and unified truth, definitively permitting a relation between man and the world based on reason. But science, bursting under the pressure of new discoveries, the principle of indetermination, the quantum theories, and relativity, became obscure and illogical. It ceased to have meaning on the human scale, and its progress seemed but a long series of lost illusions.[14]

10. L. S. Senghor, "Langage et poésie" (unpublished lecture).
11. A. Breton, quoted by Roger Vailland in Le surréalisme, p. 39.
12. G. Ribemont-Dessaignes, in Nouvelle Revue Française, June 1931, p. 868, quoted by R. M. Alberès in L'aventure, p. 167.
13. Maurice Nadeau, Histoire du surréalisme (Paris: Seuil, 1945).
14. R. M. Alberès, L'aventure, p. 15.

With science gone, philosophy and religion were no longer solid. They ceased to be "dogmas according to which one could live at peace in exchange for token payment."[15] If intellectuals thus lost faith in dogma, it was in great part because of a social and political situation so disastrous that the very principles upon which that situation was based were now in question.

Right from the start, this civilization which had tried to understand and organize the world according to pure reason had been a spectacle of massacres, colonial wars, future wars, internal dissensions. And yet France had its republic, Italy its independence, Germany its unity and England its empire. Humanist hopes had become reality; science had enabled man to dominate the universe far beyond his hopes. Industry, however, had not liberated man, freedom had only succeeded in poisoning people with rationalism. A better world had been hoped for, but it did not come. Human passions had prevented it. . . .

How this century kept its promises is sufficiently well known: two chaotic world wars, in which the popular mystiques of nationalism increased at the same time as the mysticism of literature. . . .

Disappointment thus endured turned into a pessimism which finally had to acknowledge that man had been powerless to organize his destiny and had been vanquished by his errors. . . . We shall naturally come to believe that humanism has steered the wrong course, that man is in fact dominated by superior forces: fate, instinct, his race, God, or the Devil, and that art too will abandon the peaceful depiction of a confident and reassuring humanity. . . . Everything that books, science, and intellectual mastery had promised was now rejected. Culture itself had been repudiated by reality.[16]

By a natural reaction "we surrendered to a massive intellectual pessimism. All that was real ceased to be rational. . . . This disappointment led to a general turning toward strange and irrational values, toward desires, passions, instincts, feelings, and loyalties." It was a veritable "movement toward spontaneous life. A mysterious ultimate reality was sought which could give a meaning to the world that no formula could exhaust."[17]

The search for this "ultimate reality" was encouraged by Freud's discoveries indicating a "mysterious and mystical life that existed beneath man's apparent consciousness and determined it. . . . Freud was repeating what Bergson, Unamuno, Lawrence, and Péguy had already said: that man's intelligence and awareness constantly mislead and lie, and that the final reality is an unknown force."[18]

It is in quest of this final reality—where all contradictions between

15. Ibid., p. 23.
16. Ibid., pp. 98, 100–101.
17. Ibid., pp. 16, 28, 27.
18. Ibid., pp. 67–68.

logical thought and dream, between the conscious and the unconscious, between the individual and the world around him, are abolished—that Breton rallies his contemporaries: "Abandon everything. Abandon Dada. Abandon your wife. Abandon your mistress. Abandon your hopes and fears. Abandon your children in a forest. Abandon the prey for the shadow. If necessary, abandon your comfortable life, and what you are told is your future. Follow the highways and byways."[19]

From then on, resolutely turning their backs on systems and methods, on conventions of the beaten track, "writers and artists will seize life in the raw as subject for research, convinced that the universe will not surrender its secret to logical investigation, but only to the blind questioning of life as it is lived."[20] Their guides would be the wise men of Asia or of mysterious Egypt—of those Eastern nations "which live in continuous communication with the essence of things."[21]

It is understandable to what extent this self-criticism of Western intellectuals supported the claims of the peoples Europe had previously enslaved in the name of all the values now declared bankrupt: Reason, Progress, Science, Culture. The West was destroying itself. Colonized peoples hastened to help: What they had to gain was their independence.

So it was not surprising that *Légitime Défense* should rally to the most extreme of these movements. Its ambition was less to create a new art than to attempt "a reform of knowledge and of life"[22] through the medium of art, because "thought can grasp the conceivable, while art can deal with what is essential."[23] For surrealists, poetry had a spellbinding, visionary role. Rimbaud, Nerval, Lautréamont, and Claudel had already acknowledged this, while, in Germany, Hölderlin, Stefan George, Hofmannsthal, and Rilke proposed "to use poetry as a metaphysical instrument, playing the role of mediator between man and his unknown, a role which Christ and the Passion had lost for many."[24]

But this was not the only role of poetry. "Surrealism, the ultimate product of this poetic attitude, should be an instrument both of action and of understanding."[25]

"A poet seemed to me predestined," wrote Michel Leiris; "a sort of demigod designated to carry out this vast mental transformation of a

19. M. Nadeau, *Histoire du surréalisme*, p. 56.
20. R. M. Alberès, *L'aventure*, p. 28.
21. In this connection, see M. Nadeau, *Histoire du surréalisme*, pp. 108, 109, 115.
22. R. M. Alberès, *L'aventure*, p. 178.
23. Ibid., p. 81. Quotation from Friedrich Hermann.
24. Ibid., p. 83.
25. Ibid., p. 85.

universe."[26] Taking this idea literally, René Ménil predicted the advent of a man "armed with the poetic power . . . to disrupt his country's social life with a single word." Language, he added, would have the power of action, and one might be able to conceive of politics and morals as "such that each imperative would inevitably receive the required action because spontaneous natural forces would be unleashed."[27]

This conception of the poet-as-magician restored to each word its power of "Logos," in harmony with the beliefs of primitive societies and especially with the African "action word." The words of sorcerers "produced results with the certainty of lightning," declared Ménil.[28] The words of a West Indian *hungan,* a Bantu sorcerer, or a Ruandese rainmaker were supposed to be just as efficacious. Studying the cosmogony of the Sudanese, one finds the active and creative Word of God at the origin of the world. He speaks, and his words become the sea which engenders life. He speaks again, and his words become woven threads which are the world's first technique.[29]

In *Les armes miraculeuses* Aimé Césaire makes the same magic use of the word:

> Et je dis
> et ma parole est paix
> et je dis et ma parole est terre
> ....
> et je dis:
> par de savantes herbes le temps glisse
> les branches picoraient une paix de flammes vertes.
> et la terre respira sous la gaze des brumes
> et la terre s'étira. Il y eut un craquement
> à ses épaules nouées. Il y eut dans ses veines
> un pétillement de feu.[30]

---

26. Quoted by Gaëtan Picon, in *Panorama des idées contemporaines* (Paris: Gallimard, 1957), p. 712.

27. René Ménil, "L'action foudroyante," in *Tropiques,* October 1941.

28. Ibid.

29. As in the Dogon cosmogony, for example: See Marcel Griaule's *Dieu d'eau* (Paris: Edition du Chêne, 1948). A comparison can be made with the Book of Genesis. A worthwhile study could be made of the Word in Africa and the social importance of He-who-talks-well, comparing them to ideas on surrealism. Georges Balandier has pointed out the major role of the Word in his study "Littérature de l'Afrique et des Amériques noires," in *Histoire des littératures* 1 (Paris: Encyclopédie de la Pléiade): 1536–67. As regards the religious aspect of the Word, see G. van der Leeuw, *La religion dans son essence et ses manifestations* (Paris: Payot, 1955).

30. Aimé Césaire, "Les pur-sang," in *Les armes miraculeuses* (Paris: Gallimard, 1946).

[And I speak
and my word is peace
and I speak and my word is earth.
....
And I say:
time slips through the learned grasses
the branches will scratch about for a peace of green flames.
And the earth will breathe beneath a gauze of mists
and the earth will stretch out its limbs.
There was a cracking of its stiff shoulders.
There was a crackling of fire in its veins.]

This poetry of knowledge and action innovated by the surrealists tended, in fact, to be a poetic form of living rather than an aesthetic style, and it endowed this way of living with exemplary value. It is in this sense that one can speak of "surrealist morals," of a "surrealist man."[31] "We are all moralists," said Breton.[32] Surrealism always defended the liberties of man. It proposed, among other things, to do away with "a large number of taboos which are encouraged by a belief in heaven, racism, and that supreme abjection, the power of money."[33] This again coincided with black aspirations. The more so since surrealists, on the social plane, necessarily adopted leftist tendencies[34] and violently criticized bourgeois society. It is no coincidence that almost every French surrealist at one time or another belonged to the Communist Party.

"A decadent bourgeois world . . . a ruling class which had lost faith in its mission, outdated ideals, depreciated values. From the very beginning of the movement, surrealists had encountered the Marxist explanation of their misery, and been 'tempted' by communism. . . . Strikes, riots, anti-imperialist, antimilitarist, and anticlerical demonstrations created around the young communist movement a *climate* which young dissenting bourgeois found most attractive."[35]

31. G. Picon, *Panorama*, p. 711.
32. André Breton, interview, January 1960.
33. André Breton, "Un grand poète noir," *Fontaine*, no. 35 (Paris, 1944).
34. Interview with André Breton.
35. Roger Vailland, *Le surréalisme*, pp. 36–37. It would seem to us a mistake, however, to affirm, as does this author, that " 'Communist temptation' is the entire history of surrealism, particularly from 1930 on" (p. 39). On the other hand, if many surrealists later left the party, it was in part, as Vailland remarks, due to the fact that they were all intellectuals living by their wits on the fringe of society, and, unlike workers, were not faced with concrete need. They did not therefore take part in the strikes and other demonstrations with as much enthusiasm as would a workman hoping for a salary increase or improved working conditions. It is also true that political problems do not appear very urgent to an artist (p. 42). Vailland remains silent on the lack of understanding shown to surrealists by the party. These young firebrands, encouraged by their recent successes, found in the French Communist Party nothing but obtuse criticism,

It is obvious why Negroes made use of surrealism as a revolutionary weapon. But their originality was to consist in applying it to their own condition as blacks and as a colonized people. Speaking of Aimé Césaire, Sartre wrote: "Surrealism, a European movement in poetry, [has been] stolen from the Europeans by a black man who turns it against them and gives it a well-defined purpose."[36]

Surrealism, successfully employed by Westerners to dynamite their own society, was now being used by black poets for a more fundamental revolt. More than the tight collar of rationalism, more than the impoverishment of bourgeois art, more than the debasement of a political and economic regime, their rejection would include a whole civilization, an entire race, because its wisdom, philosophies, and religions had permitted the slave markets and colonization. In contrast to the French surrealists, it was not their *own* mental structures or their *own* society they were combating, but a foreign establishment and its detested social order because it was both conqueror and oppressor. In the third part of this book, we shall show that it would be a mistake to remember only the destructive aspect of surrealism. For French West Indian intellectuals it also became an instrument for the reconquest of their original personality.

---

demands for an art conforming to "socialist realism," and a total ignorance of aesthetic problems. The party placed the accent on the *understandable* and the *useful*, the very things the surrealist revolution had rejected. Before tribunals often composed of foreigners who spoke very poor French, surrealists were called upon to justify a certain painting or poem, reports Breton. And when Breton published in his journal a drawing by Picasso or an article by Ferdinand Alquie of which the party did not approve, he was faced with questionnaires and remonstrances, and finally had to retract and apologize. This communist experience was a great disappointment for most surrealists, although several remained faithful to the party despite everything, as in the case of Aragon, even to the detriment of their art.

36. J. P. Sartre, "Orphée noir," preface to the *Anthologie de la nouvelle poésie nègre et malgache de langue française* (Paris: PUF, 1948), p. xxviii.

4/ Communism and the Black Man

French surrealists had been tempted by communism which, as they did, preached revolution and the liberation of man. For similar reasons, intensified by their particular situation as colonized persons, West Indian surrealists were also turning to communism, which at that time still enjoyed great prestige. In the chapters to come we shall discuss the hopes the Russian revolution of 1917 had aroused among black American writers. An ideology condemning racism, social differences, and man's exploitation of man would naturally appeal to generous-minded intellectuals. That appeal was heightened during 1930 and 1931 when the French communist review *Nouvel Age* devoted several issues to American Negro poetry. The magazine published folk songs of black workers, the laments of Negroes exploited by whites, along with virulent editorial comments. The interest of these songs and poems lay in the fact that, for the first time, they revealed to a European public a spirit of revolt that had been unknown in the spirituals, even though the meekness and resignation of these hymns had already suggested the unhappy condition of the black man.

The following are original English texts of some of the translated poems:*

> Ain' it hahd, ain' it hahd
> Ain' it hahd to be a nigger, nigger, nigger

*Translator's note: Madame Kesteloot quoted French translations of these folk songs from *Nouvel Age*, no. 10 (October 1931), and from a booklet *Le nègre qui chante*, ed. Eugene Jolas (Toulouse: Editions des Cahiers Libres, 1928). These texts are a close match with "Negro Songs of Protest," transcribed by Lawrence Gellert, published in the American left-wing magazine *New Masses* for November 1930 (pp. 10–11), January 1931 (pp. 16–17), and April 1931 (p. 6), which appear to have been the original sources.

Ain' it hahd, ain' it hahd
Cause you neber get yo' money when it due

If a nigger get 'rested an' cain
   has his fine
Dey sen' him out to work on
   de county line
Nigger and white man playin' seben up
Nigger win de money, fraid to pick it up.

Nigger go to white man
Ask him fo' work
White man say to nigger
Get out o' yo' shirt

Nigger throw off his coat
Went to work pickin' cotton
When time come to git pay
White folk give him nothin'.

These complaints are often accompanied by recriminations against religion, which tolerated and increased this exploitation. They thus bear out the communist theory of religion as the opiate of the people.

White folks use whip
White folks use trigger
Eart' fo' de white folks
Sky fo' de nigger

While nigger he busy
Wit' Bible and pray
White folks dey's stealin'
De whole Eart' way.

De Lawd make preacher
big an' fat
Sleek and shiny
Like a beaver hat
Dat's so

He eats yo' dinner
An' take yo' lam'
Gwine give you pay
In de promise' lan'
Oh yes.*

Finally, other songs of revolt and hatred, abandoning individual and ineffective invective like that in the first song above, make a general

*Translator's note: Lawrence Gellert, "Negro Songs of Protest," *New Masses*, November 1930, p. 11.

appeal: "All oppressed and humiliated blacks must unite!" It is no longer a question of revolt but of revolution.

> If I had my weight in lime
> I'd whip mah Cap'n till he went stone blin'
>
> Pay day come and we all git nuthin'
> Cap'n he tryin' to cheat me fo' suttin
>
> My Cap'n he so damn mean
> Ah think he come fom New Orleans
>
> I'm gonna spit in his coffee
> Spit in his tea
> De lawd help dis nigger if he catch me
>
> Sistern an' Brethren
> Stop foolin' with pray
> When black face is lifted
> Lawd turnin' away
>
> We're buryin' a brother
> They kill for the crime
> Tryin' to keep
> What was his all the time
>
> When we's tucked him under
> What you goin' to do
> Wait till it come
> They arousing fo' you too
>
> Your head tain' no apple
> For danglin' fom a tree
> Your body no carcass
> For barbecuin' on a spree
>
> Stand on your feet
> Club gripped 'tween your hands
> Spill their blood too
> Show 'em yours is a man's.*

To intellectuals in Paris, communists seemed to be the only people publicly to protest the lynchings and other crimes committed against the blacks in America. Their idea of conditions overseas is revealed in Etienne Léro's comments, in *Légitime Défense,* on the news that eight young Negroes in the United States had been accused "against all evidence" of having raped two white prostitutes and were in danger of being condemned to the electric chair.[1] "With the exception of

---

*Translator's note: Ibid., April 1931, p. 6.

1. Etienne Léro, "Civilisation," in *Légitime Défense,* p. 9. [Translator's note: The case in question was, of course, that of the Scottsboro boys, whose long and complicated

L'Humanité," writes Léro, "the French press is significantly and unanimously silent. The American colored press, sold out to whites, prisoner itself of class and political interests, is suppressing the story. The National Association for the Advancement of Colored People, obliged to deal tactfully with the capitalist criminal court system, has declared itself unable to defend the victims. The social section of the International Red Cross has had to take up the cause of the accused and is doing its utmost to alert world opinion. When will American blacks really understand that their only escape from the American hell lies in communism?"

This last sentence is illuminating. At that period, communists alone were interested in the Negroes' fate, horrified by their condition, considering them as brothers of the French or Russian proletariats—in short treating them as men.* It was rather natural for blacks to be so attracted by this ideology as to commit themselves to it. "In every country, the Communist Party's most important card has been 'the Spirit' (in the Hegelian sense of the word). The defeat of the Communist Party—should it ever appear remotely possible—would be for us the final 'I can do no more.' We believe without reservation in its triumph because we subscribe to the material dialectic of Marx as victoriously submitted to factual proof and preserved from all misleading interpretations by Lenin. On these grounds we are ready to comply with the discipline such convictions require."[2]

In connection with this attraction to communism, the influence of several black intellectuals who came just before the *Légitime Défense* group should now be mentioned.

Jacques Roumain, the Haitian ethnologist and poet who had been writing since 1926, was not only a talented writer but an ardent, militant communist. He had created the *Revue Indigène* and had been Haitian ambassador to several European countries. Jean-François Brierre, like his countryman Jacques Roumain a poet and revolutionary, had also been imprisoned because of his antigovernmental activities and had gained prestige as a result.

Léro and his friends were in sympathy with the political allegiance of the two Haitians who "give us verses filled with a dynamic of the future."[3]

---

history would continue into the 1940s. For further information see *The Columbia Encyclopedia.*]

*Translator's note: This rather overstates the truth. In the Scottsboro case, for example, the "ultimate freeing of most of the defendants was . . . the result of unceasing labor by the Scottsboro Defense Committee, formed in December 1935, which for the most part represented liberal non-Communist organizations" *(Columbia Encyclopedia).* Communist use of the case for propaganda purposes greatly complicated these efforts.

2. *Légitime Défense,* "Avertissement," p. 1.

3. Etienne Léro, "Misère d'une poésie," in *Légitime Défense,* p. 12.

The open sympathy for the Soviet Union shown by American Negro poets like Langston Hughes or an Afro-Cuban poet like Nicolas Guillen, was to have a similar effect.

Aside from these external reasons for joining the Communist Party —the prestige of the Third Internationale, the party's interest in Negroes, and the example of their predecessors of the same race—the Martiniquan students had more personal reasons for rising "against all those who are not suffocated by this Christian, capitalist, bourgeois world."[4] The first two articles of *Légitime Défense*'s manifesto were entirely devoted to denouncing the intolerable social conditions of the "earthly paradise" which Martinique was supposed to be. To "those who have dreamed of the Islands with a poet's heart," they explained that a field worker's earnings were barely enough to cover the cost of food. "The disproportion between the work performed and the few francs earned is such that the word 'wages' is inappropriate. For the skeptical let me add that a worker earns between seven and twelve francs for a day's work that often consists of thirteen hours," reports Maurice-Sabat Quitman.[5] Field laborers comprise 80 percent of the population; their clothes are generally patched together from sacking. If a peasant marries and has children, his life becomes still more difficult "until his children, on reaching the age of six to eight years, can join the struggle for their existence. Whether girls or boys, the children are hired and enrolled as helpers. Each one brings his household five francs more."

"Is it surprising then that, according to military records for 1932, 80 percent of the young men of draft age were illiterate? And yet there was no lack of schools. There were 600 elementary schools, commercial schools, a school of arts and crafts, professional schools, and a preparatory school for future lawyers. . . . As Monsieur Gerbinis, Governor of Martinique, has put it: 'The Colony has at its disposal every resource for the development of intellectual culture.' But of what use are all these schools if the children have to earn their living from the age of eight? Poor people must be given the means to send their children to these schools in order to improve their condition."

Why were the Martiniquan peasants so destitute? Jules Monnerot replies: "A hereditary white plutocracy, which no revolution has ever succeeded in ousting, owns four-fifths of the land and uses the black working class as human material to transform sugarcane into sugar and

---

4. *Légitime Défense*, "Avertissement," p. 1.

5. Maurice-Sabat Quitman, "Paradis sur terre," in *Légitime Défense*, pp. 5–6. Until further notice, the quotations given above are from this article.

rum. All the important posts in the factories as well as in the trading companies are held by members of this plutocracy. The white Creoles who once profited from slavery and still profit from a slavery of wage earners (the condition of a cane cutter in 1932 is no better than it was in 1832) form a closed, inexorable society."[6]

The white landowner, factory owner, or merchant therefore controlled all means of production. If the peasant wished to stay alive, he had to be employed by them, accepting their conditions.

"Three quarters of the Island belongs to five or six families of manufacturers, whose cupidity is matched only by the patience of the workers."[7] And, since Martinique was a French colony, "no government, even a leftist one, has ever attempted to limit this feudal power." The government today, as yesterday, still guarantees the security of French colonial "free enterprise," with the help of the army and the civil service.[8]

"Peaceful persuasion was also employed: Along with the constables, the administrators, and the tools of labor and police power imported to the colonized countries, came ideas with which the natives were conditioned in order to permit the happy exploitation of the conquered land. Among the colonist's ideas Christianity generally appears, encouraging resignation and suppressing anything among the indigenous population which might hinder the smooth conduct of business."[9]

With such protection, declares René Ménil, the European colonist can afford to "deposit a million francs in the town bank on the birth of a daughter" or assure the future education of his sons—sons "who rarely need perform their military service."[10]

Does the power of democracy ever prevent this aristocratic minority from having its members elected to Parliament? There is no obstacle here. "The aristocracy buys its legislators ready-made. Their representatives are mainly chosen from the colored bourgeoisie, whose political ideas generally defy analysis. Governors, police, colonial mag-

6. Jules Monnerot, "Note touchant la bourgeoisie de couleur française," in *Légitime Défense*, p. 3. The condition of these workers has still not greatly improved, as Daniel Guérin has shown in *Les Antilles décolonisées* ("The decolonized West Indies") (Paris: Présence Africaine, 1956).

7. M. S. Quitman, "Paradis," pp. 7, 8.

8. See articles in *Le Monde* of December 1939 on riots in Martinique caused by unemployment, low wages, and lack of opportunity. These riots were "pacified" but without bringing any solutions to the problems.

9. René Ménil, "Généralités sur l'écrivain de couleur antillais," in *Légitime Défense*, p. 7.

10. M. S. Quitman, "Paradis," pp. 5, 6.

istrates, marines, etc., take part to a man in the elections, which are always fraudulent—and occasionally people are killed."[11]

These passages in *Légitime Défense* are important, because, without actually using the word, they already denounce all the characteristics of colonialism. But even more than white capitalists, *Légitime Défense* criticizes the colored bourgeoisie with all the ferocity of an adolescent rebelling against his parents: "We spit on everything from which they derive sustenance and joy."[12]

This colored bourgeoisie was composed of small officials, white-collar workers, tradesmen—generally more or less light-skinned mulattoes—who, in order to compensate for their feeling of racial inferiority, encouraged their sons to obtain diplomas and "good jobs." They all imitated the white bourgeoisie, their morals, their manners. But was it really imitation? Is not middle-class behavior the same the world over? "Lawyers, doctors, professors, etc., who are newly arrived at this status, must, in order to 'make their way,' avoid hurting the feelings of their employers, and must demonstrate to the class which is taking them to its bosom the image of itself it desires to see. They must adopt the ideals of this class (a million francs, fierce admiration for all officials, diplomas, decorations; the habit of speaking of 'my friend the governor,' 'my friend the minister,' etc.) and its mores; an advantageous marriage, Catholicism ('my wife is a volunteer for charitable causes'; 'my daughters are having their First Communion'; 'my husband is a freemason, but broad-minded'); the awareness of what belongs to them ('my villa, my automobile, my daughter'); cultivated manners ('they don't belong to our set. He's a laborer; a cousin of my wife's. Naturally, I have family feeling, but my clientele, you understand). . . ."[13]

This ideal is proposed to youngsters as soon as they can read and write, and it is never challenged or criticized, even by the favored ones who are able to continue their studies in France. "In this they appear anxious to conform to the manners and disposition of the majority of their European fellow students. . . . Because they carry with them everywhere the incontestable mark of their race, their desire 'not to be noticed,' to 'be assimilated,' can result in lending a tragic aspect to their slightest advance."[14] Many of these young men wish to remain in France and "settle there."

"Through conforming, they succeed in whitening themselves. . . .

11. Jules Monnerot, "Note," p. 4.
12. "Avertissement," *Légitime Défense*, p. 2.
13. Jules Monnerot, "Note," p. 3.
14. Ibid., p. 4.

Those who return home have caught on. . . . Restrained, tolerant, conciliatory, now they set the tone. They know that the important thing is 'position' and that everything, from their wives to their ideas, including their car, proceeds from it. So they settle down gently, calling on people, thanking them, and being thoroughly refined. Soon they are anxious to show off: to appear on official platforms, to be decorated, to be appointed mayor, and who knows? . . . No ceremony is complete without the brilliance of their supermanners."[15]

To the pressure of the social milieu, "filled to the brim with white ethics, white culture . . . and white prejudices,"[16] is added that of the schoolroom, where "the colored West Indian's natural gifts are automatically denied" and the children are brought up on "books written in other countries and for other readers."[17]

How is it that these grandchildren of Africans think and feel like French bourgeois? Has their country assimilated the lessons of French civilization so well over the centuries? "The evil appears to me even greater," writes René Ménil. "For I am afraid that it is not the result of conscious, Machiavellian hypocrisy but of an objective, unconscious hypocrisy." He was becoming aware of the basic alienation of the cultured West Indian: "The colored West Indian progressively rejects his race, his body, his fundamental and ethnic passions, his specific way of reacting to love and death, and finally ends by living in an unreal world determined by the ideals and abstract ideas of another people."[18]

This discovery of themselves was to become a recurrent theme among the black writers of French America: Damas, Césaire, Paul Niger, Guy Tirolien, Mayotte Capécia, and Joseph Zobel evoked this phenomenon of estrangement long before Frantz Fanon made a thorough analysis of it.[19] For a colored man "cannot be other than he is, cannot be white, he will always read in a white's face that nothing is possible in that direction." Often, in fact, he only succeeds in making the white man smile. "What sometimes makes a colored West Indian appear ridiculous to an ordinary Frenchman is that the latter sees in the colored man his own deformed and darkened image."[20]

Jules Monnerot humorously condemns this caricature of French bourgeoisie to which the native of Martinique aspires: "If a documentary movie on the creation of the French colored bourgeoisie were

15. Ibid.
16. Etienne Léro, "Misère," p. 10.
17. René Ménil, "Généralités," p. 7.
18. Ibid.
19. Frantz Fanon, *Peau noire, masques blancs* (Paris: Seuil, 1952). Translated as *Black Skin, White Masks* (New York: Grove Press, 1967).
20. René Ménil, "Généralités," p. 7.

shown in sufficiently fast motion, the bent back of the black slave could easily turn into the obsequious back of the colored, refined, and kow-towing bourgeois who—in the space of a few frames—would be seen to grow a suit and a bowler hat."[21] The "successful" end product of this evolution in the opinion of *Légitime Défense* is therefore nothing but a marionette, a despicable puppet. He is not a ridiculous figure but a tragic one, the man "who dares not be himself, who is afraid, ashamed,"[22] ashamed to the point of applying this racial prejudice to his brothers and basing his hierarchy of values on the degree of black-ness of his skin. This is tragic both for himself and his people, from whom he separates himself, thus reinforcing their shackles.

The young bourgeois members of *Légitime Défense* were perfectly aware of the responsibilities of their class. If the condition of Martini-quan workers is so bad, they said, "the fault lies with those who, refusing to admit that these pariahs are their brothers, ought at least to consider them human beings. The fault lies with those who place their intelligence at the service of factory owners, who are clever ex-ploiters of that false pride which consists of denying one's origins and looking down on 'niggers.' "[23] The cowardliness of this class prevents it from seeing that if "black workers go on cutting cane and still do not think of cutting off the heads of those who continually betray them,"[24] "a day will come when these workers will revolt."[25]

The protagonists of *Légitime Défense* openly proposed, moreover, to bring this thought to mind. "Traitors to their class," they declared their intention "to go as far as possible along the path of this treason." And they urged the sons of the bourgeoisie to follow their example, at least those among them "who are not yet damned, dead, successful, settled university students, decorated, spoiled, wealthy, prudish, decorative, branded opportunists . . ., those who can still claim—with some semblance of truth—that they are alive."[26] "If we address young West Indians like this," they wrote, "it is because we consider that they especially have suffered from capitalism and that they seem to offer— insofar as their ethnic personality has been materially determined—a generally higher potential for rebellion and joy."[27]

Légitime Défense, in short, only wanted to prepare for revolution. And certain sentences have the familiar ring of communist propaganda: "The bourgeois . . . no longer wish to share . . . the profits sweated

21. Jules Monnerot, "Note," p. 3.
22. René Ménil, "Généralités," p. 7.
23. M. S. Quitman, "Paradis," p. 6.
24. Jules Monnerot, "Note," p. 4.
25. M. S. Quitman, "Paradis," p. 6.
26. "Avertissement," *Légitime Défense,* p. 2.
27. Ibid., pp. 2, 3.

for by proletarians who will not always be anesthetized by the inoculations of democracy."[28] The authors were aware of the support of the workers of the world, and, because of this, their concern extended beyond the narrow limits of the West Indies. It was more from class solidarity than racial solidarity that they denounced the summary execution of blacks in the United States. "So far only the working classes have cried out their indignation in meetings. Negroes all over the world owe it to themselves to be the first to agitate for their brothers, unjustly threatened by Yankee sexual neuroses."[29]

One can see why communism—which presented itself as antiracial and anticapitalist—seemed the only possible escape from the economic and social situation in the West Indies. Communism was opposed to precisely the twin evils from which the French West Indies were suffering and against which the young intellectuals of *Légitime Défense* were in revolt. Yet Etienne Léro and his friends retained from communism only the class struggle, rebelling specifically against the oppression of the common people effectuated by the combined action of the mulatto bourgeoisie, the French administration, and the Creole colonists. Their political conscience stopped at social demands for the black proletarian class. It had not yet reached the level of national feeling, and the question of French domination had not yet been raised. Only the methods of the French were criticized.[30]

28. "Noeud coulant" (anon.), in *Légitime Défense*, p. 15.
29. Etienne Léro, "Civilisation," in *Légitime Défense*, p. 9.
30. See chap. 8 regarding Senghor's censure on this point.

5/ Black Students in Paris and the Harlem Renaissance

"The wind rising from black America will soon sweep the West Indies clean, we hope, of all the stunted fruits of its outdated culture," cried Etienne Léro at the end of his critical examination of West Indian literature.[1] Following Léro's stirring declaration of faith was an excerpt from a rousing chapter of Claude McKay's novel *Banjo*, introduced under a new title, "L'étudiant antillais vu par un noir américain"[2] ("The West Indian student as seen by an American Negro"). In the same journal René Ménil wrote: "The poems of American Negroes are moving the whole world."[3]

Senghor, Césaire, and Damas, the founders of what came to be known as the negritude movement,[4] acknowledge that, between 1930 and 1940, African and West Indian students living in Paris were in close contact with the American Negro writers Claude McKay, Jean Toomer, Langston Hughes, and Countee Cullen, and that they read these writers' work and were personally acquainted with them. "We were in contact with these black Americans during the years 1929–34, through Mademoiselle Paulette Nardal, who, with Dr. Sajous, a Haitian, had founded the *Revue du Monde Noir*. Mademoiselle Nardal kept a literary salon, where African Negroes, West Indians, and American

1. Etienne Léro, "Misère d'une poésie," in *Légitime Défense*, p. 12.
2. Claude McKay, *Banjo* (Paris: Editions Rieder, 1928). We later discuss this work at greater length. [Translator's note: The passage was probably from chap. 16 and can be found in the 1957 Harvest edition of *Banjo* (pp. 199–218), published by Harcourt Brace Jovanovich.]
3. René Ménil, "Généralités sur l'écrivain de couleur antillais," in *Légitime Défense*, p. 8.
4. See chaps. 8 and 9 of the present book.

Negroes used to get together."[5] Around 1935, René Maran's salon came to play the same role. Professor Mercer Cook put many black French and black American intellectuals in touch with one another.

This is an important point, since the American literature already contained seeds of the main themes of negritude. Hence, one can assert that the real fathers of the Negro cultural renaissance in France were neither the writers of the West Indian tradition, nor the surrealist poets, nor French novelists of the era between the two wars, but black writers of the United States. They made a very deep impression on French Negro writers by claiming to represent an entire race, launching a cry with which all blacks identified—the first cry of rebellion. "The dominant feeling of a Negro poet is a feeling of intolerance. An intolerance of reality because it is sordid, of the world because it is caged, of life because it is deprived of the great road to the sun. And now from the dark heavy dregs of anguish, of suppressed indignation, of long silent despair, a hiss of anger is rising. On the shattered foundations of its conformities, America wonders uneasily from what atrocious hatred this cry is the deliverance."[6]

Black American writers were the first to broach the subject—until then taboo—of contacts between Negroes and whites. While West Indians were carefully avoiding these themes, hoping to solve the problem by evading the question of color, the existence of a racial problem was recognized more openly in the United States.

After the abolition of slavery, Negroes had to fight to establish their worth. "I knew that in a large degree we were trying an experiment—that of testing whether it was possible for Negroes to build up and control the affairs of a large educational institution. I knew that if we failed, it would injure the whole race. I knew that the presumption was against us."[7]

The author of these remarks, Booker T. Washington, who had known slavery, succeeded in founding Tuskegee Institute, the first industrial college for blacks, right in the state of Alabama, probably the state most hostile to blacks and the most convinced of their natural

5. L. S. Senghor, letter of February 1960. This salon was frequently attended by the famous colored American professor Alain Locke. The *Revue du Monde Noir* was published in two languages (English and French), and Félix Eboué, Jean Price-Mars, and Claude McKay contributed articles. It has been impossible for us to obtain more information concerning this review published by Mademoiselle Nardal, or to obtain any copies of it. Although there were only six issues, we know that it prepared the ground for *Légitime Défense* and that it was the cause of proceedings brought against the promoters of *Légitime Défense*.

6. Aimé Césaire, "Introduction à la poésie nègre américaine," in *Tropiques*, no. 2 (July 1941, Fort-de-France, Martinique).

7. Booker T. Washington, *Up from Slavery: An Autobiography* (1901; New York: Dodd, Mead, & Co., 1965), p. 92.

inferiority. Booker T. Washington worked unceasingly to prove that blacks were as good as whites, on condition that their education was equal. He also made famous the phrase "revival of the race." He thought it would be sufficient for Negroes to show they were capable, and racial prejudice would disappear. A great number of young educated blacks, believing in these theories, conscientiously wrote "in the manner of" the poets of the period, cultivating "the conventional melancholy tone of the late nineteenth-century romantics, and dwelt on death, dreams and the wonders of nature."[8]

Experience showed, to the contrary, that racial prejudice was increasing! And if the rise of Booker T. Washington was followed with a certain sympathy by the abolitionists, the succeeding generation of black intellectuals did not receive the same support. Was it feared that blacks would become competitors if endowed with greater cultural and economic means? Or was racial prejudice too deeply rooted in the American consciousness to disappear because of laws passed during a wave of temporary generosity? As Richard Wright bitterly observed, the fight to be integrated in the white world was futile. "The gains they won fastened ever tighter around their necks the shackles of Jim Crowism. For example, every new hospital, clinic, and school that was built was a *Negro* hospital, a *Negro* clinic, a *Negro* school! So, though Negroes were slowly rising out of their debased physical conditions, the black ghettos were growing ever larger; instead of racial segregation lessening, it grew, deepened, spread."[9]

Margaret Just Butcher explains at length the means by which segregation replaced slavery and the new series of false ideas based on pseudo-scientific arguments which victimized blacks: blood atavism, inherent primitivism, etc. Even Darwinian theory was invoked to suggest that the Negro was but a link between the ape and genuine man, thus justifying his exploitation and lynching.[10]

At the same time in the South a literature was developing that glorified antebellum life, portraying slavery in the homelike atmosphere of the master's house, in a naïve, innocent, and idyllic light.[11]

Black intellectuals reacted against these stereotyped pictures of the Negro child, the Negro clown, or the bad Negro which abounded in Southern literature. The most famous of these black intellectuals was

8. Margaret Just Butcher, *The Negro in American Culture*, based on materials left by Alain Locke (New York: Knopf, 1957; rev. ed., 1971), p. 101.

9. Richard Wright, *White Man, Listen!* (Garden City, N.Y.: Doubleday, 1957, 1964 [Anchor Books]), p. 85.

10. Margaret J. Butcher, *The Negro in American Culture.*

11. Margaret Mitchell's novel *Gone with the Wind* is a more recent example of this "Southern romanticism."

Dr. W. E. B. Du Bois, whose book *The Souls of Black Folk*[12] became "the Bible of the militant school of protest."[13] He was followed by Paul Laurence Dunbar and Charles W. Chesnutt. This was the beginning of the "Harlem Renaissance," which flourished between 1914 and 1925.

The black renaissance, moreover, coincided with a general renewal of American literature immediately after World War I. Breaking away from the romantic tradition, it turned toward critical realism and began to reflect an interest in social problems.[14] In Europe the best known American writers of this new literary orientation are Steinbeck, Hemingway, Dos Passos, Faulkner, Caldwell, and the black author Richard Wright.

For black writers, the new realism consisted of a clearer conception of their situation, exposing the injustice and prejudice that made black Americans outcasts in their own land, and demanding rehabilitation of Negro cultural values and their total independence of the white world.

There is no clearer expression of the militant nature of their stand than Langston Hughes's proud declaration:

We younger Negro artists who create now intend to express our individual dark-skinned selves without fear or shame. If white people are pleased we are glad. If they are not, it doesn't matter. We know that we are beautiful and ugly too. The tom-tom weeps and the tom-tom laughs. If colored people are pleased we are glad. If they are not, their displeasure doesn't matter either. We build our temples for tomorrow, strong as we know how, and we stand on top of the mountain, free within ourselves.[15]

At the head of this young school were Langston Hughes, Claude McKay, Jean Toomer, Countee Cullen, and Sterling Brown, whose novels and poems became a steady diet for African and West Indian students in France between 1930 and 1940. These authors themselves made a number of trips to Europe and thus had the opportunity to make personal contact with the students.

At home they took full advantage of the "Negro vogue" reigning in New York between 1920 and 1929. The new snobbery, introduced by

12. The Editions de Présence Africaine, Paris, published this book in 1959, for the first time in French, as *Ames noires*. This translation represents the twenty-sixth edition of *Souls of Black Folk*, first published in the United States in 1903.

13. Margaret J. Butcher, *The Negro*, p. 129.

14. Professor A. Baiwir describes this evolution very well in his important work *Le déclin de l'individualisme chez les romanciers américains contemporains* (Brussels: Editions Lumière, n.d.).

15. Quoted by L. S. Senghor in "Trois poètes négro-américains," in the review *Poésie 45* (Paris: P. Seghers, 1945). Statement of Hughes in an article in *The Nation*, 1926. English text as quoted in Milton Meltzer's biography, *Langston Hughes* (New York: Thomas Y. Crowell, 1968), pp. 129–30.

a successful musical comedy "Shuffle Along," spread to music and Negro dances. Jazz, the Charleston, and the blues were discovered, and people became aware that blacks were good singers, good dancers, and sometimes excellent musicians. In a wider sense, books written by blacks easily found publishers and an audience in certain avant-garde groups such as the circle of the author Carl van Vechten.

One should not, however, have any illusions about this vogue. Anti-black prejudices and segregation were in no degree lessened. New York's "high society" had merely discovered a new exotic toy—the Negro clown—and the only right of the black man that was recognized was the right to amuse whites. So, while profiting commercially from this fad, blacks were not duped, as is illustrated by the humorous text written in this connection by Langston Hughes:

White people began to come to Harlem in droves. . . . Nor did ordinary Negroes like the growing influx of whites toward Harlem after sundown, flooding the little cabarets and bars where formerly only colored people laughed and sang, and where now the strangers were given the best ringside tables to sit and stare at the Negro customers—like amusing animals in a zoo.

The Negroes said: "We can't go downtown and sit and stare at you in your clubs. You won't even let us in your clubs." But they didn't say it out loud—for Negroes are practically never rude to white people. So thousands of whites came to Harlem night after night, thinking the Negroes loved to have them there, and firmly believing that all Harlemites left their houses at sundown to sing and dance in cabarets, because most of the whites saw nothing but the cabarets, not the houses.

It was a period when local and visiting royalty were not at all uncommon in Harlem. And when the parties of A'Lelia Walker, the Negro heiress, were filled with guests whose names would turn any Nordic social climber green with envy. . . . It was a period when Charleston preachers opened up shouting churches as sideshows for white tourists. . . . It was a period when every season there was at least one hit play on Broadway acted by a Negro cast. And when books by Negro authors were being published with much greater frequency and much more publicity than ever before or since in history. It was a period when white writers wrote about Negroes more successfully (commercially speaking) than Negroes did about themselves. . . . It was the period when the Negro was in vogue.[16]

However, mixed in with the folklore, black writers sowed ideas in their books which some ten years later became the leaven of the negritude movement. They resolutely turned their backs on the preceding generation which had been "characterized by intellectual acceptance of white American values and, in literature, by sentimental lyricism over the misfortunes of an oppressed and exiled race," in order to

16. Langston Hughes, *The Big Sea: An Autobiography*, new ed. (New York: Hill and Wang, 1962), pp. 224, 225, 227, 228.

commit themselves to a "vigorous though not boastful affirmation of their original values."[17]

Claude McKay's novel *Banjo,* already mentioned, presented the broadest criticism of American society and, at the same time, a sample of the feelings and anxieties of the "new Negro." The author rebelled against the black man's obligation to act according to the morals of a society that rejects him.

"It seemed to him [Ray, the narrator] a social wrong that, in a society rooted and thriving on the principles of the 'struggle for existence' and the 'survival of the fittest' a black child should be brought up on the same code of social virtues as the white, . . . earnestly learning the trite moralisms of a society in which he was, as a child and would be as an adult, denied any legitimate place."[18]

Harshly he attacked everything which most directly wounded him and his race: racial prejudice. All young black writers were unanimous on this subject, for the wound was painful. They denounced every prejudice which weighed on colored men and justified their shameless exploitation.

"Prejudice and business! In Europe, Asia, Australia, Africa, America, those were the two united terrors confronting the colored man. He was the butt of the white man's indecent public prejudices. Prejudices insensate and petty, bloody, vicious, vile, brutal, *raffiné,* hypocritical, Christian. Prejudices. Prejudices like the stock market—curtailed, diminishing, increasing, changing chameleon-like, according to place and time, like the color of the white man's soul, controlled by the exigencies of the white man's business."[19] Prejudices which automatically led all those who did not approve of them and respect segregation to be banned by society. "Show me a white woman or man who can marry a Negro and belong to respectable society in London, New York or any place."[20] "In New York we have laws against racial discrimination. Yet there are barriers of discrimination everywhere against colored people. . . . We don't want to eat in a restaurant, nor go to a teashop, a cabaret or a theater where they do not want us. . . . And when white people show that they do not want to entertain us in places that they own, why, we just stay away—all of us who are decent-minded —for we are a fun-loving race and there is no pleasure in forcing ourselves where we are not wanted."[21]

All these authors reacted strongly to the word "nigger," which, like

17. Preface by Georges Friedmann to the French edition of Claude McKay's *Banjo.*
18. Claude McKay, *Banjo,* Harvest ed., p. 319.
19. Ibid., p. 193.
20. Ibid., p. 207.
21. Ibid., p. 194.

a slap in the face, arouses in blacks a violent emotion, described at length by Langston Hughes.

The word *nigger* to colored people of high and low degree is like a red rag to a bull. Used rightly or wrongly, ironically or seriously, of necessity for the sake of realism, or impishly for the sake of comedy, it doesn't matter. Negroes do not like it in any book or play whatsoever, be the book or play ever so sympathetic in its treatment of the basic problems of the race. Even though the book or play is written by a Negro, they still do not like it.

The word *nigger*, you see, sums up for us who are colored all the bitter years of insult and struggle in America: the slave-beatings of yesterday, the lynchings of today, the Jim Crow cars, the only movie show in town with its sign up FOR WHITES ONLY, the restaurants where you may not eat, the jobs you may not have, the unions you cannot join. The word *nigger* in the mouths of little white boys at school, the word *nigger* in the mouths of foremen on the job, the word *nigger* across the whole face of America! *Nigger! Nigger!* Like the word *Jew* in Hitler's Germany.[22]

In support of this assertion Langston Hughes quotes the poem "Incident" by Countee Cullen:

Once riding in old Baltimore,
Heart-filled, head-filled with glee,
I saw a Baltimorean
Keep looking straight at me.

Now I was eight and very small,
And he was no whit bigger
And so I smiled, but he poked out
His tongue and called me, "Nigger."

I saw the whole of Baltimore
from May until December:
Of all the things that happened there
That's all that I remember.[23]

Claude McKay also referred to this reaction in *Banjo*. The way America treated blacks was disgusting, he wrote, but the French too, even if they did it more politely, concealed "a fundamental contempt for black people quite as pronounced as in the Anglo-Saxon lands. . . . There was if anything an unveiled condescension in it that was gall to a Negro who wanted to live his life free of the demoralizing effects of being pitied and patronized. Here like anywhere . . . one black villain made all black villains as one black tart made all black tarts."[24]

22. Langston Hughes, *The Big Sea*, pp. 268–69.
23. Quoted in ibid., p. 269, from *Color* by Countee Cullen (New York: Harper & Bros., 1925).
24. Claude McKay, *Banjo*, p. 275.

Elsewhere he again denounced the apparent liberalism which had so long maintained the myth of a nonracist France.

The French are never tired of proclaiming themselves the most civilized people in the world. They think they understand Negroes, because they don't discriminate against us in their bordels. They imagine that Negroes like them. But, Senghor, the Senegalese, told me that the French were the most calculatingly cruel of all the Europeans in Africa.[25]

These prejudices are even inculcated among Negroes themselves: West Indians look down on Africans, for being more "Negro" than they are.

At the African bar the conversation turned on the hostile feeling that existed between the French West Indians and the native Africans. The *patron* said that the West Indians felt superior because many of them were appointed as petty officials in the African colonies and were often harder on the natives than the whites.

Fils d'esclaves! Fils d'esclaves! cried a Senegalese sergeant. Because thay have a chance to be better instructed than we, they think we are the savages and that they are "white" negroes. Why, they are only the descendants of the slaves that our forefathers sold.[26]

Similarly, Langston Hughes remarks on the superiority complex of the mulatto regarding a black: "Mary's friend from the West Indies said she did not like Claude McKay because he was too black. . . . Rosalie was a light-skinned Jamaican, who had a violent prejudice toward dark Negroes as, unfortunately, so many West Indian mulattoes have."[27]

The list of criticisms could be still longer. The Negro censures American civilization, not only for its prejudices, but also for its oppressive capitalist structure, and the commercial spirit that always places money above men: "Business first and by all and any means! That is the slogan of the white man's world."[28] This anticapitalist reaction was broadened to meet that of all proletarians, in a sort of humorous "prospectus" written by Langston Hughes around 1929 during the famous New York economic crash. The city's largest hotel, the celebrated Waldorf-Astoria, was being built then at a cost of twenty-three million dollars. With cruel wit, the author invites "the homeless, the starving and the colored folks" to come down to the Waldorf-Astoria, reserve a room, and stuff themselves on a menu he enumerated in detail:

25. Ibid., p. 267.
26. Ibid., p. 203.
27. Langston Hughes, *The Big Sea*, p. 165.
28. Claude McKay, *Banjo*, p. 194.

> Dine with some of the men and women who got rich off of your labor,
> who clip coupons with clean white fingers because your hands dug
> coal, drilled stone, sewed garments, poured steel to let other peo-
> ple draw dividends and live easy.
> (Or haven't you had enough yet of the soup-lines and the bitter bread
> of charity?)
> *Hallelujah! Undercover driveways!*
> *Ma soul's a witness for de Waldorf-Astoria!*
> (A thousand nigger section-hands keep the roadbeds smooth so in-
> vestments in railroads pay ladies with diamond necklaces staring at
> Cert murals.)
> *Thank Gawd A'mighty!*
> (And a million niggers bend their backs on rubber plantations, for
> rich behinds to ride on thick tires to the Theatre Guild tonight.)
> *Ma soul's a witness!*
> (And here we stand, shivering in the cold, in Harlem.)
> *Glory be to Gawd—*
> *De Waldorf-Astoria's open!*[29]

It is from this perspective that one must understand why communism at that time attracted certain black intellectuals. It seemed to
them to solve both social and racial problems.[30] The Russian revolution, still so young, seemed to promise every hope of liberty.

The end of the war! [World War I]. But many of the students at Central
[High School] kept talking, not about the end of the war, but about Russia
where Lenin had taken power in the name of the workers, who made everything, and who would now own everything they made. "No more po-
groms," the Jews said: no more race hatred. . . . The daily papers pictured
the Bolsheviks as the greatest devils on earth, but I didn't see how they
could be that bad if they had done away with race hatred and landlords—
two evils that I knew well at first hand.[31]

Even today, one discovers that most of the black writers who were
in their twenties at the beginning of the New Deal were for a short
period members of the Communist Party and are still more or less
Marxist.

In poems where the black man's sufferings and miserable condition
are freely expressed, threats begin to sound. Veiled at first, in Countee
Cullen's poem:

> We shall not always plant while others reap
> The golden increment of bursting fruit

---

29. Langston Hughes, *The Big Sea*, pp. 322–23.
30. Yet the desire to be assimilated into American society always kept the majority
of these intellectuals from joining the Communist Party. Society could then have
banned them for two reasons: their color and their opinions.
31. Langston Hughes, *The Big Sea*, pp. 51–52.

Not always countenance, abject and mute,
That lesser men should hold their brothers cheap.[32]

Then clearer, as expressed by Fenton Johnson:

I am tired of work; I am tired of building up
somebody else's civilization.[33]

And finally, poems poured forth furiously from Claude McKay:

Your door is shut against my tightened face,
And I am sharp as steel with discontent;
....

The pavement slabs burn loose beneath my feet
A chafing savage, down the decent street;
And passion rends my vitals as I pass,
Where boldly shines your shuttered door of glass.[34]

The threat becomes a song of revolt in the name of outraged dignity: "If we must die, let it not be like dogs—Hunted down and penned in an inglorious spot."[35]

With an ironic smile, Langston Hughes wrote a short poem in the "blues" style, which is a message of strength and the confidence of a man "who has faith in his people's destiny":

I, too, sing America.

I am the darker brother.
They send me to eat in the kitchen
When company comes,
But I laugh,
And eat well,
And grow strong.

Tomorrow,
I'll be at the table
When company comes
Nobody'll dare
Say to me
"Eat in the kitchen,"
Then.

Besides,

32. "From the dark tower," quoted by Margaret J. Butcher, in *The Negro*, p. 104.
33. "Tired," quoted in Hughes and Bontemps, *The Poetry of the Negro* (Garden City, N.Y.: Doubleday, 1949), p. 62.
34. "The white house," quoted by Richard Wright in *White Man, Listen!*, p. 96; Hughes and Bontemps, p. 31.
35. "If we must die," quoted by Richard Wright in *White Man, Listen!*; Hughes and Bontemps, p. 31.

> They'll see how beautiful I am
> And be ashamed—
>
> I, too, am America.[36]

Abandoning the role of victim for that of judge, Claude McKay criticized the values of which the West was so proud and in the name of which it presumed the right to colonize other peoples: Christianity, technology, and "reason."

He had no difficulty criticizing the latter. The First World War abundantly proved the impotence of "reason," which had proved unable to prevent either barbarous conflicts or the civil wars of "reasonable" nations:

[Ray] was not unaware that his position as a black boy looking on the civilized scene was a unique one. He was having a good grinning time of it. Italians against French, French against Anglo-Saxons, English against Germans, the great *Daily Mail* shrieking like a mad virago that there were still Germans left who were able to swill champagne in Italy when deserving English gentlemen could not afford to replenish their cellars. Oh it was a great civilization indeed, too entertaining for any savage ever to have the feeling of boredom.[37]

His attack on Christianity grew more virulent because this religion seemed to him a huge swindle. While in Western countries the Church tolerates materialism and the profit motive, racial pride, and social diseases like organized prostitution, it claimed the right to "civilize" colored people and purge them of their "heathen morals." In reality, religion was an alibi and a screen for the white subjection of blacks. McKay therefore rejected Christianity entirely and without exception:

As far as I have been able to think it out the colored races are the special victims of biblical morality—Christian morality. . . .

I don't think I loathe anything more than the morality of the Christians. It is false, treacherous, hypocritical. I know that, for I myself have been a victim of it in your white world, and the conclusion I draw from it is that the world needs to get rid of false moralities and cultivate decent manners—not society manners, but man-to-man decency and tolerance.

So—if I were to follow any of the civilized peoples, it wouldn't be the Jews or the Christians or the Indians. I would rather go to the Chinese—to Confucius.[38]

This cry from the heart is an echo of the speech made in 1852 by Frederick Douglass, a pioneer Negro abolitionist, who explained the aversion of blacks to Christian morality:

36. "I, too, sing America," quoted in Hughes and Bontemps, p. 64.
37. Claude McKay, *Banjo*, p. 136.
38. Ibid., p. 268.

You boast of your love of liberty, your superior civilization, and your pure Christianity, while twin political powers of the nation (as embodied in the two political parties) is solemnly pledged to perpetuate the enslavement of three million of your countrymen. You hurl your anathemas at the crown-headed tyrants of Russia and Austria and pride yourselves on your democratic institutions, while you yourselves consent to be the mere tools and bodyguards of the tyrants of Virginia and Carolina. You invite to your shores fugitives of oppression from abroad, honor them with banquets, greet them with ovations, cheer them, toast them, salute them, protect them, and pour out your money to them like water; but the fugitives from your own land you advertise, hunt, arrest, shoot, and kill. You glory in your refinement and education, yet you maintain a system as barbarous and dreadful as ever stained the character of a nation—a system begun in avarice, supported in pride, and perpetuated in cruelty. You shed tears over fallen Hungary, and make the sad story of her wrongs the theme of your poets, statesmen, and orators, till your gallant sons are ready to fly to arms to vindicate her cause against the oppressor; but in regard to the ten thousand wrongs of the American slave, you would enforce the strictest silence, and would hail him as an enemy of the nation who dares to make these wrongs the subject of public discourse![39]

We have made a point of quoting large excerpts from this speech, although it is now more than a hundred years old, because it is contemporary still in many respects. It underlines perfectly the glaring contradictions between beliefs and acts for which colored people censure whites with such constancy as to give truth to the accusation. The travesty of Christian morality, when it occurs in relations between peoples, inevitably casts discredit on an ideology which is nonetheless basically humanist and whose principles call for attitudes completely contrary to those actually adopted.

As to the technical progress so warmly extolled by Western countries as one of their most important attributes, McKay saw in technology the deterioration of human possibilities, a yoke on spontaneity, a diminishment of man, and a depersonalization particularly painful to blacks. We should remember that McKay's book was written at a time when assembly-line work was being denounced on film by Charlie Chaplin (in *Modern Times*) and by René Clair (in *A nous la liberté*). In America as in Europe, men—Mounier, Duhamel, Bernanos—were sounding an alarm. The fears raised by increasing automation concerned not only the "mechanical organization of life" but also the leveling of personalities, the "standardization" of man and the boring everyday life that would be the result. Sinclair Lewis's *Babbitt* expressed a similar anxiety, which was shared by all clear-thinking Americans. The opinion of black writers about most white American writers

39. Quoted by Margaret J. Butcher, *The Negro*, pp. 118–19.

of the period is summed up by Albert Baiwir, who declared: "The writers' attitude leads therefore to the repudiation of American civilization and, in the final analysis, to the spirit which presided over its establishment."[40]

Claude McKay's pessimism matches that of his contemporaries:

[Ray] kept wondering how [his] race would fare under the ever tightening mechanical organization of modern life. . . . The grand mechanical march of civilization had levelled the world down to the point where it seemed treasonable for an advanced thinker to doubt that what was good for one nation or people was also good for another. But as he was never afraid of testing ideas, so he was not afraid of doubting. All peoples must struggle to live, but just as what was helpful for one man might be injurious to another, so it might be with whole communities of peoples.

For Ray happiness was the highest good, and difference the greatest alarm, of life. The hand of progress was robbing his people of many primitive and beautiful qualities. He could not see where they would find greater happiness under the weight of the machine. . . .

Many apologists of a changed and magnificent machine system doubted whether the Negro could find a decent place in it. . . . [Ray] did not think the blacks would come very happily under the super-mechanical Anglo-Saxon-controlled world society of Mr. H. G. Wells.[41]

It is clear that McKay had little confidence in such a society's capacity for happiness. He was led to wonder whether the future role of the black race would not be precisely to humanize society by escaping from technical civilization. The very backwardness and unadaptability of the black race might have preserved a vital resource, the inestimable potential for happiness. "A black man, even though educated, was in closer biological kinship to the swell of primitive earth life. And maybe his apparent failing under the organization of the modern world was the real strength that preserved him from becoming the thing that was the common white creature of it."[42]

The attitude of the assimilated "black intelligentsia" appeared to him ridiculous and illogical, and no words were sufficiently contemptuous to vilify them: "The colored intelligentsia lived its life . . . 'to have the white neighbors think well of us' so that it could move more peacefully into nice white streets."[43] In similar fashion, McKay criticized black students in Europe, who, even when out to amuse themselves, were never without books "to protect themselves from being hailed everywhere as minstrel niggers, coons, funny monkeys . . . because the general European idea of the black man is that he is a

---

40. A. Baiwir (see n. 14 above), p. 383.
41. Claude McKay, *Banjo*, pp. 324, 325.
42. Ibid., p. 323.
43. Ibid., p. 320.

public performer." He poked fun at their clothes "as close as ever to the pattern of the most correctly grey respectability" and of their glasses—"a mark of scholarship and respectability differentiating them from common types."[44]

The obsession with "propriety" also existed in the literary domain, as Langston Hughes pointed out. "Black American intellectuals," he said, "when Negroes wrote books, . . . wanted them to be books in which only good Negroes, clean and cultured and not funny Negroes . . . were presented." One of them wrote in the *Philadelphia Tribune* about *Fine Clothes to the Jew:*

It does not matter to me whether every poem in the book is true to life. Why should it be paraded before the American public by a Negro author as being typical or representative of the Negro? Bad enough to have white authors holding up our imperfections to public gaze. Our aim ought to be present to the general public, already misinformed by well-meaning and malicious writers, our higher aims and aspirations, and our better selves.

Hughes comments:

I felt that the masses of our people had as much in their lives to put into books as did those more fortunate ones who had been born with some means and the ability to work up to a master's degree at a Northern college.[45]

Claude McKay studied this "alienated" reaction of black intellectuals and discovered several reasons for it. First of all, the loss of a folk tradition and folk wisdom, which are the foundations of any culture. Afro-Americans are uprooted people, twice uprooted if they are cultured men, educated and policed by Western civilization. Also, there is the deep inferiority complex from which all American Negroes suffer, the more so this elite for whom whites represent an ideal, leading them to stifle in themselves anything that might appear strange to a civilized white. This black elite so faithfully attempts to imitate the white American as to completely obliterate its own personality. McKay accused this Negro bourgeoisie of no longer being "a people believing in themselves."[46] They seemed to have lost their native spontaneity, the invigorating contact with the masses, in the attempt to obtain a "civilization" of doubtful value.

To rediscover the least distorted black values, one had to go to the masses, the laborers, the sailors, a whole working class for whom life was difficult, but which still had "that raw unconscious and the devil-with-them pride in being Negro," who represented "the irrepressible exuberance and legendary vitality of the black race" whose appar-

44. Ibid., pp. 323–24.
45. Langston Hughes, *The Big Sea*, pp. 267–68.
46. Claude McKay, *Banjo*, p. 320.

ent anarchy helps safeguard its personality.[47]

The most "genuine" black man would therefore be the one least corrupted by Western social structures and standards, the man from the masses whose very ignorance protects him from the multiple forms of alienation which threaten the educated black: "To be educated, black and his instinctive self [was] something of a big job to put over," remarks McKay. The black workingmen he had met in Harlem or Marseilles, on the other hand, lived far from the influence of a Negro press that carried ads for "skin-whitening" and "hair-straightening" remedies right next to those for training and education programs, which were also excellent "bleaching" agents.

Among these working people, there was no desire to look like a white, but there was a sense of humor, spontaneous artistic gifts, and above all, real fellowship during good and bad times. They did not act, did not try to show themselves other than they were; they were genuine and free—like the marvelous character Banjo himself, who has always had enough resilience to bounce back into the "gentle, natural jazz of life" as he calls it, despite war, despite the lynching of his brother, despite the precariousness of his life as a sailor, and of all the trades that he plies for a living. When he has no money to pay for his drink at the bar, Banjo strums his instruments, inventing blues so his friends can dance:

Shake That Thing! That jelly-roll Thing! Shake to the loud music of life playing to the primeval round of life. . . . Shake that thing! In the face of the shadow of Death. Treacherous hand of murderous Death, lurking in sinister alleys, where the shadows of life dance, nevertheless, to their music of life. Death over there! Life over here! Shake down Death and forget his commerce, his purpose, his haunting presence in a great shaking orgy. Dance down the Death of these days, the Death of these ways in shaking that thing. Jungle jazzing, Orient wriggling, civilized stepping. Shake that thing! Sweet dancing thing of primitive joy, perverse pleasure, prostitute ways, many-colored variations of the rhythm, savage, barbaric, refined—eternal rhythm of the mysterious, magical, magnificent—the dance divine of life. . . . Oh, Shake that Thing![48]

The rediscovered value of the dance inspired this piece of pure lyricism, and dance, in Africa, symbolizes the joy of living.

Finally, Claude McKay turned to Africa for hope. He felt his race would rediscover its essence only by going to the very roots. Margaret Just Butcher has testified to the indelible survival of Africa in the folklore and sensibility of American blacks, even though they have

47. Ibid., pp. 320, 324, 319.
48. Ibid., pp. 57–58.

been cut off from all contact with their continent of origin for more than three centuries.[49]

But it was through personal contact with black Africans that McKay realized both what he had missed and an enrichment in the recognition of his origins.

[Ray] always felt humble when he heard the Senegalese and other West African tribes speaking their own languages with native warmth and feeling.

The Africans gave him a positive feeling of wholesome contact with racial roots. They made him feel that he was not merely an unfortunate accident of birth, but that he belonged definitely to a race weighed, tested, and poised in the universal scheme. They inspired him with confidence in them. Short of extermination by the Europeans, they were a safe people, protected by their own indigenous culture. Even though they stood bewildered before the imposing bigness of white things, apparently unaware of the invaluable worth of their own, they were naturally defended by the richness of their fundamental racial values.[50]

The acknowledgment of Africa was one of the pervasive characteristics of the Harlem Renaissance. Countee Cullen's most beautiful poem perhaps, "Heritage," is a long evocation of African landscapes, full of the persistent, rhythmic resonance of tom-toms, and of his fascination with ancient gods:

> Lord, I fashion dark gods, too,
> Daring even to give You
> Dark despairing features where,
> Crowned with dark rebellious hair,
> Patience wavers just so much as
> Mortal grief compels, while touches
> Quick and hot, of anger, rise
> To smitten cheek and weary eyes.
> Lord, forgive me if my need
> Sometimes shapes a human creed.
> ....
> Not yet has my heart or head
> In the least way realized
> They and I are civilized.*

It was also in the name of his African heritage that Langston Hughes rejected the modern world:

> All the tom-toms of the jungles beat in my blood,
> And all the wild hot moons of the jungles shine in my soul.

49. Margaret J. Butcher, The Negro, esp. chaps. 2 and 3.
50. Claude McKay, Banjo, p. 320.
*Translator's note: For the French edition of this work, Mme Kesteloot used Léopold Senghor's translation of Cullen's poem, which can be found in Poésie 45.

> I am afraid of this civilization—
> So hard,
>   So strong,
>   So cold.[51]

> We should have a land of sun
> Of gorgeous sun
> And a land of fragrant water
> Where the twilight
> Is a soft bandana handkerchief
> Of rose and gold,
> And not this land where life is cold.

> We should have a land of trees,
> Of tall thick trees
> Bowed down with chattering parrots
> Brilliant as the day,
> And not this land where birds are grey.

> Ah! we should have a land of joy,
> Of love and joy and wine and song,
> And not this land where joy is wrong.[52]

The progress accomplished toward authenticity becomes fully evident only if one thinks of the denial of Africa ingrained in pre-Harlem Renaissance black consciences: as Phyllis Wheatley once called it, "the land of errors and Egyptian gloom."[53]

Banjo was the first novel to articulate the Negro problem fully and clearly. Blacks in Paris could not remain indifferent to so many revolutionary ideas. But they were also attracted by *Banjo*'s free and easy style, by its human warmth, the reality of its characters. Senghor, Césaire, and Damas can still cite entire chapters. "What struck me in this book," said Aimé Césaire,"is that for the first time Negroes were described truthfully, without inhibitions or prejudice."[54]

Banjo's success did not stop with the first "triumvirate" of black writers. Ousmane Socé pointed out during the same period in *Mirages de Paris*[55] that *Banjo* was displayed in black-student bookshelves right next to books by Delafosse.[56] In *La rue Cases Nègres,* Joseph Zobel

---

51. Langston Hughes, "Poem," from *The Weary Blues* (New York: Knopf, 1926); a French translation appeared in the review *Nouvel Age* in 1931.

52. Hughes, "Our Land," in *The Weary Blues* and also in *Nouvel Age.*

53. Quoted by Margaret J. Butcher, *The Negro,* p. 97.

54. Interview with A. Césaire, September 1959.

55. Ousmane Socé, *Mirages de Paris,* novel, followed by *Rythmes du khalam,* poems (Paris: Nouvelles Editions Latines, 1955).

56. See chap. 7 below.

remarked on the interest aroused in Martinique by McKay's novel.[57] Among writers of the younger generation, Sembene Ousmane in *Le docker noir*[58] was more influenced by *Banjo* than by the novels of Richard Wright, to which *Le docker noir* is occasionally compared.

The success of McKay's book was therefore due not only to its historical timeliness but also to a real literary merit, not yet surpassed by any contemporary black novelist. It is regrettable that many Europeans interested in black literature who have read Richard Wright or Peter Abrahams do not yet know the work of Claude McKay. His books are teeming with ideas, situations, and characters that are not found in such abundance or portrayed with such nuance in the books of any of his successors.

The American Negroes' contribution to young black writers in France was not limited only to new ideas. On a literary level they brought spontaneity of expression, freedom of rhythm and inner music. Léon Damas still has a veritable passion for Langston Hughes, who had a greater influence on the form of his poems than any French poet. Senghor has personally translated numerous poems by Langston Hughes, as well as those by Countee Cullen and Jean Toomer. He has moreover explained—like the good professor he still is—his interest in the Negro Renaissance poets:

What are the characteristics of this poetry? It is essentially nonsophisticated like its African sister. It remains close to song. It is made to be sung or recited and not to be read—thus the importance of the rhythm—Negro rhythm, so tyrannical under its aspect of freedom—thus the importance of its music, so difficult to retain in translating Toomer. These are the characteristics of the picture which, rare or in profusion, adhere closely to an idea or feeling. The words restored to their original purity keep their paradisiac power, and this often explains the clarity of the text.

In a word, a poetry of flesh and of the earth, to put it as Hughes does, the poetry of a peasant still in contact with tellurian forces. And that explains the cosmic rhythm, this music and these pictures of flowing water, rustling leaves, beating wings, twinkling stars.[59]

Aimé Césaire, formed by the surrealist and symbolist schools, also appreciated this poetry, but for other reasons:

From this poetry, which might seem like the sort Valéry called "loose," "defenseless," written only to the rhythm of a juvenile spontaneity, at the exact point of intersection between the ego and the world, a drop of blood oozes. A drop. But of blood. . . .

There is its value: to be open on man in his wholeness. What others bring

57. Joseph Zobel, *La rue Cases Nègres* (Paris: Editions Jean Froissart, 1950).
58. Sembene Ousmane, *Le docker noir* (Paris: Editions Debresse, 1956).
59. L. S. Senghor, "Trois poètes négro-américains," in *Poésie 45*.

to poetry is a preference for the exterior world or for man at his most noble, the finest flower of his thought or feelings. And what indicates that greater or lesser mobility is the fear of oneself, a capitulation of the being to the seeming to be, a refusal to accept one's complete nature. But such weakness is unknown to the Negro poet. His treasure lies in those depths disdained by others. . . .

Where the role of an earlier literature was to seek out the grotesque, the absurd or exotic aspects of the ordinary Negro, this Negro now becomes the poet's hero. He is described seriously, with passion, and the limited power of his art—by a miracle of love—succeeds, where more considerable means fail, in suggesting even those inner forces which command destiny. Is creating a world of minor importance? Evoking a world from the outlandish inhuman creatures that used to be displayed row after row as if in a ten-cent store? And where once we could find nothing but a vision of crude puppets, to reap new ways of suffering, dying, enduring, in a word, to carry the sure weight of human existence.[60]

More than aesthetic criteria, it was the human values of sincerity, love, and humility that touched Césaire. He was so deeply affected that without hesitation he proposed this type of poetry as a model for all Negro poets.

Senghor too has emphasized this aspect which he considers of principal importance:

[It is a] human poetry, and for this reason it deserves to be known. America is not only a land of machines and records, it is also a land of youth and hope, and among all its faces, America's black face is one of its most human.[61]

60. Aimé Césaire, in *Tropiques,* no. 2 (July 1941), pp. 41–42.
61. L. S. Senghor, "Trois poètes négro-américains."

6/ René Maran and *Batouala*

René Maran has a special place. It is impossible to rank him alongside other West Indian writers of his generation. This West Indian who lived in France and Africa effortlessly and completely assimilated French culture. There was not a trace left in him of the "Negro temperament" nor of "ancestral vestiges." His manner of thinking and feeling were French. Though he is considered today to have been a precursor of "negritude," Maran admitted he did not really understand the phenomenon and had a tendency to see racism in the term rather than a new form of humanism. Why then did the young negritude movement adopt this writer who retained nothing of being Negro but his color?

It will be remembered that in 1921 René Maran received the Prix Goncourt, a prestigious French literary award, for his novel *Batouala*.[1] The recognition immediately gave rise to violent reactions in certain quarters. "A work of hatred: *Batouala* or Slander. By awarding the prize to this pamphlet, the Goncourt Academy has committed a grave error."[2] Doors were closed on René Maran, who said bitterly: "It's hard to be a prophet; one gets stoned."[3]

Rejected by the French, the novel passed on to black African posterity. In 1928, the American writer Claude McKay mentioned that *Batouala*, considered a dangerous book, was banned in all the colonies. In 1932, the Martiniquan student manifesto *Légitime Défense* challenged

1. René Maran, *Batouala—véritable roman nègre* (Paris: Albin Michel, 1921, 1938 [édition définitive]). An English translation by Barbara Beck and Alexandre Mboukou, *Batouala: A True Black Novel*, was published in Washington, D.C., by Black Orpheus Press in 1972.
2. *La Dèpêche Coloniale*, 26 December 1921 issue.
3. Interview with René Maran, March 1959.

the ban as an example of West Indian subservience. Joseph Zobel[4] and Ousmane Socé[5] in turn declared that *Batouala* was read as a classic by all those blacks in Paris and the colonies who were interested in the African Negro renaissance. Aimé Césaire, Léopold Senghor, and Léon Damas are in agreement that this novel marked an important date for the new black generation. With *Batouala* something had changed for men of color.

Let us take a new look at this book—a work of indisputable literary merit and fully deserving of its Goncourt Prize. We shall understand why René Maran, though he thought himself too Westernized properly to appreciate his younger confreres, was adopted by them. He was the first black man in France to have dared tell the truth about certain methods of colonization and to have revealed the true mentality of blacks and what they thought of European occupation.

René Maran was in fact for thirteen years a French colonial administrator in the Ubangi-Shari.[6] He learned the language of the country and often listened to the natives talk without their being aware of it. Too Westernized to participate in their way of living,[7] he tried nevertheless to become acquainted as closely as possible with the Ubangi population. His portrayal of Batouala, the head of the Ubangi tribe, was a faithful one.[8] Maran soon understood, moreover, that the black men's criticisms were not unfounded. In his novel, Chief Batouala, drunk one night, recalls how the tribes withdrew at first when the whites arrived. When the Europeans occupied their entire territory, however, there was no possible escape. In the face of fine promises, the tribes resigned themselves to working for the whites.

What promises they made us! "You will realize later," they said, "that it was with your happiness in mind that we forced you to work. We only take a small part of the money we compel you to earn. We shall use this small part to construct villages, roads, and bridges for you, and machines which, with the help of fire, move along on steel bars! . . .

Thirty moons ago, they were still buying our rubber at three francs a kilo. Without any explanation, from one day to the next, the same quantity of "banga" brought only fifteen sous—one meya and five bi'mbas! And the governor chose just that moment to raise our taxes from five to seven and ten francs! . . .

4. Joseph Zobel, *La rue Cases Nègres* (Paris: Editions Jean Froissart, 1950).

5. Ousmane Socé, *Mirages de Paris* (Paris: Nouvelles Editions Latines, 1955).

6. A former French Equatorial African territory to the north of the former Belgian Congo.

7. Interview with René Maran, March 1959.

8. H. Baumann and D. Westermann, *Les peuples et les civilisations de l'Afrique* (Paris: Payot, 1948, 1957), pp. 294ff.

We are nothing but bodies to be taxed. We are nothing but beasts of burden. Beasts? Not even. A dog? They feed dogs and take good care of their horses. Us? We are less than these animals, we are lower than the lowest. They are slowly killing us.[9]

Batouala's virulence was not that of a mere hothead. His whole people agreed with him.

There were insults and injuries. Batouala was entirely right. Before the arrival of the whites we were happy. We worked little and for ourselves alone. We ate, drank and slept. Occasionally, we had bloody palavers, where we tore out the livers of the dead, to eat their courage and make it ours. Those were the happy days before the whites came. . . .

Now they were nothing but slaves. There was nothing to hope for from a race with no hearts. For these *boundjous* were heartless. They abandon the children they have with black women. These children, knowing they are the sons of whites, do not deign to consort with negroes. Full of hate and envy, like the *boundjouvoukos* they are, these "black-and-whites" lead vicious, lazy, evil lives and are hated by one and all.[10]

Further on, René Maran explains the Banda philosophy of the after-life.[11]

There are no mosquitoes, no mists, no cold. Work has been abolished. No more taxes, no *sandoukos*[12] to carry. No more brutalities, fines, hagglings, *nini! mata!* perfect quiet, limitless peace.[13]

This is not as mystical as Negro spirituals, but it is the same expression of relief from a life one lays down like a burden. It is particularly striking because this way of thinking is completely contrary to the temperament of these tribes, who are naturally joyous and eager for life. Most of the novel is a description of this joy of living during the small events of the year. "I showed the blacks as they were," René Maran said. "I had no intention of writing a polemic."[14]

If indeed the novel is as "objective as a police report" and dwells more on the daily life of the blacks than on their complaints, a number of more vehement pages and, especially, the preface nonetheless make *Batouala* a "committed" book. In a few introductory pages, the author —who in this novel conceals himself behind his characters—confirmed Batouala's reproaches. As an administrator, Maran had had occasion to realize the harmful effects of colonization.

9. *Batouala,* French ed., pp. 76–77.
10. Ibid., pp. 77–78. One man's cruelty is not necessarily the same as another's. Blacks in Ubangi thought it normal to eat the liver of the dead, but were scandalized that an illegitimate child should be abandoned. Many whites believe the opposite.
11. The Bandas are black tribes of the Ubangi-Shari region.
12. Cases and boxes.
13. *Batouala,* p. 99.
14. Interview with René Maran.

This area was well populated and very rich in rubber, covered with plantations of every kind. It swarmed with goats and chickens. Seven years were enough to bring about its ruin. Villages were dispersed, plantations disappeared, goats and chickens were destroyed. As for the natives, debilitated from constant, excessive, and unpaid work, it became impossible for them to spend the necessary time to sow their own crops. Sickness and famine struck, and their numbers decreased.[15]

Undoubtedly, the Ubangi-Shari region was particularly ill organized and poorly managed, for the author emphasizes the negligence, immorality, and cynicism of his colleagues.

It is they who are responsible for the harm done in certain parts of the black man's country, wrongs from which the people still suffer today. For the sake of their promotions, administrators must have no trouble. They did not have the courage to speak out. And with moral weakness added to their intellectual anemia, they have betrayed their homeland without the slightest remorse.[16]

Maran therefore called upon his "brothers in spirit, the writers of France"[17] to echo his testimony and urge that serious measures be taken. "I call on you to redress what the administration euphemistically calls 'weaknesses.' The battle will be difficult. You will encounter slave traders. It will be harder to fight them than to do battle with windmills. The task is a noble one! To work then, without delay! You owe it to France!"[18]

It showed considerable optimism to imagine naïvely that the testimony of one honest man would overturn the established disorder. Particularly when that one man happened to be black. He was made to pay dearly for his audacity. Léon Damas has explained how a press campaign was launched against René Maran that was to have cruel repercussions on his career. The day after the Goncourt vote, Paul Souday, all honey and venom, wrote in *Le Temps* that Maran's indictment of colonial administrators was so formidable that every Frenchman, and every European too, would blush for shame. In an ordinary book Souday thought this might pass unnoticed. The stir created by the Prix Goncourt and the thousand of purchasers it would attract both in France and abroad, however, made silence difficult. So the reviewer declared that the decision of the ten Goncourt members would provoke "questions in the Chamber of Deputies, an investigation and severe censure either of the administration or of . . . the author of the indictment."[19] An investigation commission did arrive in French

15. *Batouala*, p. 16.
16. *Batouala*, p. 14.
17. Ibid., p. 13.
18. Ibid., pp. 14–15.
19. L. G. Damas, "Pour saluer René Maran," *Les Lettres Françaises*, no. 825 (May 1960).

Equatorial Africa at the beginning of January 1922. "It ought to have investigated the facts to which I had called attention," René Maran declared. "The contrary occurred." Orders were given to investigate elsewhere.

Nevertheless, René Maran's book and testimony did not prove useless. His successors are in agreement as to the deep impression *Batouala* had made upon them.

II   NEGRITUDE IS BORN

7 / *L'Etudiant Noir:* A Forum for the New Ideas

Légitime Défense, the West Indian student review in Paris, had just one issue because of insufficient funds, governmental threats, and a several months' suspension of scholarships held by the editors. But the seed had been sown and reactions would follow. That was the essential. Hadn't the editors, with great foresight, announced to their readers: "Should this little review—a temporary tool—fail, we will find other instruments."[1]

Etienne Léro's group continued to exist and to defend in practice the ideas expressed in its manifesto. Its members published articles in other magazines, and as late as 1935 Jules Monnerot made a declaration to the Writers' Congress for the Defense of Culture in the group's name. The conscience of young Africans and West Indians awakened, a new group formed under the direction of Léopold Senghor from Senegal, Aimé Césaire from Martinique, and Léon Damas from French Guiana. It included the West Indians Léonard Sainville and Aristide Maugée, the Senegalese Birago Diop and Ousmane Socé. Around 1934, a small, unpretentious newspaper, *L'Etudiant Noir,* publicized the problems which preoccupied them. The group soon discovered that these problems concerned the entire black race, and the first accomplishment of the periodical was to unite African and West Indian students, as Damas points out in the following text:

L'Etudiant Noir, a corporate and combative newspaper, aimed to put an end to the tribalization and clan feeling that were strong in the Latin Quarter. One ceased to be a student from Martinique, Guadeloupe, Gui-

1. *Légitime Défense,* "Avertissement," p. 1.

ana, Africa, Madagascar, and became merely a black student. Life in isolation was over.[2]

"*L'Etudiant Noir* and *Légitime Défense*," writes Senghor,[3] "represented respectively two tendencies shared by the students. Although both reviews had been subject to the same influences, they differed on several points: *L'Etudiant Noir* believed in the priority of culture. For us," he adds, "politics was but one aspect of culture, whereas *Légitime Défense* maintained . . . that political revolution should precede cultural revolution, the latter becoming possible only if radical political change had occurred. But what political revolution? Monnerot and his friends saw salvation only in communism and consequently in the fight against colonialism. I note, however, that these curious revolutionaries did not preach the independence of Africa, and still less of the West Indies. They were content to repeat communist slogans."

It is true that the aspect of communism which had struck Etienne Léro and his friends most was the class struggle. As we have already pointed out, they had not yet questioned French domination of the West Indies.[4] Even today, the communists of Martinique are still completely subservient to French representatives of the party.[5] We should add, however, that an awareness of colonization was just beginning in 1932. *Légitime Défense* had proposed a first set of solutions to several important problems. It was normal for its successors to attempt to go further. "Monnerot and his friends rejected traditional Western values in the name of contemporary Western values, in the name of communism and surrealism . . . whereas our first move was to reject all Western values."[6]

It might be more accurate to say that the *Etudiant Noir* group used contemporary Western values with discrimination, choosing from them only what was likely to promote the dignity of black peoples. For this reason *L'Etudiant Noir* refused to belong to any party, even an international one, or to establish Marxism as an ideology, preferring to distrust—as Marx himself had wanted in *Das Kapital*—the "tendency

2. None of the writers I could reach was able to supply me with a copy of this newspaper. Therefore I was only able to read a few excerpts from L. Damas, "Notre Génération" (unpublished manuscript).

3. L. S. Senghor, letter of February 1960.

4. See chap. 4, p. 55, above.

5. This is one of the reasons Césaire left the party in 1956. In his *Lettre à Maurice Thorez* (Paris: Présence Africaine, 1956), p. 13, he wrote: "The French Communist Party thinks of its duties to colonial peoples in terms of authoritative power to be exercised and . . . French communist anticolonialism still bears the stigma of the colonialism against which it is fighting."

6. L. S. Senghor, letter of February 1960.

to transform his theories into a universally valid historic-philosophical doctrine."[7] Even today, Senghor still regards socialism as a means, "an efficient instrument for research," enabling spontaneous rebellion to be made logical. Socialism, when applied to the colonies, made it appear that man's relationship with nature (economy) and man's relationship with man (sociology) were tainted by a triple alienation: political, economic, and cultural. Because of European capitalism, of which imperialism was a foreseeable outgrowth, class exploitation of class became one people's exploitation of another people.[8] "But," Senghor warns, "to draw one's inspiration from socialism is not to adopt some sort of 'Marxist dogma,' or to borrow European solutions ready-made."[9] "It is to analyze our concrete situation dialectically . . . as Negro Africans, Madagascans, Indonesians, or colonized West Indians"[10] and to find "an original solution" to these problems, "which alone will prove effective."[11]

Thus most of the contributors to *L'Etudiant Noir* recognized socialism as a valuable "method of research" and as a "revolutionary political technique,"[12] but would not permit it to interfere in philosophical and religious domains. *"Marxist metaphysics,"* recalls Senghor, "is not the work of Marx but of his disciples. . . . Socialism's aim is not to know the essence, the thing in itself, but the phenomenon. It is not to philosophize but to act."[13] A perfectly understandable reservation for men who were mainly spiritualists. This is why Senghor, Damas, Birago Diop, and Ousmane Socé were none of them communist partisans. Césaire himself only joined the party ten years later, and returned to his original position thirteen years after that. "I am now convinced that our ways and those of communism, as they are applied, purely and simply do not blend. . . . We colored men . . . have become aware of the entire range of our uniqueness, . . . the uniqueness of our 'condition in the world,' which can be confused with no other, . . . of our problems which can be compared to no other problem, . . . of our history, interrupted by terrible misfortunes which belong to it alone. . . . What is the result if not that our paths toward the future, . . . both the political and cultural paths, are not ready made; that they are still

---

7. L. S. Senghor, "Rapport sur la doctrine et le programme du parti," given at the Constitutive Congress of the African Assembly Party (P.R.A.), mimeographed, 1959, p. 12.

8. Ibid., pp. 5, 11.

9. Ibid., p. 14.

10. Ibid., p. 13.

11. Ibid., p. 14.

12. Ibid., p. 8.

13. Ibid., p. 12.

to be discovered and that the route to this discovery must be ours alone?"[14]

As for surrealism, *L'Etudiant Noir* no longer saw it as either "a school or a master." "We accepted surrealism as a means, but not as an end, as an ally, and not as a master. We were willing to be influenced by surrealism, but only because surrealist writing rediscovered Negro African speech."[15] In fact, Senghor and Damas, although the one was very friendly with Philippe Soupault, and the other with Robert Desnos, made little use of surrealism. Césaire himself did not entirely adopt it until the beginning of the war, for reasons we will analyze in detail in part III. All three were more affected by the revolutionary spirit of surrealism than by its method[16] and also by traits it happened to share with Negro art and poetry.

The group took great interest in traditional African poetry. Senghor, for example, translated Serer[17] poems into French. Reminiscences of them can be found in his own work. Birago Diop transcribed stories by Amadou Koumba, a *griot*[18] from his village. Léon Damas and Aimé Césaire discovered the riches of a non-Western literature which charmed their imagination and harmonized with the rhythm of their feelings. In 1944 Damas was to write a series of Guianese stories[19] and delightful *Poèmes nègres sur des airs africains.*[20] As early as 1937, in *Pigments,*[21] he had sought a literary form closer to sung and danced African poems.[22]

Senghor asserts that he was more influenced by the literature of his own country than by that of France. "The truth is that for the most part I read or, to be more precise, listened to, transcribed, and commented on African Negro poems. And West Indians who were unaware of them—not Césaire—naturally rediscovered them by searching their own subconscious. . . . If our masters must be found, it would be wiser to look for them in Africa."[23]

This is how Senghor especially began to study the structure of West African poetic language, and his discoveries are worth mentioning, because they introduced West Indian poets to an Africa they had lost.

14. A. Césaire, *Lettre à Maurice Thorez,* pp. 7–8.
15. L. S. Senghor, letter of February 1960.
16. See chap. 3, above.
17. Serer is the language of Senghor's tribe, which bears the same name.
18. See the meaning of *griot* given in note 12, chap. 2, above.
19. Léon Damas, *Veillées noires* (Paris: Stock, 1943; Ottowa: Editions Leméac,1972).
20. Paris: Guy Lévi Mano, 1948. Published by Mbari Press, Ibadan, Nigeria, as *African Songs of Love, War, Grief, and Abuse,* translated by Miriam Koshland and Ulli Beier.
21. Paris: Guy Lévi Mano, 1937.
22. See chap. 11, below, on the poetry of Damas.
23. L. S. Senghor, *Ethiopiques* (Paris: Seuil, 1956), postface, p. 107.

"Negro art," said Senghor, "and particularly poetry, aims at expressing a moral world more real than the visible world . . . animated by the invisible forces that rule the universe."[24] When an artist is emotionally affected, and he is by rhythm, he comes into contact with cosmic forces and attempts to exteriorize them in his work. "In Black Africa, any work of art is at the same time a magic operation. The aim is to enclose a vital force in a tangible casing and, at the appropriate moment, release this force by means of dance or prayer."[25] The artist's aim is not therefore a "work of art," valid by its mere formal beauty. Neither does he wish to represent real objects, but to capture invisible forces and place them at man's service. Such art is functional, never gratuitous.[26] This does not mean he is only incidentally interested in beauty. Blacks assimilate beauty, goodness, and effectiveness. A work of art is effective only through its beauty.[27] For an African, art therefore becomes "knowledge and explanation of the world or, in other words, reality which sustains the world: *surreality.*"[28]

In traditional African literature this results in the use of what Senghor has called the "analogy-image," where *meaning* surpasses *symbol*: "The object does not mean what it represents, but what it suggests, what it creates. An elephant is Strength; a spider is Prudence; horns are the Moon, and the Moon is Fecundity. Any representation is an image, and the image is not the sign but the meaning, that is to say, the symbol, the ideogram."[29]

This interpretation extends to all elements of language—the sensual qualities of word and phrase, the timbre, tone, rhythm—and to all elements of the plastic arts—the materials used (stone, wood, iron, clay, fiber, etc.), the lines and colors. The black artist uses clay rather than iron or stone, for example, not by chance but because this medium, in each precise case, is the only one capable of grasping the *surreality* he wishes to express. He gives a certain color or form to his work for the same reason. It is not only because the materials, colors, and forms are symbols, but because they act magically and they alone

24. L. S. Senghor, "Language et poésie négro-africaine," Second Biennial of Poetry, Knokke, Belgium, 1954, pp. 7–8. See also "Les lois de la culture négro-africaine," in the special issue of *Présence Africaine* devoted to the First Congress of Black African Writers and Artists, nos. 8, 9, 10 (June–November 1956), p. 51.

Father Tempels has clearly shown the exceptional importance of these vital forces in *La philosophie bantoue* (Elizabethville: Editions Lovania, 1945; repr. Paris: Présence Africaine, 1949).

25. L. S. Senghor, "L'art négro-africain," unpublished lecture, 1955, p. 16.
26. Ibid., p. 9.
27. We speak here, of course, of the "work of art," not the gri-gri which the witch doctor makes powerful by other means.
28. Lecture (see note 25 above), p. 10.
29. Ibid., p. 11.

can capture nature's secrets and more or less compel them to take tangible form. This is the main function of fetishes, masks, statues of ancestors, etc.—objects both artistic and religious at the same time, the two domains are always inseparable here.[30]

Senghor tells us that "any language which is not imaginative is boring because it does not reach the feelings. What is more, the African Negro does not understand such a language."[31]

This, of course, refers to artistic language. In ordinary conversation an African uses the exact word applicable to concrete objects, and when he says "This tree is ten meters high," he means exactly the same thing we do. But the artist's language must always be understood as a fable. Beings and things are not accepted as themselves but as ideas evoked by them, just as in La Fontaine, for whom the oak tree represents proud strength and the reed humility and apparent frailty. Except for fables, whose double meaning is made clear to Westerners from their childhood, the Westerner has lost this spontaneous understanding of symbols. The greatness of modern poets is to have rediscovered this "world of correspondences" Baudelaire spoke of. It is also their tragedy, since they are incomprehensible to the general public and only accessible to an elite. "The French," Senghor observes, "always feel the need to comment and explain the meaning of images by abstract words. For the Negro poet this is rarely necessary. His public has this second sight spontaneously,[32] because it is initiated, . . . gifted with inner eyes which see through walls. . . .[33] There is no need," he adds, "to explain that the young girl who has just seen her fiancé triumph in athletic games is flooded with joy as she sings:

> I shall not sleep; I shall watch on the open square
> The tom-tom of me is decked in a white necklace.

Nor that the young man is singing of his fiancée's nobility when he says:

> The road forks in the midst of the clouds
> Of a tall house. I shall yield it to no one.[34]

30. Let us take an easily understood example: a wedding ring. The ring represents the bond uniting the husband and wife, and the gold represents their indestructible fidelity. For us these are but symbols, ineffectual ideas, whereas an African—supposing this particular symbolism is also valid for him, which we do not know—would use this shape and this metal in order to "trap" the invisible forces which ensure faithfulness in marriage. A man wearing such a ring would thus inform other men, not only that he was married, and intended to remain faithful to his wife, but that the power magically contained in the ring would really give him the virtue of fidelity.

31. L. S. Senghor, "L'art négro-africain," p. 11.

32. L. S. Senghor, "Langage et poésie négro-africaine," p. 8.

33. Ibid., p. 7.

34. Ibid., pp. 7–8.

The analogy-image we have just analyzed is close to that used by Western surrealists. Yet Senghor attempted to distinguish African from European surrealism.

What did André Breton have to say about it? "Poetic analogy," he wrote in *Signe ascendant,* "has this in common with mystical analogy; it transgresses the laws of logic so that the mind may seize the interdependence of two objects of thought operating on different levels, which are unlikely to be spanned by the logical operation of the mind and which are *a priori* even opposed to such spanning. Poetical analogy differs fundamentally from mystical analogy in that it does not presuppose in any way an invisible world which is trying to show itself through the screen of the visible world. It is completely empirical in its approach."[35]

This passage is ambiguous. Breton seems opposed to any invisible world, no matter what it may be. What has become of the surrealist attempt to liberate the unconscious, the "invisible world" peopled by impulses "that tend to reveal themselves" in abortive acts, in dreams, desires? What Breton later says, however, shows that he rejects only a supersensible, "supernatural world." "The poetic image," he writes, "tends to give a glimpse and an appreciation of the real 'absent' life, which no more draws its substance from metaphysical reverie than it considers for a moment using its conquests for the glory of a possible world 'beyond.' "[36]

But Senghor's criticism nevertheless remains accurate, *from his point of view.* European surrealism—at least as Breton conceives it—is not metaphysical, whereas Negro African surrealism, says Senghor, "presupposes and reveals the hierarchic universe of vital forces."[37]

The difference is obvious. The African artist attempts to show a religious universe peopled with objective forces, external to man, whereas European surrealism reveals only an internal, psychological world. And it is precisely because Western surrealists know nothing of this unconscious to be discovered, that their methods can only be empirical (automatic writing, the transcription of dreams, etc.).

And yet, if the difference were as clear as Senghor claims, could we easily include certain black authors in Negro African surrealism thus defined? We are thinking, among others, of Césaire, whom Senghor often quotes and who does not believe in a universe of "vital forces" outside man. Césaire, however, does possess all the other characteristics of African expression: rhythm, symbols, descriptive power, and so forth.

35. Quoted by L. S. Senghor in "Les lois de la culture négro-africaine" (mimeographed), p. 59.

36. A. Breton, *Poésie et autre* (Paris: Club du Meilleur Livre, 1960), pp. 264–65.

37. L. S. Senghor, "Les lois de la culture négro-africaine," p. 59.

Senghor also seems to say that the African artist accepts these external forces, that he submits to them without difficulty, and that his role merely consists of revealing them. (This is what we shall call a *religious* mentality.) But in Africa one also finds a *magic* mentality. By means of rites and certain practices, men try to control and tame vital forces for personal or community ends.

In European surrealism, we discover numerous traces of a similar belief in the power of magic. Words, pictures, objects, briefly, all means of expression, can serve not only to reveal the forces of the unconscious, but also to use these forces to transform the world or oneself (the alchemy of the word). Consequently, instead of differentiating between Negro African surrealism and European surrealism under the pretext that only the former accepts the existence of a metaphysical universe, would it not be more interesting to distinguish between the religious current and the magic current (in the sense we understood these adjectives above), both contained in a single surrealism? Nothing, moreover, prevents both tendencies from existing side by side in an artist's work.

Among Negro Africans, Senghor and Birago Diop are perfect examples of the *religious mentality*, whereas the incantations of a Damas and the rebellion of a Césaire belong rather to the *magic* current.[38] This magical attempt to "change life" is found in Western literature also, particularly since Rimbaud, Lautréamont, and the German romantics. And it is not *by mere chance* that many poets have been interested in the occult and esoteric sciences.[39]

In sum, Negro African surrealism is probably more complicated than Senghor imagined, and fundamentally, perhaps, it does not differ greatly from European surrealism. Yet, the expression of Negro African poets remains entirely different from that of French surrealists. The founders of *L'Etudiant Noir* always rejected the indiscriminate imitation of acknowledged masters, as Etienne Léro and his group had done before them, but were concerned above all about being authentic.

In discussing communism from a social point of view, and surrealism from a literary one, then, *L'Etudiant Noir* was moving away from even the most revolutionary Western values, in an attempt to rediscover "the values of negritude." It was in this sense that *L'Etudiant Noir* preached cultural revolution before anything else: "How can we wish

38. Perhaps the magic and demiurgic aspect is given greater emphasis by West Indian poets because of the more stifling social conditions and of less deeply rooted religious beliefs. See also chap. 18, note 29, below.

39. P. Mabille, *Le miroir du merveilleux* (Paris: Editions du Sagittaire, 1940).

for political independence if we do not have faith in the values of negritude? . . . All our articles were in this vein. Césaire led the fight, of course, primarily against the assimilation of West Indians. As for me, my aim was to analyze and exalt the traditional values of black Africa."[40]

The following passage is an example of the dominant tone and theme of this little newspaper created by student enthusiasts:

Assimilation, born of fear and timidity, always ends in contempt and hate, and carries in it seeds of battle, of like against like, which is the worst struggle of all.

That is why black Youth turns its back on the tribe of the Ancients. The tribe of the Ancients says: Assimilation. We reply: Resurrection.

What does black Youth want? . . . To live. But to really live, one must remain oneself. An actor is a man who does not really live. He gives life to a multitude of men—a matter of roles—but he does not bring himself to life. Black Youth does not wish to play any role; it wishes to be itself. Black history is a three-act drama. Negroes were first enslaved (they were called idiots and brutes). . . . Then a more compassionate eye was turned upon them, and it was said that they were better than had been supposed. An attempt was made to make something of them. They were assimilated. They were sent to the Masters' school like "grown-up children." For only children are perpetually pupils at the Masters' school.

Today's young Negroes want neither slavery nor "Assimilation." They want emancipation. They want to be men, because only a man walks without a tutor along the great roads of Thought . . .; Slavery and Assimilation are somewhat alike: they are both forms of passivity.

During these two periods, Negroes were also impotent. Emancipation, on the contrary, means Action and Creation.

Black Youth wants to act and create. It wants to have its own poets, its own novelists, who will speak to it of its own affliction and of its own greatness. It wants to contribute to universal life, in the humanizing of Humanity. And for this, once again, one must either conserve or rediscover oneself; the self is of the first importance.

But in order to be oneself, one must first do battle with the lost brothers who are afraid to be themselves: the senile mob of the assimilated. And then one must fight those who like to hear themselves: the fierce legion of assimilators.

Finally, to be oneself, one must fight against oneself. Indifference must be destroyed, obscurantism must be uprooted, sentimentality must be cut off at its source. And what is most important to cut off, Meredith tells us: "Black Youth, one hair keeps you from action: Uniformity. And you are the one who wears it. Crop your heads for fear that Uniformity will escape. Shave yourself. This is the first condition of creation. Long hair is an affliction.[41]

40. L. S. Senghor, letter of February 1960.

41. A. Césaire, passage from *L'Etudiant Noir*, quoted by L. Damas in his "Notre génération," unpublished.

Senghor's group thus went further than Etienne Léro's. First, in forging one mystique for the entire black race,[42] it went beyond the particularity of being West Indian or African. Then, too, it extended Léro's criticism of the West into a criticism of the European ideologies which challenged the West itself: communism and surrealism. Finally, it passionately urged a rediscovery of the "patrimony of African civilizations." This last difference was the most original. The presence of Africans in the group was probably one underlying reason for this, but one must not forget the genuine "search for their sources" that Césaire and Damas were undertaking.[43] Damas sought information from Africans of many different backgrounds whom he met in Paris and in his classes with Professor Paul Rivet, director of the Musée de l'Homme in Paris.[44] It was with this aim that the entire group—in addition to their literary studies—plunged into the study of African ethnology, the influence of which we shall now examine.

42. A. Viatte, in *Histoire littéraire de l'Amérique française, des origines à 1950* (Paris: PUF, 1954), p. 510, declares that between 1940 and 1945 "Guy Tirolien was a fellow prisoner, during the war, of L. S. Senghor, theorist of 'negritude.' By this means, West Indian literature was welded to that of black Africa." In reality the "welding" took place approximately ten years earlier.

43. Césaire claims that Senghor revealed Africa to him.

44. Interview with L. Damas, June 1959.

8 / How the Ethnologists Helped

Leaving the theories of Lévy-Bruhl, Gobineau, and Spengler behind, the new school of ethnology spoke about the so-called primitive peoples with greater objectivity. Leo Frobenius's *Histoire de la civilisation africaine*,[1] and *Les nègres* by Maurice Delafosse,[2] were read and discussed by black students in Paris and, for many of them, became bedside reading matter. These works by men of science conferred new value on a past long considered lacking in interest. The light shed by these books dispelled the deficiencies unjustly attributed to the black race: as a people with no history, with a primitive, idolatrous and fetishist mentality. In answer to these accusations, Frobenius declared that toward the end of the Middle Ages, the first European navigators had discovered in the ancient kingdom of the Congo[3] "swarming crowds dressed in silks and velvets, great states organized down to the last detail, powerful sovereigns, wealthy industries. Civilized to the very marrow of their bones."[4] What can be said about the West African peoples later dispersed by the slave trade? When Frobenius himself penetrated the Kassai-Sankuru territory[5] in 1906, he found "villages where the main streets were lined on either side, for miles, with quadruple rows of palm trees, and where charmingly decorated huts contained innumerable works of art. There was no man

1. Leo Frobenius, *Histoire de la civilisation africaine* (Paris: Nouvelle Revue Française, Gallimard, 1936; 3d ed. of the French translation).
2. Maurice Delafosse, *Les nègres* (Paris: Edition Rieder, 1927).
3. This kingdom included part of Angola, part of the French Congo, and Lower Congo. See Monseigneur Cuvelier's interesting study *L'ancien royaume du Congo* (Brussels: Desclée de Brouwer, 1946).
4. L. Frobenius, *Histoire*, p. 14.
5. Territory south of the Congo, between the rivers Kasai (or Kassai) and Sankuru.

without magnificent weapons of iron or brass, with inlaid blades and pommels covered with snakeskin. Velvet and silk were everywhere. Each cup, each pipe, each spoon was a work of art worthy of comparison with creations in the Roman-European style. The gestures, manners, and moral standards of all the people, from the smallest child to the oldest man, although completely natural, were full of dignity and grace."[6]

Frobenius found traces of this same culture throughout Africa. After twenty years of expeditions to Egypt, South Africa, the Congo, Dahomey, Nigeria, Senegal, and the Sudan, he declared that a civilization "bearing the same stamp" existed throughout Africa. "Everywhere we recognize a similar 'spirit,' 'characteristic,' 'essence.' "[7]

Everything has a definite aim: harsh, severe, tectonic. That is the main characteristic of African style. Anyone who comes close enough thoroughly to understand it, soon recognizes that it dominates *all of Africa* and is the very expression of its essence. It is manifest in the gestures of all Negro peoples as well as in their plastic arts. It speaks in their dances and in their masks, in their religious feelings as in their mode of existence, in their forms of government and in their destiny as peoples. It lives in their fables, their fairy tales, their legends and myths.[8]

Not content with defining these characteristics and extending them to an entire continent, Frobenius connects them directly with the most ancient civilization known: "If we compare these characteristics to those of pre-Islamic Egypt, we see that the formula for black Africa also applies to the essence of this particular civilization. Does not pre-Islamic Egypt express itself in a harsh, severe, thoughtful, direct, and solemn style?"[9]

Thus, for the first time, a Western scholar not only acknowledged that there was an African civilization, but that its value, both social and artistic, was high. He ennobled it, moreover, by tracing it back to the very cradle of culture. With what enthusiasm the young blacks read Frobenius! Césaire and Senghor confess their passion for this book,

6. L. Frobenius, *Histoire*, p. 15. It would be irrelevant to check the veracity of Frobenius's assertions—the investigations of this great ethnologist have often been shown insufficient. What counts is the impression his book made on black students in Paris.

7. Ibid., p. 16.

8. Ibid., pp. 17–18.

9. Ibid., p. 18. Following this trail, the Senegalese Cheik Anta Diop devoted a voluminous study to the Negro origins of ancient Egypt: *Nations nègres et culture* (Paris: Présence Africaine, 1954). However, the extremist conclusions reached in this book weaken an otherwise interesting documentation. The question of whether or not the origins of ancient Egypt are Negro is still not resolved. On the other hand it is certain that Meroe civilization influenced the Sudanese civilizations before colonization. See also "Le rayonnement de l'Egypte antique dans la mythologie de l'Afrique occidentale," by Luc de Heusch, in *Journal des Africanistes*, 1958.

which from beginning to end showed the richness and complexity of African civilizations, an admiration recorded in many of their own writings.[10]

Before becoming enthusiastic about Frobenius, the black students had already read Maurice Delafosse, whom Senghor called "the greatest Africanist in France, I mean the most careful and most thorough."[11] Delafosse's studies, published between 1922 and 1927, bore fruit with the young black generation only after 1933.

With greater objectivity than Frobenius and with the scrupulous honesty of a man of science, Delafosse investigated the history of West Africa. He relied on local traditions, documents left by the scholars of Timbuctoo, written reports by Arab historians and geographers of the tenth to the fifteenth centuries, (including Ibn Batouta, Ibn Haoukal, Ibn Khaldoun, and El Bekri), and in addition often checked their testimony against archeological researches. Reaching as far back as the sixth century of our era, Delafosse too discovered flourishing West African empires (Ghana, Mali, Gao, the Mossi states), well-established dynasties, solid social and political structures, and intensive commerce with North Africa.

All this was assurance of "sound administration by the state, prosperity, the courtesy and discipline of civil servants and provincial governors, an excellent state of public finance, a rich, complex, and rigorous etiquette of royal receptions, the respect of the king's decisions of justice and his sovereign authority." Taking Mali as an example, Delafosse concluded, in short, that it was: "a real state, whose organization and civilization could compare favorably with that of Moslem kingdoms and many Christian kingdoms of the same period (1353)."[12]

In addition, this Mandingo or Mali empire "occupied an area approximately equal to that of all the territories of French West Africa and the foreign colonies situated in it. . . . The master of this huge black state enjoyed friendly relations with the greatest Moslem potentates of North Africa and especially with the 'Merinide' Sultan of Morocco."[13]

10. See especially the space given to Frobenius by Césaire in his Martiniquan review *Tropiques*—a study included in part III, below—and the allusion he again makes to him, in 1955, in the *Discours sur le colonialisme* (Paris: Présence Africaine), p. 36. [Translator's note: See also "Negritude and the Germans," by Léopold Sédar Senghor, in *Africa Report*, May 1967.]

11. L. S. Senghor, "Ce que l'homme noir apporte," in *L'homme de couleur* (Paris: Plon, 1939).

12. Maurice Delafosse; *Les noirs de l'Afrique* (Paris: Payot, 1922), p. 61.

13. Ibid., pp. 60–61. See also G. Dieterlen, "Importance du Mali pour la diffusion des mythes cosmogoniques," *Journal des Africanistes* 25 (1955) and 29 (1959).

Delafosse suggested, in fact, that the African Middle Ages were comparable to ours on many levels. The thriving of black peoples did not stop here; it continued despite the slave trade. It is true that the kings of Dahomey had become famous for their human sacrifices, but they had known how to organize their state and their army, and to administer their kingdom in a way that did them honor.[14] As for the Benin kingdom—present-day Nigeria—"as far back as the fifteenth century, and perhaps farther, it formed a powerful and dreaded state, where industrial arts, and particularly bronze and ivory arts, flourished in remarkable fashion. Certain Benin bronzes are worthy to compete with the corresponding products of several famous civilizations."[15]

If the splendors of these peoples were past, Delafosse stated, this was as a result of Arab and later European invasions, whose aim was "to capture thousands as slaves" and to "drown them in the alcohol trade."[16] In spite of this, one could still find in these territories "peoples astonishingly gifted intellectually, artistically, and politically," as for example the tribes in the British Gold Coast—now called Ghana —which produced "a fantastic number of doctors in law and theology, lawyers, and writers."[17]

The author's conclusion is immediately clear from the title of the final chapter: "The so-called intellectual inferiority of blacks has never been demonstrated—numerous proofs to the contrary." Having read Gobineau,[18] Delafosse poses the following question: "Do African Negroes form a race intellectually inferior to other human races?"[19] No convincing proof has ever been brought forward to confirm this frequent statement, he replies. In order to judge correctly, the isolation of Africa must be taken into consideration, as well as the ill treatment its peoples have suffered. "Would we have done better than they had we been in the same situation?"[20]

When peoples placed in such circumstances have been able by means of their own resourcefulness alone to organize states, whose history I have attempted to trace herein; to create and maintain educational centers like Timbuctoo, for example; to produce statesmen like the Mansa Congo-Moussa[21] or

14. Maurice Delafosse, *Les noirs de l'Afrique,* p. 91.
15. Ibid., p. 92.
16. Ibid., p. 158. In spite of these assertions, Delafosse does not yet criticize the colonial system itself.
17. Ibid., p. 90.
18. Ibid., p. 160.
19. Ibid., p. 156.
20. Ibid., p. 158.
21. King of the Mandingos, who reigned from 1307 to 1332, in the heyday of the Mali empire.

the Askia Mohammed,[22] . . . scholars and educated men who, without the aid
of dictionaries or any vehicular language, have grasped Arabic sufficiently well
to read it fluently and write it correctly, to form idioms, the flexibility, richness,
and preciseness of which astonish all those who study them, idioms which
could—by the normal play of their morphological laws and without foreign
interpolation—furnish the required instrument to those speaking these idioms; if these peoples could leap fifteen or twenty centuries forward, to invent
a perfectly viable system of writing—in the same way that the Vai people of
the Coast a hundred years ago and, more recently, the Cameroon Bamouns
invented seeds—then these peoples do not deserve to be treated as intellectual
inferiors.[23]

One can see the use the black students would make of such affirmations. They knew now they had a history. Oral tradition had already
told them the great deeds of their tribes, but here was a white scholar,
after broad and thorough study, advising them that these local histo-
ries were integral parts of a history of vast empires, whose fame had
already reached as far as Arabia, Morocco, and even Spain.

Georges Hardy's work L'art nègre, published in 1927, must also be
mentioned, since it disproved certain preconceived ideas that had
been believed for centuries about African religions:[24]

For most of our contemporaries, the religion of black Africans has to do with
the adoration of fetishes, idols, images, embodying good or evil natural forces.
. . . It is understood that this fetishist, idolatrous, polytheistic religion is also
imbued with totemism. These are all errors, preconceived notions to be dis-
carded if one wishes to reach the deeply religious Negro soul. The religion of
black Africans has little in common with so crude a picture or so simplistic an
analogy. Doubtless it is full of fetishist and superstitious practices; but . . . these
must not be confused with the religion itself, any more than Catholicism
should be confused with survivals of magic that still exist in rural Europe.
. . . The better one knows these religions, the more one can assert that they
originate from a common dogma, a dogma of considerable strength and depth
to have resisted so many trials and to have maintained itself so firmly despite
a general absence of sacred books.[25]

As the title of his study indicates, Georges Hardy particularly
stresses the blacks' artistic talents, both in the literary and musical
domains, as well as in sculpture, the field in which they excell. Many
times he hints that "European influence here—no matter who the
representative may be—appears to be disastrous for Africa."[26] He

22. Chief of the Gao empire, who reigned from 1493 to 1529, at the peak of Gao's
glory.
23. Maurice Delafosse, Les noirs de l'Afrique, p. 159.
24. G. Hardy, L'art nègre (Paris: Henri Laurens, 1927).
25. Ibid., pp. 14, 16.
26. Ibid., p. 99.

expresses the same opinion about political organization, religion and the arts. These blemishes on "the blessings of civilization" led him to conclude that "Negro art [is] now completely decadent. . . . Islam began the work of destruction. But Europe did a better job, not only —as it has done occasionally in the past—by separating and destroying the races, but by systematically disorganizing; in the areas where Europe's incursion was the most pacific . . . its action has been more disastrous perhaps from an artistic viewpoint, than where the incursion was brutal."[27]

And Georges Hardy briefly mentions the stifling of local religions by Christianization, the dismembering of artisan castes by the introduction of European industry and commerce, without forgetting a political administration which reduced the "last of the native rulers to mere puppets."[28]

In short, he calls into question the entire phenomenon of the contact of civilizations. The encounter between Europe and Africa—no matter how necessary one may consider it—was far from tender. The author, who was at the time director of the Ecole Coloniale de Paris, recognizes that "the creative forces of the black race must be given time to find their balance, to recover from the staggering blow of European intervention."[29]

With the years, the moral support of ethnologists and Africanists would increase. They were discovering an ancient African civilization; they were becoming aware both of the obvious cultural impoverishment and of a need to encourage a response from African intellectuals capable of defending their threatened values.

It was in this spirit in 1935 that Robert Delavignette wrote a preface to Ousmane Socé's novel *Karim*.[30] "Karim and his friends," he said, "are authentic Wolofs,[31] proud and generous, loving display, noble sentiments, and heroic deeds. Their models were the great Lingueres, whose glory had been sung to them. But the whites arrived, and Africa changed. Karim and his friends can no longer live like their ancestors. The failure of their traditional ideal leaves them defenseless in the face of modern life which may destroy them. The efforts they are forced to make to rediscover their meaning and place in this new world—this is the real subject matter of Karim."[32]

27. Ibid.
28. Ibid., p. 154.
29. Ibid., p. 160.
30. Ousmane Socé, *Karim, roman sénégalais* (Paris: Editions Fernand Sorlot, 1935; repr. Paris: Nouvelles Editions Latines, 1948).
31. Wolof—a Senegalese tribe.
32. Preface to *Karim*, p. 12.

In fact, Ousmane Socé's novel is rather superficial, but the author of the preface felt it was now important to give blacks the floor. The rest of his preface shows this clearly. He begins by quoting another eminent Africanist, Théodore Monod,[33] on the diversity of African peoples, their languages, and their cultures. Africa, says Monod, is a world as complex as ours or as that of Asia. He laughs at the schematization forced upon it by our ignorance. "The black is not a man without a past. He did not fall out of a tree yesterday. Africa is literally covered with prehistoric vestiges, and certain experts have recently wondered whether, contrary to current opinion, it may not have witnessed the birth of original man."[34] He then enumerates the inherent and still existent values of black people: "their sense of politeness and hospitality, . . . the humor of their narrators, the pithy wisdom of their elders, their artistic talent, the inspiration of their poets, the supernatural faculties of their witch doctors, the expression of philosophical, symbolical, religious, or mystical thought."[35] Next, he evokes the method of colonial politics: "Africa exists, very definitely. It would therefore be absurd to continue to consider it a *tabula rasa*, upon which one can build anything, *ab nihilo.*"

And here Monod sets forth the first principles of cultural relativism, which today grow stronger and stronger:[36]

In our stupid and lazy passion for abstract generalization, we are sure that one educational system, one method of voting, one set of laws, a single regime are excellent "in themselves" and automatically beneficial for the whole world. . . . Convinced that [our civilization] is not only the only good one but the only possible one, we would willingly see it, in a world conquest, replace all others. . . . But this is the heart of the problem. It is by no means a question of impoverishing humanity by ensuring the triumph of only one possible aspect of human culture, but, rather of allowing each element of the earthly family to bring its best to the common assembly, in order to enrich the whole with its very best element. Consequently, after a selection, a sorting out, each

33. Théodore Monod spent all his professional life in Africa. He became director of the Institut Français d'Afrique Noire (since Senegalese independence, known as the Institut Fondamental d'Afrique Noire) at Dakar and has always used his knowledge and fame to help African cultural renaissance.

34. Most of the texts quoted by Delavignette were quoted anew by T. Monod in the preface of the French translation of a prewar book written by H. Baumann and D. Westermann, *Les peuples et les civilisations de l'Afrique* (Paris: Payot, 1948, 1957). This ethnological work is considered the most important synthesis and is also the most criticized to date, together with G. P. Murdock's book *Africa: Its People and Their Cultural History* (New York: McGraw, 1959).

35. Preface to *Karim.*

36. See Melville Herskovits, *Man and His Works: The Science of Cultural Anthropology* (New York: Knopf, 1948).

culture should retain of its own patrimony only that which is worth keeping, and should accept no influence from outside except that which is organically assimilable or can enrich its soul.[37]

Somewhat ahead of his time, Monod adds:

When all that is outdated after five centuries of the old colonial system disappears, in a milieu where new structural and mental forms emerge, it will be important to accept honestly the enormous—and in my opinion—happy differences which separate men; differences it would be foolish and vain to deny, but which must be openly recognized in order to find among them the very foundations of new spiritual progress. On the condition that it be progress we are aiming for and that we not continue to consider other systems: material, economic, political, as an end in themselves rather than what they are: a means.[38]

Delavignette concludes by acknowledging the merit of African writers, who will help to solve future problems:

By expressing and analyzing themselves, Africans are not only working for their own development, but also for ours. And they carry the problem of our relations with Africa to a higher level, obliging them, and us as well, to go beyond the ancient ideas of colonization to a period of African nationalism.[39]

The past must not be an obstacle to the adjustment imposed by the present. It is from a knowledge of the past, out of respect and love for it, that men have always received a sense of their individual and collective vocations and the strength to fulfill them. Africa will prove no exception. It will find within itself sufficient spiritual resources to accomplish the effort of synthesis which the modern world requires of all men.[40]

The merit of most French ethnologists, it is clear, was to use all their scientific authority to support black intellectuals. By 1938, Lévy-Bruhl acknowledged in his notebooks that he felt obliged to go back on his former assertions and declare that there were no qualitative differences between the so-called primitive mentality and that of more developed peoples.[41] After Delavignette and Théodore Monod, the blacks were able to count successfully on Professor Paul Rivet, Michel Leiris, Marcel Griaule, Georges Balandier, and others for support.[42]

Describing this movement, Césaire says it was so general that there was talk of "the great betrayal of Western ethnography which, for some time, with a deplorable deterioration of its sense of responsibil-

37. Preface to *Karim*, p. 15.
38. Ibid.
39. Ibid.
40. Ibid., p. 13.
41. *Les carnets de Lucien Lévy-Bruhl* (Paris: PUF, 1949), pp. 131ff.
42. The last three personally helped to launch the periodical *Présence Africaine*, to which part IV of this book is devoted.

ity, was doing its utmost to cast doubts on the omnilateral superiority of Western civilization over the exotic civilizations."[43] The colonialists who denounced this phenomenon had fully recognized its impact. Roger Caillois, for example, attacked European intellectuals who "in bitterness and disappointment" persist "in repudiating the various ideals of their culture, thus encouraging tenacious discomfort, particularly in Europe."[44] Ignoring the work of the experts, Caillois reasserts "that only the West is capable of thought. . . . At the limits of the Western world begins the dark kingdom of primitive thought, which, dominated by the idea of participation, incapable of logic, is the prototype of unsound thinking."[45]

With less hypocrisy, the Belgian periodical *Europe-Afrique* accused Messieurs Leiris, Lévy-Strauss, and Mircea Eliade of shaking the foundations of the colonial edifice. "Formerly, the colonizer conceived his relation to the colonized people as basically that between a civilized man and a savage. Colonization thus rested on a hierarchy, crude no doubt, but vigorous and secure."[46] On what could this hierarchy be based from now on, when men of science—the only ones to study African cultures without prejudice and wholly disinterestedly—were destroying the idea of "savage," so convenient to the good conscience of the colonizer?

43. Aimé Césaire, *Discours sur le colonialisme* (Paris: Présence Africaine, 1955), p. 57.

44. Ibid., p. 59, quoting Roger Caillois, "Illusion à rebours," *Nouvelle Revue Francaise*, no. 6 (December–January 1955).

45. Ibid., p. 58.

46. Ibid., quoting M. Piron's article in *Europe-Afrique*, no. 6 (January 1955).

9/ Negritude: Some Definitions, Sartre's Negativity

Negritude! The term has been discussed at such length and has elicited so many different definitions that it seems indispensable to make a detailed analysis of it, based on the work of those who invented the term around 1935, especially Léopold Sédar Senghor and Aimé Césaire.[1] We have discovered no chronological evolution in these authors' works; it would seem therefore that their understanding of the concept has not changed. Nor have we found any thorough definition. In his poems and articles, for example, Senghor emphasizes different aspects of the concept according to the needs of the moment. These partial explanations often go beyond the definition he usually quotes: "Negritude is the cultural patrimony, the values, and above all the spirit of Negro African civilization."[2]

How did Aimé Césaire and I launch the word "negritude" in the years 1933–35? Together with a few other black students, we were at the time in the depths of despair. The horizon was closed. There was no reform in the offing, and the colonizers were legitimizing our political and economic dependence by the *tabula rasa* theory. They deemed we had invented nothing, created nothing, written, sculpted, painted and sung nothing. Dancers, perhaps! . . . To institute a worthwhile revolution, *our* revolution, we first had to get rid of our borrowed clothing—the clothing of assimilation—and to assert our essential being, namely our negritude. Nevertheless, negritude, even when defined as "the total of black Africa's cultural values" could only offer us the beginning of a solution to our problem and not the solution itself. We could not go back to our former condition, to a negritude of the sources. We were no longer living under the rule of the Askias of the Songhai, or under Chaka the Zulu. We were twentieth-century students in Paris, and one of the realities

1. Damas does not use the word negritude in any of his writings of that period.
2. Interview with L. S. Senghor, June 1959.

102

of this twentieth century was the awakening of national consciousness; another, even more real, however, is the interdependence of peoples and continents. To be really ourselves, we had to embody Negro African culture in twentieth-century realities. To enable our negritude to be, instead of a museum piece, the efficient instrument of liberation, it was necessary to cleanse it of its dross and include it in the united movement of the contemporary world.

This was, after all, the conclusion of the First Congress of Black Artists and Writers, which gathered symbolically at the Sorbonne in September 1956.[3]

In this passage, dated 1959, Senghor repeats his favorite definition: Negritude is the "ensemble of black Africa's cultural values." Immediately after, he compares the "negritude of the sources"—that is to say the Negro situation before the arrival of the whites in Africa—to today's negritude, "the effective instrument of liberation." In relation to the first negritude, present-day negritude possesses an aggressiveness resulting from long years of domination. Negritude is therefore changing. It has a historic dimension which Senghor does not explain but of which he is aware.

But let us look at some of Senghor's other comments:

I have often written that emotion was Negro. I have been reproached for it. Mistakenly. I do not see how else to account for our specificity, that of this negritude which is the "whole of the black world's cultural values," including the Americas, and which Sartre defines as "a certain affective attitude toward the world."[4]

Here again we find the first definition of negritude: the ensemble of black cultural values. But in addition these values shed light upon particular characteristics which differentiate blacks from other men and give them a different "affective attitude."

Rhythm, which is born of emotion, in turn engenders emotion. And humor, *the other facet of* negritude. *This shows its multivalence.*[5]

Monotony of tone, which distinguishes poetry from prose, is the seal of negritude, the incantation enabling one to reach the truth of essentials: the Power of the Cosmos.[6]

Negritude, the sensibility peculiar to black men, gives African poetry a rhythm and qualities peculiarly its own. This monotonous, incantatory rhythm permits communication with vital forces that direct the world.

3. L. S. Senghor, "Rapport sur la doctrine et le programme du parti," given at the Constitutive Congress of the African Assembly Party (P.R.A.), mimeographed, 1959, p. 14.

4. L. S. Senghor, "*Psychologie du négro-africain,*" unpublished lecture, n.d.

5. L. S. Senghor, *Ethiopiques* (Paris: Seuil, 1956), postface, p. 116.

6. Ibid., p. 120.

What makes the negritude of a poem is less the theme than the style, an emotional warmth which brings words to life and transmutes speech into verb.[7]

In other texts Senghor comes back to "negritude of the sources," precolonial conditions in which the black man lived without alienation; or to what he also calls the "kingdom of childhood," a time when he lived happily in his distant village far from contact with the whites. He evokes the African night:

Night, delivering me from reasons, salons, sophisms, pirouettes, pretexts, from calculated hatreds, from slaughter humanized.

Night, melting all my contradictions, melting all contradictions in the primal unity of your negritude.[8]

Sometimes, however, negritude designates his entire despised race, excluded from the modern world:

. . . the nobility prohibited to black blood
And Science and Humanity setting up police lines
at negritude's borders.[9]

Senghor's negritude is a revolt against the white man, a refusal to be assimilated, an affirmation of self:

Independence is like negritude. As I have said, it is first a negation, or more exactly, the affirmation of a negation. It is the necessary moment of an historical movement: the refusal of the Other, the refusal to be assimilated, to lose oneself in the Other. But because this movement is historic, it is also dialectical. Refusal of the Other is an affirmation of self.[10]

Before drawing any conclusions from these texts, let us listen to Césaire. On a Negro encountered in a streetcar:

His nose looked like a peninsula adrift, and even his negritude was fading under the hand of a tireless tawer.[11]

Haiti, where negritude first stood up and declared it believed in its humanity.[12]

In the first text negritude merely indicates the color of the black man's skin; in the second, negritude encompasses the entire race:

My grandfather is dying, I say, hurrah! the old negritude is gradually dying.
. . . It's true, he was a good Negro, . . . a good Negro to his good master

---

7. L. S. Senghor, *Anthologie de la nouvelle poésie négre* . . . (Paris: PUF, 1948), p. 173.
8. L. S. Senghor, "Que m'accompagnent kôras et balafongs," *Chants d'ombre* (Paris: Seuil, 1956), p. 50.
9. L. S. Senghor, "Lettre à un prisonnier," *Hosties noires* (Paris: Seuil, 1948), p. 133.
10. L. S. Senghor, "Rapport" (see note 3 above), p. 25.
11. A. Césaire, *Cahier d'un retour au pays natal* (Paris: Présence Africaine, 1956), p. 65.
12. Ibid., p. 46.

. . . and it never occurred to him that he could hoe, dig, cut anything, anything other than dull uninteresting cane. . . . And stones, scrap iron, broken bottles were thrown at him, but neither the stones, the iron, nor the bottles . . .[13]

Here the word "negritude" implies an attitude to life. Césaire rejoices at the disappearance of the ancient psychology of his race, alienated in its flesh and spirit and incapable of breaking its bonds.

Let us now listen to a song in which the poet speaks of negritude as a living thing, deep, patient and indomitable, the slave's demand for justice, dignity, and humanity.

> my negritude is not a stone, its deafness hurled against
>   the clamor of the day
> my negritude is not a drop of stagnant water on the earth's
>   dead eye
> my negritude is neither tower nor cathedral
> it plunges into the red flesh of the earth
> it plunges into the ardent flesh of the sky
> it perforates opaque dejection with its upright patience.[14]

These quotations are all taken from the *Cahier d'un retour au pays natal* ("Notes on a return to the native land") written by Césaire in 1938–39, in which he experiences four aspects of negritude at the same time: color, race, psychology, and assertion of rights. Today, Césaire defines the term as follows:

the awareness of being black, the simple acknowledgement of a fact which implies the acceptance of it, a taking charge of one's destiny as a black man, of one's history and culture.[15]

Noting the different functions of the word "negritude" as used by these two authors, we can begin to isolate its meaning and content: negritude has been defined rather precisely by Sartre in Heideggerian terms, as "the black man's being-in-the-world." Sartre explains that it refers to a "definite manner of living our relation to the world surrounding us . . . which includes a certain understanding of the universe, . . . a tension of the soul, a choice of oneself and others, a way of going beyond the rough facts of experience, briefly a *scheme.*"[16]

This "being-in-the-world of blacks" involves a *constant* that Delafosse calls "black soul,"[17] which is less a question of race than of civilization and which has less to do with skin color than with the

13. Ibid., pp. 88–89.
14. Ibid., p. 73.
15. Interview with A. Césaire, June 1959.
16. J. P. Sartre, "Orphée noir," preface to L. S. Senghor's *Anthologie*, p. xxix.
17. As Jacques Taravant, one of Senghor's students, has so rightly remarked in an unpublished memoir presented in 1948 at the Ecole Nationale de la France d'Outremer.

cultural climate in which African blacks have bathed for many centuries. It is this "climate" that Senghor calls the "spirit" of African civilization or the "ensemble of the black world's values."

Just as whites are indelibly marked in their way of thinking, feeling, or expressing themselves by Western European civilization, whose key values are Reason (for the mind), Technique (for work), Christianity (for religion), Nature (for art), and Individualism (in the social life), black peoples are formed by their culture, of which we already know the principal traits: Solidarity, born of the cohesion of the primitive clan; Rhythm and Symbolism in artistic and religious manifestations; Participation in the cosmic forces, "special reasoning processes,"[18] which, although neither prelogical nor alogical,[19] do not necessarily follow the Western mind or its syllogisms.[20]

Despite the tribulations of the race since the fifteenth century, despite slavery and colonization, cross-breeding and assimilation, these characteristics remain in most individuals. Whatever their social status and the overlay of Western influence, as long as they have remained in a sufficiently large group, they retain more or less intact the traits of specifically Negro African psychology, which gives their culture an easily recognizable flavor: in music, the special rhythm of jazz, for example; in poetry, a style which transforms any foreign language it uses according to its own particular cadence and sensibility; in the organization of social life, "palaver," for example, as in Sekou Touré's Africanized Marxism, where the least decree is discussed and weighed at length by the chiefs of even the smallest villages.

It was because they wanted to escape from these particular characteristics, intent that their negritude not show, that the West Indian writers we spoke of earlier[21] ended up producing impersonal works. Their very failure proves to what extent the Negro temperament still dominates individuals anxious to become Westernized, to the point that the effort of suppressing it destroys all capacity to create.

But these characteristics of Negro culture must not be confused with the imaginary "black essence" mentioned by Sartre.[22] Race has nothing to do with this aspect of negritude. The black man is not from an "essence" different from ours. Brought up in a completely white milieu, isolated from his traditions, he will think, act, and create like a white man. The case of René Maran is typical. Having lived all his youth in France, in a boarding school, far from his parents and his

18. Maurice Delafosse, L'âme nègre (Paris: Payot, 1922), p. 8.
19. On this point, Lévy-Bruhl contradicted himself. See page 100, above.
20. See Meinrad Hebga's article in Aspects de la culture noire (Paris: Fayard, 1958).
21. See chap. 2.
22. J. P. Sartre, "Orphée noir," p. xv.

family, René Maran lost his Negro characteristics and acquired a French style, without effort, without self-alienation. His works are authentic and personal, and at the same time very French. They do not belong to Negro literature, although they influenced it. It is easy to place René Maran in the French tradition of Flaubert and Suarez, and in spite of his sympathy for his racial brothers, he regretfully confessed he was too Westernized fully to understand them.[23] On the other hand, David Diop, born in Bordeaux and raised in France, but in a family circle greatly attached to its ancient traditions, lost nothing of his negritude.

The insistence on their own cultural characteristics in authors writing in a foreign language is not special to Negroes. Rabindranath Tagore's poems in English preserve all the elegance and wisdom of India, and Khalil Gibran's *The Prophet* is full of oriental mysticism. So much so that these works, although they may have been written in French or English, belong by their spirit and style to their national literatures and not to ours.

Understood in this sense, "black soul" belongs to all time and has not been "surpassed," as maintained by Sartre[24] and others whom he influenced. No more than Slavic soul, Arab soul, or French *esprit* have been surpassed. On the contrary, one must hope that their originality will continue to bloom among the rich diversity of human cultures, "for the same reason that a variety of instruments are needed in a symphony, and a variety of colors for the harmony of a painting."[25]

It is in this sense that the efforts of Alioune Diop and his group must be understood and, by extension, those of the two recent congresses of black writers and artists who were fully aware of *negritude's irreductibility*.

Incapable of assimilating us with the English, French, Belgian or Portuguese —of eliminating certain original dimensions of our genius—for the benefit of some hypertrophied Western vocation, we will endeavor to give this genius a means of expression adapted to its twentieth-century vocation.[26]

We believe that, rather than fall in line with your systems, we may bring you something substantially new . . .; we may enrich you.[27]

"The being-in-the-world of blacks" therefore possesses one constant: the *black soul* we have just outlined. Brutal contact with the West

23. Interview with René Maran, March 1959. See also chap. 6, below.

24. J. P. Sartre, "Orphée noir," p. xliii.

25. Théodore Monod, quoted by Robert Delavignette in his preface to *Karim, roman sénégalais,* by Ousmane Socé (Paris: Nouvelles Editions Latines, 1948).

26. A. Diop, opening speech of the second congress. Published in the special issue of *Présence Africaine,* nos. 24–25 (February–May 1959), p. 41.

27. A. Diop, conference at the Centre International, Brussels, 4 March 1960.

since the fifteenth century, however, modified original negritude, adding to it the idea of race: "It is the white man who created the Negro."[28] A minimum of a 150 million men torn from Africa in the space of four centuries, slavery abolished hardly more than a hundred years ago, lynchings and segregation, poverty, prejudice of all kinds—we find many excuses for these facts: Christianity, hygiene, technology, education, economic development. Negroes have other memories of the experience: "Black peoples have endured a number of historical avatars that, under the specific form of total colonization—involving slavery, deportation, and racism—were imposed upon these peoples and on them alone, in the course of known historical time."[29]

A "community of common origins and suffering"[30] since that time has left its mark on negritude. The mortgage was so heavy that, until recent decades, black peoples were incapable of finding within themselves sufficient energy to shake it off. With the exception of Haiti, where in 1804 "negritude first stood upon its feet," slave rebellions were always repressed and runaway slaves savagely mutilated.[31] After slavery, "law and order" was maintained in Africa by policemen and guns, in the West Indies by hunger, which kept the peasants in the cane fields, and by alienation of the élite. Negroes learned fatalism and resignation. It was the era of the "good Negro and his kind master":

Misery had wounded him back and front, and they had stuffed his poor head with the notion a fatality held him by the neck in a grip he could not wrench off; that he had no power over his own destiny; that an evil Lord for all eternity had written laws of interdiction on his pelvic nature; and that he must be a good nigger, honestly believing in his unworthiness without any perverse curiosity ever to verify the prophetic hieroglyphics.

He was a very good nigger.[32]

Now negritude is taking on characteristics of the veritable "Passion" that appears in American Negro spirituals. The black man's hope found refuge in death as a deliverance:

> Un jour prochain je poserai à terre
> Le lourd fardeau qui pèse à mes épaules
> Ah! un de ces matins en pleine lumière
> J'ouvrirai mes ailes et je fendrai les airs
> Un jour prochain

28. Frantz Fanon, *L'an V de la révolution algérienne* (Paris: Editions Maspero, 1959); translated as *A Dying Colonialism* (New York: Grove, 1967).

29. "Résolutions concernant la littérature," at the second congress, in *Présence Africaine*, nos. 24–25 (February-May 1959), p. 389.

30. Ibid.

31. See chap. 17, note 19, below.

32. A. Césaire, *Cahier d'un retour*, p. 88.

Un jour prochain
Je poserai à terre
Le lourd fardeau qui pèse à mes épaules.[33]

[One of these days I'm gonna lay ma burden down
This load that weighs so heavy on my shoulders
Oh! one of these mornin's, one bright day
I'll spread ma wings and fly away
One of these days
One of these days
I'm gonna lay ma burden down.]

But this time is soon past: "The old negritude is gradually dying."[34]

We will no longer sing the sad, despairing spirituals,
Another song will spring forth from our throats.[35]

Today the black man holds up his head. We need not enumerate the reasons here: the example of other colonized peoples such as India and the Arab countries, the influence of communism, the increasing number of black intellectuals, and the impotence of the Western master to maintain order in his own territories. All these have had their effect. The black man now refuses to accept a fate imposed on him by whites, refuses servitude, rejects the prejudices from which his race is made to suffer—it is both a moral and a political revolt. He no longer wishes to "assimilate himself, lose himself in the Other." Different from the white man, he wishes to play his own role and take pride in it. He demands his rights and responsibilities as "a man-like-any-other,"[36] and finally he proclaims himself a *Negro*.

If he is oppressed for his race and because of it, he must first become aware of his race. Those who have vainly attempted for centuries because he was a Negro to reduce him to the animal level must be compelled to recognize him as a man. There is no escape from this, no possibility of cheating, no way of "crossing the line": A Jew, white among whites, may deny that he is Jewish and declare himself a man among other men. A Negro cannot deny that he is a Negro, nor claim to be part of this abstract, colorless humanity: He is black. He is thus forced to be authentic. Insulted, enslaved, he draws himself up, picks up the word "nigger" that has been thrown at him like a stone, and proudly asserts himself as a black man facing the white man.[37]

33. Negro songs translated by J. Cassadesus in the review *Minutes* (Paris), February 1931. [Translator's note: Although the themes are familiar, our English version is a retranslation and not the original text, which is unknown.]

34. A. Césaire, *Cahier d'un retour*, p. 88.

35. Jacques Roumain, *Bois d'ébène* (Port-au-Prince: H. Deschamps, 1945), p. 13.

36. *Un homme pareil aux autres*, title of a novel by René Maran (Paris: Editions Arc-en-Ciel, 1947).

37. J. P. Sartre, "Orphée noir," pp. xiii–xiv.

The black now demands everything, both for his race and his civilization. He demands to be recognized and imposes this recognition by appropriating our techniques and cultures. He demands not only equal rights in the world, but also the right to enrich it.

Western contribution to the formation of our personality remains precious. Yet we demand the right to enrich it and the right on our turn *to give*. Not only *to receive.* . . . It is important for everyone to participate in the creative work of humanity. The African presence will fit in usefully among the other "presences," to the extent that Africa's personality will have marked the development of sciences and art with the original seal of our concerns, our circumstances, and our genius.[38]

For contemporary blacks there is no question of returning to the "negritude of their origins"; they have different problems to solve than those that faced the Askias of the Songhai! Yet they find their strength in the sufferings of the recent past and in the will to regain and develop anew the cultures which had been thwarted by colonization. They rely upon their history, sum total of their experience. Included here is the constant factor of the black soul, a result of ancestral African cultures. Alioune Diop sums this up clearly in a formula indicating the two poles of negritude today: "Negritude . . . is nothing but the Negro genius combined with the desire to reveal the dignity of this genius."[39]

To sum up: "The-being-in-the-world of blacks" now comprises the constant element of "Negro genius"—namely a characteristic psychology, the result of an original civilization—to which are added the scars of the Passion of the race, which will long remain impressed upon the collective memory:

> Each of my todays has eyes
> that look upon my yesterdays
> with rancor and with shame[40]

> my race covered with stains
> my race ripe grapes for drunken feet
> queen of spittle and of leprosy[41]

> but all the tears across three continents
> all the black sweat that fertilized the
> cane and cotton fields.[42]

38. Alioune Diop, *Le sens de ce congres* (see note 26 above), p. 44.
39. Ibid., p. 41.
40. Léon Damas, "La complainte du nègre," in *Pigments.*
41. A. Césaire, *Cahier d'un retour*, p. 80.
42. L. S. Senghor, "Que m'accompagnent kôras et balafongs," in *Chants d'ombre*, p. 50.

This "being-in-the-world of blacks" also includes—particularly for twentieth-century blacks—a proud assertion of race, revolt against Western racism and imperialism, and the demand for total freedom. Once he is freed, the black man's aggressiveness will doubtless disappear. It should leave room for a new relation between blacks and the rest of the world, already anticipated and desired by them, room for a negritude which, "for the universal hunger and the universal thirst," will at last produce "the succulence of fruit."[43]

We believe, however, that the negritude to come will retain two elements, which will be added to the two constants of Negro genius and past oppression: the black man's reconquered pride and his awareness of the historic values of his race. "Negritude has been passed from the immediate state to the meditative state."[44] This awareness of self is also a definitive conquest.

In the negritude to come, blacks will express themselves freely and in their own forms. Modified by modern life, these forms will no longer be those of ancient times, but will nonetheless be different from European ones because they will be rooted once more in African culture and history, in the black man's own "epic poetry," as Sartre so beautifully expressed it. One must not forget that the psychology of a people also depends on its history, which leaves a special mark on the works of its men. In this "royal era of negritude"[45] One will recognize African art by its new and different style, just as in American or Slavic novels one perceives a soul unlike that of Western Europeans.

We must now explain the misunderstanding about negritude that has existed since Sartre's famous study "Orphée noir."

Negritude appears to be the upbeat of a dialectical progression; the theoretical and practical assertion of white supremacy is the thesis; the position of negritude, as an antithetic value, is the moment of negativity. But this negative moment is not sufficient in itself, and the blacks who make use of it are aware of this. They know its aim is to prepare a synthesis or realization of the human in a society without races. Thus negritude exists in order to be destroyed. It is a transition, not a result, a means and not a final ending.[46]

Frantz Fanon explained the effect this text had on him:

When I read that page, I felt that I had been robbed of my last chance. I said to my friends: "The younger generation of black poets has just suffered a blow

43. A. Césaire, *Cahier d'un retour*, p. 77.
44. J. P. Sartre, "Orphée noir," p. xv.
45. P. Joachim, "L'heure nègre," in *Présence Africaine*, no. 16 (October–November 1949), p. 189.
46. J. P. Sartre, "Orphée noir," p. xli.

that can never be forgiven." We had sought help from a friend of colored peoples, and that friend had found no better response than to point out the relativity of what they were doing. . . . Jean-Paul Sartre, in this work, has destroyed black zeal.[47]

Fanon was the victim of his own too subtle reasoning, as were many others. Sartre spoke as a philosopher and employed the word "negativity" in its proper sense, the Hegelian one, which is not at all pejorative. Hegel regarded Mind too as negativity, as well as Liberty and Conscience—all, in other words, that is opposed to the immediate. Sartre explicitly calls on Hegelian dialectics here, the process in which the first moment, of "thesis," necessarily results in its opposite, "antithesis." The resulting contest creates a third moment, "synthesis,"[48] which retains all the perfections of the first two terms and cancels out their imperfections. Hegel called this superior moment *Aufhebung*, from the verb *aufheben*, which means, at one and the same time, to excel, cancel, and retain. The "negative moment" of this process is not therefore a sterile opposition that is content to deny the thesis without adding anything positive to it and would be destined to disappear after the contest. On the contrary, this "negative moment" brings forth new qualities not contained in the first expression, which are imposed upon "thesis" and later conserved in the "synthesis." According to Hegel, to deny the negation does not mean to reject it—as a court dismisses a plaintiff—but rather to terminate a quarrel by recognizing the respective rights of both parties and thus reconciling them.

In "Orphée noir," however, an essay intended for the general public, the word "negativity" was bound to be misunderstood. This technical term of modern philosophy is not even mentioned in the Larousse dictionary of the period. For anyone unfamiliar with the Hegelian usage, it was inevitable to mistakenly associate it with the words negative, negatory, negation, etc., namely the "act of denying" a positive affirmation. Sartre himself unintentionally encouraged the misunderstanding. Having called the thesis an "assertion of white supremacy," he referred to the antithesis negritude only in the following terms: "negativity," "upbeat," "not sufficient by itself," and "destined to destroy itself." All this is true enough when one has Hegelian synthesis in mind and realizes that the moment of negativity is also a positive contribution which will remain! But Sartre, with a certain

47. Frantz Fanon, *Peau noire, masques blancs* (Paris: Seuil, 1952), pp. 135–36; translated as *Black Skin, White Masks* (New York: Grove, 1967), pp. 133, 135.

48. In Hegelian dialectics, "thesis-antithesis-synthesis" are usually called "the three moments." In reality, however, Hegel called them "affirmation-negation-negation of the negation."

sentimentality, accentuated the impression of negritude's transience, almost of its futility:

One more step, and negritude will completely disappear[!]: what was once the mysterious ancestral seething of black blood has been transformed into a geographical accident by the inconsistent [!] product of universal determinism, by the Negroes themselves.[49]

At the end of so rich a literary analysis, how could Sartre so limit his conception of negritude? He seemed to consider it only from an angle of opposition to the white man, thus mistaking a part for the whole concept, which he himself had first given a far broader meaning. "The being-in-the-world of blacks," according to Sartre, covered all the ways in which the black experienced his condition in the world: through rhythm, sexual pantheism, a cosmic sense, "the indissoluble unity of suffering, the erotic and joy,"[50] etc. From a general viewpoint, this situation did not necessarily imply the presence of whites. This is why, with Senghor, we can speak of a "negritude of the sources," which existed before the arrival of Europeans. It is true that blacks *became aware* of their "being-in-the-world" upon contact with whites. The black man recognized his negritude but did not *create* it in response to whiteness. Having recognized his own qualities the black man sets himself before the Other: Thesis and antithesis are thus face to face, each asserting itself. "Synthesis," we should again point out, must destroy this opposition while retaining the values of each. This had to be emphasized.

Sartre pursued his dialectical outline still further. At the moment of synthesis, black and white will in fact have disappeared, leaving only fellow creatures, men like one another, enriched by one another. Can we follow him to this point?

"The Negro," declared Sartre, "desires the abolition of all ethnic privileges wherever they come from. He asserts his solidarity with all the oppressed, no matter what their color. At once, the subjective [!], existentialist, ethnic idea of negritude 'passes over,' as Hegel would say, to the objective, positive, exact idea of a *proletariat.*"[51] Sartre adds immediately that "the idea of race does not blend with the idea of class: The former is concrete and specific, whereas the latter is universal and abstract."[52] In spite of this, just as the proletariat "seeks a society without classes,"[53] the black man "aims to prepare the synthesis or

49. J. P. Sartre, "Orphée noir," p. xli.
50. Ibid., p. xxxv.
51. Ibid., p. xl.
52. Ibid., p. xli.
53. Ibid., p. xliii.

realization of being human in a society without race."[54]

Sartre, it seems to us, is too anxious to assimilate the conflict of races with the class struggle, to consider Negroes and the working class as one and the same.[55] If proletarians are fighting for the *abolition* of the very idea of class, the Negro is fighting for the recognition of his race. His aim, in fact, is not a society without races, but a society without "ethnic privilege," namely without *racism*.

If we accept this (optimistic) view of history, that one day all men will be so closely united that all precedence among them will cease to exist, and that all will have equal rights and responsibilities, will that mean the disappearance of all cultural differences? Although both are communist and theoretically have equal rights, are the Chinese similar to the Russians? Will a society without "racism" necessarily have only one culture? Climate, geography, plant and animal environment, history, heredity, and many other factors have an influence not only on individual physical characteristics but also on psychic characteristics. These psychic elements in their turn determine sensibilities creative of a variety of cultures.[56]

Sartre himself, having spoken so well of destruction, of renouncement, of going beyond to a "future universalism which will be negritude's twilight,"[57] wonders nevertheless: "And if, some day, the sacrifice is made, what will happen? . . . Will the great black river, after all, color the ocean into which it flows?" He leaves the question

54. Ibid., p. xli.

55. In the course of our interview with J. P. Sartre in April 1960, the same tendency again clearly appeared.

56. We do not share the opinion of Mme Eliane Boucquey (thesis for the Université Libre de Bruxelles in 1959), who thinks that tomorrow's Negro will feel that his negritude is as "unimportant, for example, as citizenship to a Belgian in relation to a Frenchman, a Swiss or an Englishman" (p. 32). First of all, the comparison is not very good; she should have compared the Belgian to a Chinese, for example, or an Indian, because, if there is no obvious incompatibility between them, there are, however, many very tangible differences. Furthermore, even between Europeans there are persistent cultural and psychological differences despite centuries of close contact. In Belgium, for example, any man on the street will tell you that the French are brilliant conversationalists, accomplishing little, that hygiene is not their strong point, and that they are developing a complex of grandiosity. On the other hand, our intellectuals will praise the subtlety, the brilliance and the wide range of French minds. All this tends to prove that Belgians are different and have other qualities and faults, despite a common language and a similar culture. What can be said, therefore, of the "exotism" felt by a Belgian in contact with a Spaniard or a Sicilian?

Negritude is not therefore just "a great dream" whose "passing everyone will accept, with regret or relief" (p. 13). It is a combination of very tangible and living cultural characteristics that differentiate the blacks from Western peoples, just as Asiatics are differentiated from Americans.

57. J. P. Sartre, "Orphée noir," p. xlii.

without reply: "It does not matter. . . ."[58]

What remains, according to Frantz Fanon, is to "plead the unpredictable." Will technology, victor over other determining factors, level all cultures, or will it allow them to survive in harmonious intersubjectivity? Before reaching this question, Negro African culture has plenty of time to develop its possibilities. Unless, of course, a new war speedily suppresses all classes and races by destroying all of society. That also belongs to the unpredictable!

58. Ibid., p. xliv.

III   THE NEGRITUDE POETS

10 / The Poetry of Negritude

"Nothing is said without form!" Today's negritude was not fully revealed and understood in France until it was expressed in striking literary works.

The first person to have the honor of publication was Léon Damas. As early as 1934, his poems appeared in the magazine *Esprit. Pigments*, his book of poems, came out in 1937.[1] Two years later, the periodical *Volontés* ran much of Aimé Césaire's famous *Cahier d'un retour au pays natal*,[2] which was to become negritude's emblem.[3] Finally, in 1945 and 1948 Léopold Senghor published two collections of poems he had written between 1936 and 1945, *Chants d'ombre* and *Hosties noires*.[4]

These works illuminate negritude better than any theoretical study. With these first fruits of an authentic art, the three poets founded a cultural movement that has not ceased to grow, and of which they have become the classics. In an original language they defined the "being-in-the-world" of their entire race, as well as their personal manner of living this negritude.

We say "personal manner," for in Césaire's experience negritude was primarily "the acknowledgment of a fact, revolt, and the acceptance of responsibility for the destiny of his race"[5] in the face of compatriots who refused to assume that responsibility. For Senghor,

1. Paris: Guy Lévi Mano.
2. Paris, 1939; bilingual edition in Cuba, 1943; reprinted in 1947 by Bordas, and in 1956 by the Editions de Présence Africaine.
3. A publisher had recently refused to publish this work, not deeming it sufficiently commercial.
4. *Chants d'ombre* (Paris: Seuil, 1945); *Hosties noires* (Paris: Seuil, 1948). Reprinted in 1956 in one volume, by the same publisher.
5. Interview with Césaire, June 1959.

above all it retrieved "black Africa's cultural patrimony, that is to say, the spirit of its civilization."[6] For Damas, it consisted essentially of rejecting an assimilation that negated his spontaneity, and "defending his condition as a Negro and a Guianese."[7]

Far from being incompatible, these three meanings completed and reinforced each other, just as the three friends were helping each other in a common humanistic action, whose aim was to restore the worth of the name, the person, and the values of the Negro. In the course of analyzing these three poetic works, we shall see that nostalgia for Africa and the evocation of its cultures are far from absent in Césaire and Damas, while Senghor too has moments of revolt and discouragement. From the very beginning, negritude thus formed a whole, of which each poet was more or less deeply affected by one aspect or another, according to his temperament, social condition, or country of origin.

To understand this better, let us take a brief look at the past of these poets before tackling their poems.

In the opinion of those who know him well, Senghor is a sober, conscientious, and methodical man, naturally inclined to conciliation. Born into a wealthy family of business people, he never knew the material want his companions suffered, and his generosity was proverbial in the black student world. Senegal, moreover, had nurtured him on a still living culture, and, of all his companions, Senghor felt the least deprived of his original personality.

Césaire recognizes in himself a temperament completely different from that of Senghor. Aimé Patri goes as far as to say they are like day and night. "Night's maternal gentleness naturally triumphs in Senghor, who loves the echo in his poems of the muted tom-tom, whereas Césaire grows enthusiastic in the fierce heat of a martial sun."[8] Naturally impatient and uncompromising, Césaire had a difficult childhood, sharing the hard-earned family bread with six brothers and sisters. Numerous traces of this childhood are found in the *Cahier*. Even as a scholarship student in Paris, Césaire often lived on short rations. Having suffered under the colonial regime, it was normal for him to react against it with greater violence and to feel more deeply the unhappiness of his people. If hope and humanism tip the balance in the *Cahier*, it is at least in part because Césaire by this time—married and a father —had a stable and happy personal life.

As for Léon Damas, whose paternal uncle was white and a writer, he too had grown up under particular circumstances. Damas was born in

6. Interview with Senghor, June 1959.
7. Interview with Damas, June 1959.
8. Aimé Patri in the *Anthologie . . .* by Senghor, p. 147.

Cayenne of a bourgeois family. His father was a composer of classical music and his mother had her heart set on teaching her son "good white manners." *Pigments* reveals over and over how heavily this upbringing weighed upon the child. In addition, he suffered from asthma, which kept him bedridden until he was six, and he began to talk only a year later. As a result of his delicate health as a child, Damas remained whimsical and touchy, with a sharpened sensitivity that made him very vulnerable to the teasings and mockery of his Parisian companions. "Oh, you're from Guiana! Was your father a convict?"* How many times did he hear such stupid questions.[9] He folded himself into his loneliness, and very soon a reaction took place which led him to defend his color and, after two years of studying law and oriental languages, to take up the study of ethnology in the hope of reestablishing his original roots. With this aim, he sought out Africans of every possible milieu in Paris. His parents, from their point of view deciding that their son was not serious about his studies, cut off his allowance. To make a living, Damas was reduced to working at Les Halles, then as a laborer in a nickel-plating factory, as a dishwasher, as a paper boy. He now knew real poverty, the poverty of Paris with its cold and loneliness, until a petition made on his behalf by black students won him a scholarship. All these factors gave his negritude special nuances that time and again appear in his writings.

Finally, because Césaire and Damas were West Indians,[10] they knew more than Senghor the frustration of a distant lost Africa, the sufferings of exile, the despair of never having seen their countrymen free of the profound alienation caused by their ancient slavery. As the search for their roots became more difficult, so their bitterness against Europe became greater, and their words of forgiveness fewer.

If today's negritude has become, not a "complex that defies analysis,"[11] but at least a "source of misunderstanding,"[12] it was not so at the beginning. For its official founders it was an obvious, necessary idea, even though they each stressed different aspects of it.

In analyzing the works, we have had to give up the traditional division of substance and form—a separation always impoverishing when it comes to poetry, "the alchemy of language," where ideas and feelings are inseparable from the words which reveal them. But if this distinction can be avoided in analyzing a poem, it seems impossible when it concerns a man's entire work. We do not wish to neglect either

*Translator's note: Though today French Guiana boasts a Space Research Center, historically it is best known as a French penal colony.

9. Interview with Damas, June 1959.
10. See chap. 20, note 11, below.
11. J. P. Sartre, "Orphée noir," p. xliii.
12. Interview with J. Rabemananjara, June 1959.

of the two aspects, nor to flounder in confusion. What makes the poets we are going to present interesting is that they are truly *creators*. Their words and pictures, syntax and rhythm, constantly reinforce or nuance themes that are not present in French literature. And we are fascinated by their ideas as much as by their way of bending the French language to a sensibility foreign to it. These writers use other symbols, another rhythm, and have other reactions than French authors do; at each moment we are liable to misunderstand their vision of things, and particularly to be offended by their special conception of the West.

To approach the first poetic works of these black writers of the new school, one must remain alert and beware of one's instinctive reflexes. Sartre's advice is pertinent.

Strong in our thousand years of literature, our Villons, our Racines, our Rimbauds, what I particularly fear is that we will look down upon our black friends' poems and stories with the charmed indulgence shown by parents for their offspring's birthday compliments. Let us guard against seeing in these products of the mind an homage to French culture. It is something quite different. Culture is an instrument; we must not believe that they have chosen ours. Had the English occupied Senegal rather than the French, the Senegalese would have adopted English. The truth is that the blacks are trying to get themselves together through a cultural world that was thrust upon them and which is foreign to them. They must reshape this ready-made clothing. Everything in it irks them and feels awkward, even the syntax, and yet they have learned to make use of this tool with all its deficiencies.[13]

13. J. P. Sartre, "Présence noire," in the first issue of *Présence Africaine*, November–December 1947, p. 29.

11 / Léon Damas: *Pigments*

Pigments, the first collection of poems in French to carry the mark of the new negritude, earned the author considerable prestige among the black students in Paris, a prestige reinforced by the volume's appearance in a deluxe edition with a preface by the French surrealist poet Robert Desnos.[1] Apart from the ideas it contained, the originality of *Pigments* lay in the fact that for the first time a Caribbean poet was calling attention to the color of his skin. The title referred to it directly, and Desnos dwelt on the fact before going on to point out the social significance of Damas's poems:

> His name is Damas. He is a Negro. . . . Damas insists on his Negro-ness and his condition as a Negro. This is what will raise the eyebrows of a certain number of civilizers who deem it right that in exchange for their freedom, their land, their customs and their well-being, persons of color ought to be honored by the name of "black." Damas refuses this title and takes back his own. What this consists of will be revealed to you in the poems that follow. . . .
>
> They do honor, these poems, to the whole immense native proletariat of our colonies. They signify that the time has come for us to seek the conquest of these lands and of these peoples. Are they not exploited just as ours are, these lands? And are these people not exploited? . . . Notice where the pen and common sense are leading us. These poems are therefore also a song of friendship offered in the name of his entire race by my friend Damas the Negro, to all his white brothers. A gift from the field to the factory, from the plantation to the farm, from tropical workshop to European foundry.

1. Léon Damas, *Pigments* (Paris: Guy Lévi Mano, 1937). Preface by Robert Desnos. [Translator's note: French texts of the poems cited in this chapter, however, conform to those of the *édition définitive* of *Pigments,* published in Paris by Présence Africaine in 1962; reprinted with *Névralgies* in 1972. Many of the translations appeared in *Black World,* January 1972.]

Damas begins by rejecting everything Europe had made him and his ancestors swallow by force. The poems reflect a veritable "indigestion," ranging from nausea to regurgitation, from despair to insults and threats.

A nausea that comes at first for no apparent reason:

> Un goût de sang me vient
> un goût de sang me monte
> m'irrite le nez
> la gorge
> les yeux[2]

> Il est des nuits sans nom
> il est des nuits sans lune
> où jusqu'à l'asphyxie
> moite
> me prend
> l'âcre odeur de sang
> jaillissant
> de toute trompette bouchée
> ....
> où le dégout s'ancre en moi
> aussi profondément qu'un beau poignard malais.[3]

> [A taste of blood comes
> a taste of blood rises
> irritates my nose
> eyes
> throat

> There are nights with no name
> there are nights with no moon
> when a clammy
> suffocation
> nearly overwhelms me
> the acrid smell of blood
> spewing
> from every muted trumpet
> ....
> when the sickness sticks within me
> like an oriental dagger.]

The nausea is particularly strong in those nightclubs and cabarets where blacks entertain whites with their music and dancing, through which, beyond the exotic, Damas detects all the lamentations and sobs that those muted trumpets contain:

2. "Obsession."
3. "Il est des nuits" ("There are nights").

Trève de blues
de martèlements de piano
de trompette bouchée
de folie claquant des pieds
à la satisfaction du rythme

Trève de séances à tant le swing
autour de rings
qu'énervent
les cris de fauves[4]

[Enough of blues
pianos banging
muted trumpet
mad feet tapping
to satisfy the rhythm

Enough of those sessions
of swing
around rings
aggravated by
the cry
of wild things]

The Negro is too often delivered as a spectacle, like a puppet or a clown. And even Damas, the West Indian, who has witnessed the abasement of his race, isn't he too playing the white man's game? He becomes aware of his inauthenticity:

Trève de lâchage
de lêchage
de lèche
et
d'une attitude
d'hyperassimilés[5]

[Enough letting-go-of
licking-up-to
taking-the-leavings
and
enough
of that attitude
of super-assimilation]

The nausea then takes shape, and the poet sees himself lucidly, without any concession: the elegant Léon Damas, strutting about to

4. "Trève" ("Temporary relief").
5. Ibid.

impress his friends with the refinement of his clothes; Léon Damas parading in drawing rooms, suddenly catching sight of himself.

> J'ai l'impression d'être ridicule
> dans leurs souliers
> dans leur smoking
> dans leur plastron
> dans leur faux-col
> dans leur monocle
> dans leur melon
> ....
>
> J'ai l'impression d'être ridicule
> dans leurs salons
> dans leurs manières
> dans leurs courbettes
> dans leurs multiple besoin de singeries[6]
>
> [I feel ridiculous
> in their shoes
> their dinner jackets
> their starched shirts
> and detachable collars
> their monocles and
> their bowler hats
> ....
> I feel ridiculous
> in their drawing rooms
> in their manners
> their bowings and scrapings
> in their manifold need of monkeyshines]

He understands that these customs and mores belong to an ethical system he rejects:

> J'ai l'impression d'être ridicule
> parmi eux complice
> parmi eux souteneur
> parmi eux égorgeur
> les mains effroyablement rouges
> du sang de leur ci-vi-li-sa-tion[7]
>
> [I feel ridiculous
> among them
> like an accomplice
> among them
> like a pimp

6. "Solde" ("Sellout").
7. Ibid.

> like a murderer among them
> my hands hideously red
> with the blood of their
> ci-vi-li-za-tion]

More than his friends Césaire (closer to ordinary people) or Senghor (raised in Africa), Léon Damas was an "assimilated Negro." His spontaneity had been suppressed since his earliest childhood. He used to envy his country cousins who spoke Creole and could throw themselves into the noisiest games without being reprimanded,[8] while he was patiently inculcated with "good manners," religion, and the violin, together with all the bourgeois prejudices of his mulatto milieu. One must read again the brightly original poem "Hoquet" ("Hiccups"), which so well earns Damas the adjective "unsophisticated" that Senghor used to describe him:[9]

> J'ai beau avaler sept gorgées d'eau
> trois à quatre fois par vingt-quatre heures
> me revient mon enfance
> dans un hoquet secouant
> mon instinct
> ....
>
> Ma mère voulant d'un fils très bonnes manières à table
> ....
>
> une fourchette n'est pas un cure-dents
> défense de se moucher
> au su
> au vu de tout le monde
> et puis tenez-vous droit
> un nez bien élevé
> ne balaye pas l'assiette
>
> Et puis et puis
> et puis au nom du Père
>   du Fils
>   du Saint Esprit
> à la fin de chaque repas
> ....
>
> Ma mère voulant d'un fils mémorandum
>   Si votre leçon d'histoire n'est pas sue
>   vous n'irez pas à la messe
>   dimanche
>   avec vos effets du dimanche

8. See Léon Damas, *Black-Label* (Paris: Gallimard, 1956), p. 64.
9. L. S. Senghor, *Anthologie de la nouvelle poésie nègre et malgache*, p. 5.

Cet enfant sera la honte de notre nom
....

 Taisez-vous
 Vous ai-je ou non dit qu'il vous fallait parler français
 le français de France
 le français du français
 le français français

Désastre
parlez-moi du désastre
parlez-m'en

Ma mère voulant d'un fils
fils de sa mère
 Vous n'avez pas salué voisine
 encore vos chaussures de sales
 et que je vous y reprenne dans la rue
 sur l'herbe ou sur la Savane
 à l'ombre du Monument aux Morts
 à jouer
 à vous ébattre avec Untel
 avec Untel qui n'a pas reçu le baptême

Désastre
parlez-moi du désastre
parlez-m'en
....

Il m'est revenu que vous n'étiez encore pas
à votre leçon de vi-o-lon
Un banjo
vous dîtes un banjo
comment dîtes-vous
un banjo vous dites bien un banjo
Non monsieur
vous saurez qu'on ne souffre chez nous
ni *ban*
ni *jo*
ni *gui*
ni *tare*
les *mulâtres* ne font pas ça
laissez donc ça aux *nègres*

[I gulp down seven drinks of water
several times a day
and all in vain
instinctively
like the criminal to the crime
my childhood returns

in a rousing fit of hiccups
....

My mother wanted a son with good manners at the table:
....

A fork is not a tooth-pick
Don't blow your nose
in front of the whole world
and sit up straight
a well-bred nose
doesn't sweep the plate

And then
and then
there was in the name of the Father
   and the Son
   and the Holy Ghost
at the end of every meal
....

My mother wanted her son to have the very best marks:
   If you don't know your history
   You won't go to mass
   tomorrow
   in your Sunday suit

This child will bring disgrace upon our family name
This child will be our . . . in the name of God
   Be quiet
   Have I or have I not
   told you to speak French
   the French of France
   the French that Frenchmen speak
   French French

Calamity
Disasters
And how!

My mother wanted her son to be a mama's boy:
   You didn't say good evening to our neighbor
   What—dirty shoes again
   And don't let me catch you any more
   playing in the street or on the grass or in the park
   underneath the War Memorial
   playing
   or picking a fight with what's-his-name
   what's-his-name who isn't even baptized

Disaster
talk about disaster

> I'll tell you
> ....
>
> I see you haven't been to your vi-o-lin lesson
>   A banjo
>   Did you say a banjo
>   What do you mean
>   a banjo
>   You really mean
>   a banjo
>   No indeed young man
>   you know there won't be any
>   *ban*—
>   or
>   *jo*
>   or
>   *gui*
>   or
>   *tar* in our house
> They are not for *colored* people
> Leave them to the *black* folks!]

With witty pen, Damas caricatured the absurdities of the education he had received as an "assimilated black." The caustic tone thinly disguises a deep bitterness; his education had "bleached" him with a whitewash of morals, manners, ways of thinking and feeling alien to his true nature. This "assimilation-alienation" of the élite, cause of the century-old surrender of his race, rushes back upon him in a wave of shame:

> De n'avoir jusqu'ici rien fait
> détruit bati
> osé
> à la manière du Juif
> du Jaune
> pour l'évasion organisée en masse
> de l'infériorité[10]
>
> [From having done nothing up to now
> destroyed nothing
> dared nothing, built nothing
> like the Jew
> or the yellow man
> for the organized escape
> from mass inferiority]

Doesn't he know that these whites, who have been held up to him as models, at bottom despise him? He is a "Negro." His fine manners

10. "Réalité."

cannot change this. His fine education may pass muster in the West Indies among the natives, but in France there is no escape: "All negroes are niggers."[11] Frantz Fanon has well described this phenomenon:

The evidence was there, implacable. My blackness was there, dense and indisputable. . . . I was walled in; neither my polished manners, my literary knowledge, nor my understanding of the quantum theory mattered. . . . There was the myth of the Negro. . . . I was repeatedly told about cannibalism, mental backwardness, fetishism, racial defects. . . .[12]

When Damas wore a tuxedo, he was treated like someone "whitewashed," while during the unhappy days when his parents cut off his allowance, he saw whites

   . . . se gausser
de mes hardes de clochard
et se régaler
de voir un nègre les yeux le ventre creux[13]

[. . . mocking, laughing
at my beggar clothes
amused
to see a nigger with
empty eyes and belly]

Here, in Europe, any clear-thinking black knew it was impossible to cross the line; he understood that he had been deprived, "robbed" of his country, his culture, his very personality. Damas laments this loss in his beautiful poem "Limbé":[14]

Rendez-les moi mes poupées noires
que je joue avec elles
les jeux naïfs de mon instinct
....
Redevenu moi-même
nouveau moi-même
de ce que Hier j'étais
hier
      sans complexité
            hier
quand est venue l'heure du déracinement.

11. Letter from Frantz Fanon to M. J. Beclard, quoted in "La poésie noire de langue française et l'évolution de la littérature africaine," unpublished thesis submitted for licentiate's degree at the Institut Universitaire des Territoires d'Outre-mer, Brussels, 1953.

12. Frantz Fanon, *Peau noire, masques blancs,* pp. 120 and 116.

13. "Un clochard m'a demandé dix sous" ("A beggar asked me for a dime").

14. *Limbé* is a Creole word meaning "spleen" or, more colloquially, "blues."

Le sauront-ils jamais cette rancune de mon cœur
à l'œil de ma méfiance ouvert trop tard
ils ont cambriolé l'espace qui était mien
la coutume
les jours
la vie
la chanson
le rythme
l'effort
le sentier
l'eau
la case
la terre enfumée grise
la sagesse
les mots
les palabres
les vieux
la cadence
les mains
la mesure
les mains
les piétinements
le sol

Rendez-les-moi mes poupées noires
mes poupées noires
poupées noires
noires.

[Give me back
my black
dolls so that I can play
the simple games of my instincts
....
I become myself once more
myself again
out of what I used to be
once upon a time
   once without complexity
      once upon a time
when the hour of uprooting came

Will they never know the rancor in my heart
opened to the eye of my distrust too late
they did away with what was mine
ways
days
life

```
song
rhythm
effort
foot path
water
huts
the smoke-grey earth
the wisdom
the words
the palavers
the elders
the cadence
the hands
beating time
the hands
the feet marking time
upon the ground

Give them back
to me
my black
dolls
black
dolls
black black
dolls.]
```

In this evocation of what he has lost, the poet rediscovers the rhythm of Negro tom-toms, expressing a manner of suffering that is non-European, authentic at last. From the same Negro rhythm, Senghor would extrapolate a law of African culture to uncover all its richness:

It is the architecture of the being, the inner dynamic which gives it form, the system of waves which it emits to others, the pure expression of the vital force. Rhythm is the vibrating shock, the force which, through the senses, reaches to the root of our being . . . directing all tangible things toward the light of the spirit.[15]

If Damas still has this rhythm, it is the last thing he has left. The West Indian, infinitely more than the African, is dispossessed, the middle class more so than the working man. Damas knows the tragic past of his race:

```
. . . coups de corde noueux
de corps calcinés
de l'orteil au dos calcinés
de chair morte
```

15. L. S. Senghor, "L'esprit de la civilisation ou les lois de la culture négro-africaine," *Présence Africaine*, nos. 8, 9, 10 (June–November 1956).

> de tisons
> de fer rouge
> de bras brisés
> sous le fouet qui se déchaîne
> sous le fouet qui fait marcher la plantation
> et s'abreuver de sang de mon sang de sang la sucrerie
> et la bouffarde du commandeur crâner au ciel.[16]

> [. . . blows with the knotted cord
> bodies burnt
> charred from head to toe
> dead flesh
> branded
> by the red hot iron
> arms broken
> beneath the lashing whip
> beneath the whip that made plantations move
> and quenched their thirst for blood my blood sweet blood
> and the overseer's bravado as he swaggered it to heaven.]

The slavery of yesterday has given way to the subservience of the "good nigger" who "lays down upon his pallet every night the ten to fifteen hours of his factory day,"[17] waiting for tomorrow, perhaps for new persecutions. Racism was at the threshold of France in 1937, and Damas was not unmindful of the alarming developments in Germany.

> bientot cette idée leur viendra
> de vouloir vous en bouffer du nègre
> à la manière d'Hitler
> bouffant du juif
> sept jours fascistes
> sur
> sept[18]

> [Soon it will come to them
> the idea of ridding you of niggers
> just as Hitler
> does away with Jews
> seven fascist days a week]

When at last he has clearly seen and recognized the oppressors of his race, the poet grits his teeth, hatred replaces nausea:

> La peine qui m'habite
> m'oppresse

16. "La complainte du nègre" ("The black man's lament").
17. "Rappel" ("Reminder").
18. "S.O.S."

La peine qui m'habite
m'étouffe[19]

Ma haine grossit en marge
de leur scélératesse
en marge
des coups de fusil
en marge
des coups de roulis
des négriers
des cargaisons fétides de l'esclavage cruel
....

Ma haine grossit en marge
de la culture
en marge
des théories
en marge des bavardages
dont on a cru devoir me bourrer au berceau
alors que tout en moi aspire à n'être que nègre
autant que mon Afrique qu'ils m'ont cambriolée.[20]

[The pain that inhabits me
presses
The pain that inhabits me
chokes

My hatred swells
at the scope of their villainy
the scope of the fleecing
the pitching
of cruel slaveships
and their fetid cargoes
....

My hatred swells
around the limits of the culture
the limits of the theories
the tales
they thought they ought
to stuff me with
from the cradle onward
while
everything within me
wants only to be black
as negro as the Africa they robbed me of.]

19. "Il est des nuits" ("There are nights").
20. "Blanchi" ("Whitewash").

He utterly rejects this borrowed personality that makes him an accomplice:

> Alors
> je vous mettrai les pieds dans le plat
> ou bien tout simplement
> la main au collet
> de tout ce qui m'emmerde en gros caractères
> colonisation
> civilisation
> assimilation
> et la suite[21]

> [Then
> I'll put your feet in it
> or simply rub your nose in it
> in all that capital letter shit
> Colonization
> Civilization
> Assimilation
> and the rest]

The rejection is purposely vulgar. Damas's reaction is all the more violent because of his perfect upbringing:

> . . . autant que vous qui m'a donné le goût des mignardises
> des politesses
> le ton des entrechats
> le chic des ronds de jambe
> ....
> autant que vous
> sinon plus exercés
> l'odorat chatouilleux
> les mots de circonstances
> le clin d'œil entendu
> ....
> le sens bourgeois des convenances
> qui veut qu'on se découvre au corbillard qui passe[22]

> [. . . as much as you who gave me
> the taste for
> dainty ways
> for courtesy
> an ease at making small talk
> cutting capers

21. "Pour sûr" ("Surely").
22. L. Damas, *Black-Label*, p. 27.

....
as much as you
if not more practiced at it
I have a nose for social nuance
the word for each occasion
the understanding wink
....

the bourgeois sense of decency
that makes one doff the hat as a hearse goes by]

Damas wants to shock the whites and make them say: "What, such a well-bred fellow!" Twenty years after *Pigments,* the same theme returns in *Black-Label:*

malgré les rafles
malgré les flics
malgré les fouilles
....

malgré l'attentat raté sur la Ligne
Paris–Le Havre–New York
bon gré mal gré
....

voilà
qu'il recommence
qu'il recommence à dire
Merde.[23]

[in spite of the round-ups
the cops
the searches
....

in spite of the attempt that failed on the
Paris–Le Havre–New York Line
willy-nilly
....

there he goes
he's at it again
back to saying
Shit.]

In *Pigments,* he ironically entitled a poem "Savoir vivre" ("Good manners") in order to reject the upbringing he had received:

On ne bâille pas chez moi
comme ils bâillent chez eux
avec
la main sur la bouche

23. Ibid., p. 29.

Je veux bâiller sans tralalas
le corps recroquevillé
dans les parfums qui tourmentent la vie
que je me suis faite
de leur museau de chien d'hiver
de leur soleil qui ne pourrait
pas même
tiédir
l'eau de coco qui faisait glouglou
dans mon ventre au réveil

Laissez-moi bâiller la main
là
sur le cœur
à l'obsession de tout ce à quoi
j'ai en un jour un seul
tourné le dos.

[We don't yawn the way they do
behind a hand

I want to yawn without a fuss
my body curled
in fragrances that plague the life
I've made myself of
their wintry dog faces
in their sun that couldn't
even
warm
the coco milk that gurgles
in my belly when I waken

Let me yawn with a hand
here
upon my heart
to the consternation of all
on which in just one day
I turned my back.]

Although Damas was usually satisfied with biting sarcasm, occasionally he was unable to contain his anger:

Si souvent mon sentiment de race m'effraie
autant qu'un chien aboyant la nuit
une mort prochaine
quelconque
je me sens prêt à écumer toujours de rage
contre ce qui m'entoure
contre ce qui m'empêche

à jamais d'être
un homme

Et rien
rien ne saurait autant calmer ma haine
qu'une belle mare
de sang
faite
de ces coutelas tranchants
qui mettent à nu
les mornes à rhum[24]

[If often my feeling of race
strikes the same fear
as the nighttime howling of a dog
at some approaching death
I always feel
about to foam with rage
against what surrounds me
against what prevents me
ever
    from being
          a man

And nothing
nothing would so calm my hate
as a great
pool
of blood
made
by those long sharp knives
that strip the hills of cane
for rum]

And now hatred really spurs him on, draws him upright. Proudly standing, eyes open at last, he proclaims his negritude:

Avec d'autres
des alentours
avec d'autres
quelques rares
j'ai au toit de ma case
jusqu'ici gardé
l'ancestrale foi conique

Et l'arrogance automatique
des masques
des masques de chaux vive

24. "Si souvent" ("If often").

jamais n'est parvenue à rien enlever jamais
d'un passé plus hideux
debout
aux quatre angles de ma vie

Et mon visage brille aux horreurs du passé
et mon rire effroyable est fait pour repousser
   le spectre des levriers
                        traquant le marronnage
et ma voix qui pour eux chante
est douce à ravir
l'âme triste
de leur por-
        no-
           gra-
              phie

Et veille mon cœur
et mon rêve qui se nourrit du bruit de leur
   dé-
      gé-
        né-
          rescence
est plus fort que leurs gourdins d'immondices
brandis[25]

[With others
from the neighborhood
a few rare friends
till now I've kept
the conical ancestral faith
high among the rafters of my hut

And the automatic arrogance
of masks
masks of living chalk
never has been able to remove
anything
ever
of a past
more hideous
here
at the four corners of my life

And my face gleams with the horrors of the past
and my dreadful laughter would repel
   the specter of the hounds
                   pursuing runaways

25. "Shine."

and my voice which sings for them
is sweet enough to soothe
the soul saddened by their
  por-
     no-
       gra-
         phy

And my heart keeps watch
and my dream feeding on the noise of their
  de-
     pra-
       vi-
        ty
is stronger than their clubs besmeared with foulness]

This time Damas rejects the degenerate and pornographic West in the name of his entire race. He denounces the age-old oppression, appropriates the whole past of slavery, maintaining his belief in the "conical ancestral faith" of traditional Africa, and, in final threats, he anticipates a future victory over the cudgels of colonizers whose faces are "masks of living chalk." No longer will the Negro be taken advantage of. Damas's collection of poems ends with the theme of revolt still veiled:

Ils ont si bien su faire
si bien su faire les choses
les choses
qu'un jour nous avons tout
nous avons tout foutu de nous-mêmes
tout foutu de nous-mêmes en l'air[26]

[They did their thing so well
did their thing so well
that one day we let all
all that once was ours
go
we threw it all away]

The idea of revolt returns in many of his poems. Damas had no intention of remaining on a purely personal and literary level, but meant to be part of a tangible historical context. He did not confine himself to recalling his personal experiences and the historic misfortunes of his race, but wished to act in the present and to share with other blacks his rejection of the West. Why should they care about the

---

26. "Ils ont." [Translator's note: Mme Kesteloot perhaps misreads this poem as a threat. See rather such poems of Damas as "Et caetera," "Si souvent," and "Sur une carte postale."]

fate of a civilization that had crushed them and was slowly disintegrating? The tide of racism was growing in Europe. France and Germany were wearing themselves out, raising one generation of children after another "living the obsession with some revenge to take."[27] Already the two countries were preparing new sacrifices to the patriotic and capitalistic myth:

Rien que pour le fonctionnement
d'usines à canons
obus
balles
la guerre
elle
elle va bientôt venir
s'enivrer encore à la marseillaise
de chair fumante[28]

[For nothing else
just to keep
the gun
shell
bullet
factories going
war
war will soon be here
getting high again
on the Marseillaise
reeking with flesh]

Why should this concern the blacks? Haven't they better things to do, more important and more urgent tasks in their own lands?

Aux Anciens Combattants Sénégalais
aux Futurs Combattants Sénégalais
à tout ce que le Sénégal peut accoucher
de combattants sénégalais futurs anciens
de quoi-je-me-mêle futurs anciens
de mercenaires futurs anciens
....
Moi je leur demande
de commencer par envahir le Sénégal[29]

[To the Senegalese veterans of war
to future Senegalese soldiers
to all the Senegalese veterans or soldiers

27. "Sur une carte postale" ("Written on a postcard").
28. "Des billes pour la roulette" ("Balls for a game of roulette").
29. "Et caetera."

that Senegal ever will produce
to all the future veterans
former and future regulars
what do I care, future, former
. . . .

Me
I ask them
to begin
by invading Senegal]

The final poem in *Pigments,* therefore, is an invitation to direct action. Damas, a West Indian, was speaking directly to the Senegalese. Paradoxically, it was in the Ivory Coast that his message was heard. Translated into Baoulé,[30] his vivid, rhythmic, incisive style struck home in 1939 with Ivorians, who recited his poems while resisting the military draft. *Pigments* was immediately banned. From its first publication, the new poetry of negritude revealed itself as revolutionary—and effectively so, because it touched the feelings of the entire black race. The words of a West Indian were inspiring Africans. A new idiom had been created that all Africans could understand despite their six hundred different languages and dialects. The response gave the young poets in Paris confidence that they had hit upon the right tone of voice. No matter what language they wrote in, they felt "black," they were talking "black."

Damas knew he was a precursor. He has called *Pigments* the forerunner to Césaire's *Cahier d'un retour au pays natal.* Both Césaire and Senghor, as a matter of fact, were later to build on Damas's experience, although Damas as a poet remained silent for years. He did not cease to write, however. In 1938 he published a virulent book of articles, *Retour de Guyane.* In 1943, he published a collection of Guianese stories.[31] In 1947, it was Damas who edited the first anthology of poets from the French colonies.[32] In 1948 he published adaptations of African folk songs,[33] and in 1952, a collection of delicate love lyrics, *Graffiti.* But he had abandoned his original inspiration and accepted the conspiracy of silence he alludes to in *Black-Label. Black-Label* did not appear until 1956, although Damas had begun it many years earlier.[34] It

30. Baoulé is one of the important dialects of the Ivory Coast.

31. *Veillées noires* (Paris: Stock; Ottowa: Editions Leméac, 1972).

32. *Poètes d'expression française d'outre mer* (Paris: Seuil). [Translator's note: Or, with the nuance a more literal translation gives it, "poets of overseas France."]

33. *Poemes nègres sur des airs africains* (Paris: Guy Levi Mano). [Translated by Ulli Beier and Miriam Koshland as *African Songs of Love, War, Grief and Abuse* (Nigeria: Mbari, 1961).]

34. *Graffiti* (Paris: Seghers, 1952); *Black-Label* (Paris: Gallimard, 1956). A few poems from these two works had already appeared in the anthology published by Damas in 1947.

marks a return to the itinerary of *Pigments,* which we will next consider from a more strictly literary point of view.

The first few poems in *Pigments,* which we have not yet discussed, were influenced by surrealism. They enclose a secret or attempt to seize a fleeting impression. Damas was tempted by the hermetic manner, particularly through the poetry of Mallarmé, which he had read a great deal between 1920 and 1930.[35] Damas was more closely attached to the French surrealist poets—Aragon and Desnos, for example—than his colleagues were, but he managed rather early to detach himself enough from their influence to develop a personal style. The majority of the poems in the *Pigments* have the Damas "stamp": their beat; the use of everyday words, occasionally crude, but never prosaic; the inimitable offhand humor, full of disrespectful banter; the sensitivity to every nuance. "Damas's poetry is essentially unsophisticated. . . . It is direct, crude, brutal at times, but never vulgar."[36] This was Senghor's opinion of his friend. He grasped the fundamentals.

Unlike his two fellow poets, Damas definitely did not have a bent for amplification. The soft, hazy drapery of Senghor's verse is foreign to him; he has none of Césaire's splashing imagery, extensive vocabulary, or visionary gifts. This is doubtless why Damas's star paled before the more dazzling works of his successors. It is regrettable, because in rereading *Pigments* one realizes that no one has replaced Damas. No other poet has matched his dry, vivid style, extraordinarily effective in its very starkness; his astonishing flippancy, the audacity and elegance even of his insults; in short, his freedom! Some of Damas's poems are so close to the spoken word that one seems to hear him personally reciting them, even inventing them as he goes along. Notice, for example, the amazing spontaneity of this tirade written, it would seem, under the lash of emotion, after reading a newspaper item announcing that "in response to a German threat, Senegalese War Veterans have cabled an expression of their unremitting loyalty to France":

> Aux Anciens Combattants Sénégalais
> aux Futurs Combattants Sénégalais
> à tout ce que le Sénégal peut accoucher
> de combattants sénégalais futurs anciens
> de quoi-je-me-mêle futurs anciens
> de mercenaires futurs anciens
> de pensionnés
> de galonnés
> de décorés

35. Interview with Léon Damas, June 1959.
36. L. S. Senghor, *Anthologie,* p. 5.

de décavés
de grands blessés
de mutilés
de calcinés
de gangrenés
de gueules cassées
de bras coupées
d'intoxiqués
et patati et patata
et caetera futurs anciens

Moi
je leur dis
merde et
d'autres choses encore

Moi je leur demande
de remiser les
coupe-coupe
les accès de sadisme
le sentiment
la sensation
de saletés
de malpropretés à faire

Moi
je leur demande
de taire le besoin qu'ils ressentent
de piller
de voler
de violer
de souiller à nouveau les bords antiques
du Rhin

Moi je leur demande
de commencer par envahir le Sénégal

Moi je leur demande
de foutre aux "Boches" la Paix[37]

[To the Senegalese veterans of war
to future Senegalese soldiers
to all the Senegalese veterans or soldiers
that Senegal ever will produce
to all the future veterans
former and future regulars
what do I care, future, former
    pensioners

37. "Et caetera."

```
            n.c.o.'s
            broken-down
            decorated
            mutilated
            poison-gassed
            disabled
            disfigured
            alcoholic
            amputee
            past and present soldiers
            et cetera et cetera

      Me
      I say SHIT
      and that's just half of it

      Me
      I ask them to
      shove
      their bayonets
      their sadistic fits
      the feeling
      the knowing
      they have
      filthy
      dirty
      jobs to do

      Me
      I ask them
      to conceal the need they feel
      to pillage
      rape
      and steal
      to soil the old banks of the Rhine anew

      Me
      I ask them
      to begin
      by invading Senegal

      Me
      I call on them
      to leave the Krauts in peace!]
```

The lean, incisive spoken style exactly expresses his ideas. And if Damas had but one thought, he did not wrap it up in ribbons and fog:

```
      De n'avoir jusqu'ici rien fait
      détruit
      bati
```

osé
à la manière
du Juif
du Jaune
pour l'évasion organisée en masse
de l'infériorité

C'est en vain que je cherche
le creux d'une épaule
où cacher mon visage
ma honte
de
   la
      Ré-
         a-
           li-
              té.[38]

[From having done nothing up to now
destroyed nothing
built nothing
dared nothing
like the Jew
or the yellow man
for the organized escape
from mass inferiority

I look in vain for
the hollow of a shoulder
in which to hide my face
my shame of the
   Re-
      al-
        i-
          ty.]

There is nothing excessive in this short poem. It is impossible to omit even one word of these naked, almost skeletal lines. Lack of words? The art of Damas lies in having made a style of terseness. He is perfectly aware of this characteristic and intentionally accentuates it. This is why he so often uses ellipses and short cuts:

Les jours eux-mêmes ont pris la forme
des masques africains
indifférents à toute profanation
de chaux vive
qu'encense

38. "Réalité."

un piano répétant la rengaine
d'un clair de lune à soupirs
tout format
dans les halliers
gondoles
et caetera[39]

[The days themselves
assumed the shape
of African masks
indifferent
to any profanation
of quick lime
the hommage of
moonlit sighs
any size
played on a piano
the refrain
repeated in
shrubbery
gondolas
et cetera]

The movement is so rapid that one has to pause a while to understand that Damas, sickened by the syrupy, banal sentiment of ready-made European cliches, is calling for the inflexible dignity of African masks.

The same allusive process appears in this gay, apparently inoffensive refrain. Here again, one grasps the point later. It is the song of the black race, which threatens with an innocent air:

Bientôt
je n'aurai pas que dansé
bientôt
je n'aurai pas que chanté
bientôt
je n'aurai pas que frotté
bientôt
je n'aurai pas que trempé
bientôt
je n'aurai pas que dansé
chanté
frotté
trempé
frotté

39. "Position."

chanté
dansé
  Bientôt[40]

[Soon
I'll not only have danced
soon
I'll not only have sung
soon
I'll not only have polished
soon
I'll not only have sweated
soon
I'll not only have danced
sung
polished
sweated
polished
sung
danced
  Soon]

Damas poses riddles and lets the reader complete his thoughts, cleverly drawing him into the game. His style has the advantage of being very flexible; it is the style of a juggler who adapts himself marvelously to any trick, especially to any turn of wit. Damas is full of ellipses and allusions, unexpected associations and puns:

avec ces maux de tête qui cessent
chaque fois que je salue quelqu'un
....
. . . ils vous servent l'aprés-midi
un peu d'eau chaude
et des gâteaux enrhumés

Mes amis j'ai valsé
valsé comme jamais mes ancêtres
les Gaulois
au point que j'ai le sang
qui tourne encore
à la viennoise

[with this head that aches
but stops
each time I greet someone
  (implied: because I take off my tight hat)
....

40. "Bientôt."

> . . . they serve each afternoon
> a bit of tepid water
> and tea-cakes snuffling rum*

> I've waltzed my friends
> waltzed
> more than any
> of my ancestors
> the Gauls†
> to such a point my blood
> still beats
> three-quarter time]

Occasionally, however, the humor grates. We no longer feel like smiling when Damas predicts that German fascism might lead other Europeans to

> couper leur sexe aux nègres
> pour en faire des bougies pour leurs églises

> [cut the niggers' parts off
> to make candles for their churches]

Even the half-smile which ends the poem "Pareille à ma légende" is full of bitterness:

> occcidentalement avance mon ombre
> pareille à ma légende
> d'homme-singe

> [my shadow moves forward occidentally
> like the legend
> of my ape-man past]

The humor in the monologue "Hoquet" ("Hiccups")—the masterful digest of the principles of middle-class education in the West Indies —is less bitter:

> Le pain ne se gaspille pas
> le pain de Dieu
> le pain de la sueur du front de votre père
> le pain du pain
> ....

> un estomac doit être sociable
> et tout estomac sociable se passe de rots

*Translator's note: Pun: In French, rum as in rumcake is spelled *rhum*, while *enrhumé* is the word for having a cold, i.e., the rumcakes are drippy, as if they had a cold.

†Translator's note: At the time Damas wrote *Pigments*, the same history books were used in all elementary schools throughout France and the French colonies. The first sentence was "Nos ancêtres le Gaulois . . ." ("Our ancestors the Gauls . . .").

et que je vous y reprenne dans la rue
....

a vous ébattre avec Untel
avec Untel qui n'a pas reçu le baptême

[We don't waste bread
God's bread
the bread your father sweats his brow for
our daily bread
....

a stomach has to have good manners too
and a well-bred stomach never burps

and don't let me catch you in the street again
....

picking a fight with what's-his-name
what's-his-name who isn't even baptized]

How ever special this wit is, we would not dare call it "Negro." It is rather, as Senghor puts it, "a reaction to human imbalance." Is not "white" wit often the same thing? Think of Jacques Prévert or Charlie Chaplin? Damas has much in common with them.

Another aspect of Damas's poetry, another string of his "banjo," is nostalgia and tenderness. The two most beautiful poems in *Pigments*, "Regard" and "Limbé," are in this minor tone. In "Regard," the bohemian, his weapons abandoned, finding anew his brother Ruteboeuf, says with the same sincere voice, full of emotion:

Quand sur le tard
quand sur le tard mes yeux
mes yeux se brideront

Quand sur le tard
quand sur le tard j'aurai
de faux yeux de Chinois

Quand sur le tard
quand sur le tard
tout m'aura laissé
tout m'aura laissé jusqu'à la théorie
jusqu'à la théorie choir

Quand sur le tard
quand sur le tard
suivra la pente
suivra la pente le bâton
qui soutient les vieux corps

M'achèterez-vous
m'achèterez-vous dites

des fleurs
que sais-je
pour qu'au bistrot de l'angle
pour qu'au bistrot de l'angle
j'aille
ranimer l'âtre
d'un grand verre de bordeaux

[Later on
later on in life
when my eyes are shrivelled

Later on
later on in life
when my eyes are mock Chinese

Later on
later on in life
when everything is gone
when everything has left me
but the theory
when everything but the theory
has let me down

Later on in life
later on
when the bent back
is preceded by the cane
that keeps old bodies going

Tell me
will you buy
will you buy
my flowers
who knows
so I can go
down to the corner bar
down to the corner bar
to light this old hearth up
with a big glass of bordeaux]

We have already quoted "Limbé" ("Blues"). We can see how Damas's style, stark as it is, is often the result of long labor. Words which
seem to have been assembled haphazardly, nevertheless call to and
complete each other, as the thought develops, to form a definite idea
in each verse:

la coutume
les jours
la vie

la chanson
le rythme
l'effort
le sentier
l'eau
la case
la terre enfumée grise
la sagesse
les mots
les palabres
les vieux
la cadence
les mains
la mesure
les mains
les piétinements
le sol

[ways
days
life
song
rhythm
effort
footpath
water
huts
the smoke-grey earth
the wisdom
the words
the palavers
the elders
the cadence
the hands
beating time
the hands
the feet
marking time
upon the ground]

Customs rule the days of which life is made. Song, by its rhythm, encourages work and effort. In two lines Damas evokes the hut with its path to the water and the open, smoky fire. The elders, too, whose wisdom is expressed in the words they speak at the "palavers." Finally, the dance with hands beating time—note the repetition—and feet stamping the ground!

And this brings us to the rhythmic features of Damas's poetry, apparently the foremost stylistic concern in his work, which always seems to have been written in a single rush of words. This rhythm—the seal of negritude, according to Senghor—is achieved by Damas in many ways. The first most common one is to begin each new line with the words of the preceding one, as in the poem "Ils ont":

> Ils ont si bien su faire
> si bien su faire les choses
> les choses
> qu'un jour nous avons tout
> nous avons tout foutu de nous-mêmes
> tout foutu de nous-mêmes en l'air

> [They did their thing so well
> they did their thing so well
> that one day we let all
> all that once was ours go
> we threw it all away]

Another way is to repeat a single phrase or a few words several times ("I too", "empty belly—empty eyes" . . .) as in "Un clochard m'a demandé dix sous":

> Moi aussi un beau jour j'ai sorti
> mes hardes
> de clochard

> Moi aussi
> avec des yeux qui tendent
> la main
> j'ai soutenu
> la putain de misère

> Moi aussi
> j'ai eu faim dans ce sacré foutu pays
> moi aussi j'ai cru pouvoir
> demander dix sous
> par pitié pour mon ventre
> creux

> Moi aussi
> jusqu'au bout de l'éternité de leurs
> boulevards à flics
> combien de nuits ai-je dû
> m'en aller
> moi aussi
> les yeux creux

> Moi aussi
> j'ai eu faim les yeux creux

moi aussi j'ai cru
pouvoir demander dix sous
les yeux
le ventre
creux
jusqu'au jour où j'en ai eu
marre
de les voir se gausser
de mes hardes de clochard
et se régaler
de voir un nègre
les yeux ventre creux

[I too one fine day I took to
beggar clothes
with eyes that hold
the hand out

I too
pimped
for poverty the whore

I too have gone hungry in this
    rotten lousy land
I too thought I
could beg a dime
for pity of my empty
belly

I too
to the end of the eternity
of their cop-filled streets
how many nights have I
too had to turn away
with hollow eyes

I too went hungry hollow-eyed
I too thought I
could beg a dime
for empty
eyes
and belly
until the day I'd had enough
of seeing them make fun
of my shabby clothes
feasting on the sight
of a nigger
with eyes

and belly
empty]

Again, in "Obsession," Damas begins each verse with the same phrase: "a taste of blood comes"; similarly in "Il est des nuits" each stanza begins "There are nights with no name," and in "Solde" each begins with "I feel ridiculous."

In "Limbé," besides using this same method, Dames employs a very suggestive "diminuendo" finale.

Rendez-les-moi mes poupées noires
mes poupées noires
poupées noires
noires

[Give me back my black
dolls my black
dolls black
black
dolls]

To emphasize his rhythms, Damas made use of typographical innovations:

Ils sont venus ce soir où le
tam
   tam
      roulait
        de
          rythme
            en
              rythme
                la frénésie. . . .

[They came that night as the
tom
   tom
      rolled
        from
          rhythm
            to
              rhythm
                the frenzy. . . .]

In this poem, Damas gives greater emphasis to the rhythmic beat of his verses by repeating the same group of words after short intervals. He uses both exact repetitions and reversed repetitions in "En file indienne":

Et les sabots
des bêtes de somme
qui martèlent en Europe
l'aube indécise encore
me rappellent
l'abnégation étrange
des trays[41] matineux
repus
qui rythment aux Antilles
les hanches des porteuses
en file indienne

Et l'abnégation étrange
des trays matineux
repus
qui rythment aux Antilles
les hanches des porteuses
en file indienne
me rappellent
les sabots
des bêtes de somme
qui martèlent en Europe
l'aube indécise encore

[And the wooden shoes
of beasts of burden
beating out
the still uncertain dawn
in Europe
remind me of
the strange self-sacrifice
of morning trays
brimful
which sway in the Antilles
to the rhythm of the hips
of women walking Indian file

And the strange self-sacrifice
of brimful morning trays
that sway in the Antilles
to the rhythm of the hips
of women walking Indian file
reminds me of
the boots

41. In Guiana and in the West Indies, the "tray" is a large, rectangular, wooden tray with high sides.

in Europe
of beasts of burden
beating out
the still uncertain dawn]

Damas: trickster-poet, a poet sensitive to irony, with an unpretentious tenderness, a poet of sincerity. Hopefully, we have sufficiently highlighted the temperamental qualities his style reveals. Césaire's great cries, the chords of Senghor's organ, are not for Léon Damas, who prefers a simple song to a symphony. We do not reproach him this. He is infinitely fascinating, and his poetry is effective to such an extent that it aroused an entire people to the rediscovery of its "negritude," as we showed earlier.

It is to be regretted, on the other hand, that Damas's most recent collection appears to be greatly influenced by Césaire and Jacques Roumain. His own rare qualities—soberness, ellipsis, allusiveness—are drowned in a long epic poem that is too often wordy in spite of excellent passages.[42] *Veillées noires* and *Graffiti*, which would do credit to any worthwhile library, are much more representative of negritude because they are more authentic.

Let us hope that Damas rediscovers his original direction and gives up his wandering. Should he again want to take up the fight he has so long abandoned, may he return with his own weapons, those short poems sharp as an "oriental dagger," those lively, biting, tender verses. Surely they will better serve both his "cause" and literature. No one has yet replaced the author of *Pigments*. Will he himself leave his place empty?

42. For example, the one quoted by Senghor in his *Anthologie*, p. 18.

12/ Aimé Césaire:
Cahier d'un retour au pays natal

The *Cahier d'un retour au pays natal* reveals stages of its author's own life story, the painful "parturition"[1] of his self-discovery as a Negro. In a single, violent poetic effort, Aimé Césaire brings together his own experience and the destiny of his race, fusing them so completely as to render any future separation impossible.

In 1938, before writing the *Cahier*,[2] Césaire "burned all the books within him." He began by destroying all the classical verse he had composed up to that time. It was, of course, impossible for him to ignore the profound knowledge of French culture and language he had acquired at the Ecole Normale Supérieure. He had read and liked the surrealists, though he preferred to them Mallarmé, Péguy, the Claudel of *La tête d'or*, and above all Rimbaud. When he began the *Cahier*, however, Césaire had no intention of writing "poetry." He was intensely preoccupied at the time by concerns far from literary. He was living a predicament that seemed as intolerable to him in Paris as in Martinique. It was in an "extraordinary state of excitement" that he began a work which was to help him to become fully aware of his revolt and to analyze it. He set about it determined to free himself of all acquired form, in order to discover his very own.[3]

The *Cahier* opens with a description of the West Indies quite different from those "Happy Isles" whose languid graces, tropical paradise,

---

1. The word is Senghor's. He was present at the birth of *Cahier* and called it a "parturition in suffering" (*Ethiopiques* [Paris: Seuil], p. 104).

2. Aimé Césaire, *Cahier d'un retour au pays natal* (Paris: Présence Africaine, 1956). The quotations given are taken from this last edition, which we indicate as *Cahier*. The page numbers given in parenthesis are those of that edition.

3. Details given by Césaire in the course of an interview in March 1959.

159

and Creole charm[4] had oft been repeated by other poets. How dis-
cordant this voice speaking of the "hungry Antilles, these pock-marked
Antilles, Antilles dynamited by alcohol, shipwrecked in the mud of this
bay, in the dust of this town, dismally stranded" (p. 26); this voice
tersely denouncing the lies of some, the illusion of others:

> Au bout du petit matin, l'extrême, trompeuse désolée eschare sur la bles-
> sure des eaux; les martyrs qui ne témoignent pas; les fleurs du sang qui se
> fanent et s'eparpillent dans le vent inutile comme des cris de perroquets
> babillards; une vieille vie menteusement souriante, ses lèvres ouvertes d'an-
> goisses désaffectées; une vieille misère pourissant sous le soleil, silencieuse-
> ment; un vieux silence crevant de pustules tièdes . . .[p. 26]

> [Shortly after dawn, this last deceptive desolated scab, this wound upon the
> waters; martyrs who do not bear witness, flowers of blood that fade and scatter
> in the wind as useless as the cries of babbling parrots; an old life deceitfully
> smiling, its eyes open on alienated anguish; an old hovel silently rotting under
> the sun; an old silence bursting with lukewarm pustules . . .]

How confusing! Who is telling the truth? Marceline Desbordes-
Valmore and Saint-John Perse, or this twenty-five-year-old Martiniquan? One must turn to the evidence and accept the disenchanting
reality, because since the *Cahier* there has been ample testimony.
Frantz Fanon assures us that "Césaire was magnanimous. . . . This
town of Fort-de-France is truly flat, stranded. The description given by
Césaire is anything but poetic."[5] So, we cannot censure gloomy lyricism. Césaire has merely described reality, removing our rose-tinted
glasses. But perhaps the natives? So much has been made of their
natural insouciance, their gaudy clothes, their happy chatter. What
does Césaire say?

> Dans cette ville inerte, cette foule criarde si étonnament passée à côté de son
> cri . . . cette foule à côté de son cri de faim, de misère, de révolte, de haine,
> cette foule si étrangement bavarde et muette . . . [pp. 27–28]

> [In this inert town, the noisy crowd so surprisingly missing the point of its
> noise . . . this crowd that overlooks its cries of hunger, misery, revolt and hate;
> this crowd so strangely talkative and mute . . .]

But if these people do not rise in rebellion, it is because they have
not found their condition too intolerable. Unless, replies Césaire, four
centuries of oppression have taught them lasting fatalism. Looking
closely, what does one see behind the parrots, the bougainvillea, the
multicolored madras headscarves? "Fear cowering in the ravines, fear
roasting in the trees, fear furrowing the ground, fear floating in the

4. See chap. 2, above.
5. Frantz Fanon, *Peau noir, masques blancs,* p. 35.

sky, a mass of fear" (p. 29) and also "these worn-out men," "this accelerated stench of corruption," and, dominating them all, pervasive Hunger:

Et ni l'instituteur dans sa classe, ni le prêtre au catéchisme ne pourront tirer un mot de ce négrillon somnolent, malgré leur manière si énergique à tous deux de tambouriner son crâne tondu . . .
car sa voix s'oublie dans les marais de la faim,
et il n'y a rien, rien à tirer vraiment de ce petit
vaurien,
qu'une faim qui ne sait plus grimper aux agrès
de sa voix
une faim lourde et veule,
une faim ensevelie au plus profond de la Faim de ce morne
famélique.[6] [pp. 30–31]

[And neither the teacher in his classroom nor the priest at catechism can get a word out of this sleepy little nigger, in spite of the energetic way they both have of drumming on his close-cropped head . . .
for his voice is forgotten in a quicksand of hunger
and there is nothing really nothing to be had
from this worthless little nobody
but hunger a hunger that no longer cares to
clamber up the rigging to his voice
dull, sluggish hunger
a hunger buried in the deeper Hunger
of this famished hill.]

Of course, there are always the feast days, when the "wild and foolish ways to revive the golden splash of happy moments" (p. 32) are rediscovered, when exuberance takes its revenge on quotidian restrictions and bursts into song, dance, and revelry. This is what the foreigner remembers, talks about, takes pictures of: the natives' gaiety.[7] But the morning after such drunken nights, what do these people waken to? "A prostrate life, with no place to put its snuffed-out dreams, the dream of life disconsolately torpid in its bed" (p. 37) and the resignation of this city which "creeps on its hands without ever any wish to pierce the sky with a stance of protest" (p. 37); "the shack blistered like a peach tree suffering from blight, and the worn roof, patched with bits of kerosene cans, . . . and the bed of planks from which my race has sprung . . . its mattress of dried banana leaves and rags" (pp. 38–39).

This is the setting! For actors, let us take any average family: "an-

6. *Mornes:* hillocks on the outskirts of Martiniquan towns, on which the slum areas are usually located. For Césaire, these *mornes* are the very symbol of West Indian poverty.
7. Even the best movies do not avoid this fault—Marcel Camus's *Black Orpheus,* for example.

other stinking little house on a very narrow street, a tiny house that harbors in its guts of rotting wood dozens of rats and the turbulence of my six brothers and sisters, a cruel little house whose intransigence made us panic at the end of every month . . . and my mother, whose limbs for our tireless hunger pedal, pedal day and night" (p. 37). This is the true face of the "happy Antilles," Césaire's Martinique, his anguish, his passion:

> Iles cicatrices des eaux
> Iles evidence de blessures
> Iles miettes
> Iles informes [p. 80]

> [Island scars upon the waters
> Island evidence of wounds
> Island crumbs
> Imperfect isles]

"This bulk, this plunder, this earth" where "men have abandoned their courage," "deaf land brutally sealed off at every opening," he writes elsewhere.[8]

Césaire spent his childhood in the setting we have just described; he was the little pickaninny drowsy with hunger; his was the poverty-stricken family in the village of Basse-Pointe! In the single word "partir" ("to leave"), which ends his description of the West Indies, Césaire summarizes the dreams of his youth. Stifled and disgusted, it was "with voluptuous pleasure" that he left Martinique to continue his studies in France.

The rest of the *Cahier* retraces the stages of Césaire's self-discovery. What position would he take toward this prostrate homeland of his? What was it, and what ought he to do?

His first impulse was "to leave" in order to take up the burden of *all* oppressed people of the world:

> Je serai un homme-juif
> un homme-cafre
> un homme-hindou-de-Calcutta
> un homme-de-Harlem-qui-ne-vote-pas
> L'homme famine, l'homme insulte, l'homme torture [p. 39]

> [I shall be a Jew Man
> a Kaffir
> a Hindu from Calcutta
> a Harlemite who doesn't vote
> the starving man, insulted man, the tortured]

8. Aimé Césaire, *Ferrements* (Paris: Seuil, 1960), pp. 46 and 23.

To save them he wishes to be the magic Word to re-create the world:

Je retrouverais le secret des grandes communications et des grandes combustions. Je dirais orage. Je dirais fleuve. Je dirais tornade. Je dirais feuille. Je dirais arbre. . . . Qui ne me comprendrait pas ne comprendrait pas davantage le rugissement du tigre. [p. 40]

[I shall rediscover the secret of great communications and combustions. I shall say storm. I shall say river. I shall say tornado. I shall say leaf. I shall say tree. . . . They who do not understand me would not understand the roaring of a tiger either.]

But at the heart of this redemptive ideal, there was a secret weakness. Refusing to look it in the face, Césaire was submerging the lowliness of *his* people in the great current of universal pain. He was taking on the noble role of Pure Hero come to save the powerless, but one who holds himself above them because he is not of their race.

> . . . Mon cœur bruissait de générosités emphatiques. . . .
> j'arriverais lisse et jeune dans ce pays mien et je dirais à ce pays
> . . . « J'ai longtemps erré et je reviens vers la hideur desertée de vos plaies. » [p. 41]

> Et je lui dirais encore:
> « Ma bouche sera la bouche des malheurs qui n'ont point de bouche, ma voix, la liberté de celles qui s'affaissent au cachot du désespoir. » [p. 42]

> [. . . My heart throbbed with emphatic generosities. . . .
> I would come young and polished to this country of mine and I would say to it. . . : "Long have I wandered and I return to the abandoned horror of your wounds."

> And I would say more:
> "My lips shall speak for miseries that have no mouth,
> my voice shall be the liberty of those who languish in the dungeon of despair."]

Then Césaire realized the insufficiency of his "gesture." Face to face with "the dazzling pettiness of the death" which is life in his country, "grandeur runs pitifully aground." "This death that limps from insignificance to insignificance; these spadefuls of petty greeds . . . of petty flunkeys . . . of petty souls" (p. 42), would quickly bury such neophyte enthusiasm.

The protagonist takes fright: Is he called to save only "these few thousand humiliated souls circling round inside a Calabash island"? (pp. 43–44). No—"I have no right to reduce myself to this little ellipsoidal nothing trembling a few inches above the horizon" (p. 43). After all, he is not only Martiniquan; he is also Negro and his empire is huge: "There is nowhere on this earth without my finger-print" (p. 44). He counts up his treasures: "Haiti where negritude stood upon its feet for the first time," its hero, Toussaint Louver-ture,[9] "a man alone who defies the white screams of white death"; Africa, "where death cuts a wide swath"; and all the blacks of the Americas, their trumpets ridiculously muted (pp. 43–44). Every-where the Negro suffers; "death breathes madly in the ripe cane-field of his arms" (p. 46).

In order to begin, Césaire must identify the oppressor of his race. In a passage now famous he "undertakes . . . systematically to destroy what has been acquired from Europe, and the idea of this spiritual destruction symbolizes the great future call to arms by means of which blacks will destroy their chains."[10]

> Parce que nous vous haïssons vous et
> votre raison, nous nous réclamons de la
> démence précoce de la folie flambante
> du cannibalisme tenace [pp. 47–48]

> [Because we hate you
> you and your reason, we call upon the
> dementia praecox, the blazing insanity
> of stubborn cannibalism]

Césaire strikes at the very heart of Western civilization, at its key value, Logic, in the name of which Europe had arrogated the right to enslave peoples it called "prelogical." Yes, indeed, Negroes are sav-ages for whom "two and two are five," who identify themselves with trees and rivers:

> Je déclare mes crimes et qu'il n'y a rien à
> dire pour ma défense.
> Danses. Idoles. Relaps. Moi aussi
> J'ai assassiné Dieu de ma paresse de
> mes paroles de mes gestes de mes chansons
> obscènes
> J'ai porté des plumes de perroquet des
> dépouilles de chat musqué
> J'ai lassé la patience des missionaires
> insulté les bienfaiteurs de l'humanité.
> Défié Tyr. Défié Sidon.

9. Toussaint (1743–1803), called Louverture: Haitian statesman and general, born in Santo Domingo; leader of the Haitian revolutionaries from 1796–1802; was captured by General Brunet, and soon died in France, a prisoner at the fort in Joux. See further Aimé Césaire's *Toussaint Louverture* (Paris: Club Français du Livre, 1960).

10. J. P. Sartre, "Orphee noir," p. xvii.

Adoré le Zambèze.
L'étendue de ma perversité me confond! [p. 50]

[I confess my crimes and admit there is nothing
to say in my defense.
Dances. Idols. Apostasy. I too
killed God with my laziness
my words my deeds my obscene
songs.
I have worn parrot feathers
musk cat skins
I have exhausted the missionaries' patience
insulted the benefactors of mankind.
Defied Tyr. Defied Sidon.
I have worshipped the Zambezi.
The extent of my perversity confounds me!]

To deepen his scorn of Europeans, he reverts to the practice of
(black) magic and plays witch doctor:

Voum rooh oh
voum rooh oh
à charmer les serpents à conjurer
les morts
voum rooh oh
à contraindre la pluie à contrarier
les raz de marée
voum rooh oh
à empêcher que ne tourne l'ombre
voum rooh oh que mes cieux à moi
s'ouvrent [p. 51]

Alors voila le grand défi et l'impulsion
sataniques et l'insolente
dérive nostaligique de lunes rousses,
de feux verts, de fièvres jaunes! [p. 54]

[Voom rooh oh
voom rooh oh
charming snakes and conjuring the
dead
voom rooh oh
bringing down rain, provoking
tidal waves
voom rooh oh
preventing the darkness from coming
voom rooh oh may my heavens
open

> Here is the great defiance and
> impulse of Satan
> and the insolent nostalgic drifts of red moons,
> green fires and yellow fevers!]

After the suffering, the snuffed-out revolts, all the evils of phantom Africa[11] are summoned to begin "the only thing in the world worth beginning—the end of the world, of course" (pp. 53–54). This is an open declaration of war: "Accommodate yourself to me. I shall not accommodate myself to you!" (p. 55).

The West Indies do not consist only of the picturesque, on which whites feast their eyes and ears: lagoons covered with water lilies, "women with madras about their hips, rings in their ears, and smiles on their lips" (p. 54).

Dans ma mémoire sont des lagunes. Elles sont couvertes de têtes de morts. Elles ne sont pas couvertes de nénuphars.
Dans ma mémoire sont des lagunes. Sur leurs rives ne sont pas étendus des pagnes de femmes.
Ma mémoire est entourée de sang. Ma mémoire a sa ceinture de cadavres! [pp. 57–58]

[There are lagoons in my memory. They are covered with heads of the dead. Not with water lilies.
There are lagoons in my memory. Women's clothes are not spread out along their banks.
My memory is surrounded with blood. My memory has a belt of corpses.]

The Negro has not forgotten the rebellions crushed and his race's enslavement in the name of convenient prejudices:

> (les nègres-sont-tous-les-mêmes, je-vous-le-dis
> les vices-tous-les-vices, c'est-moi-qui-vous-le-dis
> l'odeur-du-nègre, ça-fait-pousser-la-canne
> rappelez-vous-le-vieux-dicton:
> battre-un-nègre, c'est le nourrir) [p. 58]

> [(Niggers-are-all-alike, I-tell-you
> vices-all-the-vices, I-tell-you
> the-smell-of-nigger makes-the-cane-grow
> remember-the-old-saying:
> beat-a-nigger-and-you-feed-him)]

He has not forgotten the humiliation of nigger clowns amusing the wealthy in search of entertainment:

> Obscènes gaiment, très doudous de jazz
> sur leur

11. Michel Leiris, *L'Afrique fantôme* (Paris: Gallimard, 1951).

excès d'ennui
Je sais le tracking, le Lindy-hop et les
claquettes. [p. 58]

[Gaily obscene, mad for jazz
to relieve their
awful boredom
I know the tracking, the lindy-hop, the tap dance.]

But being reminded of these accumulated deaths and humiliations leads to a third brutal awakening. The poet becomes excited by his negritude; it reclothes him with all the grandeur of a virile past, with the energetic virtues of all those blacks who resisted the whites. An abstract negritude envelops him like a halo. Draping himself in this heroic abstraction is another way of escaping his destiny and his responsibility. Césaire's negritude was that of the Martiniquan people, "the sweet green flow of abject waters" (p. 59). He cannot renounce his native land:

Mais je me suis adressé au mauvais sorcier.
....

Quelle folie le merveilleux entrechat par
moi rêvé au-dessus de la bassesse! [p. 59]

[But I went to the wrong witch doctor.
....

How mad my dream of a marvelous
leap above the baseness!]

His proud cries, his spectacular exorcisms, his threats cannot be heard by his countrymen; for they are stuck in "the accumulated dung of our lies" (p. 59). Césaire understands that he must give up the idea of being a Knight, the Herald of a race covered with glory. He must cease boasting in the face of a reality painful to describe and still more painful to accept.

Par une inattendue et bienfaisante révolution intérieure, j'honore maintenant mes laideurs repoussantes. . . .
Et je ris de mes anciennes imaginations puériles.
Non, nous n'avons jamais été amazones du roi du Dahomey, ni princes de Ghana avec huit cents chameaux, ni docteurs à Tombouctou Askia le Grand étant roi. . . . Nous ne nous sentons pas sous l'aisselle la démangeaison de ceux qui tinrent jadis la lance . . . je veux avouer que nous fûmes de tout temps d'assez piètres laveurs de vaisselle, des cireurs de chaussures sans envergure . . . et le seul indiscutable record que nous ayons battu est celui d'endurance à la chicotte. . . . [pp. 60 and 61]

[Due to an unexpected and salutary inner revolution, I honor now my repulsive ugliness. . . .

And I laugh at my childish old imaginings.

No, we were never Amazons to the king of Dahomey, nor princes of Ghana with eight hundred camels, nor doctors in Timbuctoo when Askia the Great was king. . . . We do not feel the armpit itch of those who once upon a time bore lances. . . . I wish to confess that we have always been rather mediocre dishwashers, shoeshine boys of little scope . . . and the only indisputable record we have ever broken is that of endurance to the whip. . . .]

Nothing could induce the Martiniquan to revolt once and for all against the worst humiliations:

. . . et l'on nous marquait au fer rouge et nous dormions dans nos excréments et l'on nous vendait sur les places et l'aune de drap anglais et la viande salée d'Irlande coûtaient moins cher que nous, et ce pays était calme, tranquille, disant que l'esprit de Dieu était dans ses actes. [p. 62]

[. . . and they branded us with hot irons and we slept in our excrement and they sold us in the public squares and a bolt of English cloth or a side of salted meat from Ireland cost less than we did, and this land was calm, tranquil, proclaiming that the Spirit of the Lord was in its actions.]

Césaire must now admit that he recognizes himself in these people, that his pride has been concealing a weakness he unexpectedly discovers on a streetcar. A poor, unkempt Negro, a tramp in rags "was trying to dispose his gigantic limbs and his trembling hungry boxer's hands on this greasy trolley seat." Women were snickering at the sight of him.

Il était COMIQUE ET LAID
COMIQUE ET LAID pour sûr.
J'arborai un grand sourire complice . . .
Ma lâcheté retrouvée!

Mon héroisme, quelle farce!
Cette ville est à ma taille.
Et mon âme est couchée. . . . [p. 65]

[He was COMICAL AND UGLY
COMICAL AND UGLY to be sure.
I unfurled a great big guilty smile . . .
My cowardice discovered!

My heroism, What a farce!
This town is just my size.
And my soul is asleep. . . .]

Césaire, the rebel who was defying the white man with great shouts bursting from the strength of his race, no longer attempts to escape his reality. He is is part of it like all the others:

Tiède petit matin de chaleur et de peur
ancéstrales

je tremble maintenant du commun tremblement
que notre sang docile chante dans le madrépore.

Et ces têtards en moi éclos de mon ascendance
prodigieuse!
Ceux qui n'ont inventé ni la poudre ni la boussole
ceux qui n'ont jamais su dompter la
vapeur ni l'éléctricité
ceux qui n'ont exploré ni les mers ni le ciel
mais ils savent en ses moindres recoins
le pays de souffrance
ceux qui n'ont connu de voyages que de
déracinements
ceux qui se sont assoupis aux agenouillements
ceux qu'on domestiqua et christianisa
ceux qu'on inocula d'abâtardissement
tam-tams de mains vides
tam-tams inanes de plaies sonores
tam-tams burlesques de trahison tabide

  Tiède petit matin de chaleurs et de peurs
ancéstrales
par dessus bord mes richesses pérégrines
par dessus bord mes faussetés authentiques. [pp. 67–68]

  [Tepid dawn of ancestral heat and
fear
I tremble now with the collective trepidation of our docile blood
pulsing in the Madrepore.

And these tadpoles within hatched by my prodigious
ancestry!
Those who invented neither gunpowder nor
compass
those who never harnessed steam or
electricity
those who explored neither sea nor the
sky
but who know in its uttermost corners
the landscape of pain
those who've known no voyages other than
uprootings
those who were stupefied from falling on their knees
those who were Christianized and tamed
those who were inoculated with decay
tom-toms of empty hands
futile tom-toms echoing with wounds
tom-toms made absurd by atrophied betrayals

    Tepid dawning of ancestral heat and
fear
overboard my alien riches
overboard my authentic falsehoods.]

There is no question here, as Sartre believes,[12] of a "haughty vindication of nontechnical cultures," but only the objective, humble, re-
gretful acknowledgment of a genuine inferiority, to be charged, together with all the rest, to the debit of his race and assumed as such
by Césaire!

    Je me cachais derrière une vanité stupide
    ....

    Voici l'homme par terre
    et son âme est comme nue
    et le destin triomphe qui contemple se
    muer
    en l'ancestral bourbier cette âme qui le
    défiait. [pp. 66–67]

    [I was hiding from myself in stupid vanity
    ....

    Behold the man brought low
    his soul naked
    and destiny triumphant
    at the sight of this defiant soul
    stripped in the ancestral mud.]

From this moment, accepting true participation in his race, its sufferings and its humiliations, Césaire understands it better; he now has
access to the real "reserves" of his people's humanity. Their virtue
does not lie in pride or a capacity to vanquish the world, nor in the
grandiose rebellions the poet has just sung of! Their virtue lies precisely in all that he rejected: the "landscape of pain" whose uttermost
recesses have been explored by the former slaves; the ancestral values
maintained despite exile and servitude; the capacity to understand the
world intuitively, to adapt oneself to it rather than try to dominate it;
and the never forgotten contact with cosmic forces, symbols, and
myths.

    Césaire draws from these sources the courage to accept the deficien-
cies of his people. As "earth more and more abandons the earth," that
is to say, as the white world becomes dehumanized, these deficiencies
seemed to him all the more precious.[13]

    12. J. P. Sartre, "Orphée noir," p. xxx.
    13. Césaire takes up an idea already expressed by Claude McKay: the excesses of
technology and reason which have led to a dehumanization in the West, which the black
man has avoided to the extent that he has "lagged behind" European progress!

Ecoutez le monde blanc
horriblement las de son effort immense
ses articulations rebelles craquer sous les
étoiles dures
ses raideurs d'acier bleu transperçant la
chair mystique
écoute ses victoires proditoires trompeter
ses défaites
écoute aux alibis grandioses son piètre
trébuchement [pp. 72–73]

[Listen to the white world
horribly weary from its enormous effort
its rebellious joints crack beneath the
harsh stars
its rigid blue steel penetrates
mystic flesh
hear its boastful victories trumpet
its defeats
listen to the grandiose alibis for its sorry
stumblings]

On the contrary, blacks have remained

ignorants des surfaces mais saisis par le
mouvement de toute chose
insoucieux de dompter, mais jouant le jeu
du monde [p. 72]

[ignorant of surfaces but caught by the
movement of all things
indifferent to conquering
but playing the game of the world]

No, negritude is not "a speck of dead water on the earth's dead eye."

elle plonge dans la chair rouge du sol
elle plonge dans la chair ardente du ciel
elle troue l'accablement opaque de sa
droite patience [p. 71]

[it plunges into the red flesh of the earth
it plunges into the ardent flesh of the sky
it perforates the opaque dejection with its
upright patience]

The poet gathers all these strengths of his black people; he becomes
their spokesman before the Universe; he solemnly vows to arouse them
from their torpor, to defend them and help them to develop:

> donnez-moi la foi sauvage du sorcier
> donnez à mes mains puissance de modeler
> donnez à mon âme la trempe de l'épée
> je ne me dérobe point.
> ....
> voici le temps de se ceindre les reins
> comme un vaillant homme— [pp. 73–74]

> [give me the sorcerer's wild faith
> give my hands the power to shape
> give to my soul the temper of the sword
> I do not shrink.
> ....
> now is the time to gird one's loins
> like a valiant man—]

He wishes, however, to accomplish this without hating other races, out of pure love for his own:

> . . . ce que je veux
> c'est pour la faim universelle
> pour la soif universelle
> la sommer libre enfin
> de produire de son intimité close
> la succulence des fruits. [p. 75]

> [. . . what I wish
> for the universal hunger
> for the universal thirst
> is to shake it free at last
> to summon from its inner depths
> the succulence of fruit.]

This is how Césaire has described the successive phases of discovering *his* negritude. The physical and moral destruction of his countrymen aroused immense pity in him. He wished from then on to devote all his strength to helping them. While their distress appalled him, he had no desire to reduce himself to these few derelict people; his youthful ideal had been to take up the cause of all oppressed peoples. Quickly, however, he realized his vanity. He was a Negro, and his strength not too great for his brothers. At least he would be *their* herald, *their* cantor! A fearless one, who would dare confront the whites, because he felt sustained by the power of a glorious past and glorious ancestors. The memory of his country's humiliation, however, was sufficient to bring him down to a much less grandiose reality. He was not the prideful Negro, he was the vanquished Martiniquan who submitted.

Having found the strength to accept this, and reimmersing himself in the roots of his own people, Césaire understands that only this "descent into hell"[14] makes him capable of saving, through his countrymen, the entire black race. So he no longer refuses his destiny:

> J'accepte . . . j'accepte . . . entièrement, sans
> réserve . . .
> ma race qu'aucune ablution d'hysope et
> de lys mêlés ne pourrait purifier
> ma race rongée de macules
> ....
>
> J'accepte. J'accepte.
> et le nègre fustigé qui dit: « Pardon mon maître »
> et les vingt-neuf coups de fouet légal
> et le cachot de quatre pieds de haut
> et le carcan à branches
> et le jarret coupé à mon audace marronne[15]
> et la fleur de lys qui flue du fer rouge
> sur le gras de mon épaule . . . [pp. 77–78]

> [I accept . . . I accept . . . entirely without reserve
> my race that no ablution of hyssop and lilies
> could purify
> my race corroded with stains
> ....
>
> I accept. I accept.
> the flogged nigger who cries "Forgive me master"
> and the twenty-nine legal blows of the whip
> and the dungeon four feet high
> and the spiked iron collar
> and the hamstring cut for my runaway audacity
> and the fleur-de-lis streaming from the brand iron
> on my shoulder . . .]

And the poet's total identification with his people finally produces a miracle:

> Et voici soudain que force et vie m'assaillent
> ....
>
> Et nous sommes debout maintenant, mon pays et moi,
> les cheveux dans le vent, ma main petite maintenant
> dans son poing énorme et la force n'est pas en nous,

14. A recognized expression since Sartre compared the black poet to Orpheus. The success of this expression is also due in part to the analogy to the title of the poem, "Une saison en enfer" ("A season in hell") by Rimbaud, a poet to whom, not without reason, Césaire has often been compared. In any case, it appears to us perfectly valid: The tortured inner experience of the author of the *Cahier* is truly a painful descent into hell.

15. See our definition of the escaped slave, chap. 17, note 19, below. In our text we refer to punishments really inflicted on slaves and mentioned in the Black Code: See Victor Schoelcher's book, *Esclavage et colonisation* (Paris: PUF, 1948).

mais au-dessus de nous, dans une voix qui vrille la
nuit et l'audience comme la pénétrance d'une guêpe
apocalyptique. Et la voix prononce que L'Europe
nous a pendant des siècles gavés de mensonges et
gonflés de pestilences,
car il n'est point vrai que l'œuvre de l'homme
est finie
que nous n'avons rien à faire au monde
que nous parasitons le monde
qu'il suffit que nous nous mettions au pas
du monde,
mais l'œuvre de l'homme vient seulement
de commencer
et il reste à l'homme à conquerir toute
interdiction immobilisée aux coins de sa
ferveur
et aucune race ne possède le monopole de
la beauté, de l'intélligence, de la force
et il est place pour tous au rendez-vous
de la conquête et nous savons maintenant
que le soleil tourne autour de notre terre
éclairant la parcelle qu'a fixée notre
volonté seule et que toute étoile chute de
ciel en terre à notre commandement sans
limite. [pp. 82–83]

[And now suddenly strength and life charge through me
....

And we are standing now, my country and I,
hair in the wind, my hand little now in its
enormous fist and the strength is not in us
but above us, in a voice that pierces the night and
the audience like an apocalyptic hornet. And
the voice proclaims that Europe for centuries
has stuffed us with lies and bloated us
with pestilence,
for it is not true that the work of man is finished
that there is nothing for us to do in this world
that we are parasites on this earth
that it is enough for us to keep in step with the world
but the work of man has only just begun
and it is up to man to vanquish all the
deprivations immobilized in the corners of his fervor
and no race has the monopoly of beauty, of
intelligence or strength.
And there is a place for all at the rendezvous
of conquest
and we know now that the sun turns around
our earth illuminating the portion that our will

alone has determined and that any star falls
from sky to earth at our limitless command.]

To face this new destiny, renewed strength is needed, "not date hearts, but men's hearts" (p. 84). The old negritude of the "good nigger to his kind master," that of the docile slaves or the assimilated Negroes who say to Europe: "Look, I know how to kow-tow like you, and like you, pay homage. After all, I'm no different than you. Pay no attention to my black skin: It's suntan" (p. 85)—that type of negritude must disappear.

Césaire predicts a future negritude when blacks will have won, along with their freedom, the right to be themselves:

> Je dis hurrah! La vieille négritude
> progressivement se cadavérise
> l'horizon se défait, recule et s'élargit
> et voici parmi des déchirements de nuages la
> fulgurance d'un signe
> le négrier craque de toute part . . . [pp. 86–87]

> La négraille aux senteurs d'oignon frit
> retrouve dans son sang répandu le goût
> amer de la liberté
> Et elle est debout la négraille
> ....
>
>   debout
>   et
>   libre [pp. 87–88]

> [I say hurrah! The old negritude is
> gradually dying
> its horizon breaks, recedes and broadens
> and through the shredding of the clouds the
> flashing of a sign
> the slave ship is breaking into pieces . . .

> Smelling of fried onions the niggertrash
> once more in their shed blood
> find the bitter taste of freedom
> And they stand tall the niggertrash
> ....
>
>   upright
>   and
>   free]

The poem concludes with this prophecy in a frenzied rhythm of happiness and dancing in the midst of which Césaire foresees the arrival of a time of brotherhood[16] and renews his vow of loyalty to his race:

16. Césaire has no desire to see blacks fall into the error of racism, for which he blames Europeans: "Keep me, my heart, from any hatred."

et le grand trou noir où je voulais me
noyer l'autre lune
c'est là que je veux pêcher maintenant
la langue maléfique de la nuit en son
immobile verrition! [p. 91]

[and the deep dark hole in which
I would have drowned myself
a moon ago
There is where I want to fish now
for the evil tongue of night
in its immutable truth!]

The *Cahier* traces a sure and certain dramatic progression. We confess, however, that it was only after several careful readings that we were able to discover the various connecting links of its drama. Carrying the reader along as if in the current of a wild, swift stream, broken here and there by rapids, it appears to have been written in a single sitting. But one must not forget that Césaire worked on it for more than a year.

It begins with slowly flowing stanzas in prose, reciting each rosary bead of the ills and afflictions of "this city, flat, exposed." A short phrase, constantly repeated, connects these sad pictures: "Au bout du petit matin . . ." ("Shortly after dawn"). The phrase evokes the clear, lucid but occasionally cruel gaze of the young Césaire who frankly admits his country's ugliness and the apathy of its inhabitants. Beneath his gaze, Martinique rotting in quagmire appears monstrous, and Césaire's tone, which tries to be detached, allows his anguish and disgust to seep through as he describes these "stranded Antilles" and their sinister retinue: "the maimings, the itchings, the rashes, the warm hammocks of degeneracy" (p. 31). One solitary moment of intense joy, when he evokes festivities at Christmas, does not counterbalance the poet's feeling of repulsion; it scarcely interrupts the flow of his painful memories.

The style exactly matches "scrofulous glandular swelling" (p. 31) of this tide. It creeps along, it too trapped on this absurd, beggarly island, this "little ellipsoidal nothing" (p. 43), where anguish accumulates like heaps of rubbish.

Une détresse cette plage elle aussi, avec ses tas d'ordure pourrissant, ses croupes furtives qui se soulagent, et le sable est noir, funèbre, on n'a jamais vu un sable si noir, et l'écume glisse dessus en glapissant, et la mer la frappe à grands coups de boxe, ou plutôt la mer est un gros chien qui lèche et mord la plage aux jarrets, et à force de la mordre elle finira par la dévorer, bien sûr, la plage et la rue Paille avec. [pp. 38–39]

[The beach appalling too with its heaps of rotting garbage, furtive rumps relieving themselves, and the sand black, funereal—never has one seen sand so black—with sea-froth slithering over it with a yelping sound, and the sea striking great blows, or rather the sea is like a huge dog licking and biting the beach, biting it so fiercely that it will finally devour it, the beach and the rue Paille along with it.]

Césaire's prose, usually so rich, so abundant, seems completely paralyzed here. He seeks in vain for words powerful enough to express his loathing and disgust. Nor are the images strong enough or precise enough. He strings them together with a lot of "ands" and "or rather," as if the very awkwardness of his style was more appropriate to the impression he wished to create, and as if this casual way of writing could better show us the customary filth and ugliness of his beach.

The whole of his literary effort is to free himself from this too sickening reality, in order to prophesy and re-create, by the magic of the Word, the new desired world. Not an idealistic, abstract, absolute attempt! Césaire is not one to be satisfied with verbal pictures. He does not abandon his people. It is *with* them that he wishes to create this new purified world. His words will attempt to "regenerate his fellow men,"[17] to call upon their secret energies, summon them to action and a return to life.

The long description of Martinique's afflictions leads to the exceedingly weary desire "to leave"!

The course of the poem, regular and monotonous up till now, breaks into rapids, omitting conjunctions and adverbs, leaping from one image to another without any commas, knocking out uneven lines, continuing on very jerkily, occasionally reaching more tranquil, recitative passages where punctuation often becomes more normal:

> . . . et toi terre tendue
> terre saoule
> terre grand sexe levé vers le soleil
> terre grand délire de la mentule de Dieu
> terre sauvage montée des resserres de la mer avec dans la bouche une
>   touffe de cécropies
> terre dont je ne puis comparer la face houleuse qu'à la forêt vierge
>   et folle que je souhaiterais pouvoir en guise de visage montrer aux
>   yeux indéchiffreurs des hommes
> il me suffirait d'une gorgée de ton lait jiculi pour qu'en toi je découvre
>   toujours à même distance de mirage—mille fois plus natale et
>   dorée d'un soleil que n'entame nul prisme—la terre où tout est
>   libre et fraternel, ma terre [p. 41]

17. The Yugoslav scholar P. Guberina's original phrase, used in his preface to the 1956 edition of the *Cahier*.

[. . . and you taut earth
drunken earth
great phallus earth thrusting toward the sun
great delirious earth of God's mentula
wild earth risen from the sea's hold with a clump of cecropia trees in
   your mouth
earth whose hostile face I can only compare to the mad virgin forest
   I would like to show to men's indecipherable eyes in place of a face
one drop of your jiculi milk would suffice
   for me to discover in you the ever distant
   mirage—a thousand times more native
   and golden from a sun no prison can
   alter—that earth where all are
   free and fraternal, my earth]

From this point on, the *Cahier* continues, alternating rhythmic poetry with prose passages never more than two pages long. Was there
an organic reason for this construction, or is it only a literary device?
This is what we must now discover.

We have said Césaire wished to disengage himself from a reality that
was obsessive. Senghor writes that Césaire used his pen "the way Louis
Armstrong uses his trumpet, or more exactly perhaps, as the Voodoo
faithful use their tom-toms. Césaire needs to lose himself in a *verbal*
dance to the rhythm of a tom-tom, in order to rediscover himself in
the cosmos."[18] We fully agree with Senghor's judgment, adding that
Césaire's method, even if it is a more natural one, has no other aim,
and is of the same kind as Rimbaud's use of opium or Henri Michaux's
of mescaline. Césaire's "verbal tom-tom" follows a fairly simple
rhythm, dictated by the poet's emotion or by his search for a corresponding harmony. It is often marked by a downbeat on the first
words, repeated at the beginning of the line.[19]

Ce qui est à moi
c'est un homme seul emprisonné de
blanc
c'est un homme seul qui défie les cris
blancs de la mort blanche
(TOUSSAINT, TOUSSAINT
LOUVERTURE)

c'est un homme qui fascine l'épervier blanc de la mort
   blanche
c'est un homme seul dans la mer inféconde de sable blanc
c'est un moricaud vieux dressé contre les eaux du ciel

18. L. S. Senghor, *Ethiopiques* (Paris: Seuil, 1956), p. 118.
19. Mme Elyane Boucquey has carefully emphasized this in her thesis, already quoted.

La mort décrit un cercle brillant au-dessus de cet homme
la mort étoile doucement au-dessus de sa tête
la mort souffle, folle, dans la cannaie mûre de ses bras
la mort galope dans la prison comme un cheval blanc
la mort luit dans l'ombre comme des yeux de chat
la mort hoquète comme l'eau sous les Cayes
la mort est un oiseau blessé
la mort décroît
la mort vacille
la mort est un patyura ombrageux
la mort expire dans une blanche mare
   de silence. [pp. 45–46]

[This is mine
a man alone
imprisoned in white
a man alone who defies the white
cries of white
death
(TOUSSAINT, TOUSSAINT
LOUVERTURE)

a man who fascinates the white
hawk of white
death
a man alone in a sterile sea of white
snow
an old darky standing tall
against the waters of the sky
Death traces a shining circle
above this man
gently sprinkling stars about his head
Death breathes madly in the ripe canefield of his arms
Death gallops in the prison like a white horse
Death gleams in the darkness
with cat's eyes
Death hiccups
like the water underneath the quays
Death is a wounded bird
Death wanes
wavers
Death is a great shady tree
Death expires in a white
pool of silence.]

"A man alone," repeated at the beginning of the introductory lines, emphasizes the poet's admiration for his hero. But death appears and from this point on, it is death that gives urgency to the rhythm. It circles above Toussaint, embraces him, penetrates him and soon possesses him entirely. The rhythm grows slower, more staccato as he succumbs—until finally it expands outward in the last two lines suggesting final peace and silence!

A word, an image, can also unleash in the poet a violent reaction that results in a change of rhythm. As we have seen, the very mention of leaving the West Indies is so disturbing that the poem suddenly reflects that sharp emotion. Césaire reacts in the same manner when he recalls the resignation of the "good nigger toward his kind master" in the face of injustice and ill treatment. We feel his anger gradually mounting. With the ending of his evocation on the word "négraille" ("niggertrash"), the insult stings him personally. He breaks loose, hurling his shouts at us as if to the beat of African war drums:

> Et elle est debout la négraille
> la négraille assise
> inattendument debout
> debout dans la cale
> debout dans les cabines
> debout sur le pont
> debout dans le vent
> debout dans le soleil
> debout dans le sang
>   debout
>   et
>   libre [pp. 87–88]

> [And the niggertrash rises
> the niggertrash that was sitting down
> unexpectedly rises
> rises in the hold
> rises in the cabins
> rises on the bridge
> rises into the wind
> rises into the sun
> rises in blood
>   upright
>   and
>   free]

Not only is the rhythm closely wed to the emotion, but it provokes and maintains it. The poet uses it to reach, by degrees, a sort of secondary state, in which he will participate in the creative power of the cosmos.[20] His poetry takes on the aspect of incantation. Held in

20. A ritual process fairly common to many religions, with the aim of putting man in

thrall by the power of words and images which increase his inner tension, the poet gives free rein to his thoughts, becoming a magi or medium. His words seem charged with supernatural power. They cease to be words and become "parts of a world . . . delirious continents . . . swamp fevers . . . lavas . . . blazing cities" (p. 55).

He makes threats and his anger is dreadful. Words lose their usual meaning to take on an obscure significance and form baffling pictures.

> Parfois on me voit d'un grand geste du
> cerveau, happer un nuage trop rouge
> ou une caresse de pluie, ou un prélude
> du vent,
> ne vous tranquilisez pas outre mesure:
> Je force la membrane vitélline qui me
> sépare de moi-même,
> Je force les grandes eaux qui me ceinturent de sang
> C'est moi rien que moi qui arrête ma
> place sur le dernier train de la dernière
> vague du dernier raz de marée
> C'est moi rien que moi
> qui prends langue avec la dernière
> angoisse
> C'est moi oh, rien que moi
> qui m'assure au chalumeau
> les premières gouttes de lait virginal! [pp. 55–56]

> [Sometimes I am seen with a vast mental
> gesture to grab a too red cloud,
> or the rain's caress, or a prelude
> of the wind
> Do not calm yourselves unduly:
> I am breaking the vitelline membrane which
> separates me from my self,
> I am breaking the waters which girdle me with blood
> It is I, I alone who can hold my
> seat on the last train of the last
> billow of the final tidal wave
> It is I, I alone
> who can give tongue at the final
> anguish
> It is I, oh I alone
> who with a straw will sip
> the first drops of virginal milk!]

---

contact with the higher Powers. Indispensable in African ceremonies and especially in voodoo rites, where "possession" is obtained only by means of a series of incantations. This is also present in litanies, in the telling of beads and in Christian prayers.

But these hypnotic trances are not the ultimate state of Césaire's poetic impulse. Through them he tries to attain ecstasy. The attempts often fail, the inspiration carrying the poet sinks and abandons him, disappointed, once more immobilized.

Sur cette terre exorcisée, larguée à la dérive de sa précieuse intention maléfique, cette voix qui crie, lentement enrouée, vainement, vainement enrouée et il n'y a que les fientes accumulées de nos mensonges—et qui ne répondent pas. [p. 59]

[Upon this exorcized world, cast off to the drifting of its precious, evil purpose, this shouting voice, slowly getting hoarse, vainly, vainly hoarse and there is nothing left but the accumulated droppings of our lies—which do not reply.]

Césaire now returns to recitative prose, describing, enumerating or reasoning. His words are tame once more. He becomes as precise and detailed in describing reality as he was previously surreal in the poetry. Take, for example, the few lines describing a "comical and ugly Negro" marked by poverty and misfortune, "whose clawmarks on his face had healed in scabby islands."

On voyait très bien comment le pouce industrieux et malveillant avait modelé le front en bosse, percé le nez de deux tunnels parallèles et inquiétants, allongé la démesure de la lippe, et par un chef-d'œuvre caricatural, raboté, poli, verni la plus minuscule mignonne petite oreille de la création.[21] [p. 64]

[The industrious malevolent thumb, one could see, had shaped his forehead with a lump, pierced the nose with two parallel alarming tunnels, elongated the huge lip, and in a masterstroke of caricature had planed, polished, and varnished the tiniest, most adorable little ear in all creation.]

But the description of this reality quickly provokes loathing and revolt, dynamic feelings that call for the transformation of a situation now unbearable. Once more the rhythm changes from prose to verse. Once more Césaire becomes witch doctor, Oracle. He makes prophesies, exorcizes, conjures. At last the trances lead to a "state of grace." The prophet then becomes a demigod, re-creating in words the world of his desire, marvelously crystallized in his poems. No longer anger, clenched hands, or gnashing teeth, but a free gushing forth of joy, where the soul is peaceful, releasing tenderness and love.

> il y a sous la réserve de ma luette une bauge de sangliers
> il y a tes yeux qui sont sous la pierre grise du jour un conglomérat
> frémissant de coccinelles

21. Occasionally the qualities of this prose form real poems which could be taken out of the context of the *Cahier* because of their individual merit, as for example, the picture of the Negro, a passage of which we quote, and the description of Christmas in the West Indies (pp. 33–36) or the parable of the Martiniquan horse traders (pp. 60–61).

il y a dans le regard du désordre cette hirondelle de menthe
et de genêt qui fond pour toujours renaître dans le raz-de-maree de
    ta lumiére

Calme et berce ô ma parole l'enfant qui ne sait pas que la
carte du printemps est toujours à refaire
les herbes balanceront pour le bétail vaisseau doux de l'espoir
le long geste d'alcool de la houle
les étoiles du chaton de leur bague jamais vue
couperont les tuyaux de l'orgue de verre du soir
puis répandront sur l'extrémité riche de ma fatigue
des zinnias
des coryanthes
et toi veuille astre de ton lumineux fondement tirer lémurien du
sperme insondable de l'homme
la forme non osée
que le ventre tremblant de la femme porte tel un minerai! [pp. 69–70]

[Beneath the discretion of my uvula there is a lair of wild boars
There are your eyes, ladybirds quivering in the grey stone day

there in the disorderly look is this swallow made of mint
and gorse which melts in order always
to be reborn in the tidal wave of your light

May my words calm and soothe the child who does not know the
map of springtime must always be drawn anew
the grasses will sway for the cattle, gentle vessels of hope
the long drunken swell of the sea
the stars in the setting of a never-seen ring
will cut through the crystal organ pipes of evening and
then spread across the rich extremity of my fatigue
zinnias
coryanthases
and you star from your luminous buttocks may you draw forth a
    family
of lemurs
from the unfathomable sperm of man
inaudacious shape
that woman's trembling womb carries like a mineral!]

These moments are rare, alas! One—midway in the *Cahier*—begins
with the above quoted excerpt; another consists of the last three pages
of the poem and shows very well how, emerging from the violent
incantatory rhythm that follows the line "And the niggertrash rises,"
Césaire becomes a demigod, master of life who has the power to call
forth the forces of nature:

et . . .
par la mer cliquetante de midi

par le soleil bourgeonnant de minuit
écoute épervier qui tiens les clefs de l'orient
par le jour désarmé
par le jet de pierre de la pluie
écoute squale qui veille sur l'occident
écoutez chien blanc du nord, serpent
noir du midi
qui achevez le ceinturon du ciel
Il y a encore une mer à traverser
oh encore une mer à traverser
pour que j'invente mes poumons
pour que le prince se taise
pour que la reine me baise
encore un veillard à assassiner
un fou à délivrer
pour que mon âme luise aboie luise
aboie aboie aboie
et que hullule la chouette mon bel ange curieux
Le maître des rires?
Le maître du silence formidable?
Le maître de l'espoir et du désespoir?
Le maître de la paresse? Le maitre des danses?
C'est moi! [p. 89]

[and . . .
through the noontime clicking of the sea
through the budding sun at midnight
listen sweepnet that holds the keys to the orient
disarmed by the day
by the hurtling stones of rain
listen dogfish that guards the occident
listen white dog of the north
black serpent of noon
who complete the girdling of the sky
there is still an ocean to cross
still a sea to cross
so that I may invent my lungs
so that the prince will be quiet
so that the queen will kiss me
still an old man to assassinate
a madman to rescue
so that my soul may shine bark shine
bark bark bark
and so that the owl my beautiful serious angel may hoot
Master of laughter?
Master of formidable silence?

Master of hope and despair?
Master of laziness? Dancing master?
It is I!]

These moments are also very brief. Scarcely are they reached but the poet already feels they are escaping him and tries to prolong them with a prayer. It is not to God that Césaire prays.[22] He draws from these too brief moments of ecstasy the strength to continue the mission he has given himself and vows to remain faithful to his race, to give it access to the pure universe he has glimpsed:

Mais avant d'aborder aux futurs vergers
donnez-moi de les mériter sur leur ceinture de mer
donnez-moi mon cœur en attendant le sol
....

donnez-moi sur cet océan divers
l'obstination de la fière pirogue
et sa vigueur marine. [pp. 75–76]

Et pour ce, Seigneur,
les hommes au cou frêle
reçois et perçois fatal calme triangulaire. [p. 90]

[But before reaching the orchards of tomorrow
let me deserve them on their girdle of sea
give me my heart while awaiting the earth
....

give me on this various ocean
the stubborness of a proud canoe
and its nautical vigor.

And for this, oh Lord,
may men with frail necks
receive and perceive fatal triangular calm.]

Such are the main points in the structure of the *Cahier*, its relation to what we might call Césaire's psychological motivation. Let us now examine the style.

We have already spoken of the *Cahier*'s rhythm—an important characteristic, for Césaire is a Negro and therefore does not separate poetry from rhythm, as we will demonstrate later at length with Senghor. Many pages of the *Cahier* are in prose, however, and Césaire does not have so personal a poetic rhythm as Senghor. How is it, then, that we immediately recognize his stamp?

Above all by the images, the first and principal quality of which is the brutal expression of the poet's desire and obsession. Césaire's

22. Interview with Césaire, June 1959.

emotions coagulate in poetic pictures that are often surprising, revealing an alien reality with an extraordinary precision. Words and feelings have rarely fused to such a degree.

> la rauque contrebande de mon rire . . . [p. 47]

> Iles tronçons côte à côte fichés sur l'épée flambée du Soleil . . . [p. 80]

> Et le navire lustral s'avancer impavide sur les eaux écroulées . . . [p. 88]

> Et maintenant pourrissent nos flocs d'ignominie! [p. 89]

> Sous la syzgie suppurante des ampoules, merveilleusement couché le corps de mon pays dans le desespoir de mes bras, ses os ébranlés et, dans ses veines, le sang qui hesite comme la goutte de lait végétal à la pointe blessée du bulbe . . . [p. 82]

> [the harsh contraband of my laughter . . .

> Island stumps thrust side by side upon a flaming sword the Sun . . .

> And the lustral ship fearlessly advancing on the tumbled waters . . .

> And now our splashes of ignominy are rotting!

> Beneath the suppurating syzygy of blisters, the body of my country marvelously recumbent in the despair of my arms, its bones shaking and in its veins the blood hesitating like a drop of vegetal milk at the wounded point of the bulb . . .]

When his emotion is too sharp and he wishes to describe the still nonexistent world of his desire, where we would be wordless because ordinary vocabulary would prove insufficient, Césaire finds the rare words, invents neologisms, creates baffling associations. It is not necessary to understand the meaning: The words are chosen for what we may call their texture, for their sound. To pronounce them is sufficient to make "palpable" the emotion that inspires them.

Those gluey pictures describing the West Indies result in the following text:

Ici la parade des risibles et scrofuleux bubons, les poutures de microbes très étranges, les poisons sans alexitère connu, les sanies de plaies bien antiques, les fermentations imprévisibles d'espèces putrescibles. [p. 31]

[Here the parade of ludicrous scrofulous bubos, the cultures of very strange microbes, the poisons with no known antidotes, the pus of very ancient wounds, the unpredictable fermentations of putrescible species.]

We share the author's disgust at this mass of suffering and foul rot, at the mere sound of these exceptional words—scrofulous, bubos, cultures, antidotes, pus—even if their exact meaning escapes us.

Further on, his exacerbated revolt seeks the destruction of this "horizon of mud" (p. 79) projecting pictures of a world in a state of disorderly fusion:

> nous chantons des fleurs vénéneuses
> éclatant dans des prairies furibondes;
> les ciels d'amour coupés d'embolie, les matins épiléptiques; le
> blanc embrasement des sables abyssaux, les déscentes d'épaves dans
> les nuits foudroyés d'odeurs fauves. [p. 53]

> [we sing of poisonous flowers
> blooming in furious fields;
> skies of love interrupted with embolisms, epileptic mornings, the
> white fiery glow of abyssal sands, flotsam and jetsam descending
> into thundering nights filled with wild odors.]

Occasionally Césaire is satisfied to apply the usual surrealist technique of haphazardly associating odd pictures. The result reminds one of certain Salvador Dali paintings, but to the extent that internal consistency is not required, it seems a practice without originality:

Et vous fantômes montez bleus de chimie d'une forêt de bêtes traquées de machines tordues d'un jujubier de chairs pourries d'un panier d'huîtres d'yeux d'un lacis de lanières découpées dans le beau sisal d'une peau d'homme j'aurais des mots assez vastes pour vous contenir [pp. 40–41]

[And you phantoms rise chemically blue from a forest of hunted animals of twisted machines of jujube trees of putrefied flesh of baskets of oysters of eyes of a lacing of leather strips cut from the beautiful sisal of human skin I shall have words vast enough to contain you]

Reality speaks with another voice! Fortunately, however, these passages occur rarely. Usually the text reveals a new, free universe where each word has a precise, often symbolical weight, reinforcing the image:

Les herbes balanceront pour le bétail vaisseau doux de l'espoir le long geste d'alcool de la houle. [p. 70]

[Grasses will wave for the cattle gentle vessels of hope the long alcoholic swell of the sea.]

Grasses and plants represent for Césaire nature's spontaneous life, and cattle are a sign of prosperity, just as the swell, which indicates water and the sea, is a promise of intoxicating fecundity ("long alcoholic swell").

Il y a tes yeux qui sont sous la pierre grise du jour un conglomérat frémissant de coccinelles [p. 69]

[There are your eyes, quivering swarm of ladybirds on a grey stone day]

Hope, which floods the preceding pages, is concentrated here in the luminous eyes of his young wife. Where we might be content to say sparkling with a "thousand lights," Césaire finds the word "ladybirds." The promise of happiness becomes even more palpable when we know that while Césaire was composing the *Cahier,* his wife was pregnant[23] —a fact evoked again a little later.[24]

The importance of symbols is so great in the *Cahier* that many images need to be clarified in order to be fully appreciated. This happens when one understands the secret overtones of certain key words which reappear throughout the text. The following excerpt includes many of them:

j'entendais monter de l'autre côté du désastre, un fleuve de tourterelles et de trèfles de la savane que je porte toujours dans mes profondeurs à hauteur inverse du vingtième étage des maisons les plus insolentes et par précaution contre la force putréfiante des ambiances crépusculaires, arpentée nuit et jour d'un sacré soleil vénérien. [p. 25–26]

[from the other side of the disaster I could hear a stream of doves and of savannah clover which I always carry deep within me to the reverse height of the twentieth story of the most insolent houses and as a precautionary measure against the putrefying power of twilight atmosphere, surveyed day and night by a sacred venereal sun.]

The disaster represents the past horrors of colonization; the stream, as running water, brings purification that will permit a new life.[25] Birds and plants are always symbols of hope and untrammeled life. Savannahs and virgin forests indicate sources of freedom and authenticity, in contrast to cities, tall buildings and the like—for Césaire, synonyms of European domination. Finally, twilight atmospheres and nocturnal shadow accompany misfortune and despair. The sun and the stars, on the other hand, represent the light of exultant joy; in the West Indian night "the stars are more dead than a broken *balafong*"[26] (p. 32),

23. Interview with Mme Suzanne Césaire, January 1960.
24. See complete text, pp. 236–37: "May my words calm and soothe the child who. . . ."
25. See detailed application of the symbol of purifying water, p. 241.
26. *Balafong:* a xylophone with thin wooden slats, the frame of which is fixed on calabashes which form the sound boxes.

whereas we see them participate, with the sun and the wind, in the final apotheosis* (p. 91).

Together with the use of personal images, a second particularity of Césaire's style is his syntax. To use Senghor's expression, Césaire is "the magnificent master of his language."[27] He breaks it, mixes it, forges and rebuilds it. His sentences often appear rough, knotty, heavily laden. One could describe Césaire's poetry as "sculptured"; he uses language as a substance carving shapes from it as if in wood or stone. Without fear of subverting established grammatical usage, he displaces adjectives, omits verbs to make his images more suggestive, just as Picasso deforms objects in order to give them more truly the shape of his own perceptions.

Au bout du petit matin, ce plus essentiel pays restitué à ma gourmandise, non de diffuse tendresse, mais la tourmentée concentration sensuelle du gras téton des mornes avec l'accidentel palmier comme son germe durci. . . . [pp. 32–33]

[Shortly after dawn, this most essential land returned to my greediness, not tenderly diffuse, but the tormented sensuous concentration of these fat, teat-like hillocks with an accidental palm tree as their hardened offshoot. . . .]

Elsewhere he accumulates adjectives to emphasize the picture and fix it in our minds, or else he will use simple enumeration—an incantatory litany:

Au bout du petit matin, cette ville plate—étalée, trébuchée de son bon sens, inerte, essouflée sous son fardeau géométrique de croix éternellement recommençante, indocile à son sort, muette, contrariée de toutes façons, incapable de croître selon le suc de cette terre, embarrassée, rognée, réduite, en rupture de faune et de flore. [p. 27]

[This flat city shortly after dawn, exposed, stumbling commonsensically along, inert, breathless beneath its geometric load of crosses eternally renewed, intractable before its fate, mute, thwarted in every way, incapable of growing according to the essence of this earth, cut down, encumbered, reduced, ruptured from fauna and flora.]

Virginie. Tennessee. Géorgie. Alabama.
Putréfactions, monstrueuses de révoltes
inopérantes,
marais de sang putrides
trompettes absurdement bouchées

* Translator's note: With regard to Césaire's symbolism, see Mme Kesteloot's study of the poet in the Seghers "Poètes d'Aujourd'hui" series.
27. L. S. Senghor, *Ethiopiques*, p. 115.

Terres rouges, terres sanguines, terres
consanguines. [p. 45]

Au bout du petit matin, flaques perdues,
parfumes errants, ouragans échoués, co-
ques, dématées, vieilles plaies, os pour-
ris, buées, volcans enchaînés, morts mal
racinés, crier amer. [p. 81]

[Virginia. Tennessee. Georgia. Alabama.
Monstruous putrefaction of inoperative
revolts,
swamps of putrid blood
trumpets absurdly stopped
Red lands, sanguine
consanguine.

Shortly after dawn, lost puddles,
vagrant odors, stranded hurricanes
dismasted hulls, old sores, rotting
bones, vapors, chained volcanos, ill-
rooted dead, bitter cries.]

One must not, however, imagine that Césaire was incapable of being
classical. If he does violence to the French language to express an
extraordinary emotion, he also knows how to ply it with order and
harmony, to tighten his style into more regular lines:

voum rooh oh
pour que revienne le temps de pro-
mission
et l'oiseau qui savait mon nom
et la femme qui avait mille noms
de fontaine de soleil et de pleurs
et ses cheveux d'alevin
et ses pas mes climats
et ses yeux mes saisons
et les jours sans nuisance
et les nuits sans offense
et les etoiles de confidence
et le vent de connivence. [p. 52]

[voom rooh oh
so that the pro-
mised times return
and the bird who knew my name
and the woman with a thousand names
of fountain of fun and tears

and her hair made of sea creatures
and her footsteps my climate
and her eyes my seasons
and the days without injury
and the nights without offense
and the intimate stars
and complicitous wind.]

The third characteristic of Césaire's style to which we must call attention is the "always major quality of tone" André Breton discovered in his work, by means of which, Breton said, one recognizes great poets. Césaire has a sense of grandeur. Whether he grieves or hopes, is ironic, accusing or triumphant, he is never mean or petty; his insults are never vulgar, nor his demands shabby. As we have seen, he is not afraid of words, nor does he disdain the colloquial turn of phrase: "Poverty certainly had done its best to finish him off"[28]—"and we eat well and drink the cup that cheers, and there's sausage. . . ."[29] But no matter how he humbles himself, burdens himself with shame, his stature is greater than ours, even in the moments of defeat: "We vomited from the slaveships—We hunted in the Calebars. . . ."[30]"I prefer to admit that I have been gallantly raving, my heart in my brain like a drunken knee—my star now, the funereal menfenil."[31]

In Césaire we rediscover the mobility of Greek tragedy, and we are tempted to say of him, with the chorus of his *Et les chiens se taisaient* ("And the dogs grew silent"):

Il est Roi. . . .
il n'en a pas le titre, mais bien sûr il est roi[32]

[He is King. . . .
he doesn't have the title, but he surely is a king]

The *Cahier* was published almost *in toto* in 1939 in the journal *Volontés*, but went unnoticed by the Parisian public. A first bilingual (French-Spanish) edition of the work appeared in 1944 in Cuba, and was not published in full in France until 1947 in the Bordas edition, prefaced by an article on Césaire that André Breton had written in

28. "Portrait d'un nègre," *Cahier*, p. 64.
29. "Noël antillais," p. 34.
30. Ibid., p. 63.
31. *Cahir*, p. 66. The menfenil is a West Indian bird of prey.
32. Aimé Césaire, "Et les chiens se taisaient," in *Les armes miraculeuses* (Paris: NRF, Gallimard, 1946), p. 164.

1944 for the magazine *Fontaine*.[33] Présence Africaine published a new and revised edition of the *Cahier* in 1956. Sartre did not hide his own lyrical admiration for the poem in the 1948 essay "Orphée noir." Nonetheless, this black poet "who manipulates the French language as no white man can today"[34] remains almost unknown to the general public, and barely known in literary circles.[35]

It is true that Césaire is a difficult poet. Compared to collections of his later poems, in which his language becomes increasingly hermetic and surrealist, as will be shown in chapter 18, the *Cahier* is easily accessible. Several pages in the later books are so magnificent that the style of the *Cahier* seems rather simple and impoverished. Yet this did not bring Césaire closer to a general readership. *Les armes miraculeuses, Et les chiens se taisaient* (1946), and *Soleil cou coupé* (1948) are full of precious stones that one discovers only if one has the courage to penetrate wild jungle. In *Corps perdu* (1950) and *Ferrements* (1960) Césaire goes beyond the surrealism which nourished his early development to achieve a completely personal poetry, free of any influence, thus reaching the summit of his art.

Césaire's poems must be approached as gently as wild birds: They cannot be grasped immediately, they must be tamed. After understanding their general sense by means of the tone and dominating images, we must dig for the meaning of each association of words and ideas. Even then, many details escape us. Césaire often includes in his poems events from his personal life, memories which he alone can explain. Sometimes, as with many writers, the entire poem is built around such an event without its being clearly mentioned. For example, the poem "Séisme" ("Earthquake") in *Ferrements* was written after the poet's break with the Communist Party.

> tant de grands pans de rêve
> de parties d'intimes patries
> effondrées
> tombées vides et le sillage sàli sonore de l'idée [p. 10]

> [so many great sections of dreams
> parts of fallen secret homelands
> fallen empty and their soiled wakes echoing the idea]

33. André Breton, "Un grand poète noir," *Fontaine*, no. 35 (1944). [Translator's note: A small and little known bilingual French and English edition of the *Cahier* (translated by Ivan Goll and Lionel Abel as *Memorandum on My Martinique*) was published with the Breton preface by Brentano's in New York, also in 1947. The Cuban edition was illustrated by Wifredo Lam.]

34. A. Breton, "Un grand poète noir."

35. It is only during the last few years, that Pierre de Boisdeffre and Gaëtan Picon, two of the best French literary critics, have finally broken their silence.

In similar fashion the poet makes frequent allusion either to West Indian history (Toussaint Louverture, Messrs. de Fourniol and de la Mahaudière, the Black Code and runaway slaves), or to West Indian folklore. He includes names of equatorial fauna and flora (mangrove fruit, spondias, payturas, icacos, manchineel trees, "coccolobes") which are part of his universe, just as the Duke of Alba's oak tree and the reeds in "Till Eulenspiegel" are part of Europe's.

All of these are foreign elements that may easily discourage a Westerner, particularly if one adds to them the unusual words and symbols we have already mentioned. Césaire has an extraordinarily wide vocabulary. An "agrégé de lettres,"* the poet works without a dictionary, but his readers often have to refer to one in order to understand his poems! The liberties taken by Césaire are not, however—as Sartre once thought—meant to "destroy" the colonizer's language,[36] but to remold it, as Sartre later suggests,[37] in order to fit it exactly to his negritude. In this, Césaire does not differ from other Western poets, because

poetry worthy of the name is judged by its degree of abstention, the refusal it implies. . . . It is reluctant to accept the already seen, heard, agreed upon, or to employ what has already been used. Césaire in this respect is particularly hard to please, not only because he is integrity itself, but still more because of the greater scope of his knowledge.[38]

The French language emerges considerably enriched, but is no longer a vehicle of Western thought. Other themes, another style, another sensibility! It is quite a foreign universe that is revealed to us. "Before Césaire, West Indian literature was a literature by Europeans."[39]

If Césaire's work requires effort—as does the poetry of Mallarmé or Eluard—what recompense is ours when we penetrate the secrets of these poems "always accessible to the sincerity of great thirst."[40]

* Translator's note: similar to the Ph.D. in literature.
36. J. P. Sartre, "Orphée noir," p. xx.
37. J. P. Sartre, "Présence noire," in the first issue of *Présence Africaine*.
38. A. Breton, "Un grand poète noir."
39. Frantz Fanon, quoted by D. Guérin in *Les Antilles décolonisées*, p. 91.
40. Aimé Césaire, "Patience des signes," in *Ferrements*, p. 39.

13/ Léopold Senghor:
Chants d'ombre and *Hosties noires*

Léopold Sédar Senghor was attracted to poetry very early. As a lycée student in Dakar, he was composing romantic verse even before he developed an enthusiasm for Corneille and Racine. In Paris, Senghor discovered Péguy, then the modern European and American Negro poets. Later on, while studying for his degree in literature, he read the works of the medieval troubadors and a great deal of Claudel, but experimented with his own talent as a writer mainly by translating into French the poems of his homeland, Senegal.[1]

Much has been made of the profound influence of Saint-John Perse on Senghor. In the part of this chapter devoted to literary analysis, we shall show to what extent the discovery of Saint-John Perse influenced Senghor's style. Senghor did not yet know Perse's work when he composed his own first two books of poems, *Chants d'ombre* and *Hosties noires*,[2] whose major themes we now propose to analyze.

These poems were written between 1936 and 1945, not all at once like Césaire's *Cahier,* but at long intervals. Nor do they follow a psychological progression, like Damas's poems. Only a few of them are dated. Though we can place in time those which were written during World War II and perceive a definite evolution in the thinking, this is possible only occasionally in the other poems. The very first poem, "A l'appel de la race de Saba," which dates from 1936, already reveals the principal themes of Senghor's entire work.

1. The details given in this introduction were obtained in the course of an interview with L. S. Senghor in June 1959.
2. *Chants d'ombre* (Paris: Seuil, collection Pierres Vives, 1945). *Hosties noires* (ibid., 1948). Both reissued as one vol. in 1956. We give the title of each poem, indicating the collection to which it belongs by the letters *CO* or *HN.*

The downbeat of Senghor's negritude is unquestionably his "pilgrimage to the ancestral fountains," his return to Mother Africa, for him not at all "the imaginary continent"[3] invented by West Indians in the depths of their exile. Senghor did not need to make a great effort to rediscover his origins; they were close to him and nourished his youth. He had the privilege of being born in 1906 to a family of very un-Europeanized landowners who lived in an opulent "villa" that sheltered more than sixty persons, including servants. For many years he lived in Djilor and Joal, rural Senegalese villages, and did not attend a "white school" until the age of seven, when he entered the seminary at Ngasobil; he later on went to Dakar for his Latin humanities.[4] During that period, he used to come home to the village for his vacations.

Senghor thus knew his country, his "childhood kingdom," as he called it, extremely well, and was impregnated with its culture.

J'y ai vécu jadis, avec les bergers et les paysans . . . J'ai donc vécu en ce royaume, vu de mes yeux, de mes oreilles entendu les êtres fabuleux par delà les choses: les Kouss[5] dans les tamariniers,[6] les Crocodiles, gardiens des fontaines, les Lamantins,[7] qui chantaient dans la rivière, les Morts du village et les Ancêtres, qui me parlaient, m'initiant aux vérités alternées de la nuit et du midi. Il m'a donc suffi de nommer les choses, les éléments de mon univers enfantin, pour prophétiser la Cité de demain, qui renaîtra des cendres de l'ancienne, ce qui est la mission du poète.[8]

[I lived there long ago, among the shepherds and the farmers . . . I lived then in this kingdom, saw with my eyes, with my ears heard the fabulous beings beyond things; the ancestral spirits (the *Kouss*) in the tamarind trees; the crocodiles, guardians of the springs; the seacows who spoke to me, initiating me in turn to the truths of night and noon. It has therefore been enough for me to name these things, the elements of my childhood universe, to prophesy the City of tomorrow, which shall be born from the ashes of the ancient, which is the poet's mission.]

Senghor was rooted in this civilization which had survived the ancient Mali empire, assimilating both Islam and Christianity without losing any of its original traditions. His Africa was living, profuse, completely unlike Césaire's ("Bambara ancestors," his evocation of "the king of Dahomey's amazons") or Damas's ("till now I've kept the conical an-

3. This expression Sartre's, in "Orphée noir," p. xvi.
4. He wished to become a priest or a professor.
5. *Kouss:* genies, reminding one of the first inhabitants of black Africa, the Pygmies, who were exterminated or driven away by the Great Negroes.
6. Tamarind trees: large trees which grow in equatorial countries.
7. *Lamantins:* one of the herbiverous Sirenian mammals found in Africa and America, in river estuaries. In West African mythology they play a role similar to our Sirens. See Camara Laye's novel *Le regard du roi* (Paris: Plon, 1955).
8. L. S. Senghor, *Ethiopiques* (Paris: Seuil, 1956), p. 111.

cestral faith high among the rafters of my hut"), visions of a mother continent reduced to ethnological reminiscence or disembodied symbols.

Senghor's return to his native land was thus accomplished without any of the pain typical among the West Indians. His were only pleasant memories of a coddled childhood in the bosom of a family which formed a "large household, with its grooms, stablemen, shepherds, servants, and artisans."[9]

At nightfall, the house at Djilor was a veritable painting of biblical opulence.

> Je suis sur les marches de la demeure profonde obscurément.
> Mes frères et mes sœurs serrent contre mon cœur leur chaleur nombreuse de poussins.
> Je repose la tête sur les genoux de ma nourrice Ngâ, de Ngâ la poétesse.
> Ma tête bourdonnant au galop guerrier des dyoung-dyoungs, au grand galop de mon sang de pur sang.
> Ma tête mélodieuse des chansons lointaines de Koumba l'Orpheline.
> Au milieu de la cour, le ficus solitaire
> Et devisent à son ombre lunaire les épouses de l'Homme de leurs voix graves et profondes comme leurs yeux et les fontaines nocturnes de Fimla.
> Et mon père étendu sur des nattes paisibles, mais grand mais fort mais beau
> Homme du Royaume de Sine, tandis qu'alentour sur les kôras voix héroiques, les griots font danser leurs doigts de fougue
> Tandis qu'au loin monte, houleuse de senteurs fortes et chaudes, la rumeur classique de cent troupeaux.[10]

> [Dimly I am on the steps of the deep house
> My brothers and sisters press their incubating warmth against my heart
> I rest my head upon the knees of Ngâ my nurse, Ngâ the poetess
> Head throbbing with the warrior gallop of the dyoung-dyoung drums, with the racing of my blood's pure blood
> Head humming with the distant songs of Koumba—the Orphan Girl
> In the center of the court the solitary fig tree
> And chatting in its moonlit shade the Man's wives, voices grave and deep as their eyes and the nightime fountains of Fimla.
> And my father stretched out on peaceful mats so tall so strong so handsome a
> Man of the Kingdom of Sine, while about him on their kôras, griots with heroic voices make their ardent fingers dance

9. "Le retour de l'enfant prodigue," *CO*, p. 72.
10. "A l'appel de la race de Saba," *HN*, pp. 88–89. *Kôra* (line 9): a kind of Senegalese harp.

> While from afar with a sense of warm strong smells the classic sound
> of a hundred cattle rises.]

Senghor conserves the memory of a society deeply rooted in its traditions, its values and its history. One can certainly detect the traces of ethnology. It was surely not from the griots that Senghor learned that Pharoah "seated people on his right"[11] or that the glorious Gongo Moussa reigned from 1307 to 1332.[12] But certainly local myths and the genealogies of the dyalis[13] sang the glory of his forbears, who were cousins of Prince Koumba Ndofène, and recounted the sixteen-year struggle against the powerful Almamy of Fouta Djalon.[14]

> On nous tue, Almamy! On ne nous déshonore pas.
> Ni ces montagnes ne purent nous dominer ni ses cavaliers nous
> encercler ni sa peau claire nous séduire
> Ni nous abâtardir ses prophètes.[15]

> [They slaughter us, Almamy! We are not dishonored.
> Neither could these mountains rule us, nor his
> horsemen surround us, nor his bright skin seduce us
> Nor his prophets corrupt us.]

Two princesses of royal blood and their servants were able to escape the massacre:

> Et parmi elles, la mère de Sira-Badral, fondatrice de royaumes
> Qui sera le sel des Sérères, qui seront le sel des peuples salés[16]

> [And among them the mother of Sira-Badral, founder of kingdoms,
> Who would be the salt of the Serers, the salt of these salty people]

This historical past explains the moral values of that warrior and pastoral people—sobriety, a sharp sense of honor, scorn of money but love of the vital riches, children, and cattle:

> . . . minces étaient les désirs de leur ventre.
> Leur bouclier d'honneur ne les quittait jamais ni leur lance loyale
> Ils n'amassaient pas de chiffons, pas même de guinées à parer
> leurs poupées.
> Leurs troupeaux recouvraient leurs terres, telles leurs demeures
> à l'ombre divine des ficus

11. "Que m'accompagnent kôras et balafongs," *CO*, p. 49. Certain ethnologists, especially Frobenius, link African civilizations to those of ancient Egypt. See chap. 8 above.

12. Gongo Moussa: a prince of the Mandingo empire which covered the entire territory of former French West Africa.

13. *Dyali:* a griot attached to a Lord. See chap. 2, note 12, above.

14. Almamy: a Sudanese chief. Fouta Djalon: a mountain range in Guinea, and an ancient kingdom, conquered by the French in 1896, of which the capital was Timbe.

15. "Que m'accompagnent kôras et balafongs," *CO*, p. 46.

16. Ibid., p. 47.

Et craquaient leurs greniers de grains serrés d'enfants.
Voix du Sang! Pensées à remâcher![17]

[. . . sparse were the wants of their bellies.
Their shield of honor never left them nor their loyal lance
They amassed no silks not even cottons to decorate their darlings.
Their herds covered their lands, like their dwellings
   in the divine shade of fig trees
And their granaries creaked with grain stowed by children.
Voices of the Blood! Thoughts to ruminate upon!]

A simple and vigorous morality which was developed in an harmonious social order—disparaged by the West for reasons of their own[18]—where the prince was not a tyrant but the defender and guarantor of his subjects:

Tu n'es pas plante parasite sur l'abondance rameuse de ton
   peuple!
Ils mentent; tu n'es pas tyran, tu ne te nourris pas de sa graisse.
Tu es l'organe riche de réserves, les greniers qui craquent pour
   les jours d'épreuve
....
Voilà, tu es, pour écarter au loin l'ennemi, debout, le tata[19]
Je ne dis pas le silo, mais le chef qui organise la force qui forge le bras,
   mais la tête qui reçoit coups et boulets.
Et ton peuple s'honore en toi . . .[20]

[You are no parasitic plant on the vegetable abundance
   of your people!
They lie; you are no tyrant, you do not feed yourself upon their fat
You are the rich instrument of savings, granaries swollen for the days
   of sorrow
....
Behold you are upright, fortress to keep the enemy at bay
I do not call you silo but chief who gathers up the strength who
   strengthens the arm, but head who receives the blows and bullets
And you do honor to your people . . .]

Religious values give meaning to this universe and animate the cosmic life. The ancients initiate the young to these "forests of symbols"[21] whose poetry Senghor feels extremely deeply. The following poem, perhaps one of the most beautiful he has written, bears witness:

17. "Le message," *CO*, p. 26.
18. This is a thesis dear to Senghor. See, for example, his contribution to the joint work *L'homme de couleur*, and chap. 8 above.
19. *Tata*: fortress.
20. "Que m'accompagnent . . . ," *CO*, p. 48.
21. Baudelaire.

Tokô'Waly mon oncle, te souviens-tu des nuits de jadis quand
  s'appesantissait ma tête sur ton dos de patience?
Ou que me tenant par la main, ta main me guidait par ténèbres
  et signes?
Les champs sont fleurs de vers luisants; les étoiles se posent
  sur les herbes sur les arbres.
C'est le silence alentour.
Seuls bourdonnent les parfums de brousse, ruches d'abeilles
  rousses que domine la vibration grêle des grillons
Et tamtam voilé, la respiration au loin de la Nuit.
Toi, Tokô'Waly, tu écoutes l'inaudible
Et tu m'expliques les signes que disent les Ancêtres dans la
  sérénité marine des constellations
Le Taureau le Scorpion le Léopard, l'Eléphant les Poissons
  familiers
Et la pompe lactée des Esprits par le tann céleste qui ne finit
  point.[22]
Mais voici l'intélligence de la déesse Lune et que tombent les
  voiles des ténèbres.[23]

[Toko-Waly, my uncle, do you remember those long ago
  nights when my head grew heavy on your patient back?
Or how you took my hand in yours and guided me
  through signs and shadows?
The fields blossom with glow worms; stars alight
  in grass and trees.
There is silence all around
The only stirrings are the perfumes of the bush, hives
  of russet bees that dominate the crickets
And, muffled tom-tom, the distant breathing of the night.
You Toko-Waly, you hear what is inaudible
And explain to me the signs our forbears make
  in the marine serenity of the constellations
The Bull, the Scorpion, the Leopard, the Elephant
  and the familiar Fish
And the Spirits' milky splendor in the infinite celestial tann.
But here as veils of darkness fall is the Goddess Moon's intelligence.]

The poet, like every other African, learned nature's language very
early and lived in close relationship to Ancestors, whom he held in
veneration:

Je m'allonge à terre à vos pieds, dans la poussière de mes respects
A vos pieds, Ancêtres présents. . . .[24]

---

22. *Tann:* flat ground covered over by the sea during spring tides.
23. "Que m'accompagnent . . . ," *CO*, pp. 51–52.
24. "Le retour de l'enfant prodigue," *CO*, p. 73.

> [I stretch upon the earth at your feet, in the dust of my respect
> At your feet, Ancestors who are present. . . .]

He knew that the dead were not dead, that he himself was the "the grandfather of his grandfather . . . his soul and his ancestry,"[25] and he kept preciously secret "in [his] most intimate vein" the name of his totem, "My ancestor with the lightning-scarred, the stormy skin,"[26] the third name given at his initiation, which no African dares reveal for fear of putting himself in the hands of an enemy. Senghor acquired this knowledge during the long nights of Sine, nights which he evokes with warm fervor:

> Femme, allume la lampe au beurre clair, que causent autour les
>   Ancêtres comme les parents, les enfants au lit.
> Ecoutons la voix des Anciens d'Elissa. Comme nous exilés
> Ils n'ont pas voulu mourir, que se perdît par les sables leur
>   torrent séminal.
> Que j'écoute, dans la case enfumée que visite un reflet d'âmes
>   propices
> Ma tête sur ton sein chaud comme un dang au sortir du feu et
>   fumant
> Que je respire l'odeur de nos Morts, que je recueille et redise leur
>   voix vivante, que j'apprenne à
> Vivre avant de descendre, au-delà du plongeur, dans les hautes
>   profondeurs du sommeil.[27]

> [Woman, light the limpid butter lamp, so around it Ancestors can
>   come to chat like parents when their children are in bed.
> Let us listen to the Ancients of Elissa. Exiled, like us,
> They did not wish to die, or lose their fertile torrent
>   in the sands.
> Let me listen in the smoky hut where friendly souls
>   have come to visit
> My head upon your breast, warm as *couscous* newly
>   steaming from the fire
> Let me breathe the odor of our Dead, let me gather
>   and repeat their living voices, let me learn
> To live before I sink, deeper than a diver, into the
>   lofty depths of sleep.]

The nearness of the dead in no way depreciates life. Senghor tastes its fruits both as poet and artist. *Chants d'ombre* contains at least eight love poems, of which the most famous glorifies "Black woman":

25. "Que m'accompagnent . . . ," *CO*, p. 46.
26. "Le totem," *CO*, p. 33
27. "Nuit de Sine," *CO*, p. 18.

Femme nue, femme obscure
Fruit mûr à la chair ferme, sombres extases du
    vin noir, bouche qui fais lyrique ma bouche
Savane aux horizons purs, savane qui frémis aux
    caresses ferventes du Vent d'Est
Tamtam sculpté, tamtam tendu qui grondes sous les
    doigts du Vainqueur[28]

[Naked woman, dark woman
Firm fleshed ripe fruit, dark ecstasies of black wine,
    mouth that makes mine lyrical;
Savanna with pure horizons, trembling at the ardor
    of the East Wind's touch
Sculpted tom-tom, taut tom-tom murmuring
    beneath the Conqueror's fingers]

But in addition to love, there were the festivals, high points of community life, where Christian rites and native ceremonies mingled:

Je me rappelle les festins funèbres fumant du sang des troupeaux
    égorgés
Du bruit des querelles, des rhapsodies des griots.
Je me rappelle les voix païennes rythmant le *Tantum Ergo*,
Et les processions et les palmes et les arcs de triomphe.
Je me rappelle la danse des filles nubiles
Les chœurs de lutte—oh! la danse finale des jeunes hommes,
    buste
Penché élancé, et le pur cri d'amour des femmes—*Kor Siga!*[29]

[I remember funeral feasts steaming with the blood of
    slaughtered herds
The noise of quarrels, the griot's rhapsodies.
I remember pagan voices beating out the *Tantum Ergo,*
And the processions and the palms and the triumphal arches.
I recall the dance of the nubile girls
The battle songs—and oh!—the final dance of the young
    men, slender
Chests bent, and the women's pure love cry—*Kor Siga!*]

Yes, Africa truly lives in Senghor's poems! Yet he left it "for sixteen years of wandering" through a Europe he learned to know firsthand "in the narrow shadow of the Latin Muses,"[30] before becoming "a shepherd of blonde heads" at the lycée in Tours, and later in Paris: "good civil servant . . . good colleague, elegant, polite . . . Old France,

28. "Femme noire," *CO,* p. 21.
29. "Joal," *CO,* pp. 19–20.
30. "Que m'accompagnent . . . ," *CO,* p. 42.

old university, the works."[31] To all appearances, Senghor was perfectly assimilated.

Then why his unusual activity with *L'Etudiant Noir*? Why his defense of Africanism and support of anticolonialism as early as 1928?[32] For personal reasons, first of all. In Europe, Senghor felt lonely. There were very few African students in Paris in those days. Most of the blacks there were West Indians, and although they succeeded in creating a unity around a New Negro ideology, the various mentalities differed on many points. Damas regretted that he had never had a free childhood. Césaire—whose wife was expecting a second baby when the *Cahier* was published—was not homesick for his country but wished to transform it: His memories were painful. As for the solitary Senghor, "left to the hypocritical silence of this European night, held prisoner by white, cold, well-smoothed sheets and all the anguish and qualms which inextricably encumber me,"[33] he turned to the "paradise of his African childhood,"[34] to his friends there, crying out his immense nostalgia:

> Je t'écris parce que mes livres sont blancs comme l'ennui comme
> la misère et comme la mort.
> Faites-moi place autour du poêle, que je reprenne ma place
> encore tiède.
> Que nos mains se touchent en puisant dans le riz fumant de
> l'amitié
> Que les vieux mots sérères de bouche en bouche passent comme
> une pipe amicale.
> Que Dargui nous partage ses fruits succulents—foin de toute
> sécheresse parfumée!
> Toi, sers nous tes bons mots, énormes comme le nombril de
> l'Afrique prodigieuse.
> Quel chanteur ce soir convoquera tous les Ancêtres autour de
> nous
> Autour de nous le troupeau pacifique des bêtes de la brousse?
> Qui logera nos rêves sous les paupières des étoiles?[35]
>
> [I write to you because my books are white
> as boredom, misery and death.
> Make room for me around the pot, let me sit
> once more in the place still warm for me,
> Hands touching as we share the rice

31. Ibid., pp. 44–45.

32. Claude McKay mentions Senghor as representing the new ideas in Paris in *Banjo*, published in 1929.

33. "A l'appel de la race de Saba," *HN*, p. 87.

34. "Que m'accompagnent . . . ," *CO*, p. 41.

35. "Lettre à un prisonnier," *HN*, pp. 133–34.

that steams with friendship.
Let the old Serer words pass from mouth
to mouth like a friendly pipe.
May Dargui share his juicy fruits with us—
a harvest of all scented dryness!
You, serve us your good words, as big as
the umbilicus of prodigious Africa.
What singer will call the Ancestors tonight,
Will bring the peaceful jungle beasts about us?
Who will send our dreams to lodge
beneath the eyelids of the stars?]

But these too tangible memories make his exile seem more terrible and intensify his homesickness:

Je me rappelle, je me rappelle . . .
Ma tête rythmant
Quelle marche lasse le long des jours d'Europe
où parfois
Apparaît un jazz orphelin qui sanglote sanglote
sanglote.[36]

[I remember, I remember . . .
My head in motion with
What weary pace the length of European days
where now and then
An orphan jazz appears sobbing sobbing
sobbing.]

Beneath his European clothes, Senghor felt like a foreigner. How far he was from his own clothes, from his own customs! The reproach Senghor puts on the lips of a Senegalese prince in his poem "Le message" testifies to his ridiculous appearance as a man "assimilated and uprooted":

Enfants à tête courte, que vous ont chanté les kôras?
Vous déclinez la rose, m'a-t-on dit, et vos ancêtres les Gaulois.
Vous êtes docteurs en Sorbonne, bedonnants de diplômes.
Vous amassez des feuilles de papier . . .
Vos filles, m'a-t-on dit, se peignent le visage comme des courtisanes
Elles se casquent pour l'union libre et éclaircir la race!
Etes vous plus heureux? Quelque trompette à wa-wa-wa
Et vous pleurez aux soirs là-bas de grands feux et de sang.
Faut-il vous dérouler l'ancien drame et l'épopée?
Allez à Mbissel à Fa'oy; récitez le chapelet de sanctuaires qui ont
jalonné la Grande Voie
Refaites la route royale et méditez ce chemin de croix et de gloire.

36. "Joal," *CO,* p. 20.

Vos grands-prêtres vous répondront: Voix du Sang![37]

[Children with short memories, what did the kôras sing to you?
You decline the rose, they tell me, and your ancestors the Gauls.
You are doctors of the Sorbonne, paunchy with diplomas
You collect pieces of paper
Your daughters they tell me paint their faces like whores
They wear their hair in chignons, go in for free love to elucidate the
    race!
Are you happier? Some trumpet goes wa-wa-wa
And you weep there on the great holiday and family feasts.
Must the ancient epic story be unfurled for you?
Go to Mbissel and Fa'oy; say the rosary of the
    sanctuaries that marked out the Great Way
Walk upon the royal road again and meditate upon
    the way of cross and glory.
Your high priests will answer: Voices of the Blood!]

Yet Senghor's stay in France was far from useless. First, it taught him where his heart was; second, that the suffering of his race was vast. As a child, Senghor had been so happy and docile by nature that he had never criticized his teachers. In Paris, the contact with French intellectuals and West Indians and Americans of his race awakened his conscience. At the Lycée Louis-le-Grand, he was first listed among the "talas,"[38] but then he went through a violent crisis and became a socialist. It was then that he met Aimé Césaire, whose rebellion had begun to smoulder while he was still in Martinique. Along with Césaire, Senghor questioned Western values to such a point that for more than a year he lost his religious faith.[39]

All the themes of present-day negritude appear in Senghor's work from this moment on. First, the affirmation of his color! This is clearly shown in the titles of his poems: *Chants d'ombre* ("Shadow songs," or "Songs of darkness")—*Hosties noires* ("Black hosts" or "Black victims") —*A l'appel de la race de Saba"* ("At the call of the race of Saba")—*Masque nègre* ("Negro mask")—*Femme noire* ("Black woman"), etc. Second, the feeling of solidarity with all oppressed peoples of the world. It has been said that Senghor was moved by the poverty and misery of the proletariat before becoming aware of the passion of his own race. Certainly, however, one encounters his loyalty to his original culture even in his first poem:

37. "Le message," *CO,* pp. 25–26.
38. *Talas:* student slang expression applied to those who went to church (ceux qui vont-à-la-messe).
39. Interview with Senghor, June 1959.

Mais je n'efface pas les pas de mes pères ni des pères de mes
    pères dans ma tête ouverte à vents et pillards du Nord.
....
Qu'ils m'accordent, les génies protecteurs, que mon sang ne
    s'affadisse pas comme un assimilé comme un civilisé.[40]

[I do not erase the footsteps of my father nor of the
fathers of my fathers in my head open to the winds and plunderers
    of the North.
....
May my guardian spirits not permit my blood to grow insipid
    like some assimilated, civilized soul.]

His wish for the liberation of Africa can be seen as a proletarian
emancipation where there would be

Ni maîtres désormais ni esclaves ni guelwars[41] ni griot de griot
Rien que la lisse et virile camaraderie des combats et que me soit
    égal le fils du captif, que me soient copains le Maure
    et le Targui congénitalement ennemis.[42]

[Neither masters any more nor slaves nor knights nor griots of griots
Nothing but the smooth and virile camaraderie of battles
    And may the son of the captive be my equal
    the Moor and Targui, those congenital enemies, my companions.]

Senghor included in this struggle

. . . tous les travailleurs blancs dans la lutte fraternelle.
Voici le mineur des Asturies le docker de Liverpool, le Juif chassé
    d'Allemagne, et Dupont et Dupuis et tous les gars de Saint-Denis.[43]

[. . . all white workers in the fraternal struggle
the miner from Asturia, the Liverpool docker,
the Jew chased out of Germany, and Dupont and Dupuis
and all the boys from Saint Denis.]

And hailed it with the classical slogan (printed in capital letters):

L'AUBE TRANSPARENTE D'UN JOUR NOUVEAU.[44]

---

40. "A l'appel de la race de Saba," *HN*, p. 39.

41. *Guelwars* or *guelowars:* Serer warriors in the noble sense of "knights" as compared with "soldiers."

42. "A l'appel de la race de Saba," *HN*, pp. 90–91.

43. Ibid., p. 93.

44. Ibid., p. 94. One will remember that the *Légitime Défense* team also at first demanded emancipation of the proletariat and included in it the Negro problem. Senghor acted the same way. His text (1936) reminds us of Jacques Roumain's poems, dated 1939 but published only in 1945, *Bois d'ébène* (Port-au-Prince: Imprimerie H. Deschamps):

[THE TRANSPARENT DAWN OF A NEW DAY.]

Only later was Senghor to realize the particular oppression of which his race had been the victim: slavery, the looting of Africa, the humiliation and servitude of colonization. Gradually, he too accepted these, and to the general indictment against Europe he would add the ancient wounds

> . . . d'une terre vidée de ses fils
> Vendus à l'encan moins cher que harengs, et il ne lui reste que son
>   honneur.[45]

> [. . . of a land emptied of its sons
> Sold at public auction cheaper than herring, and with nothing left but
>   its honor.]

He denounced

> Les mains blanches qui tirèrent les coups de fusils qui croulèrent
>   des empires
> Les mains qui flagellèrent les esclaves, qui vous flagellèrent
> Les mains blanches poudreuses qui vous giflèrent, les mains peintes
>   poudrées qui m'ont giflé
> Les mains sûres qui m'ont livré à la solitude et à la haine
> . . . les diplomates qui montrent leurs canines longues
> Et qui demain troqueront la chair noire.[46]

> [White hands that pulled the trigger on guns that crushed
>   empires
> Hands that whipped slaves, that whipped you
> White powdery hands that slapped you, painted
>   powdery hands that slapped me
> Sure hands that delivered me to solitude and hate
> . . . diplomats who show white teeth
> And tomorrow will barter black flesh.]

Senghor learned all this and would not forget it, even if he did not wish to "bring out his stock of hatred."[47] Too often he has been called the man of conciliation. His words of peace ("Oh! do not say that I do not

---

"Mineurs des Asturies, mineur nègre de Johannesburg, metallo de Krupp, dur paysan de Castille, vigneron de Sicile, paria des Indes" ["Asturian miners, black miner of Johannesburg, Krupp's metalworker, hard Castillian peasant, Sicilian vine grower, Indian untouchable"].

Contrary to what Sartre thought ("Orphée noir," pp. xl–xli), it would therefore seem that socialism or communism had been a phase on the way toward the claim for specifically Negro rights, rather than the reverse.

45. "Au Gouverneur Eboué," *HN*, p. 118.
46. "Neige sur Paris, *CO*, p. 30.
47. Ibid.

love France")[48] have been boasted of in contrast to those of his rebellious brothers, particularly Césaire. The indictment against colonization that runs throughout Senghor's poems, however, is not so easily overlooked. His disillusioned contempt of the "mud of civilization"[49] which dehumanizes "the boulevard crowds" of Europe, "sleepwalkers who have rejected their identity as men,"[50] as well as Africa, where "on the Sudanese plain, dessicated by the East Wind and the Northern masters of Time,"[51] men deprived of freedom are slowly suffocating, are too quickly forgotten.

> . . . rien que les sables les impôts les corvées la chicotte
> Et la seule rosée des crachats pour leurs soifs inextinguibles en souvenir des verts pâturages atlantidiens
> Car les barrages des ingénieurs n'ont pas apaisé la soif des âmes dans les villages polytechniques.[52]

> [. . . nothing but sand taxes forced labor the whip
> And spittle the only dew for their inextinguishable thirst in memory of green Atlantic pastures
> For barrages of engineers have not satisfied the thirsty souls in polytechnic villages.]

Senghor's bitterness, increased by his personal experience of segregation, has never been sufficiently recognized:

> Je ne reconnais plus les hommes blancs, mes frères
> Comme ce soir au cinéma, perdus qu'ils étaient au delà du vide fait autour de ma peau.[53]

> [I no longer recognize my brothers, the white men,
> Lost as they were this evening at the films, beyond the emptiness they left about my skin.]

In the crucible of war, Senegalese soldiers were "caught in the toils, delivered to civilized barbarity, exterminated like warthogs"[54] or abandoned at the time of France's downfall in 1940 and deposited in German prison camps:

> Haines et faim y fermentent dans la torpeur d'un été mortel.
> ....
> Et les nobles guerriers mendient des bouts de cigarette[55]

48. "Poème liminaire," *HN*, p. 82.
49. "Le retour de l'enfant prodigue," *CO*, p. 73.
50. "Lettre à un prisonnier," *HN*, p. 133.
51. Ibid.
52. "Désespoir d'un volontaire libre," *HN*, p. 104.
53. "Lettre à un prisonnier," *HN*, p. 133.
54. "Au guelowar," *HN*, p. 115.
55. "Camp 1940," *HN*, pp. 119–20.

> [Hunger and hatred fermented there in the torpor of one mortal
> summer.
> ....
> And noble warriors were begging cigarette butts]

And the Negro continued to do K.P. and latrine duty for the "great
pink children." "Who else but the high born will do the lowly jobs?"
asks Senghor.[56] But his witticism hides only thinly a pain and bitterness
he was not always able to contain:

> L'Europe m'a broyé comme le plat guerrier sous les pattes pachy-
> dermes des tanks[57]

> Dans la nuit nous avons crié notre détresse. Pas une voix n'a
> répondu.
> Les princes de l'Eglise se sont tus, les hommes d'Etat ont clamé
> la magnanimité des hyènes
> «Il s'agit bien du nègre! Il s'agit bien de l'homme! non! quand
> il s'agit de l'Europe.»[58]

> [Europe has crushed me like the flat warrior beneath the
> pachydermal feet of tanks

> We cried out our pain in the night. Not a single voice
> gave answer.
> The Princes of the Church were silent, statesmen claimed the
> hyenas were magnanimous
> "It certainly concerns the Negro! It certainly concerns
> mankind! Not when Europe is involved!"]

To present Senghor as a tender elegiac, as Aimé Patri has done,[59]
is to weaken him. Can he have forgotten Senghor's shouts of virile
rebellion?

> . . . je déchirerai les rires banania sur tous les murs de France[60]

> En avant! Et que ne soit pas le pean poussé o Pindare! mais
> le cri de guerre hirsute et le coupe-coupe dégaîné.[61]

> [. . . I shall tear the banana laughter from all the walls of France

56. Ibid., p. 121.
57. "Ndessé," *HN*, p. 130.
58. "Au guelowar," *HN*, p. 116.
59. Aimé Patri, "Deux poètes noirs en langue française: A. Césaire et L. S. Senghor,"
Présence Africaine, no. 3.
60. "Poème liminaire," *HN*, p. 91.
61. "A l'appel de la race de Saba," *HN*, p. 93.

Forward! And may there be no song of praise o Pindar! But shaggy
war shout and quick sword thrust!]

To call Senghor a "man of civilization"[62] seems to us ambiguous.
The last poem in *Hosties noires*, although entitled "Prière de paix"
("Prayer for peace"), is the one with the most violent accusations.
Reading it, one realizes to what extent the poet's "pardon" is the
opposite of "compromise." Senghor forgives while remaining very
much aware of his race's suffering and the misdeeds of political and
missionary France. His forgiveness is great only because it is offered
with complete lucidity:

> Au pied de mon Afrique crucifiée depuis quatre cents ans et
>   pourtant respirante
> Laisse-moi Te dire Seigneur, sa prière de paix et de pardon.
>
> Seigneur Dieu, pardonne à l'Europe blanche!
> Et il est vrai, Seigneur, que pendant quatre siècles de lun ières,
>   elle a jeté la bave et les abois de ses molosses sur mes terres
> ....
> Seigneur pardonne à ceux qui ont fait des Askia des maquisards,
>   de mes princes des adjudants
> De mes domestiques des boys et de mes paysans des salariés,
>   de mon peuple un peuple de prolétaires.
> Car il faut bien que Tu pardonnes à ceux qui ont donné la chasse
>   à mes enfants comme à des éléphants sauvages.
> Et ils les ont dressés à coups de chicotte, et ils ont fait d'eux les
>   mains noires de ceux dont les mains étaient blanches.
> Car il faut bien que Tu oublies ceux qui ont exporté dix millions
>   de mes fils dans les maladreries de leurs navires
> Qui en ont supprimé deux cents millions.
> Et ils m'ont fait une vieillesse solitaire parmi les forêts de mes
>   nuits et la savane de mes jours.
> Seigneur la glace de mes yeux s'embue
> Et voila que le serpent de la haine lève la tête dans mon cœur,
>   ce serpent que j'avais cru mort . . .
>
> Tue-le Seigneur, car il me faut poursuivre mon chemin, et je
>   veux prier singulièrement pour la France.
> Seigneur, parmi les nations blanches, place la France à la droite
>   du Père.
> Oh! je sais bien qu'elle aussi est l'Europe, qu'elle m'a ravi mes
>   enfants comme un brigand du Nord des bœufs, pour engraisser
>   ses terres à cannes et coton, car la sueur du nègre est fumier.
> ....

---

62. On a formal level, this is one of Senghor's least good poems; Claudel's influence
is too apparent, to the detriment of African feeling. The purpose, however, is noble, and
many of the lines are concise.

Oui Seigneur, pardonne à la France qui dit bien la voie droite
et chemine par des sentiers obliques
Qui m'invite à sa table et me dit d'apporter mon pain, qui me
donne de la main droite et de la main gauche enlève la
moitié.
Oui Seigneur, pardonne à la France qui haït les occupants et
m'impose l'occupation si gravement
Qui ouvre les voies triomphales aux héros et traite ses Sénégalais
en mercenaires, faisant d'eux les dogues noires de
l'Empire
Qui est la République et livre les pays aux Grands-Concessionnaires
Et de ma Mésopotamie, de mon Congo; ils ont fait un grand
cimetière sous le soleil blanc.[63]

[At the foot of my Africa, crucified these four hundred years
yet breathing still
Lord, let me repeat its prayer of pardon and of peace.

Lord God, forgive white Europe!
It is true, Lord, that for four centuries of enlightenment
she threw her yelping, foaming dogs upon my lands
....
Lord, forgive those who made guerrillas of the Askias,
who turned my princes into sergeants,
Made houseboys of my servants, and laborers of my country
folk, who turned my people into a proletariat.
For you must forgive those who hunted my children like
wild elephants
Who trained them to the whip and made them the black hands
of those whose hands were white.
You must forget those who stole ten million of my sons in
their leprous ships
And who suppressed two hundred million more.
A lonely old age they've made me in the forest of my
nights and the savannah of my days.
The glass before my eyes grows misty, Lord.
And the serpent Hatred stirs his head within my heart,
the Serpent I'd thought dead . . .

Kill it, Lord, for I must proceed upon my way
and strangely, it is for France I want to pray.
Lord, among the white lands, set France upon the
Father's right.
Oh, I know she too is Europe, she too like some northern cattle
rustler raped my children to swell the cane and cotton
fields, for negro sweat is like manure.

63. "Prière de paix," *HN*, pp. 148–52.

....

Yes, Lord, forgive France, who expresses the right way so
    well and makes her own so deviously
Who invites me to her table, and tells me to bring my own
    bread, who gives with her right hand while the left
    takes half back again.
Yes, Lord, forgive France, which hates all occupations
    and imposes hers so heavily on me
Who throws open her triumphal routes to heroes and
    treats her Senegalese like hired hands;
    making them the black dogs of her empire
Who is the Republic and delivers her countries
    to the concessionary companies
That have made my Mesopotamia, the Congo, a vast
    cemetery beneath the white sun.]

It was not that Senghor made peace with the West over the dead bodies of his victimized race,[64] but that war had revealed to him all the horror of racism.[65] The spectacle of French people in their turn bruised and ravaged and struggling against oppression enabled him to rise above his resentment and to recognize aspects of France he could love—the faces of its suffering:

Et la fiancée pleure sa viduité, et le jeune homme voit sa
    jeunesse cambriolée
Et la femme lamente oh! l'œil absent de son mari, et la mère
    cherche le rêve de son enfant dans les gravats.[66]

[The fiancée who mourns her widowhood
The boy robbed of his youth
And the woman weeping, oh, for her husband's
    absent eye, and the mother seeking
    her child's dream among the rubble.]

and that of its freedom:

Bénis ce peuple garrotté qui par deux fois sut libérer ses mains
    et osa proclamer l'avènement des pauvres à la royauté
....
Bénis ce peuple qui rompt ses liens, bénis ce peuple aux abois
    qui fait front à la meute boulimique des puissants et des
    tortionnaires.[67]

64. To use Césaire's expression from the *Cahier*, p. 82: "I shall not make my peace with the world upon your backs," i.e. at your expense.
65. Interview with Senghor, June 1959. He feels that the barbarity of the European war he lived through was so shocking that he can no longer bear anything which has the semblance of racism.
66. "Prière de paix," p. 152.
67. Ibid.

[Bless these captive people who twice have known how to liberate
  their lands and dared proclaim the advent of the poor
  to those of royal lineage
  ....

Bless these people who break their bonds, bless these people
  reduced to their last extremity who confront the wild
  greed of the powerful, the torturers.]

This is why Senghor forgives more easily than Damas or Césaire—also, because he benefits from that basic psychological equilibrium due to his happy childhood and, in addition, because he feels strong with the strength of Africa's future.

But if, for the edification of a world henceforth without hate or racism, Senghor asks his Dead, "Oh, black Martyrs, let me say the words of forgiveness,"[68] it is not a matter of forgetting blood so abundantly spilled, but rather one of making it bear fruit.

Non, vous n'êtes pas morts gratuits ô Morts! Ce sang n'est pas
  de l'eau tépide.
Il arose épais notre espoir, qui fleurira au crépuscule.
Il est notre soif notre faim d'honneur, ces grandes reines
  absolues.
Non, vous n'êtes pas morts gratuits. Vous êtes les témoins de
  l'Afrique immortelle.[69]

[No, you have not died in vain, O Dead! This blood is no
  tepid water.
It moistens our thick hope which will blossom at twilight.
It is our thirst, our hunger for honor, those great
  absolute queens.
No, you did not die in vain. You are the witnesses of
  Africa immortal.]

Senghor's devotion to his people remains total. It was to the black lands he came in search of "earthy virtues" to arm himself with the qualities of Sudanese heroes, with the "fervent science of Timbuctoo's great doctors"[70] and the "courage of the Guelwars." To dedicate himself, this modern knight spontaneously rediscovered the religious tone appropriate to solemn oaths: "Permit me to die for the cause of my people."[71] What love for the race whose ambassador he aspires to be, what faith in its reserves of life, joy and hope!

68. "Assassinats," *HN*, p. 123.
69. "Tyaroye," *HN*, p. 144.
70. Timbuctoo, the great Sudanese city, was a famous intellectual center during the Middle Ages, and its scientists were in contact with those of Morocco and Egypt.
71. "Le retour de l'enfant prodigue," *CO*, p. 77.

Du couple primitif vous êtes la charnure, le ventre fécond la
    laitance[72]

Ainsi le levain qui est nécessaire à la farine blanche.
Car qui apprendrait le rythme au monde défunt des machines
    et des canons?
Dites, qui rendrait la mémoire de la vie à l'homme aux espoirs
    éventrés?
Il nous disent les hommes du coton du café de l'huile.
....
Nous sommes les hommes de la danse, dont les pieds reprennent
    vigueur en frappant le sol sur.[73]

[You are the flesh of the primitive couple, the fertile
    belly, the soft roe

Like the leaven necessary to white flour.
For who shall teach rhythm to a world dead from
    cannon and machine?
Say who shall revive the memory of life to the man
    with disemboweled hope?
They call us men of cotton, coffee, oil.
....
We are men of the dance whose feet take on new
    strength by striking the hard ground.]

When Senghor declares his conviction that "any great civilization,
any true culture is the result of cross-breeding," we must not infer
from this that he wished to give up any of the African Negro values nor
that he was disposed to welcome everything Europe might offer.

The problem we blacks of 1959 now face is to discover how we are going
to integrate *African Negro values* into the world of 1959. It is not a question of
resuscitating the past, of living in an African Negro museum; it is a question
of animating the world, *here and now*, with the values of our past. This, after
all, is what the Negro Americans have begun to do.[74]

Senghor does not fail to warn African politicians that "cultural colonialism, in the form of assimilation, is the worst of all."[75] And if today
he declares himself in favor of mixed civilizations, this involves—to use
his own expression—"confrontation" and "symbiosis." As in Hegelian
synthesis, the two contrary assertions—Negro values and Western values—must purify each other, retaining only the best traits of each, in
order to achieve the harmonious amalgamation desired by Senghor.

72. "Assassinats," *HN*, p. 122.
73. "Prière aux masques," *CO*, p. 32.
74. Report to the Second Congress of Black Writers and Artists, p. 277.
75. Ibid., p. 279.

Senghor has a style as different from his confreres as it is possible to imagine. His poems are more elaborated. He knows them by heart and willingly recites them, being somewhat the "man of letters." Like all true poets, however, he composes in response to an inner need. To sing, he must feel deeply moved. He writes his poem in a single out-pouring, then reads it, seeks the high points and sometimes the meaning, because when he takes up his pen he does not always know what he will write.[76]

The poems in *Chants d'ombre* and *Hosties noires* quickly attained the breadth of those of his mature period; the well-formed characteristics of Senghor's style are already recognizable.

In the poems one finds a universe where the harmonious background of his Senegalese childhood—the Ancients of Elissa, Joal-the-Shady, the kings of Sine, the griots, the dances, the great house at Djilor, and the black woman with "hands with the scent of balsam"—become corroded by the anxieties of a Prodigal Son torn between two cultures who laments, threatens, or forgives, but who, whether happy or bruised, always returns to drink deep at the fountain of Kam-Dyamé near his "sober-eyed ancestors who understand all things."[77]

We discover a sensuous love of his country's names, names of places and people that have solemn and mysterious sonorities:

> Dyob!—du Ngabou au Walo, du Ngalam à la Mer s'élèveront
> les chants des vierges d'ambre
> Et que les accompagnent les cordes des kôras! . . .[78]

> Toi entre tous Eléphant de Mbissel, qui parait d'amitié ton poète
> dyâli[79]

> Je me rappelle les fastes du Couchant
> Ou Koumba N'Dofène voulait faire tailler son manteau royal[80]

> [Dyob!—from the Nagabou to the Walo, from Ngalam
> to the sea the songs of amber virgins will rise
> And may the stringèd kôras accompany them! . . .

> You among all Elephant of Mbissel, who adorn
> your poet-praise maker with friendship

76. Details obtained during an interview with Senghor, June 1959.
77. "Que m'accompagnent . . . ," *CO*, p. 42.
78. "Taga de Mbaye Dyob," *HN*, p. 128.
79. "Le retour de l'enfant prodigue," *CO*, p. 73
80. "Joal," *CO*, p. 19.

I recall the splendors of the setting sun
From which Koumba N'Dofene would have cut his royal cloak]

Next his marked taste for transpositions, which lighten biblical-style verses:

Que vaste que vide la cour à l'odeur de néant[81]

Me conduise la note d'or de la flûte du silence, me conduise le
pâtre mon frère de rêve de jadis[82]

Et tressaillent les cendres tièdes de l'Homme aux yeux de foudre,
mon père.[83]

[How vast how empty the courtyard with the smell of nothingness

The golden note of the flute of silence leads me, the shepherd,
my long ago dream brother leads me

And the warm ashes of the man-with-lightning-eyes, my father,
tremble.]

We said that Senghor had read and imitated a good deal. If we recognize from time to time definite analogies with Claudel or Saint-John Perse—it should be remembered that his discovery of the latter occurred considerably after his first poems—we must not forget the influence of Senegalese poets, whose literary methods he assimilated. Senghor's manner of celebrating in song a person he wishes to honor, for example, is the same as that of the Senegalese griots, for whom the repetition of a name is as important as the praise itself and who never fail to call upon the meritorious ancestors:

Sall! je proclame ton nom Sall! du Fouta-Damga au Cap Vert[84]

Mbaye Dyôb! Je veux dire ton nom et ton honneur[85]

Et je redis ton nom: Dyallo![86]

Noble devait être ta race et bien née la femme de Timbo qui te
berçait le soir au rythme nocturne de la terre[87]

---

81. "Le retour de l'enfant prodigue," *CO*, p. 72.
82. Ibid.
83. Ibid., p. 71.
84. "Teddungal," in the *Ethiopiques* collection (Paris: Seuil, 1956), p. 20. (Henceforth, we shall merely indicate *Eth.*)
85. "Taga de Mbaye Dyob," *HN*, p. 97.
86. "Mediterranée," *HN*, p. 97.
87. Ibid., p. 96.

[Sall! I proclaim your name Sall! from the Fouta-Damga
　　to Cap Vert

Mbaye Dyob! I want to speak your name and tell your worth

And I repeat your name: Dyallo!

Noble must your race be and well-born the woman of Timbo
　　who rocked you in the evenings to the nocturnal rhythm of the
　　earth]

This is true to such an extent that, wishing to honor the heroism of a
simple soldier, Mbaye Dyob, the poet almost apologizes for not being
able to sing his genealogy or to mention any of his ancestors.[88] The
custom of lauding the ancestors of anyone one wishes to praise is so
usual in Senegal that suitors for the hand of a maiden always pay a griot
to celebrate the great deeds of their ancestors, and the nobility of their
beloved's lineage.

Senghor's ambition, moreover, following the example of the griots,
was to become the "dyâli" of his people,[89] their "Master of Language"
as well as their ambassador.[90]

Yet Senghor's style is distinguished above all by the swing of its
rhythm and the length of the verses—the length of a respiration—
which gives his poems the monotonous motion of the waves of the sea:

Je ressuscite la théorie des servantes sur la rosée
Et les grandes calebasses de lait, calmes, sur le rythme des
　　hanches balancées.[91]

[I summon forth the theory of servants on the dew
And great calabashes of milk, calm above the rhythm
　　of their swaying hips.]

This style lends itself to prayers, natural to Senghor's religious spirit:[92]

O bénis ce peuple, Seigneur, qui cherche son propre visage sous
le masque et a peine à le reconnaître[93]

[O bless this people, Lord, who seek their own face beneath
the mask and scarcely recognize it]

88. "Taga de Mbaye Dyob," *HN*, p. 126.
89. See note 13 above.
90. "Le retour de l'enfant prodigue," *CO*, p. 77.
91. Ibid., p. 76.
92. This is where Claudel's influence is particularly noticeable and where Senghor's
poetry is often least musical.
93. "Prière de paix," *HN*, p. 132.

as well as to nostalgic songs of regret:

> Nous ne participerons plus à la joie sponsorale des moissons!
>
> ....
>
> Nous répéterons pour une fête fanée déjà la danse autrefois des
> moissons, danse légère des corps denses
>
> ....
>
> A l'aube devinée, quand des chœurs la voix plus faible des
> vierges se fait tendre et tendre le sourire des étoiles!
> Nous n'avancerons plus dans le frémissement fervent de nos
> corps égaux épaules égales
> Vers les bouches sonores et les los et les fruits lourds de
> l'intime tumulte![94]

> [We shall no longer take part in the sponsorale joy of harvests
>
> ....
>
> We shall rehearse for a feast already faded the old-time harvest
> dance, the light dance of heavy bodies
>
> ....
>
> At the hint of dawn, when in the choir the weaker voices of the maids
> grow tender and tender the smile of the stars!
> We shall move forward shoulder to shoulder,
> bodies fervently quivering
> Toward the resonant mouths and the praises and
> the heavy fruits of the intimate tumult!]

It is also suitable for evoking the mystery that hovers over villages
haunted by the ancestors:

> Enclos méridien du côté des tombes!
> Et toi Fontaine de Kam-Dyamé, quand à midi je buvais ton eau
> mystique au creux de mes mains
> Entouré de mes compagnons lisses et nus et parés des fleurs
> de la brousse!
> La flûte du pâtre module la lenteur des troupeaux
> Et quand sur son ombre elle se taisait, résonnait le tamtam
> des tanns obsédés.[95]

> [And you pool, of Kam-Dyamé at noon I
> used to drink your mystic water from the hollow of my hands
> Surrounded by companions smooth and nude
> and decked in flowers from the bush
> The shepherd's flute would modulate the slow
> pace of the herds

94. "Prière des tirailleurs sénégalais," *HN*, pp. 107–8.
95. "Que m'accompagnent . . . ," *CO*, pp. 40–52.

> And in its shadow as it ceased drums would echo in the haunted
> tanns.]

But Senghor's verse is better than any other at "singing a noble subject":

> Ah! me soutient l'espoir qu'un jour je coure devant toi,
> Princesse, porteur de ta récade à l'assemblée des peuples.
> ....
> Et tel le blanc méhari de race, que mes lèvres de neuf jours en
> neuf jours soient chastes de toute eau terrestre, et
> silencieuses.[96]

> [Ah! I am sustained by the hope that one day I shall run
> before you, Princess, bearer of your staff of honor to
> the assembled populace.
> ....
> And like the white dromedary's, may my lips for nine days at a time
> be chaste of all terrestrial water, and silent.]

If we had to choose among several adjectives, we might call Senghor's style "processional." The verses spin out, without crests, in groups of about fifteen waves; the words proceed regularly, at a rhythm kept slow by the insertion of deep-toned syllables.

The device is especially noticeable, for example, in the lines repeated below, where the "low note" of the deep-toned French -*an* and -*al* sounds is in contrast to the high-pitched tone of the vowels—*é, i, u*—and to the "occlusive" consonants—*c, d, t, thm, lm, lb:*

> Je ressuscite la théorie des serv*an*tes sur la rosée
> Et les gr*an*des c*al*eb*as*ses de lait, c*al*mes, sur le rythme des
> h*an*ches bal*an*cées.[97]

To give added rhythm to this "processional" style, Senghor often uses alliteration. He either chooses as a dominant note the first consonants, such as the *r, s, t,* of the first line above, or he emphasizes a single consonant or vowel as follows:

> Voici que dé*cl*ine *l*a *l*une *l*asse vers son *l*it de mer éta*l*e.[98]

> [And now the weary moon sinks into her slack sea bed.]

Sometimes the echoes of two (or three) sounds call and answer one another:

> A tr*a*vers C*a*y*o*r et B*a*ol de sécheresse où se *t*ordent les br*as* les
> b*a*ob*a*bs d'*a*ng*o*isse.[99]

---

96. Ibid., p. 49.
97. "Le retour de l'enfant prodigue," *CO*, p. 76.
98. "Nuit de Sine," *CO*, p. 17.
99. "Tout de long du jour," *CO*, p. 16.

[Across Cayor and Baol dryness that twists the arms of
baobabs in pain.]

Sometimes a harmony is begun in an early line and the poet gets
caught in his own trap. In the following verse, for example, the diphthongs of one line release a series of further soft diphthongs in the
next:

Ses paup*iè*res comme le crépuscule rapide et ses *y*eux vastes qui
s'emplissent de nuit.
Oui c'est b*ie*n l'*aï*eule n*oi*re, la Claire aux *y*eux v*io*lets sous
ses paup*iè*res de n*ui*t.[100]

[Her eyelids like rapid twilight and her vast eyes filling
filling up with night.
Yes, it is she, the dark ancestor, Bright with violet eyes
beneath her lids of night.]

Of course, it may be a case of imitative harmony:

Et seize ans de guerre! Seize ans le battement des tabalas de
guerre des tabalas des balles![101]

Seuls bourdonnent les parfums de brousse, ruches d'abeilles
rousses que domine la vibration grêle des grillons.[102]

[And sixteen years of war! Sixteen years of war drums beating,
beating out like bullets!

The only humming is the perfumes of the bush, swarms of russet
bees that dominate the crickets' thin vibrato.]

Most of the time, however, the device has no other aim but the
sensual. The author is attracted by the plastic qualities of certain consonants and repeats them, not in imitation of nature, but because they
stimulate or sustain his inner rhythm, even independently of the subject matter involved.

The rhythm is not always the same. It can rise to the syncopated beat
of the American Negro jazz Senghor is so fond of:

Mais s'il faut choisir à l'heure de l'épreuve
J'ai choisi le verset des fleuves, des vents et des forêts
L'assonance des plaines et des rivières, choisi le rythme de sang
de mon corps dépouillé
Choisi la trémulsion des balafongs et l'accord des cordes et des

100. "Chant d'ombre," *CO*, p. 60.
101. "Que m'accompagnent . . . ," *CO*, p. 46. *Tabala:* a large war tom-tom.
102. Ibid., p. 51.

> cuivres qui semble faux, choisi le
> Swing le swing oui le swing![103]

> [But if one must choose at the hour of affliction
> I chose the flow of rivers, wind and forests
> The assonance of plains and streams, I chose the pulsebeat
>   of my unclothed body
> The vibrations of the balafong, the harmony of strings and
>   brasses that sound out of tune
> I chose swing, swing, yes swing!]

More often, the beat quickens to a dance rhythm—strangely enough, a typically African dance, which doubles a skipping step, one-two on one foot and one-two on the other. Senghor re-creates this step by redoubling and emphasizing the accentuated syllables:

> Et quand sur *son ombre* elle se *taisait*, résonnait le *tamtam* des tanns ob*sédés*.[104]

> Nous n'avancerons plus dans le frémissem*ent* ferv*ent* de n*os* c*orps* é*gaux* ép*aules* é*gales*.[105]

> Ma tête bourdonnant au *galop* g*uerrier* des *dyoung-dyoungs*, au *grand* *galop* de mon *sang* de pur *sang*.[106]

> Qui *sera* le *sel* des *Sérères*, qui *seront* le *sel* des peuples *salés*.[107]

> [And when at its shadow she grew silent, the drums of the haunted tanns were echoing.

> No more shall we move forward shoulder to shoulder fervent bodies quivering

> My head humming with the warrior gallop of the dyoung-dyoung drums, with the racing of my blood pure blood.

> Who will be the Serer salt, who will be the salt of the peoples who've been soiled.]

He can also re-create this dance step by repetition of the consonants marking the downbeats. The dentals and explosive labials play the role of hands beating the tom-tom:

103. Ibid., pp. 43–44.
104. *Ibid.*, p. 42.
105. "Prière des tirailleurs sénégalais," *HN*, p. 108.
106. "Appel de la race de Saba," *HN*, p. 88.
107. "Que m'accompagnent . . . ," p. 47.

*Des peaux précieuses des barres de sel, de l'or du Boure de l'or
du Boundou.*[108]

[Precious skins, bars of salt, of gold from Boure, of gold
from Boundou.]

Senghor's rhythm is processional, but it is often a dancing procession, like the procession of the Brazilian Negroes in Marcel Camus's film, who are already vibrating with the carnival dances as they descend from their hills toward the Bay of Rio. It is no accident that Senghor took such pleasure in the movie *Black Orpheus*, whose "incontestable negritude"[109] he so much appreciated.

Music is one of the basic elements of Senghor's poetry, and he is aware of it: "I persist in thinking that a poem is complete only if it becomes song, with words and music at the same time."[110] "A poem is like a jazz score where the execution is as important as the text!"[111]

To understand the crux of a Senghor poem, it is not enough to have understood the meaning of the words and images, which seem to us even secondary in importance. Rather one must communicate with the poet's emotion by discovering the rhythmic throbs of his work, never forgetting that: "Strangely enough, the Negro belongs to a world where speech spontaneously becomes rhythm as soon as a man is moved to emotion, restored to himself and his authenticity. Yes, speech then becomes a poem."[112]

We have doubtless noticed the assimilation of rhythm and poetry: "Speech becomes *rhythm*, speech becomes *poem*," says Senghor. "Negro poets," he also writes, "are above all *cantors*. They are tyrannically obedient to an 'inner music.'"[113] One final example. The title of Senghor's longest poem in *Chants d'ombre* is "Que m'accompagnent kôras et balafongs." In this title, the very names of the instruments give rhythmic resonance to the poetic line: repetition of the hard *c* (Que m'acc . . . ko . . .) and the final "-ong," of which the "g" must be sonorous (. . . agn . . . fong).

This verse must therefore be accented as follows:

Que m'accompagnent kôras et balafongs[114]

This small example brings out a major difficulty for us Westerners. To "grasp" the rhythm of a Senghor poem, we must first get rid of our

108. Ibid., p. 46.
109. Interview with Senghor, June 1959.
110. L. S. Senghor, *Ethiopiques*, postface, p. 123.
111. Ibid., p. 121.
112. Ibid., p. 104.
113. L. S. Senghor, *Ethiopiques*, postface, p. 112.
114. *Kôra:* a kind of harp. *Balafong:* a kind of xylophone.

French manner of accentuating words. In the above line, we spontaneously place the accent on the syllables *pa, ras,* and f*ong,* or on the final syllables. We thus miss the *basic rhythm of the line.*

Senghor himself calls our attention to the importance of this scansion: "Rhythm," he says "does not arise merely from an alternation of short and long syllables. It can also rest upon—and one too easily forgets that this was partly true of Greco-Latin verses—the alternation of accented and unstressed syllables, of downbeats and upbeats. This is the way it is with Negro African rhythm." But he immediately points out that "in a regular poem, each verse has the same number of accents," whereas the basic rhythm of a Negro African poem, the one which gives it its specific character, "is not that of speech, but of the percussion instruments accompanying the human voice, or, to be more exact, those which beat out the basic rhythm."

It is typical of Senghor to indicate, at the head of many of his poems, the instruments which should accompany them: "*Woi* for three kôras and a balafong,"[115] "For Khalam,"[116] "To a sonorous background of funeral drums," "For three tabalas or war drums."

For these reasons, it is difficult for French-speaking people to recite a Senghor poem. They have to abandon their natural accentuation and avoid emphasizing what seems important to them: "The fashionable diction called expressive, in a theatrical or ordinary style, is anti-poetry."[117] It is because he has not understood this, that Mr. Clancier, too French-minded no doubt, has hoped that "Senghor will succeed in creating a language with a more varied rhythm, where a picture, a word, will suddenly raise its crest around which the figure of the poem will take shape; then we shall really penetrate into his poetic universe, which is original and richly human."[118] We hope we have shown with sufficient clarity how right Senghor was to reply: "Don't you see that you are asking me to organize poetry in the French manner, as a *drama,* whereas for us it is a *symphony.*"[119]

With Senghor music and poetry are inseparable. Several attempts have been made in Paris to reproduce the musical rhythm of his poems with the instruments indicated by him. Recently, during a recital of Negro poetry at the Congolese University of Lovanium, the poem "Chaka" was chanted by a black student to the accompaniment of a tom-tom. It was an astonishing success, and all Kinshasa was talking about the "Senghor concert," obvious proof that this author's poetry

115. *Woi:* a Serer word meaning both poem and song.
116. *Khalam:* a tetracord guitar.
117. L. S. Senghor, *Ethiopiques,* p. 123.
118. Quoted by Senghor, ibid., p. 119.
119. Ibid., p. 120.

loses its apparent atonality when correctly recited.

We have explained above how to interpret the *poetic phrase,* an expression we use intentionally to suggest the "musical phrase." We have shown how certain sounds give the "tone" and their repetition the "beat" to Senghor's poetry. Also, how this poetry is built on a rhythm whose discovery is essential if one wishes to reach not an external, rationalized understanding of the poem but its creative source, its original impulse.

One realizes then that the screen of "monotony," of which the author is so often accused, has been pierced: that his emotions were not always calm, peaceful, serene, as has so often been said. Senghor can be as intensely affected as Césaire, for example, but he exteriorizes less. The emotion is felt deeply, by a "tightness in the stomach and the throat."[120] Senghor does not have an explosive temperament. "With me, an emergency makes me ill, my face becomes ashen,"[121] he has said. In the same way, various emotions are hidden in his poems. Their monotony is not due to incapacity of expression, nor lack of strong feelings; it is an integral part of Senghor's personality. It is the monotony of the savannas, whose rhythm is broader, less hurried than that of the forest, akin to those interminable modulated chants of the Batutsi[122] and close also to the Bantu[123] poems.

> Feu que les hommes voient seulement dans la nuit, dans la nuit
>   profonde,
> Feu qui brules sans consumer, qui brilles sans bruler,
> Feu qui voles sans corps et sans ailes, qui ne connais case ni
>   foyer
> Feu transparent des palmes, un homme sans peur t'invoque.[124]

> [Fire men see only in the night, on the darkest nights,
> Fire that burns without consuming, that sparkles without burning,
> Fire that flies without body, without wings, knowing neither
>   hearth nor hut,
> Fire, transparent palm-tree fire, a fearless man invokes thee.]

Besides, was not even Césaire considered monotonous? And Edouard Glissant? Western ears that have not learned to listen to the tom-tom and Negro chants, ears that have not yet absorbed their rhythm,

120. Ibid., p. 106.
121. Ibid., p. 105.
122. Songs re-created by Alexis Kagame in his *Divine Pastorale* (Brussels: Editions du Marais, 1952).
123. Quoted by the Rev. P. J. Trilles in *Anthropos* (Vienna, 1909), a Bena-Kanioka poem (from the former Belgian Congo).
124. "Chant du feu follet" ("Song of the will-o'-the-wisp") quoted by Senghor in "Langage et poésie négro-africaine" (mimeographed).

will find them monotonous. Yet the monotony of Negro poets, Senghor says, "is the seal of their negritude."[125]

If rhythm is of such importance to the Negro poet, Senghor has often repeated, it is because through his incantations it "permits access to the truth of essential things: the forces of the Cosmos."[126]

These forces, Africans believe, are propagated in the form of *waves*. And Senghor added: "And, since contemporary physics has discovered the energy contained in matter, the waves and radiations, this is no simple metaphor."[127] For modern physicists, too, the "world's substance is made up of rhythmic energy waves."[128] In Sudanese cosmogonies, waves represent water, and water is life: They also represent *technique* (the to-and-fro motion of the weaver's shuttle) and *speech*, which is also propagated in the form of waves. Waves thus represent all the various manifestations of creative energy.

Rhythm enables the artist to participate in the vital cosmic forces thus endowing him with creative power. The object created—be it sculpture, painting, or poem—is a work of art only if this rhythm is apparent. "To respond to and be in harmony with the rhythm of things is the Negro's greatest joy and happiness, his reason for living. In black Africa, a work of art is a masterpiece and fully answers its purpose, only if it is rhythmic."[129]

And this is true not only of works of art, but also of dances, "to dance is to create";[130] or of work: Negroes weave, sow, reap, always accompanied by voices singing or the sound of the tom-tom. Not only to encourage effort, but to make the work effective. This characteristic is still so deeply rooted today—even when rapport with the cosmogony is lost—that both the West Indian peasant and the African worker still feel the need to sustain their effort with rhythmic songs.

It is also by means of this participation in world forces that rhythm is an instrument of knowledge. Africans only know the Other, only "penetrate" the Other, be it person or object, because they instinctively seize the waves emanating from it. Comparing Descartes to a black African, Senghor would have the latter say: "I feel the Other, I dance the Other, therefore I am."[131] He thus emphasizes the fundamental difference between European logic, "analytic through use,"

125. L. S. Senghor, *Ethiopiques*, p. 120.
126. Ibid.
127. L. S. Senghor, "Eléments constructifs d'une civilisation d'inspiration négro-africaine," in a special issue of *Présence Africaine* on the Second Congress of Black Writers and Artists, p. 255.
128. L. S. Senghor, "L'art négro-africain" (unpublished lecture, 1955), p. 12.
129. Ibid.
130. L. S. Senghor, "Eléments constructifs," p. 255.
131. Ibid.

and Negro logic, "intuitive through participation."[132]

Largely inspired by aboriginal cosmogonies, Senghor, one can see, has developed his thoughts on African rhythm to the level of a philosophy. In any case, he has emphasized the importance of rhythm in poetry, and especially in his own work. Not all of his rhythmic poetry, in truth, is successful. Occasionally music that is too facile makes his poems banal:

> Rythmez clochettes, rythmez langues rythmez rames la danse du
> Maîtres des rames.[133]

> [Set the bells in rhythmic motion, the tongues, the oars, the
> dance of the master oarsmen.]

The difference is palpable in the following line:

> Paissez mes seins forts d'homme, l'herbe de lait qui luit sur
> ma poitrine.[134]

> [Feed upon my strong man's breast, the milky grass that gleams
> upon my chest.]

On the other hand, particularly in recent poems, the image is stronger than the rhythm. It is in this, above all, that one could talk of the influence of writers such as Claudel and Saint-John Perse. We must not forget that Senghor himself admits he is an "intellectual crossbreed,"[135] and it is inevitable that he should be marked by Western poetics. Occasionally he regrets it. For example, in replying to a criticism quoted earlier of Clancier: "I may have yielded to your advice, since repeated by others. I would regret it if I were aware of it."[136] And one must admit that the use of Western images that are almost clichés weakens certain of his poems which have a well-marked rhythm:

> Que l'on allume chaque soir douze mille étoiles sur la Grand-
> Place.[137]

> [May twelve thousand stars be lit each night about the Main
> Square.]

or sometimes destroys their originality:

> Je sais le Paradis perdu—je n'ai pas perdu souvenir du
> jardin d'enfance où fleurissent les oiseaux.[138]

132. Ibid., p. 256.
133. L. S. Senghor, "Congo," in *Ethiopiques*, p. 12.
134. "Le Kaya-Magan," ibid., p. 14.
135. Ibid., p. 120.
136. Ibid.
137. "Le Kaya-Magan," ibid., p. 14.
138. "Vacances," *CO*, p. 63.

Fauchés les lilas blancs, fané le parfum des muguets.[139]

[I know the Paradise lost—I have not lost my memory of the
childhood garden blossoming with birds.

The white lilac is mown, and the scent of lilies-of-
the-valley has faded.]

On the other hand, Senghor has succeeded in writing admirable
verses which he would be wrong to disown, even though they are in
a typically French manner:

Mon empire est celui d'Amour, et j'ai faiblesse pour toi femme
L'Etrangère aux yeux de clairière, aux lèvres de pomme cannelle
au sexe de buisson ardent.
. . . Toi la flûte lointaine qui réponds dans la nuit
De l'autre rive de la mer intérieure qui unit les terres opposées
Les cœurs complémentaires: l'une est couleur de flamme et
l'autre sombre, couleur de bois précieux.[140]

[Love is my empire and I have a weakness for thee woman
Stranger with gladelike eyes, cinnamon apple lips and
sex like an ardent thicket.
. . . You the distant flute that answers in the night
From the other shore of the inshore sea that joins opposing lands
Complementary hearts: one the color of flame, the other
dark, the color of precious wood.]

Should we confess that we regret Saint-John Perse's influence on
Senghor? Certainly his poems have become more polished; he has
eliminated the clumsy prosaics that mar certain poems in *Hosties noires*.
More refined today, Senghor's style cloaks several layers of meaning.
On the other hand, the emphatic, occasionally declamatory character
of Senghor's poetry has increased. Amid this pomp and ceremony, one
sometimes misses certain accents of *Chants d'ombre*, so moving in their
simplicity.

139. "Camp 1940," *HN*, p. 119.
140. "Le Kaya-Magan," *Ethiopiques*, p. 16.

1. René Maran, author of the controversial novel *Batouala*. (From Brian Weinstein's *Eboué* [New York, 1972]; reprinted courtesy of the author.)

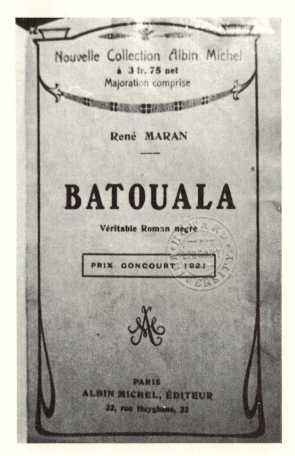

2. Cover of the first edition of *Batouala*, Prix Goncourt winner in 1921. (Photograph by Roy Lewis, reprinted by permission of the Moorland-Spingarn Research Collection, Howard University.)

3. Countee Cullen (1903–46), lyric poet and author of *Color* (1925). Photograph taken in June 1941.

4. Langston Hughes (1902–67), author of *The Weary Blues* (1926), a book of poems, and *The Big Sea* (1940), an autobiography. Photograph taken in June 1939.

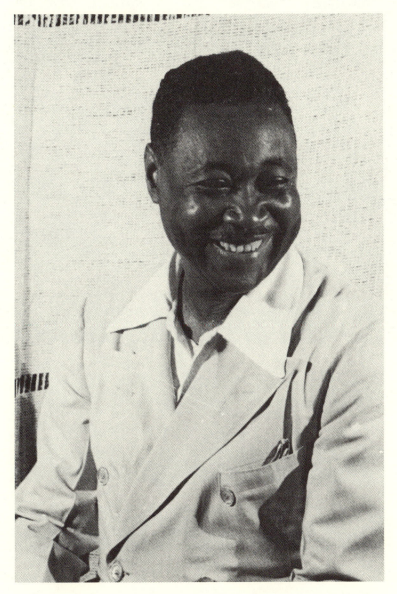

5. Claude McKay (1890–1948), poet, novelist, and author of *Banjo* (first published in the United States in 1929). Photograph taken in July 1941.

6. Léon Damas, author of *Pigments* (1937), during an interview with *Jeune Afrique* magazine in 1970. (Photograph © Guy Le Querrec, Viva, reprinted by permission.)

L - G DAMAS

■   ■

pigments

■   ■

AVEC UNE PREFACE DE ROBERT DESNOS
ET UN BOIS GRAVE DE FRANS MASEREEL

G · L · M   1 9 3 7

7. Title page of the first edition of *Pigments*. (Courtesy of Léon Damas.)

8. Aimé Césaire and Léon Damas, in a Fort-de-France, Martinique, bookstore during the summer of 1973, autographing books just after Damas's *Pigments* and *Névralgies* had been published in a new edition. (Photograph by Fernand Bibas.)

9. A rather formal photograph of Aimé Césaire taken in 1940 in Fort-de-France, after his return to Martinique to teach at the Lyceé Victor Schoelcher and a year after he had published fragments of *Cahier d'un retour au pays natal*. (Courtesy of Editions Seghers.)

AIMÉ CÉSAIRE

CAHIER
D'UN
RETOUR
AU
PAYS NATAL

précédé par
UN GRAND POÈTE NOIR
par
ANDRÉ BRETON

with translations by
Lionel Abel and Ivan Goll

BRENTANO'S

10. Title page of the 1947 bilingual edition of *Cahier d'un retour au pays natal*. (Photograph by Roy Lewis, reprinted by permission of the Moorland-Spingarn Research Collection, Howard University.)

11. Aimé Césaire and his wife Suzanne, July 25, 1959, on a street in Paris. (Courtesy of Editions Seghers.)

12. Léopold Sédar Senghor, president of Senegal, listening to Duke Ellington during the First Festival of Negro Arts in Dakar in 1966. (Photograph by Charlotte Kahler, reprinted by permission.)

13. Cover of L. S. Senghor's book of poems *Hosties noires* (1948). His first book of poems *Chants d'ombre* was published in 1945. (Photograph by Roy Lewis, reprinted by permission of the Moorland-Spingarn Research Collection, Howard University.)

14. Two future presidents, L. S. Senghor (*second row, third from left*) and Georges Pompidou (*first row, second from left*) at the Lyceé Louis-le-Grand in Paris, 1931, with fellow students. (Courtesy of Editions Seghers.)

15. Alioune Diop, founder and editor of *Présence Africaine*. (Courtesy of Service Information de la Côte-d'Ivoire.)

PRÉSENCE AFRICAINE

1

SOMMAIRE

CHRONIQUES

16. Cover (*left*) and Contents page (*above*) from the first issue of *Présence Africaine*, November–December 1947. (Reprinted by permission of Présence Africaine.)

17. Frantz Fanon (1925–61), heir of the negritude generation and also its critic in *Black Skin, White Masks* (1952). (Courtesy of Grove Press.)

18. *From left to right*, Richard Wright, L. S. Senghor, and three black American scholars, John A. Davis, William H. Fontaine, and Horace Mann Bond, at the First Congress of Black Writers and Artists, held in September 1956, at the Sorbonne in Paris. (Courtesy of Editions Seghers.)

19. Aimé Césaire and the author, Lilyan Kesteloot, with students at l'Université Laval, Quebec, in 1972.

IV THE WAR YEARS

14 / Extraliterary Activity and Two Important Essays

Between 1935 and 1940, the only means of expression the *Etudiant Noir* group had was literary. The poets were often carried away by their lyricism and went from lamentation to imprecation, from nostalgia to hope. Right from the start, however, this new romanticism, negritude, was intended by its creators to be an "effective instrument" of both moral and material "freedom." Through their journal, the young writers openly demonstrated their negritude on social and political issues. Side by side with cultural articles, others more matter-of-factly favored an increase in the number of scholarships, which at that time were being doled out in driblets and at very irregular intervals, or else criticized the politics of West Indian legislators, as *Légitime Défense* had done. The authors of these articles hoped for a union of black African students—still few in number at the University of Paris —and West Indians, despite the prejudices of the latter.[1] They were demonstrating in all this that they considered the unity of their race the basic prerequisite for obtaining results. On several occasions they joined French leftist students, once, for example, to protest the Ethiopian war. In 1936, they took part in an Ethiopian Action Committee, together with representatives of all the colored groups throughout the world. This proved that the *Etudiant Noir* team did not cling only to a narrow cause, their minds set on the condition of Negroes and deaf to the condition of all proletarians. Here, again, they emulated Etienne Léro's group and, whenever necessary, knew when to take up more universal battles. The attitude of many of these young men during the war was also ample demonstration.

Their cultural and sociopolitical activity was supported by discus-

1. Regarding these prejudices, see chap. 5 above.

229

sion meetings. There were exchanges of ideas on France's colonial policy, cultural problems, assimilation, the validity of African and West Indian cultures, etc. The conclusions of the debates were often published in the review, reaching only a limited number of readers. A larger audience developed later, thanks to two important essays which reflected the spirit of the group: one a study by Senghor, "Ce que l'homme noir apporte"[2] ("What the black man brings"), and the other, a report by Léon Damas, *Retour de Guyane*[3] ("Back from Guiana").

Senghor's essay was part of a collective work under the aegis of Cardinal Verdier, entitled *L'homme de couleur.*[4] The Belgian Canon J. Leclercq, the Haitian Price-Mars, and more particularly several intellectual Indochinese were contributors. The volume is so vigorously paternalistic that it is difficult to believe it is only one generation distant from us:

> Nothing is more moving than this gesture of the Frenchman, taking his black brother by the hand and helping him to rise. This hierarchic but nonetheless real collaboration, this fraternal love stooping toward the blacks to measure their possibilities of thinking and feeling; this gradual initiation to all the sciences and arts; this care that the natives should not be too suddenly removed from their milieu, their habits and their traditions; this art, in a word, of helping them progress through wise development of their personality toward an improved physical, social, and moral well-being; this is how France's colonizing mission on the black continent appears to us!
>
> May this work of colonization maintain its purity, its respect for human personality, its truly fraternal love inspired by that most Christian idea of the fundamental equality of all races and the divine essence of all men!
>
> May it continue carefully to avoid what has so odiously been called "man's exploitation of man."[5]

The blindness of the prelate who wrote these lines upon his return from Dakar is nothing compared with the testimony of a missionary ("Témoignage d'un missionaire") we meet up with soon after.

> Those who profess a fundamental scorn for the colored peoples do not lack arguments. We shall stop with the main one: the state of intellectual degradation and moral depravity in which whites found the African populations.[6]

These "arguments" were not mentioned to be disproved, quite the contrary! More lucid Frenchmen who participated in this work mention a tenacious "assimilationism": "Its goal is to act so that the civili-

2. L. S. Senghor, "Ce que l'homme noir apporte," in *L'homme de couleur* (Paris: Plon, 1939).

3. Léon Damas, *Retour de Guyane* (Paris: Librairie José Corti, 1938).

4. Cardinal Verdier, J. Leclercq, Dr. Price-Mars, L. S. Senghor, The Rev. Aupiais, and others, *L'Homme de couleur.*

5. Cardinal Verdier, Introduction, ibid., p. xi.

6. R. P. Aupiais, Provincial of the African Missions in Lyon, ibid., p. 59.

zation being born in Africa should develop under the aegis of France and within the framework of its spirit."[7]

These preliminary remarks are mentioned to show the attitude of the best-intentioned Europeans of that period and to emphasize the originality of Senghor's study—and even his attitude. Without a single reproach or hint even of what is said elsewhere in the work, in an always courteous and refined tone, Senghor undertakes an apology for African societies. He praises the black man whose personality "gives the impression that he is easily assimilable, whereas he is the one who assimilates," and patiently he explains African institutions to European readers: The blacks' religion? Monotheism, cults of their Ancestors, participation in cosmic forces, and moral values where love, charity, and the solidarity of the clan are preeminent. Sociopolitical systems? Personal needs, "the original human needs of true liberty, responsibility and dignity, find fulfillment in these systems;[8] the working of the soil, a noble task,[9] allows a harmony of man and creation."[10] The chief's authority is based on spiritual preeminence and controlled by nonrevocable ministers; the system of "palavers" permits peaceful settlement of conflicts, and the equality of all the members of the group is effective. Everywhere hospitality, respect for the stranger and for one's parents, flourishes.

Following this, Senghor attacks. He compares these so-called primitive societies to those of Western countries: governments in Europe which are maintained thanks to the police, governments with no authority, subject to the hands of schemers or puppets. Men there feel that they are becoming cogs in a machine and their work is alien and painful.[11] Growing individualism produces crises that become more and more serious.[12]

He concludes with a eulogy of Negro art, detailing its characteristics and contrasting it with classical Western art, to the detriment of the latter.

All this is expressed with considerable tact, for Senghor is a born diplomat, but nonetheless with perfect clarity. Your "black brother," he declares in answer to the other contributors, has no need of a helping hand to "assist him in his ascent," nor to be initiated "into all the arts and sciences," nor even to reach a "greater degree of physical,

7. Jacques Weulersse, "La vraie solution: l'école," ibid., p. 71.

8. L. S. Senghor, "Ce que l'homme noir apporte," ibid., p. 304.

9. This is valid only for agricultural civilizations. From a strictly ethnological point of view work is not an *asset* as such in Africa.

10. L. S. Senghor, "Ce que l'homme noir apporte," p. 114.

11. Senghor rediscovers an idea already expressed by Claude McKay in *Banjo*, and by numerous Europeans. See chap. 5 above.

12. L. S. Senghor, "Ce que l'homme noir apporte," p. 306.

social, and moral comfort," because in the societies created by blacks, quite as good as those the West wishes to impose, he can attain his full stature.

Senghor thus denies the state of "intellectual degradation and moral depravity" in which Father Aupiais claimed he had found African populations, and forced the unaware reader of 1939 to ask himself questions. Whom, indeed, should we believe? Senghor, a Negro certainly, but nevertheless a cultured intellectual speaking of a continent he knew well? Or the missionary, whose sincerity and good faith could not be doubted? May not the latter have been ascribing to all French Africa the conditions of life of a few particularly backward tribes? Or was he referring to certain tribeless urban centers or coastal sections, heavily marked by contact with the first white slave ships? Senghor generalizes too, concluding that the harmonious and peaceful civilizations of the Sudan extend to all black societies. Was he unaware of the barbaric practices—human sacrifice, torture, trial by poison—being performed when the whites arrived among such well-organized peoples as those of Dahomey?

Nevertheless, such an essay gave one food for thought.

The previous year, Léon Damas had published *Retour de Guyane.* Sent as head of a mission to his native country by the Musée d'Ethnographie de Paris,[13] he returned with a detailed report enumerating the social wounds due to colonization, and above all the curse of the penal colony, which humiliated all Guianese abroad[14] and corrupted society in the country itself. European convicts, far from being kept apart from social life there, Damas wrote, had considerable influence on it. They were used as domestic help by the civil servants in the colony and, when necessary, as technicians: masons, mechanics, chauffeurs, writers, nurses. Furthermore, after he had served his sentence, a convict was obliged to remain in Guiana for a period equal to that of his sentence: "He becomes a tramp, terrorizes us, rapes our children, imposes his customs and morals on our society, degrades, corrupts, and debases it instinctively."[15] Because of the high incidence of robbery and other crimes, the people in Guiana lived in a perpetual state of insecurity. Damas questioned what right France had to corrupt a colony in this manner, reducing it to the level of a "cesspool" for the protection of the mother country.

But he did not stop there. Apart from the presence of the convicts

13. Now the Musée de l'Homme.

14. Damas personally suffered from offensive teasing on the subject. See chap. 10 above.

15. L. Damas, *Retour de Guyane*, p. 52.

and its deplorable consequences, Damas denounced the appalling state of the country where hygiene, public utilities, and the police force were concerned. He revealed the inadequacies of the medical system, the scandal of the leper hospitals, the administrative waste and disorder, the absence of roads and railroads, and the paucity of industries, farms, or mines despite the richness of the soil and subsoil. Colonization could not therefore be justified by the official argument: the development and improvement of a virgin country for the good of the human community. On the contrary, colonization had brought a corrupt social order, on the one hand, through the excessive power granted to a governor who could issue "decrees whose uncontrolled and limitless action affect people's private status, political rights, and property";[16] and, on the other hand, by the racism of white settlers and civil servants, and the stratification of social classes among the black and mulatto populations. The petty bourgeois in Guiana, said Damas, swore only by the France of 1789, clothed themselves in every ridiculous aspect of assimilation, and suffered from a French education, "the cunning but certain instrument of domination."[17] They despised the rural population—of which they were nonetheless the descendants—which were the only group to have preserved an authentic culture and folklore rich in African traditions.[18] The sole point of contact between the native social classes was religion. As in Haiti, everyone belonged to the Catholic faith, which, although unable to resorb the voodoo beliefs, had willy-nilly learned to live with them. But even this unifying factor itself was threatened by a civil-servant–clergy affiliated with the French government.

Damas concluded his report with a forceful attack on French assimilation projects. He analyzed the case of American blacks, in whom a long period of assimilation had not succeeded in erasing basically African traits. Damas rebelled against the very principle of assimilation: Why attempt to destroy the ancient roots? Why try to "bleach" oneself? Not only is the attempt in vain, but it is revolting, humiliating:

A Serer, professor of grammar, is an eminent specialist in the French language. . . . It is an exceptional tribute for a country and a culture to be capable of specializing a foreigner to such a degree. But why the devil would anyone want our Serer to abandon his condition as a Serer in order to achieve this prize, supposing that he could?*

16. Ibid., p. 39.
17. Ibid., p. 97.
18. Damas found this folklore so interesting that he personally translated the most beautiful tales and published them under the title *Veillées noires* (Paris: Stock, 1943).
*Translator's note: The Serer Damas refers to is, of course, his friend Léopold Senghor.

Among the young elite, assimilation collides with a hostility masked for the moment as indifference.[19]

In addition, Damas denounced the duplicity, as much moral as political, behind the assimilation efforts:

Ignoring the quality of the people they would assimilate, the French with a certain enthusiasm see their assimilation as a reparation, a declaration that they consider the man facing them to be their equal. This ennobling of their work does indeed afford them a certain amount of pride. What they do not clearly understand is that the colonized man whom they hope to assimilate is perhaps an equal but that he is certainly different.[20]

Assimilation, moreover, solves no problem. Analyzing the proposed law for transforming the West Indies and Guiana into French departments, Damas sums up their spirit:

Assimilation will be the affirmation and proof to the civilized world of the excellence and triumph of France's traditional policy toward her colonies.[21]

Damas reacts sharply:

No and no. France's colonial policy is not admired by the civilized world. No. When 600,000 Negroes have been turned into assimilated Frenchmen, it will not bring back those who have preferred exile, it will not revive those who have died of hunger, it will not even clothe decently the future assimilated people. Assimilation will do nothing for the waves of disgust felt by Americans, Brazilians, Englishmen, or Dutchmen as they pass through Guiana.[22]

And when the terms of the law include the necessary nuances—"a wise and well understood assimilation in no way prevents consideration of circumstances and a variety of needs"—Damas lucidly comments:

Of course! It won't whitewash miners or cane cutters; the "variety of needs" will continue, more than ever, to serve as an excuse for maintaining Guiana as a septic tank for the mother country. See the guile of it, Guiana will be part of the mother country. To whom will she complain after that, I ask you? . . . Finally, this is only a new demagogy: to give it a title without worrying about what remains.[23]

Retour de Guyane, too sincere for its time, was considered a political pamphlet by French authorities.[24] One can see how "negritude" in the

---

19. L. Damas, *Retour de Guyane,* p. 167.
20. Ibid., p. 163.
21. Ibid., p. 167.
22. Ibid., p. 168.
23. Ibid., p. 174.
24. In 1939 Damas again wrote an important article, "Misère noire," which appeared in the review *Esprit,* in which he denounced race prejudice and briefly compared conditions of blacks in America and in French and British colonies. He insisted on the dangers of assimilation for the elite, which thus becomes separated from the mass and becomes

hands of Senghor and Damas[25] became a polyvalent tool, employed by each in a personal manner to obtain the same result: liberation of the colonized black and recognition of his own values. A rejection of assimilation and criticism of the West are far from absent in Senghor's writings, while the renewed esteem for ancestral African cultures is also present in Damas's work. But the new Negro consciousness was an edifice where each one assigned himself a special task.

Although the contributors to *L'Etudiant Noir* became known mainly by their literary works, already their sociopolitical activities, their articles, and their essays were creating a new spirit among the colored intellectuals of Paris. Between 1937 and 1940, they were joined by the West Indian students Guy Tirolien, Paul Niger, and René Bélance, the Madagascan Rabemananjara, and the Senegalese Alioune Diop.

"Naturally Paris is small," Senghor wrote, "at least for black intellectuals, who always end up meeting each other either in the Latin Quarter or at Saint-Germain-des-Près. This is how I made contact with a number of second-generation black intellectuals during the German occupation. This is how after the second World War, *Présence Africaine* was born."[26]

In 1940 war broke out. Damas retired to his ivory tower and for five years gave up all official activity. Senghor was drafted into the army and taken prisoner right at the beginning of war. As for Césaire, who had returned to Martinique a few months before the outbreak of hostilities, he founded the review *Tropiques* to spread the new ideas throughout his homeland.

---

completely harmless to the colonizer. This article was part of a longer essay which Damas never published.

25. Aimé Césaire later wrote a short essay, counterpart of the first two, entitled *Discours sur le colonialisme* (Paris: Editions Réclame, 1950).

26. L. S. Senghor, letter of February 1960. Senghor therefore recognizes the direct relationship between his group and Alioune Diop's. The latter, as well as Paul Niger and Jacques Rabemananjara, also confirm this fact. Since the founding of *Présence Africaine*, both Senghor and Césaire have served as members of the board. (See part V below.)

15 / Vichy Martinique and *Tropiques*

André Breton arrived in Martinique in 1941, spending his first week in the Lazaret concentration camp close to Fort-de-France. This is how he describes his feelings and his discovery of the magazine *Tropiques:*

Free at the end of a week, with what eagerness I plunged into the streets, seeking what they offered me of the heretofore unseen, the splendor of the markets, voices like hummingbirds, women whom Paul Eluard, returning from a trip around the world, had described as more beautiful than any others.

Yet soon a paralysis became apparent, threatening once more to overcome the scene. Nothing seemed to be holding this town together; it seemed bereft of its vital organs. The commerce, all in shop windows, had a hypothetical, uneasy air. Traffic was slower than it should have been, noises too distinct, as if heard across a junkyard. In the fragile air there was the distant continuous ringing of an alarm.

It was in these circumstances, as I was trying to buy a ribbon for my daughter, that I happened to glance through a magazine displayed in a store. Between its very modest covers, here was the first issue, just out in Fort-de-France, of a new review called *Tropiques.* Knowing how far ideas had degenerated here during the past year and having experienced the brutal manners of the Martiniquan police, I glanced through it with great suspicion.

I could hardly believe my eyes. What was said was what had to be said, not only as well, but as loudly as one could say it. The grimacing shadows faded; all the lies and mockeries grew limp; the voice of mankind had not then been cut off or silenced; it rose up again here like the very thrust of light. Aimé Césaire was the name of the man who spoke.

In complete contrast to what had been published in France during the past months, which bore the marks of masochism when it was not simply servile,

236

Tropiques was continuing to hollow out the royal road. "We," proclaimed Césaire, "are among those who say NO to darkness."[1]

When one opens *Tropiques,* then, it is important to remember the atmosphere in which the journal was born: Europe was at war; in France, the Vichy government was collaborating with the Nazis, and Martinique owed allegiance to Vichy representatives. There was no freedom of the press or of speech, and those who rebelled were usually arrested, Breton explained. Césaire almost became the victim of his expressed desire for independence when both he and his wife were professors at the lycée in Fort-de-France. The day always began with a salute to the flag. Suzanne and Aimé Césaire regularly missed this ceremony. This was enough for Mme Césaire to be threatened with dismissal. Her husband was about to suffer the same fate when an unexpected petition, signed by parents of the students, was received by Admiral Robert. The children adored this professor who was teaching them Rimbaud and Mallarmé, and his courage in the face of foreign authority gave him the sort of prestige to which youth is always sensitive. Under pressure from important Martiniquan personalities, Admiral Robert yielded and Césaire was "tolerated."

The difficulties were many in 1941 when Césaire decided to create a magazine. Cut off from all contact with Europe, Martinique had to fall back upon its own resources. Intellectual life was considerably weakened due to the lack of French books, magazines, and newspapers, the more so in a country which in normal times merely reflected the ideas of the motherland. Only local talent could supply the magazine with its material. This is why the Césaires took upon themselves not only the writing of many articles but also the recruitment of contributors. They served as proofreaders, dealt with the printers, and took care of other business problems such as procuring paper, which was at the time expensive and difficult to find.

Since they were anxious for the magazine to propagate new ideas, they were obliged to eliminate all contributors who were too bourgeois-minded and seek help and a readership only among those young people of their own age who had not been drafted into the war effort. In fact, only René Ménil, who had previously contributed to *Légitime Défense,* was able to lend them serious and regular aid.

From beginning to end, they were obliged to resort to innumerable tactics to get around government censorship. *Tropiques* was supposed to be nonpolitical and to deal only with "folklore." Although the allusive style of the articles misled them for a while, the authorities rapidly became aware of the subversive grain the young magazine was

1. André Breton, Preface to Aimé Césaire's *Cahier d'un retour au pays natal.* It appeared as an article in the review *Fontaine,* no. 35 (1944), pp. 542ff.

scattering. On the other hand, the reactions of the West Indian bour-geoisie, whose cultural subservience was being directly attacked, were violent and led to a clever form of sabotage. It was not possible to forbid the magazine officially, but under government pressure and out of fear of becoming compromised, one after another the island's print-ers refused to print it. These intrigues, however, took time and for three years, one way or another, the review managed to get published, sowing the seeds of new ideas in the minds of its readers.

The young read *Tropiques* with passion, and from their generation have come men like Frantz Fanon, Edouard Glissant, Joseph Zobel, and, lastly, Georges Desportes, an old student of Césaire's who, faith-ful to his master's spirit, founded the journal *Caravelle* in Martinique in 1947. In addition, *Tropiques* established cultural contacts with neigh-boring countries like Cuba and Venezuela. Césaire's reputation spread as far as Haiti, where in 1944 he was invited to deliver a series of courses and lectures over a period of eight months. It was also in Haiti in 1946 that Pierre Mabille founded an important cultural review *Con-jonctions*, which took over from *Tropiques* not only the surrealist flag but also its aims of cultural originality and the development of native personality.

From the very first issue, with courageous lucidity, *Tropiques* placed itself on a level that was both national and international. Martinique was a derelict island: "No city. No art. No poetry," as Césaire put it. Awareness of the mediocrity need not, however, lead to resignation, but must stimulate the energy of those who no longer wish to be universal parasites.

Silent and sterile land. I am speaking of our land. And across the Caribbean my ears consider the terrifying silence of Man. Europe. Africa. Asia. I can hear the shriek of steel, the sound of tom-toms in the jungle, the temple praying amid the Banyan trees. And I know man is speaking. Again and always I listen. But here there is monstrous atrophy of the voice, century-old prostration, prodigious silence. No city. No art. No poetry. No civilization, true civilization. I mean the projection of man upon the world, the shaping of the world by man: a stamping of the universe with the likeness of man.

A death more horrible than death itself toward which the living are drifting. Elsewhere science makes progress, new philosophies rise and aesthetics change. Vainly in this land of ours does the hand sow grain.

No city. No art. No poetry. Not a seed, not a single young shoot. Or else the hideous leprosy of imitations. Truly a mute and sterile land. . . .

But there is no longer time to be a parasite upon the world. Rather we must save it. It is time to gird our loins like valiant men.

World conditions were less favorable than ever. Everywhere there were threats, violence, acts of barbarity. If in the Islands men were diminished, in Europe they were killing each other.

Wherever we look the darkness is winning. One after the other the fires are going out. The circle of shadows is closing in upon the cries of men and the howlings of wild beasts. And yet we are among those who say NO to darkness. We know that the salvation of the world also depends upon us. That the world needs all and any of its sons. Even the most humble.

The darkness wins. . . .

—Ah! all hope is not too much to face the century with!

Men of good will will create a new light for the world.[2]

Right from the start, then, *Tropiques* assumed the task of describing brutal reality and combating it. Some called it the optimism of youth, and others thought it depressing pessimism. Yet it was simply manly courage! Césaire used to say then: "Everything is as bad as can be, so it is time to call up the men of good will and say NO." Twenty years later his appeal found an unexpected echo in the play by Ionesco in which the hero, facing an army of rhinoceroses, cries out: "No, I shall not capitulate!"

"What was said in *Tropiques*," Breton realized, "was what had to be said."

2. Aimé Césaire, Introduction to the first issue of *Tropiques*, April 1944.

16/ Cultural Sterility: Denial of the Self

In order to do battle with their monsters, the editors of *Tropiques* had to find new arms. First they undertook a systematic inventory of West Indian problems, continuing it for the entire duration of the magazine. Next, they attacked the mediocrity and deception of local art, its polished imitations, "useless mirror images," and simultaneously they called for a personal art which could be the true expression of the Martiniquan people.

To a people "with three centuries of recitation behind them, who have always come empty-handed to the seats of culture, never having created anything, in the belief that culture is something that occurs in the memory," what would a personal art be? René Ménil gives a definition:

Art attempts to penetrate and seize reality: It begins with impressions and images formed by the contact of our sensibility with the world, which takes on a life of its own.

When the artist cultivates his difference, he does not isolate himself but, quite the contrary, reaches men and things by a true path in order to truly express them.

The tree has access to the world not from outside but from within itself, through its roots. In man, the paths of communion with the world also necessarily come from within. . . .

And one penetrates the reality of men and things to the exact depth that one has penetrated oneself. . . .

There is one way of reaching reality outside of which one misses everything. Whoever loses awareness of himself knows nothing. When one takes nature as a guide, one inevitably becomes one's own main reality. Beyond the ego and through the ego, when one reaches the universe step by step, without losing touch, plunging deeper and deeper into one's true roots, one discovers those realities that tightly encompass and which, depending on our distance from

240

them, we describe as local, regional, social, etc.

The particularities that make up individual lives, whether petty or grandiose, are not obstacles to universal expression; they are moments which lead to it. . . .

Art is the expression of what is universal through the expression of the individual man rooted in his own existence, perhaps in his village life. And universality is attained not by suppressing the artist's most private self, but by its expression in adequate language. Language is the form of the universal.[1]

Ménil then draws the obvious conclusion: To be in a position to create an authentic art, one must commit oneself to finding one's bearings in one's actual situation.

In order to create, one must follow not the clouds of the conceptual life but the path of one's real life, the real life of one's community. One must take a chance and bet on the present course of events.

The climate and habitat, the extraordinary internal mixing of our communities, the particularities of our arrival in this world, the original life we lead and which leads us, all of this creates in us fears and hopes, desires and passions, acts and dreams, sadness and joys, which are unique in this world. . . . We have a special note to sound which so far we have not been able to send forth. . . . If we express ourselves well, and completely, we shall—by a necessity of nature—have expressed more than ourselves.

Ménil concludes his exposition with an appeal to national pride:

If we do not wish to be mere spectators of the human adventure, if we believe that we must give of ourselves merely to participate in true humanity . . . we know the task before us and the road that leads to its attainment.[2]

In the name of such criteria, this professor of philosophy thus condemns the classical activities of his country's artists and calls for a new and authentic art:

Up to now those who have spoken have not expressed themselves, and those who had something to say have been voiceless. It will require a complete turnabout in our aesthetic attitude for us to move from a formal conception of our art to art itself. There is no question of improving the condemned art. To improve what is bad is to increase its badness. There must be a change in quality. And this is what we are predicting.[3]

Tropiques stated that one of the main causes of artistic sterility in Martinique was the alienation resulting from social relations.[4] The magazine did not specifically attack colonization, but blamed Martiniquans who condoned it by allowing themselves to be completely assimilated. Suzanne Césaire explains the historical process of this

1. René Ménil, "Naissance de notre art," *Tropiques,* no. 1.
2. Ibid.
3. Ibid.
4. The alienation had already been denounced in *Légitime Défense,* as we have shown.

"pseudo-morphosis." The laws and attitudes of the settlers in a hundred different ways prevented black slaves from comparing themselves to whites. They were not allowed to wear the same clothes as whites, nor to work as anything but farm laborers, domestics, etc. As a result, it became the main object of colored men to resemble their masters as closely as possible. As long as the slave's condition was associated with a differentiation between slave and master, the black man would associate the idea of freedom with resemblance. Thus, after the emancipation of 1848, those few slaves who had the opportunity undertook by all and any means a race toward the assimilation represented by money, studies, marriages, intrigue.

"Unscrupulous ambition. A crusade reduced to the level of being middle class. Vanity fair!" This is how Suzanne Césaire sums up this period. The ideal of each Martiniquan was to become a petty bourgeois, just like the Frenchman, and he overlooked the colonial, psychological, and racial premises which had conditioned him in spite of himself. The poverty of artistic and intellectual endeavors in the West Indies stemmed from this alienation.

The Martiniquan has failed because, unaware of his real nature, he tries to lead a life which is not his own. The gigantic phenomenon of a collective lie. . . . No advanced Martiniquan would ever admit that he was merely a mimic, so natural, spontaneous, and born of legitimate aspirations did his present situation seem. And he would be sincere in this. He honestly does not *know* he mimics. He is *unaware* of his true nature, which nevertheless exists.

Suzanne Césaire calls for a new awareness from this "formidable mass of varied energies till now locked within us." She demands "the mobilization of all the living strength mixed upon this earth," in order "to use it to its maximum without deviation or falsification."[5]

If Suzanne Césaire took the trouble patiently to explain this sociological estrangement, René Ménil merely denounced it in haughty, vengeful terms. He explained nothing. He practiced caricature and assassination by means of it.

Here he comes cautiously, the most "successful" man of the region: the West Indian petty bourgeois. A laughable encounter . . . Smiles, bows, receptions, words, toasts, parades, speeches, bows, discussions, conferences, bluster, smiles, clothes . . .
Bows . . . Greetings, polite shadow!
But when is the season of men?[6]

Or else he loses patience and hurls insults:

You who have never known a lofty thought nor a strong passion, you who have never committed yourself to a venture which would have exalted you, you

5. Suzanne Césaire, "La psychologie du Martiniquais," in *Tropiques*, no. 5 (April 1942).
6. René Ménil, "Laissez passer la poésie," ibid.

who are incapable of either great courage or great cowardice, you carry on your forehead a fatal mark. . . . You lack resilience. . . . You have no character . . .

You have no faith in yourself. You invariably take yourself for less than a man since you say: "Not bad for a Martiniquan" when one of your brothers occupies a minor official post. . . . The Martiniquan petty bourgeois is incapable of writing fiction, for the simple reason that he himself is a fictitious character.

A literature is taking shape here. Whether you like or not is the least of our worries. Aware of what you are, by means of skillful geometrical projection we shall show precisely what you are not upon the Caribbean screen. Martiniquan poetry will be virile.[7]

A poet would say the same thing more symbolically:

> O terre de cimaise dénuée
> Terre grasse gorgée d'eau lourde
> Votre jour est un chien qui jappe après une ombre[8]

> [Oh deprived and concave land
> Rich land swollen with heavy water
> Your day is a dog yapping at a shadow]

Is there anyone who does not see that the denigration of this alienated society was so intense only because the editors and contributors of *Tropiques* were so painfully both judge and plaintiff? It was in themselves they found the alienation they were fighting: It was theirs because of their education, their family ties.

On the other hand, their condemnations were not without appeal. They were rejecting and shaking off old bonds, but in so doing wounding their parents, friends, and colleagues. That was why even their most vehement criticisms were always accompanied by prayers and appeals. They possessed a truth they were anxious to share, and were convinced it was transmissible. Practically every controversial article contained a note of hope: "There is still that small number of men, if not of will, at least of 'good will,' from whom we still hope to obtain something."[9] Or else justifying questions: "Could we decently come to the encounter with art holding the borrowed favors of a borrowed poetry in our hands? Did we have to have the impudence to bring copies whose originals would betray us?"[10]

Occasionally the poet sings softly to tame his ignorant and timid brethren. He asks for their trust; he becomes their patient and clear-sighted guide:

7. Ibid.
8. Aimé Césaire, "Le grand midi," in *Les armes miraculeuses* (Paris: NRF, Gallimard, 1946), p. 80.
9. R. Ménil, "Laissez passer la poésie."
10. R. Ménil, "Naissance de notre art."

Et mes doigts caressent la corde de vos doigts
vos doigts de cul de fosse
vos doigts de voix basse
vos doigts d'ainsi-soit-il
vos doigts d'Atlantide effondrée
....

Cependant—ah! la coupure fétide du ruisseau
prostitué—un cri, le même, s'éleva, violant
toutes les gorges taraudées:
Qui est-il? Qui est-il?
Qui je suis? Vous demandez qui je suis
La lagune qui fait pressentir la tiédeur dernière de son alcove; l'herbe
    folle qui fait crépiter et claironner la sonnerie des graminées . . .
Cœurs d'argent, cœurs d'argent, d'argent mat, n'entendez-vous pas
    mon ombre lovée dans le nid tempétueux de l'or jeune?
Allons, à mon oreille—quand sur la route de jadis le dernier cheval
    s'enfoncera dans l'ouest fangeux, globulera une lueur étrange: le
    ciel! le ciel tendre et jeune, le ciel nouveau-né, le ciel qu'il fallait
    contre les balles et les crachats cuirasser d'un sourire impénétra-
    ble.[11]

[And my fingers stroke the cords of yours
your ditch-bottom fingers
your soft-voiced fingers
your amen fingers
your fingers of a buried Atlantis
....

And yet—oh! the fetid drain of the
prostituted stream—one cry, the same, rises outraging
all the force-fed throats:
Who is he? Who is he?
Who am I? You ask who I am
The lagoon announcing the recent warmth of its bed; wild weeds
    crackling and trumpeting the sound of grass . . .
Silver hearts, silver hearts, of unpolished silver, can you not hear my
    shadow coiling in the stormy nest of young gold?
Whisper in my ear—when the last horse plunges into the slimy West
    on the road of days gone by, a strange light will glow: the sky! the
    young and tender sky, the newborn sky, the sky which must be
    armed against bullets and spittle with an impenetrable smile.]

Beneath the armor of wit and apparent obscurity, Césaire was predicting a young sky of hope, the newborn heaven of freedom.

11. Aimé Césaire, "En rupture de mer morte," *Tropiques*, no. 3 (October 1941), p. 75.

17 / Weapons: Africa and the Race

If Martiniquan art lacked personality and was therefore worthless, it was necessary to rediscover, behind all modifications, the true realities. The most evident reality was the racial one! Martiniquans are essentially black, more or less crossbred after three centuries of colonization. One of the first things *Tropiques* acknowledged was that "once upon a time there was a black man, clinging to the black earth."

The chief way of reaching these realities was through the revaluation of African culture: West Indians are black and the blacks were once slaves. But they were not always slaves. The Negro had been imported from Africa, which had known brilliant civilizations. This reasoning shows through like a watermark in the long articles devoted to Leo Frobenius, a man of established authority: "Here is a man who knows: a historian, an archaeologist, an ethnologist, and, it is not too much to say, a poet."[1] And this man of science discovered that "the idea of constant progress, dear to the nineteenth century, which showed civilization advancing along a single line from primitive barbarity to modern high culture, was false."[2] Whether the Païdeuma theory of an abstract power creating civilizations somewhat haphazardly in space and time was accurate or not was of little importance! The essential thing was that the concrete idea of the absolute supremacy of Western civilization was being challenged, and that primitive civilizations were being revaluated or, better still, magnified. And, indeed, Frobenius took as an example the African civilizations he had so much admired that he had devoted himself to studying them and claimed to have

1. Suzanne Césaire, "Léo Frobénius et le problème des civilisations," *Tropiques,* no. 1 (April 1941).
2. Ibid.

245

created for himself "an African soul, a way of thinking and feeling properly African."[3]

Wasn't this enough to scandalize assimilated Martiniquans who swore only by Europe? For what did this scientist discover after "numerous exploration trips, a detailed study of rupestral drawings throughout the African continent and Europe, a comparison of religions, morals, customs, habitat, tools, objects of current use, among most peoples of this earth?"[4] He discovered that the mysterious Païdeuma power had developed more slowly in Africa than elsewhere, but deeply and with fewer changes, "giving birth in certain parts of Africa to civilizations as brilliant as those of the Gao empire, at a period when Europe was covered with impenetrable forests and swamps."

Frobenius's *Histoire de la civilisation africaine*[5] is a tremendous effort of synthesis toward the understanding of all these very ancient forms of civilization, which today seem primitive and frozen, whereas in reality they were often the astonishingly rich and complex symbols of grandiose cultures of which we know nothing.[6]

Black Martiniquans had no need, then, to be ashamed of their African origins. On the contrary, insofar as three centuries of slavery and exile had cut them off from their origins, "those grandiose cultures of which we know nothing," it was urgent that they attempt a rediscovery. "Africa does not only mean for us an enlargement toward somewhere else, but also the deepening of our sense of self."[7]

"The deepening sense of self" is the phrase too that echoes from the article by René Ménil from which we have already quoted:[8] "The tree has access to the world not from outside but through its roots"—"One penetrates the reality of man and things only as deeply as one penetrates oneself"—"There is one path to reality outside of which one misses everything. Whoever loses contact with himself, knows nothing."

Here again the reasoning is simple: The Martiniquan, African in origin, has lost his personality under the influence of Europe. To rediscover himself as he was originally, he must rediscover Mother Africa!

Suzanne Césaire's utilization of Frobenius had a definite aim. She referred to the two forms of civilization which Frobenius believed he

---

3. Ibid.

4. Ibid.

5. *Tropiques* reproduced in full the introduction to this work, of which we have given several excerpts in chap. 8 above.

6. Suzanne Césaire, "Léo Frobénius."

7. Ibid.

8. René Ménil, "Naissance de notre art, *Tropiques*, no. 1.

had discovered in Africa,[9] emphasizing their psychological angle: The one, Ethiopian civilization, linked to plant life, to the vegetative cycle, is dreamy, mystical, assimilating; while the other, Hamitic civilization, is linked to animal life and to violent conquest of the right to live.

She gives examples, developing the idea that Martiniquans belong to the "Ethiopian civilization":

> What is a Martiniquan fundamentally, intimately, unilaterally? A plant-man. Like a plant, he abandons himself to the rhythm of universal life. No effort is made to dominate nature. . . . His indolence is that of a vegetable. . . . Obstinate as only a plant knows how to be. Open your eyes. A child is born? To which god shall he be entrusted? To the Tree god. Coconut tree or Banana tree, under whose roots the placenta is buried. Open your ears. According to popular Martiniquan folklore the grass which grows on a grave is the living hair of the person buried beneath, who is protesting against death. The symbol is always the same: a plant. It is a sharp feeling of a life-death community. In short, it is the *Ethiopian feeling of life.*[10]

It is because they have misunderstood their true nature and adopted the colonizer's manner of life, concludes Suzanne Césaire, that Martiniquans fail to produce valid work.

This opinion was corroborated by another contributor to *Tropiques:* "Most of the time the aesthetic of a colored Martiniquan is not ethnic but European. This is an exaggerated attitude because it implies the renunciation of part of oneself, and the result, for a personality thus repressed, mutilated and contradicted, is a powerlessness to express itself on an artistic level. Africa takes its revenge!"[11]

But must Western civilization be rejected in its entirety? No. Martiniquans are mulattoes: "We stand at the crossroads. The meeting point of races and cultures." It is useless to deny the West's profound influence. "It is evident that all our conscious reactions are determined by European culture: arts, science, technology. And we are determined to use these precision weapons with all their latest improvements."[12] Europe has supplied Martinique with means of expression which it would be vain, and impossible too, to refuse. But this Western culture must be reduced to its proper level: that of a means, no more, of

9. When asked about this, Michel Leiris replied that Frobenius's theories are still too vast for today's ethnological science to adopt or refute. Today's knowledge is insufficient to dare form such theories regarding a little-known civilization.

10. Suzanne Césaire, "Léo Frobénius." It is unimportant that Frobenius's classifications are no longer considered valid by modern ethnologists. The important thing is that they were fruitful for the *Tropiques* team.

11. René Hibran, "Le problème de l'art à la Martinique," *Tropiques,* no. 4 (October 1941).

12. We see here the germination of the myth of the "additional-African-soul," which the modern, too technical world needs—a myth which will later be nourished by the writings of Alioune Diop, Senghor, and many others.

expressing something which is *not* Western: Martiniquan reality. For "in our veins flows a blood which demands an original attitude to life." The man of color must "respond to the special dynamic of his complex biological reality," and to understand this reality completely, he must go back along one of the power lines of the race right up to this immense thing, Africa—Africa of unique poetical talents, of unique artistic production!"[13]

From this point on, it is obvious that West Indians cannot do without "the extraordinary cultural enrichment that must result from their understanding of the African fact." Only under this condition will they be able to express "everything their negritude implies" and through this "attain their complete humanity." Africa will thus give to Martiniquans, first their titles of nobility, the restoration of their dignity, and then the forgotten path to their innermost being, to the rediscovery of themselves. Finally, Africa contains a hope for the future of the European world itself, which, after a crisis of colonialist imperialism, seems to be possessed of a "truly insane craving for power and domination that plunges humanity into disasters as terrible as the two world wars."

The "return to Africa" would be insufficient, however, if it were not accompanied by an awareness of the problems of all racial brothers, beginning with those who were the closest, black Americans.

Since *Tropiques* could not officially take up politics, it decided to study the poetry of black Americans. But what would it call attention to? The art, the style? Certainly, but above all to the cry, the message: "It is by his cry that man is recognized." "Here is the cry of the Negro poet":

> Nous crions parmi les gratte-ciel
> Comme nos ancêtres
> criaient parmi les palmiers d'Afrique
> Car nous sommes seuls
> Et nous avons peur.

> [We shout among the skyscrapers
> As our ancestors
> cried among the palm trees of Africa
> Because we are alone
> And we are afraid.]

"This shows that the poet's master-feeling is one of uneasiness, or better still of intolerance. Intolerance of reality because it is sordid; of the world because it is caged; of life because he has been robbed of it on the highway to the sun."[14]

13. Suzanne Césaire, "Léo Frobénius."
14. Aimé Césaire, "Introduction à la poésie nègre-américaine," *Tropiques*, no. 2 (July 1941).

Indirectly through this poetry, Aimé Césaire evokes the black man's situation in the New World; this entire race condemned to "a sordid reality": plantation workers, vagabonds, prostitutes, "marching past men, women, children, pell-mell, with the stubborn dust of poverty and hunger clinging to their ankles." What he sees, beyond the blues and the Negro spirituals is the wait for the "coming of the Lord," compensation in eternity for a fate unbearable in this world.

"Ah, the Negro paradise! How clearly one feels it is the poetic escape of a sad, bruised people, for centuries held in material poverty and spiritual hell, in the custody of vigilant executioners!"[15]

"Grape jelly and golden biscuits" make up for the hunger that accompanies the Negro throughout his life. The kindness of the saints and prophets, the courtesy and politeness of Saint Michael and the attentions of Jesus himself are compensation for all the brutalities here on earth inflicted on the Negro, son of slaves.

But the new American Negro poets have stopped lamenting and rebelled against their "vigilant executioners":

And against the dark background of anguish, suppressed indignation, long stifled despair, anger rises and whistles, and America, on the shaky bed of its conservatism, is concerned about the dreadful hatred this cry is venting upon them. . . . The black court of miracles has risen.

The black poet has no desire to paint or describe this pitiful humanity, but is enlisted in the same adventure as his heroes. He lives their life. He does not watch them struggle or fight, he himself takes part in the struggle and fight. He is not above them but among them. He is not judge but comrade. And this comradeship explains the astonishing ease with which the poet can put himself in humanity's place, his virtuosity at unraveling the skein of fundamental and primary energies which motivate the people to whom he belongs.[16]

At the same time, Césaire defines the role of the black poet. Spokesman of his people, he need not choose as material "man's noblest part, the finest thoughts or feelings" but must "accept responsibility for man's entire nature" and paint earnestly and with passion so as to "make a hero of the everyday Negro, despite an entire literature whose mission is to ferret out all his grotesque and exotic aspects," just "like an African jeweler who has only brass and iron for his rarest masterpieces." The Negro poet must be humble, he must also remain loyal in spite of temptations: "How many opportunities for escape! . . . civilization's thousand exits called science, ethics, culture, which lead to the ego's surrender to appearances, for fear of the self."[17]

The allusion here to the bourgeois and Westernized writers that

15. Ibid.
16. Ibid.
17. Ibid.

Tropiques habitually attacked was transparent. But this time the attack was not merely negative: It pointed out the way or, better still, outlined the mission. If the black poet has the courage to accept himself, his color, and his social origins, to admit he is the racial brother of this wretched mass, if he faces the fact that he must represent these people and live their problems, then he can "call forth a world . . . accept a new manner of suffering, dying, in a word, carry a man's load." Then perhaps he will accomplish what all the virtuosity and talent of the "alienated" poets has not succeeded in: He will awaken the primitive energies, the psychological incentives which will enable this battered race to rise and undertake the conquest of its liberty. "By a miracle of love" he will succeed "in influencing even the innermost forces that order destiny."[18]

We can see how Césaire led his readers from the study of Negro literature to a more general view. The American Negro was but a symbol of the entire black race, rejected, enslaved, humiliated because it was black. And the Negro poet in the United States is authentic only because he is willing to express his people's defects. His poetry is valid only to the extent that "it allows a drop of blood to show." From then on one must be deaf not to hear the call, fixed as if by a branding iron: Writers of Martinique, you too are black, your people too are enslaved and humiliated, do not shrink from yourselves and your responsibilities!

In its next issue, *Tropiques* emphasized the recognition of the historical and racial reality by means of direct comments about West Indian folklore. In a lyrical style, René Ménil and Aimé Césaire examined the pivots on which fables and folktales center: Hunger, Fear, Defeat, Guile. After vain rebellions, Hunger and Fear engender Guile, the final result of a civilization imposed by force.

We offer some long excerpts of this social interpretation of West Indian literature: Bitterness is mixed with tenderness, occasionally creating veritable poems:

Once upon a time . . .

Don't expect to find cosmogonies or metaphysics here. Nor even the expression of those great adventures of the heart that mark mankind. Thinking, like sentiment, is a luxury.

Once upon a time, an unfortunate time, a time of poverty and shame, there was a black man clinging to a black land. . . .

Take it as you will, these people are hungry. There is not a single story where it does not occur—visions of feasting and drunkenness—this obsession with empty bellies. . . .

18. Ibid.

Drinking, eating, always the same incessant dream. Let us not smile at this "naïveté." In a form at first childish, but nonetheless direct, these are valuable historical documents. After searching through the archives, examining each file, studying every paper left by the abolitionists, anyone who wants to grasp the eloquent and pitiful destitution of our enslaved fathers must return to these folktales.

And now the secret mechanism of the marvelous is revealed. When man, crushed by a wicked, unjust society, looks around for help in vain, discouraged and powerless, he projects his wretchedness and his revolt toward a sky full of promises and dynamite.

After the cycle of hunger comes the cycle of fear. The slave's master and his companions, the whip and the stool pigeon. This is the era when white and black adventurers became experts in hunting escaped slaves.[19]

The time when bloodhounds combed gullies and mountains. The period when informers were guaranteed their freedom. In other words, the time of Fear, of the great Fear and universal suspicion.

This explains the strange and characteristic mythology of the Zombi. Everything is Zombi. Translate this into: "Be suspicious of everything; understand that the whole of humanity, animals, and nature conspires against you."

A drum beats. The great voodoo laugh rolls down from the hills. In the course of the centuries, how many revolts have begun this way? How many fleeting victories! But also how many defeats! And what repressions! Hands cut off, bodies broken on the rack, tortured, and the gallows; this is what fills the byways of colonial history. Would nothing of this have seeped into the folklore? . . .

And now, what remains? Hunger, Fear, Defeat. The great triangular circuit and its monotonous slaves. What remains? Colibri, the valiant Colibri is thoroughly dead. His drum no longer beats out the order to attack. . . . What is left? . . . The Rabbit, the weak, but sly, crafty, wily—and unreliable rabbit. The degeneration of the race. This is the great fact. Personal solutions replace those of the group. Cunning replaces strength.

What is left? The foxy, crafty guys, the ones who can wangle things. From then on, humanity is divided into two groups: those who know how to shift for themselves, and those who don't. The admirable result of two centuries of civilization!

Once upon a time there was a black man clinging to a black land . . .[20]

The aggressive tone is obvious. Social and political problems are plainly exposed here: oppression, torture, loss of freedom, physical and moral unhappiness. The whole business of colonization is challenged again: Civilization is "unmasked." The smart, foxy guy is the

19. *"Nègres marrons,"* runaway slaves, fled the plantation in order to live free in the forests. They used to be hunted with specially trained dogs. If caught, the runaways would be branded with a hot iron. A second escape attempt would be punished with hamstringing, a third by death.

20. R. Ménil and A. Césaire, Introduction to special issue of *Tropiques* devoted to Martiniquan folklore, no. 4 (January 1942).

admirable type produced by three centuries of Western occupation. To survive, a man had to do away with his dignity, annihilate his rebellion, submit his awareness to an apprenticeship of lies: These were the principles every Martiniquan sucked in with his mother's milk, extracted from his nurse's stories, from the evening legends. The people of Martinique were a "degenerate race!"

But the interest *Tropiques* had in West Indian folklore was not always so negative. If the tales told Martiniquans about alienation, they were also a source of positive knowledge. They contained survivals of African customs, for example: the role of witch doctors, metamorphoses of the devil, the custom of asking riddles, animal symbolism. *Tropiques* proposed all these as subjects for study in order to reestablish the bonds between Africa and the West Indies, long broken by exile.

Also to be found in the tales and legends were lessons of courage, a fighting spirit and heroism, as in the story of Colibri, the proud, free Negro to whom God sent various animals one by one, to rob him of his tom-tom, symbol of creative power. Colibri withstood everything until the arrival of the Armed-Fish (symbolizing the European and his technical power), whom Colibri fought to the death rather than yield his freedom. The implications of this fable still prevail, stressed *Tropiques:* The people of Martinique are still capable of resistance, as the escaped and rebellious slaves were in the past, as are all those who will say "No" to the hated masters.

18 / Surrealist Poetry: Césaire's "Miraculous Weapon"

Tropiques had thus far proposed three weapons to West Indians for the reconquest of their true personality: the return to African sources, racial originality, and the lessons of folklore. But there existed a fourth weapon, supplied by Europe itself, that would enable the Negro poet to carry out the prescribed changes in himself and in his people: surrealism.

We saw in chapter 3 how surrealism influenced the *Légitime Défense* group, with which René Ménil had been so closely associated, and how, less directly, it had influenced the Césaire-Senghor-Damas trio. Césaire's *Cahier d'un retour au pays natal*, however, was not surrealist, although some of its incantations made use of the movement's techniques. *Tropiques* was to recommend surrealism as *poetry's way of salvation*. The very first issues pleaded its cause and, without actually naming the movement, described its method.

Poetry is an incantation, a magic, a taking possession of a being's most inward life: its mysterious and secret core. . . . The magic of poetry; is the expression too strong? Let Mallarmé speak:

"To evoke a secret object intentionally in darkness, by indirect allusive words, reducing them to equal silence, comprises an attempt close to creation."

The secret is out.

The basic function of poetry since Baudelaire and Rimbaud is no longer to create a work of art as understood by the Parnassians. What does the poet now seek? Not to model, carve, or fashion a jewel. He wishes to create a world, a universe. Poetry now launches into the infinite mystery. As Paul Reverdy says: "I am as obscure as feeling . . ."

And from then on, the reader is asked to take part. To take part in obscurity. To take part with the mind and the soul. Consenting with the mind and the soul. Permitting the being to communicate with the world. A world. The poet's world.

Is nature then so clear? Its reality so understandable? The poet who has stolen its creative fire, . . . will not he too need mystery and the indescribable? Poetry is creation.[1]

Ménil's first articles on surrealism in *Tropiques* resembled a course in literature. Patiently he initiated his public to the most orthodox elementary ideas, from Reverdy's "recipe"—"The more distant and the more exact the relations between two realities that are brought together, the stronger will be the image, and the greater its emotional power"—to theories on poetic activity:

Turning one's back on the world, without ever ceasing to lean against it, the poet attempts to grasp its imaginary complement. . . .

Reality and make-believe are contrary to one another, not as the individual and nothingness, but as being and becoming. Make-believe is that which, still abstract, tends to become real, or rather, more real. It becomes so when we have the necessary courage. . . . Poetic activity is not an escape from reality, it can only be a limitless enlargement of reality, an attempt to seize it in its entirety, an attempt to reach an infinite vision of the universe. . . .

We rediscover thus a kingdom which our laziness and the little faith we have in the reality of the spirit has degraded and diminished, and we rule it, at the hellish pace of a man who reaches essential simplicity, basic truths, early youth, first origins, mad hopes which are the only hopes, and infinite confidence.[2]

Ménil speaks next of the idea of "surreality," the rediscovered unity of spirit and the benefits of automatic writing:

The poet holds the reality of every day on the point of his pen, but he glows all over with a secret fire won from that counterreality in the imagination, and delivers to man an absolute reality, a surreality if you prefer, where a primitive unity, the real and the imaginary, are animated by the same breath of life.

The multiplication of these poetic discoveries, which are discoveries of reality, depends entirely on the poet's audacity. This audacity can happily be borne by the ground swell of psychic automatism, which, left to its natural movement, necessarily leads the mind to confront its own truths which become real when they are attained.[3]

These didactic, somewhat scholarly articles were meant to introduce the West Indian reader to modern poetry and to promote parallel movements locally. At the same time, *Tropiques* regularly published the poems by Césaire that were later brought together under the title *Les armes miraculeuses*. These pages seem to have served as illustrations for the theoretical articles, whereas in fact it was, rather, the articles that

1. Aristide Maugée, "Poésie et obscurité," *Tropiques*, no. 2 (July 1941).
2. René Ménil, "Orientation de la poésie," *Tropiques*, no. 2 (July 1941).
3. Ibid.

explained the poems, which were difficult and frankly surrealistic in treatment.

For a writer like Aimé Césaire so completely to adopt surrealistic writing, having been the fiercest adversary of French cultural influence, may seem surprising. The change is often attributed to the influence of André Breton, whom Césaire met in Martinique.[4] It is a fact that Breton first recognized and then encouraged Césaire's surrealism. But that he was not the cause of it is quite simply proved by historical circumstances: The two principal poems of *Les armes miraculeuses* entitled "Le grand midi" ("High noon") and "Les pur-sang" ("The thoroughbreds"), which are already clearly surrealistic, appeared in *Tropiques*[5] before Breton ever met Césaire.[6] Moreover, Breton knew Césaire for only two months before moving on to the United States. A brand new style is not assimilated in so short a time. Breton's statement is sufficient in any case to show that between these two men there was an encounter, mutual admiration, but no influence. Speaking of *Tropiques*, Breton wrote:

These pages were written in the tone of those who do not deceive, confirming that a man wholly engaged in his adventure at the same time had every means at his disposal, not only on the aesthetic, but also on the moral and social level, to make his mediation necessary and inevitable.

One became aware that every word that crossed his tongue, from the simplest to the most unusual, was *naked*. From this in his work that culmination in the concrete, that constantly *major* quality of tone that so easily permits one to distinguish great from lesser poets. What I learned that day was that the verbal instrument had not even gone out of tune in the turmoil.[7]

Breton compared Césaire to a "human vat brought to its highest boiling point, in which knowledge—again of the highest quality—intervenes with magic gifts," and he recognized in Césaire's writings a conception of life akin to his own: "Nothing he expressed was strange to me." Breton's enthusiasm, however, did not stem only from Césaire's surrealistic poems. For when he read the still unpublished *Cahier d'un retour au pays natal*, Breton declared:

This poem is nothing less than the greatest lyrical monument of this time. . . . One discovers above all else the abundant movement, the exuberance in the thrust and the spilling forth, the faculty of constantly and utterly alerting

4. As does, for example, Madame Eliane Bouquey in "Négritude et poètes noirs (thesis for Licence ès Lettres degree, at l'Université Libre de Bruxelles, 1959).

5. *Tropiques*, no. 1 (April 1941), and no. 2 (July 1941).

6. See passage by André Breton, introducing chap. 15 above.

7. André Breton, "Un grand poète noir," *Fontaine*, no. 35 (1944).

the emotional world to the point of upsetting it completely, that are typical of authentic in contrast to false poetry. . . .

Césaire's poetry, like all great poetry and all great art, reaches the heights by the power of transmutation it sets in motion, which consists—from a base of the most disreputable subject matter, including even ugliness and servitude —of producing what we know is no longer gold or the philosopher's stone, but liberty.[8]

As for the impression Breton made on Césaire, it can be felt in the very next issue of *Tropiques*. Breton is praised to the skies, often quoted and commented on, and surrealism is extolled as a superior means of liberation.

The adoption of surrealist method was also due to the political circumstances that forced Martiniquans to speak in innuendos. From 1941 to 1943, surrealism became the stronghold of the spirit of resistance. Most of *Les armes miraculeuses* was written during the war, under the Vichy government. It was impossible to criticize the established order openly, but it was also impossible for Césaire to silence his exacerbated feeling of intolerance of all forms of oppression and cowardice. Surrealism permitted a sort of code language through which the members of the review could express their revolt and hopes without too much fear of reprisal. A literary means thus became an indispensable vehicle for expressing opposition ideas, the only possible vehicle under the circumstances, since it was allusive enough, indeed obscure enough, to prevent one's adversaries and those in authority from catching the meaning.

From among the powerful war machines the modern world now places at our disposal . . . our audacity has chosen surrealism, which offers the greatest chances for success.

During those difficult years of Vichy domination, there was not a moment when the picture of liberty was ever totally extinguished here, and we owe this to surrealism. We are happy to have maintained this image even in the eyes of those who thought they had destroyed it forever. Blind because they were ignorant, they did not see it laugh insolently, aggressively in our pages. Cowards later, when they did understand, fearful and ashamed.

So, far from contradicting, diminishing, or diverting our revolutionary feeling for life, surrealism encouraged it. It nourished in us an impatient strength, endlessly sustaining this huge army of negations.[9]

But surrealism did not serve only as an instrument of rebellion and propaganda against the West in general and the pro-Nazi government in particular. It was also used to right the Martiniquan bourgeoisie and to awaken a population degenerate from too many years of slavery.

8. Ibid. [Translator's note: The *Cahier* had not been published in its entirety, though portions had appeared in *Volontés* in 1939.]

9. Suzanne Césaire, "1943: le surréalisme et nous," *Tropiques*, no. 8 (October 1943).

We know where we stand here in Martinique. Our task as men was clearly set out for us by the arrow of history: A society, corrupt at its very roots, relying for the present on injustice and hypocrisy, fearful of the future because of its guilty conscience, must morally, historically, and inevitably disappear.[10]

That surrealist poetry was expressly to be used in order to wipe out this society was declared by Aristide Maugée, contributor to the journal:

"Le grand midi" is a poem of rebellion and hatred. Against the stagnation of a life of lies and prejudices. Against the stupidity, cowardice, surrender, immorality of a debased world.[11]

Elsewhere Césaire addressed his compatriots with these words:

Vous
O vous qui vous bouchez les oreilles. C'est à vous, c'est pour vous que je parle, pour vous qui écartelerez demain jusqu'aux larmes la paix paissante de vos sourires pour vous qui un matin entasserez dans votre besace mes mots et prendrez à l'heure où sommeillent les enfants de la peur l'oblique chemin des fuites et des monstres.[12]

[You
Oh you who stop up your ears. It is to you, for you that I speak, for you who tomorrow will shred your browsing peaceful smiles until tears flow, for you, who one morning will hoard my words up in your rucksack and while the fearful children sleep will take the crooked path of flight and monsters.]

Thus, because of "his charge of gunpowder, rout, madness, vertigo," Césaire's poetry became an instrument of combat. "Here poetry equals insurrection." Revolt against Western rationalism! Revolt against colonialism! Revolt against the "browsing peacefulness" of the Martiniquans. A fundamental revolt against "a world torn by its own contradictions," the modern world.

To defend oneself against all Society by creating an incandescent zone, beyond which, inside of which, in terrible safety, the extraordinary flower of "I" may blossom; to strip oneself of all material things in silence in the cold bright fires of humor; to conquer through rebellion the free part from which one's self arises, whole . . .

Up to now we have considered only the destructive role of surrealism. But the end of our last quotation permits a glimpse of something new: A poetry of revolt does not mean only negative poetry, but also poetry triumphant. It is a power which opposes the "all that-is-to-be-accomplished" *life* and *person,* to the "ready-made and ready-found

10. Ibid.
11. Aristide Maugée, "Un poète martiniquais, A. Césaire," *Tropiques*, no. 4.
12. Aimé Césaire, "En guise manifeste," *Tropiques*, no. 8 (October 1943).

aspects of existence and the individual person."[13] "A power, the only one that permits us to rediscover the unique, original faculty that primitive peoples and children still have traces of, that removes the curse of an impassable barrier between the interior and exterior worlds,"[14] the barrier of Western rationalism.

This was of capital importance! Surrealism becomes here a major, irreplaceable tool, liberating the unconscious, giving access to the deeper self. Of course, this was already valid for Europeans, and Breton complains a good deal about the loss of subconscious values caused by rationalism and the resulting amputation of the self. The first article of the surrealist program, he said, had always been "a desire to give the death-blow to so-called 'good sense,' which has even shown the impudence of calling itself 'reason,' a compelling need to end this deadly dissociation of the human spirit, one of whose components has succeeded in giving itself every liberty at the expense of the other. . . . Our dreams are more than half of the nature we're deprived of."[15]

Quoting several authors, *Tropiques* called attention to these possibilities of investigating surrealism:
Lautréamont:

Le premier a avoir compris que la poésie commence avec l'excès, la démesure, les recherches frappées d'interdit, dans le grand tam-tam aveugle, dans l'irrespirable vide absolu, jusqu'à l'incompréhensible pluie d'étoiles.[16]

[The first person to have understood that poetry begins with excess, immoderation, study of the forbidden, in the great blind drumming, the unbreathable absolute vacuum, as far as the incomprehensible shower of stars.]
Breton:

Un poème doit être un débâcle de l'intellect. . . . Après la débacle tout recommence—sable, chalumeaux oxydriques.

[A poem should be a breakdown of the intellect. . . . After the breakdown, everything begins anew—sand, oxyhydrogen blowpipes.]
Eluard:

Sonnant les cloches du hasard à toute volée
....
Il brula les racines les sommets disparurent
Il brisa les barrières du soleil des étangs

13. Aimé Césaire, "Maintenir la poésie," *Tropiques*, no. 8 (October 1943).
14. Suzanne Césaire, "1943: le surréalisme et nous."
15. André Breton, "Un grand poète noir," p. 546.
16. Aimé Césaire, "Isidore Ducasse, Comte de Lautréamont," *Tropiques*, no. 7 (February 1943).

Dans les plaines nocturnes le feu chercha l'aurore
Il commença tous les voyages par la fin
Et sur toutes les routes
Et la terre devint à se perdre nouvelle.[17]

[Setting all the bells of chance a-ringing
....
He burned the roots the summits disappeared
He broke the barriers of the sun and the pools
In nocturnal plains the fire sought the dawn
He began each voyage with its end
And along all the roads
And by losing itself the earth was born anew.]

In search of the essential self, the surrealists conceived a passion for psychoanalysis and ethnography, whose "most obvious interest was that they clearly show that neither individuals nor peoples act according to motives they are consciously aware of. The impulse without which action does not exist, from which it springs, is outside the sphere of our reason, our logic."[18]

That is why surrealists violently criticized the logic and "lucid ideas" of classic French thought.

Those logical reasons for real causes are a deceptive fantasy. From here on in it is apparent that all socratic speculations on the conduct of individual persons and peoples are miserably misleading in the stagnant mud of "lucid ideas"! . . . [The new sciences] are finally opening new paths enabling man to reach man, that is to say, enabling us to bypass the absurd zone of our false reasoning and to reach the level where essential and vitally preoccupying energies come into play.[19]

West Indian poets were to share this antirationalism, but in surrealism they found a still more concrete and, for them, more vital interest, in view of their tragic situation. The West Indian was a man deprived of his culture and its traditions; nonetheless, he refused French assimilation in the name of his "negritude," which was above all a sudden awareness of the fate of an exiled race oppressed and reduced to slavery for centuries. To accept assimilation would seem to him the tacit approval of too many ill deeds. Yet he understood perfectly that a simple burst of energy, a cry of rebellion or hatred was not enough to recover one's human values. One might even say that it was only *after* this burst of energy that West Indians felt completely deprived: Africa, their motherland, was far away, and its traditions had degene-

17. Breton and Eluard quoted by Suzanne Césaire, "André Breton, poète," *Tropiques*, no. 3 (October 1941).
18. René Ménil, "L'action foudroyante," *Tropiques*, no. 3 (October 1941).
19. Ibid.

rated. What was left of it that was still pure and alive? A "temperament" peculiar to blacks? This was really very little to base a culture on! Even this temperament had been modified by crossbreeding, Christianity, and middle-class education. To this throbbing nostalgia for the past, however, surrealism brought a breath of hope. It would open "the roads of yesterday and tomorrow and thereby renew . . . forgotten ties. Bright clear roads where man, freed from the bonds of time and space, might *see* clearly, clearly into a past which is at the same time his future."[20]

Speaking earlier of this "power . . . that removes the curses of an impassable barrier between the outer and inner worlds," Suzanne Césaire was thus referring not only to a Cartesian logic that was stifling the treasures of the unconscious, but also to real barriers of time and space (three centuries of exile and thousands of miles) which separate the colored West Indian from his African past.

Surrealism appeared to West Indians, then, not only as a means of exteriorizing their rebellion against the Western world, but also as the only instrument available with which they could find themselves and, from the depths of their separate unconscious, could attempt to bring forth an apparently forgotten past. This was "an adventure which may prove deadly, from all one can tell, but which one may hope—and that is the essential—will lead to total spiritual victory."[21] *Surrealism was the only possible solution at the time for the cultural alienation of Martinique.*

This was no gratuitous or experimental game, as it often was for French surrealists. On the contrary, it was Orpheus with his torch in search of Eurydice, according to Sartre's famous comparison. In the same manner, referring to Césaire's poem "Le grand midi," Aristide Maugée would speak of a descent into hell:[22]

The poet seeks a new world: a world of truth and beauty. *Where will he find it if not in the depths of his consciousness? It is at this moment that the fantastic "rise" of this descent into one's self occurs.* . . .

This search for knowledge through the tangle of earthly connections, amid the seaweed of habits, instincts, inhibitions, the anxiety of impatience, is extraordinary.

In this search for spirituality, the poet's desire is to break all shackles that hold his consciousness in bondage. To plunge deeper and deeper in order, like an exquisite rose, to welcome the supreme moment when man need no longer compromise, lower himself, grovel, but on the contrary rise and grow with the strength of his energy: "I grow like a plant. . . ." The thing is to await

20. Suzanne Césaire, "André Breton, poète."
21. Suzanne Césaire, "1943: le surréalisme et nous."
22. The two poems "Les pur-sang" and "Le grand midi" form a diptych originally published under the title of the former. Aristide Maugée's text therefore also refers to the poem "Les pur-sang," which we shall discuss at the end of this chapter.

the ecstasy that will make a bridge between the Communicable and the Incommunicable. What spiritual vengeance for the bitterness of humiliations and rancor over tortured bodies![23]

Europe had called it "accursed," this poetic movement that was trying to strip veils from the Unconscious to arrive at man's real identity despite social prohibitions and taboos. It was doubly accursed in Martinique, since here it enabled Negroes to claim a humanity that all social organization refused them and thus set themselves up as the equals of white men, predicting "a new heaven, a new world":

A poetry cursed . . . because it was knowledge and no longer entertainment. Cursed because it was a caravel from distant inner selves. Cursed because it lifted the ban on all things black. Cursed in the wake of world discoverers. Cursed because the poet's ears from now on will echo the very voice that obsessed Columbus: "I shall found a new heaven and a new earth so fine that no one will think any more of what was there before."[24]

Poetry is indeed now "this power which opposes the everything-to-be-done of life and each person to the ready-mades and ready-founds of existence and of individuals."[25] The poet becomes the prophet of the new world, as Suzanne Césaire said.[26] But he is not content merely to prophesy; his words become action and "will then take on an aura of terrible power because they will become indissolubly bound to man's secret impulses. . . . Language will have the same power as gesture."[27] As we have already shown, at the same time as surrealist methods reveal to the poet the secret energies of the unconscious, they enable him to influence those secret energies and dominate them. René Ménil can thus imagine the possibility of a new policy and new ethics, since the right word or expression will inevitably obtain the wished-for reaction from the audience. Of course, it is naïve to imagine "a man armed with the power of poetry rising far above his people and turning the social order of his country topsy-turvy by pronouncing but a single word!"[28] Yet in politics and advertising, to mention only two areas, certain psychological campaigns have proved to be highly effective. Could not a poet, acting directly on his reader's subconscious, upset him to such a point that he would completely remodel his conception of life?[29]

23. Aristide Maugée, "Un poète martiniquais, A. Césaire."
24. Aimé Césaire, "Maintenir la poésie."
25. Ibid.
26. Suzanne Césaire, "André Breton, poète."
27. René Ménil, "L'action foudroyante."
28. Ibid.
29. This conception supposes, of course, the existence of a collective Unconscious as described by Jung, that is to say identical for all men and penetrating each individual unconscious. In addition, this unconscious would have to have definite, recognizable

After being of use in the black poet's rebellion, the liberation of his personality, and the recovery of his past; after giving him the means to act upon his people to free them in turn, would surrealism outgrow its usefulness? Indeed not!

Tomorrow,

Through the angry clouds of world war, millions of black hands will spread terror everywhere. Roused from a long torpor, this most deprived of all peoples will rise from the plains of ashes. . . .

Our surrealism will then produce the bread from its depths. . . . The powerful magic of the rainmakers drawn from the very wellspring of life will be recovered. Colonial asininities will be purified by the blue flame of autogenous welding. The quality of our metal, the keen edge of our steel, our unusual communions—all this will be recovered.[30]

---

laws, expressed in a spontaneous language. By analyzing this language, its rhythms and its images, one might discover certain laws controlling the unconscious! Studies have been made in this direction. Césaire, for example became interested in the works of Gaston Bachelard (*L'eau et les rêves* [Paris: Editions J. Corti, 1942]) showing how each of the four elements impose a certain number of images on the artist's apparently free imagination: There would thus be a kind of material objectivity in the poetic knowledge of the world, as suggested by Georges Gusdorf in *Mythe et métaphysique* (Paris: Flammarion, 1953, esp. pp. 209 ff.). *L'histoire des religions* by Mircea Eliade (Paris: Payot, 1959) seems to confirm this hypothesis by showing the universality of certain symbols and even occasionally their connection with identical economic and social forms, no matter the time and the place. For example, all agricultural civilizations establish a relationship between the creation of the world, the sexual act, and sowing. One may also note the frequency of the sun cult in absolute monarchies or theocratic societies, whether they be in ancient Egypt, among the Incas, in seventeenth-century Dahomey or twentieth-century Japan.

These studies lead to the recognition that today "on the level of images there is one irreducible substance which seems part of human reality"; and also that "if the reign of material imagination has no scientific basis, it nonetheless has definite anthropological meaning . . . as a way of achieving humanity that surely corresponds to a certain form of reality" (Gusdorf, pp. 210–11). This is how Césaire understood the role of poetry and poetic images. According to him, one must "give the image its true importance, greater than the semantics of each word. One must not be put out by its arbitrary appearance. Images are never *arbitrary*, that is to say *without significance.* I am not referring here to *comparison*, but to the image which is the language of the unconscious and expresses it by its own symbols and logic. A criticism too often made is that an image which is too personal can prevent communication and close the poet in upon himself. One must not forget the store of images in the collective unconscious. One must not forget that all, or almost all, of them derive from *primordial images*—engrained in the collective unconscious—which are universal, as the language of dreams has demonstrated being identical among all peoples, no matter what their language or conditions of life. The West has for too long forgotten that images are the true universal language" (letter from A. Césaire, June 1959). If Césaire has today left orthodox surrealist thought behind, this recent text proves that he has kept one of its principal aspects.

30. Suzanne Césaire, "Le surréalisme et nous." One may note that the tone of the articles in this issue is generally more aggressive. The contributors began to express

In this impassioned text, Suzanne Césaire singles out a further goal of the surrealist revolution. After eliminating the sediment of Western alienation from black awareness in order to clear the ground for an authentically Negro culture to take root, surrealism would still serve an educational function. Not only the poet would be saved, but he in turn would liberate others, down to his very humblest black brother, by showing him concrete examples of authentic blackness and furnishing the means to attain it.[31]

When we consider the extent of poetic, philosophical, and ethical material *Tropiques* was able to draw from surrealism, the amount of space devoted to it in the journal becomes less surprising. Surrealism seemed to these young Martiniquans a panacea, a complete cure-all for their troubles. "In art as in life, the surrealist cause is the very cause of liberty," wrote Suzanne Césaire just before the journal was suppressed.[32] For the creators of *Tropiques,* the word surrealism was synonymous with revolution; if they preferred the former, it was not only because of political censorship, but because they wanted to show that it referred not merely to social reform but to a more radical change aimed at the very depths of individual awareness.

Although articles elaborating on the multiple possibilities of surrealism appeared throughout the duration of *Tropiques,* Aimé Césaire himself wrote only one brief theoretical piece on the subject. His prose was devoted more to Martiniquan folklore, black American writers, and French poets. On the other hand, in each issue of the review Césaire's poems gleamed darkly, intelligible only to those who understood their symbols and allusions, understandable only to the "thoroughbreds." "Les pur-sang" ("The thoroughbreds") is in fact the title of a poem by Aimé Césaire, from which we shall quote at length, with some commentary. It provides an excellent illustration of some of the stages of his approach that we have been attempting to outline. Let us now follow him step by step.[33]

---

their thoughts clearly; they knew the review would not appear any more, since the printers, under government pressure, were refusing to print it.

31. Regarding the educational role of the black writer, see chap. 21 below, as well as the opinions of various writers who have been questioned on the subject, and which we shall also take up in chap. 21. See also A. Césaire's speech at the Second Congress of Black Writers and Artists (Rome 1959), published in the special issue of *Présence Africaine,* nos. 24–25 (February–May 1959).

32. Suzanne Césaire, "Le surréalisme et nous."

33. This interpretation of the poem has met with Aimé Césaire's approval. We use the version published in *Tropiques,* no. 1 (April 1941), pointing out the few differences to the version published in *Les armes miraculeuses* (Paris: NRF, Gallimard, 1946), pp. 10–22, except where only the punctuation has been changed.

Voici les cent pur-sang hennissant du soleil
parmi la stagnation.
Ah! je sens l'enfer des délices
et par les brumes nidoreuses imitant les floches
chevelures—respirations touffues de vieillards
imberbes—la tiédeur mille fois féroce
de la folie hurlante et de
la mort
Mais comment, comment ne pas bénir
telle que ne l'ont point rêvée mes logiques,
dure, à contre-fil lézardant leur pouacre amas
et leur saburre, et plus pathétique
que la fleur fructifiante,
la gerce lucide des déraisons?

[Here are the sun's one hundred thoroughbreds
neighing amid the stagnation.
Ah! I feel the hell of sensual delights
and through nidorous mists imitating
flossy hair—the labored breathing of beardless elders
the thousandfold ferocious warmth
of death and howling madness
But how, how not bless
what all my hard logic never dreamed of,
splitting their scurvy bulk against the grain
and their gastric wastes, and more pathetic
than the fructifying flower
the lucid fissures of unreason?]

The thoroughbreds in the sun are really men, thirsting for freedom. They proclaim the revolution which will sweep away the stagnation of established order. More powerful than reason, which counsels submission to the law of he who is strongest, lucid, calculating madness can split the scurvy bulk of beardless elders, namely all those who, though still young, conduct themselves like resigned old men, accepting their place, not finding the condition of Negroes intolerable.

The repetitive harmony of the first line (in the original French) accumulates *s* sounds to give an impression of whistling speed, and also *ant* sounds to evoke horses neighing. But the new note of the second line immediately plunges us again into a world without air or light. The pictures Césaire paints—filthy heaps, rank smelling mists, labored breathing, flossy hair—are contrasted with the unleashed powers that will destroy them: ferocious warmth, shrieking madness, the hard and lucid fissures of unreason.

Et j'entends l'eau qui monte
la nouvelle, l'intouchée, l'éternelle,

vers l'air renouvelé.

[And I hear the water rising
new, untouchable, eternal
toward the fresh new air.]

Running water, whose flowing, murmuring effect is rendered by the
repeated *l* sound in these three lines, wells up to purify the swamps
of this stagnant world. Running water is the symbol of the new life a
transformed world would engender.

Et voici passer
vagabondage sans nom
vers les sûres nécropoles du couchant
les soleils, les pluies, les galaxies
fondus en fraternel magma

[And now
the nameless wandering
moves on
toward the sure necropolis
of the sunset
suns, rains, galaxies
fused in fraternal magma]

An apocalyptic vision: The wiping out of the ancient world, announced by the horsemen and the murmur of welling water, begins
with a stampede of nature's elements. The safe cities of the dead are
those from which one never returns: The liquidation is final.

et la terre . . .
. . . .
s'éteignit

et la mer fait a la terre un collier de silence
la mer humant la paix sacrificielle
où s'enchevêtrent nos râles, immobile avec
d'étranges perles et de muets mûrissements
d'abysse,
la terre fait à la mer un bombement de silence
dans le silence
. . . .
vide
vide comme au jour d'avant le jour . . .
—Grâce! grâce!
Qu'est-ce qui crie grâce?
Poings avortés, amassements taciturnes, jeûnes
hurrah pour le départ lyrique
brûlantes métamorphoses
dispenses foudroyantes

[and the earth . . .
....
dies out

and the sea makes a ring of silence about the earth
the sea sucking in the sacrificial peace
in which our death rattles lie entangled
motionless with strange pearls and
mute ripenings of chasms
the earth swells the sea with silence
in silence
....

empty
empty as the day before the day . . .
—Mercy! mercy!
What cries out for mercy?
Abortive fists, taciturn piles, fastings
Hurrah for the lyrical departure
the burning metamorphoses
the lightning dispensations]

With the disappearance of all light, the world dies and is surrendered to the purifying properties of water. Emptiness and silence. The sea, a necklace to the earth—Martinique is an island—promises unknown life, whose overflow, "mute ripenings of chasms," permits a better sounding of the depths. Yet all life is not extinct: The poet hears cries for mercy that unleash his anger. He calls upon all those whose rebellions were quelled and whose resentment has silently increased to break loose; all dispensations will be granted them.

feu, ô feu
les volcans tirent à bout portant
les villes par terre dans un grand bruit d'idoles
dans le vent mauvais des prostitutions
et des sodomies
les villes par terre et le vent soufflant
parmi l'éclatement fangeux de leur chair
le rugissement excrémentiel[34]

34. In the NRF, Gallimard edition, this text was replaced by the following, p. 11:
feu ô feu
éclair des neiges absolues
cavalerie de steppe chimique
retiré de mer à la marée d'ibis
le sémaphore anéanti
sonne aux amygdales du cocotier
et vingt mille baleines soufflant
à travers l'éventail liquide
un lamantin nubile mâche la braise des orients

[fire, oh fire
volcanoes shoot point blank at cities
bringing them to earth with a great crashing of idols
in the evil wind of sodomies
and prostitutions
cities hit the earth and the wind
among the filthy burstings of their flesh
blowing its excremental roar]

Fire, another purifying element! The volcanoes symbolize Martinique, its authentic reserves of strength and revolt which will destroy cities, always symbols of European civilization comprising everything artificial and unnatural: the idols (false gods of foreign religions: Money, Profit, White Supremacy . . .) and the decay and corruption which inevitably follow.

Sous l'œil du néant suppurant une nuit
la terre saquée doucement dérive
éternellement
La grisaille suinte à mes yeux, alourdit mes
jarrets, paresse affreusement le long de mes bras

[Beneath the eye of pus-secreting nothingness one night
the sacked earth gently drifts
eternally
The greyness oozes into my eyes
weighs upon my legs
shockingly frittering away my arms]

In the nothingness in which he finds himself, the poet has a feeling of suffocation, of impotence, of being stuck in some morass.

à l'heure des faillites frauduleuses, nourri d'enfants occultes
et de rêves de terre il y a notre oiseau de clarinette
luciole crépue au front fragile des éléphants
et les amazones du roi de Dahomey de leur pelle restaurent
le paysage déchu des gratte-ciel de verre détient, de voies
privées, de dieux pluvieux, voirie et hoirie de roses brouillées

---

[fire, oh fire
lightning of absolute snows
cavalry of chemical steppes
taken from the sea at the Ibis tide
the humbled Semaphore
vibrates in the tonsils of the coconut palm
and twenty thousand whales blowing
across the liquid fan
a nubile seacow chews upon the embers of the east]

—des mains du soleil cru des nuits lactées
Mais Dieu? comment ai-je pu oublier Dieu?
je veux dire la Liberté

[At the hour of bankruptcy, fed on occult children
and dreams of earth there is our clarinet bird
fuzzy glow worms on the fragile brow of elephants
and the Royal Amazons of Dahomey with their spades
restore the fallen landscape of faded glass skyscrapers
of private roads, of rain-soaked gods, inheritance
and sewer of jumbled roses—-the sun's
hands raw with milky nights
But God? How have I forgotten God?
I mean Liberty]

In the general drifting, the secretly nourished hopes of the black race (fuzzy glow worms, clarinet bird) echo nonetheless. Despite its lack of technology (the only tools the Royal Amazons of Dahomey have are spades), Africa will give life and color (hands of the raw sun) to the bloodless West (faded glass, rain-soaked gods, inheritance and thoroughfares, jumbled roses).

Yet this African weakness (a bird with flutelike voice) will vanquish European power (the elephant is an African symbol of blind and stupid power)—a power that is physical and technical but not spiritual: Fuzzy glow worms will attack the elephant's "fragile brow."

O Chimborazo violent
prendre aux cheveux la tête du soleil
36 flûtes n'insensibiliseront point les mains d'arbre à pain
de mon désir de pont de cheveux sur l'abîme
de bras de pluies de sciure de nuit
de chèvres aux yeux de mousse remontant les abîmes sans rampe
de sang bien frais de voilures au fond du volcan des lentes termitières

[Oh violent Chimborazo
to take the sun's head by its hair
36 flutes will not anaesthetize the bread tree hands
of my desire for a bridge of hair across the depths
for arms, for rain, for sawdust, for night
for goats with foamy eyes climbing up the the slopeless depths
for fresh blood for sails at the bottom of the volcano of sluggish
      termite nests]

The Chimborazo is a volcano in the Andes. The poet, evoking future liberty, feels a surge of sharp desire, the desire to at last throw a bridge across the chasm which separates him from his motherland (Africa is far away) and from himself (West Indians are alienated). The desire for a life purified, filled with fresh air (rain, moss, goats, fresh blood, sails) that would at long last cleanse the bottom of this volcano (Martinique) still eaten away by the termites of resignation, subservience and alienation.

> mais moi homme! rien qu'homme!
> Ah! ne plus voir avec les yeux.
> N'être plus oreille a entendre!
> N'être plus la brouette à évacuer le
> décor!
> N'être plus une machine à déménager
> les sensations!

> [but me man! nothing but a man!
> Ah! no longer eyes to see with
> No longer to be ears for listening
> No longer to be a wheelbarrow for carting the
> scenery away!
> No longer to be a machine for stirring up the senses!]

But faced with the enormity of his task, what a feeling of solitude and weakness he has! The task is a crushing one, and he wishes he might never again see or hear this real world, wishes he were rid of his mission as purifier. But another interpretation of this passage does not exclude the first: Césaire feels robbed of his own personality here. Outwardly he had rid himself of this alienating world, but he had borne it for so long that the old Negro attitudes are stuck to him like glue, saturating his retina, his ears, hindering his creation of the new world he desires.

> Je veux le seul, le pur trésor
> celui qui fait largesse des autres

> [I want the true, the only treasure
> the one that bounteously makes all others]

In the face of this environment which overwhelms him, the poet maintains and cries out his demands: freedom and a retrieved authentic sense of self, without which there is no possibility for happiness or worthwhile creation.

> Homme!
> Mais ce début me fait moins qu'homme!
> Quelle torpeur! Ma tête stupidement ballotte
> Ma tête rongée est déglutie par mon corps
> Mon œil coule à pic dans la chose
> non plus regardée mais regardante.

> [Man!
> But this beginning makes me less than man!

What torpor! My head wobbles stupidly
My gnawed head is swallowed by my body.
My eye sinks down in the thing
no longer looked at but looking.]

Has this "nothing but a man" become discouraged? But the depersonalized Negro is no longer even a man! There is a moment of confusion, of disgust with the self, in the face of things perceived as foreign, hostile. (Here we recall the famous passage in Sartre's novel, *La nausée*, when Roquentin contemplates a root in the park.)

Homme!
Et voici l'assourdissement violent
qu'officie ma mémoire terrestre,
mon désir frappe aux états simples
je rêve d'un bec étourdi d'hibiscus
et de vierges sentences violettes
s'alourdissant aux lézards avaleurs
du soleil
l'heure bat comme un remords
la neige d'un soleil
aux caroncules crève la patte levée
le monde . . .

[Man!
And here is the violent deafening
my earthly memory officiates at,
my desire strikes at simple things
I dream of beaks stunned by hibiscus
and purple virgin judgments
growing heavy with sun-swallowing lizards
the hour strikes like remorse
the snow of a wattled sun
bursts that raised paw
the world . . .]

To escape from this discouragement, this doubt, before a world he must resuscitate, the poet "deafens" his earthly memory; in other words, he forgets the things he has learned and knocks at the gates of the Unconscious. At first it is a sort of formless raving, a profusion of images where red (hibiscus, wattles) and purple dominate, colors that dazzle the eyes when one looks directly at the sun.

Ca y est. Atteint. Comme frappe
la mort brutale . . .
....

Je m'ébroue en une mouvance d'images
de souvenirs néritiques, de possibles
en suspension, de tendances-larves,

d'obscurs devenirs;
les habitudes font à la vase liquide
de traînantes algues—mauvaisement,
des fleurs éclatent.
Floc!
On enfonce, on enfonce comme dans
une musique.

[It's happened. Struck. As
brutal death strikes . . .
....
I bathe in ever-changing images
of neritic memories, suspended
possibles, larval tendencies,
obscure becomings
habits form trailing algae in the
liquid slime—evilly,
flowers burst.
Plop!
One sinks, sinks as if
into music.]

The poet has found the door that gives access to the depths of his soul. Walking slow-motion as if he were floating through fog, as the languid style suggests, he attempts the descent into his self, despite the resistant glue of habit.

Radiolaires,[35]
Nous dérivons à travers votre sacrifice
Refoulements enfouis! désirs, désirs
Processionels désirs . . .[36]

[Radiolarias.
We drift through your sacrifice
Buried inhibitions! desires, desires
Processional desires . . .]

On the way, he meets stifled, unformed aspirations, which live on within him in a larval state.

d'un dodelinement de vagues, je saute
ancestral aux branches de ma
végétation.
Je m'égare aux complications
fructueuses.
Je nage aux vaisseaux

35. *Radiolaria:* aquatic protozoa, the protoplasm of which send out radiating pseudopods (Larousse dictionary).
36. These last two verses are missing in the Gallimard edition.

Je plonge aux écluses.

[with the rocking of the waves, I make the
ancestral leap to the branches of my
trees.
I lose my way in fruitful
complications.
I swim to the ships
I dive through the floodgates.]

The way becomes more open, as he plunges deeper. He can more easily explore the complicated ancestral kingdom of his being. The poem reflects this smoother rhythm of his passage.

Où, où, où vrombissent les hyènes
fienteuses du désespoir?
Non. Toujours ici torrentueuses
cascadent les paroles.
Silence
Silence par delà les rampes
sanguinolentes,
par cette grisaille et cette
calcination inouïe.

[Where, where, where do the
hyenas hum dung-smeared with despair
No. Always here the torrential
cascades of words
Silence
Silence beyond the
blood-stained slopes
through this grayness
and outrageous calcination.]

But he still hears the pessimistic voices prophesying failure. He must go farther still to find true silence, where all things learned are finally forgotten, and with them all shame and baseness erased.

Enfin lui,
ce vent des méplats, bonheur,
le silence
....
Ah
Le dernier des derniers soleils tombe
Où se couchera-t-il sinon en Moi?
A mesure que se mourait toute chose,
je me suis, je me suis élargi[37]

37. In the Gallimard edition: "Je me suis, je me suis élargi—comme le monde" ("I, I grew and stretched forth—like the world").

et ma conscience plus large que la mer!
Dernier soleil
J'éclate. Je suis le feu, je suis la mer. Le
monde se défait. Mais je suis le monde!

[At last
this flat wind, happiness,
silence
....
Ah!
the last of the last suns is falling
Where will it set if not in me?
As gradually all things died
I, I grew and stretched forth
and my awareness larger than the sea!
The last sun
I burst. I am the fire, I am the sea. The
world is breaking up. But I am the world!]

At last the hoped-for annihilation of the ancient world has occurred
in the very heart of the poet's awareness. This means the end of all the
alienations that separate him from himself. As the barriers between
him and his true self fall, they also fall between him and the world.
Once more he can be part of the elements: fire and sea, merging with
the world's creative forces.

La fin, la fin disions-nous.
Quelle sottise! Une paix proliférante
d'obscures puissances. Branchies opacules,
palmes, syrinx, pennes. Il me pousse
invisibles et instans par tout le corps,
secrètement exigés, des sens,
et nous voici pris dans le sacré
tourbillonnant ruissellement primordial
au recommencement de tout.

[The end, were we saying the end.
What foolishness! A peace proliferating
from dark powers. Opaculous gills,
palms, syringes, quills. They grow
covering my body invisibly and immediately,
secretly desired by the senses,
and here we are caught in this precious
primordial whirling streaming
in which everything begins anew.]

Was this the end of everything, death? No, it was the unveiling of
the true self in contact with deep sources and the spontaneous germination of new desires, new "senses" which earthly life until how had

atrophied. The poet thus reaches the very beginning of creation, which will permit him to transform the world. The two final lines with the repetition of *r* and *ant* sounds (in the original French), suggest the centrifugal vortex of molten, vital energy that flows from the crucible of the cosmos.

> La sérénité découpe l'attente en prodigieux
> cactus.
> Tout le possible sous la main.
> Rien d'exclu.
> Le monde véritablement pour la première
> fois total.[38]

> [Serenity cuts up the waiting into prodigious
> cactus.
> Everything possible is at hand.
> Nothing excluded.
> The world truly for the first
> time complete.]

A pause. In expectation of a miracle. The poet savors the serenity of one who knows it is only a question of time now, because the secrets of his being have revealed to him the mystery of the universe and because he now possesses re-creative power.

> Et je pousse, moi, l'Homme
> stéatopyge assis
> en mes yeux des reflets de marais, de honte,
> d'acquiescement
> —pas un pli d'air ne bougeant aux
> échancrures de mes membres—
> sur les épines séculaires
> je pousse comme une plante
> sans remords et sans gauchissement
> vers les heures dénouées du jour
> pur et sûr comme une plante·
> sans crucifiement
> vers les heures dénouées du soir!
> La fin!
> Mes pieds vont le vermineux cheminement
> Plante!
> mes membres ligneux conduisent d'étranges sèves
> Plante! Plante!
> Le vieil esprit de la terre passe . . .[39]

> [And I, I the seated steatopygous Man

38. These last two lines are missing in the Gallimard edition.
39. This last verse is missing in the Gallimard edition.

I grow
glimmers of swamps, of shame, of acquiescence
in my eyes
—not a puff of air at the articulations
of my members—
on the age-old thorns
I grow like a plant
remorseless and without warping
toward the unfettered hours of day
pure and sure as a plant
without crucifixion
toward the unfettered hours of night!
The end!
My feet follow the verminous path
Plant!
my woody members contain strange sap
Plant! Plant!
The ancient spirit of the earth is dying . . .]

Here is the Negro, seated, resigned, humiliated, suffering from centuries of moral and intellectual sclerosis, growing now in accordance with his own law, like a plant which has found its sap once more,[40] toward an existence finally free, "unfettered," human. "The ancient spirit of the earth is dying. . . ." With this symbol of esoteric ancestral rites the Negro is once again connected to his past, to his ancestors, and once more part of the world's Vital Forces.

Linked thus to the Creative Power, the Word of authentic man is henceforth all-powerful, like the word of God.[41] It brings forth a world re-created in Man's measure. In tender, hopeful images, the poet sings of this new world's awakening, the birth of the elements on purified, virgin islands. Revolt and the thirst for destruction are necessary no longer. Now he can be happy.

Et je dis,
et ma parole est paix
et je dis et ma parole est terre
et je dis
et la Joie
éclate dans le soleil nouveau!
et je dis:
par de savantes herbes le temps glisse
les branches picoraient une paix de flammes vertes
et la Terre respira sous la gaze des brumes.

40. This recalls Frobenius's theories on the plant-man. See chap. 17 above.
41. According to Senghor's idea, which is close to Césaire's, it is sufficient to "name things . . . to prophesy the City of tomorrow which will be born from the ashes of the ancient city, that is the poet's mission" (*Ethiopiques*, p. 111).

Et la Terre s'étira. Il y eut un craquement
a ses epaules nouées. Il y eut dans ses veines
un pétillement de feu.
Son sommeil pelait comme un goyavier d'août
sur de vierges îles assoiffées de lumière
Et la terre accroupie dans ses cheveux
d'eau vive
au fond de ses yeux attendit les
étoiles . . .

« Dors ma cruauté,» pensai-je
L'oreille collée au sol, j'entendis
passer Demain.

[And I speak,
and my word is peace
I speak and my word is earth
I speak
and Joy
bursts in the new sun!
and I say:
time slips through the clever grass
branches foraged for a green-flamed peace
and the Earth breathed beneath gauze-like mists.
And the Earth stretched. There was a cracking
of its knotted shoulders. A fiery sparkling
in its veins.
Its sleep peeled off like August guava trees
on virgin islands athirst for light
And Earth crouched in its hair of
running water
with stars waiting deep within its eyes . . .

"Sleep, my cruelty," thought I
My ear to the ground, I heard
Tomorrow passing.]

V   AN END TO COLONIZATION

19 / In Paris: Founding *Présence Africaine*

While Césaire continued to develop the New Negro ideas in Martinique, in occupied France his friends were condemned to silence. Yet soon after Senghor's release from a German prisoner-of-war camp in 1941, a new group took shape around him and Alioune Diop. They were joined by the West Indians Paul Niger, Guy Tirolien, and Lionel Attuly; the Madagascan Jacques Rabemananjara; and, shortly after, by two Dahomeans named Apithy and Behanzin. Their debate and discussion of black world problems continued for four years. "This marked our personality and created a common awareness," Paul Niger declared.[1]

But alas, with no possibility of expressing themselves in a periodical or of making their ideas public, black intellectuals in wartime Paris were left in an isolation that emphasized the romantic aspect of their negritude. They dreamed of the black continent as a distant paradise.

With the liberation of France, reality quickly corrected their illusions. Paul Niger and Guy Tirolien, who set off on a "pilgrimage to the ancestral sources," sang a different tune after a confrontation with Africa's "yes-men," "the Africa of sleeping men, waiting for the favor of being booted awake; the Africa of tom-toms waving like flags of surrender to dysentery, the plague, yellow fever, and jiggers (to say nothing of the whip)."[2] It was with some bitterness that Niger recalled those discussions in Paris: "We had been living an unreal Negro-ness, cooked up from the theories of the ethnologists, sociologists, and

1. Conversation with Paul Niger in March 1959. (Paul Niger is the pseudonym of André Albert Béville.)

2. Paul Niger, "Je n'aime pas l'Afrique," 1944, in *Anthologie de la nouvelle poésie nègre et malgache de langue française,* ed. L. S. Senghor, p. 9.

279

other scholars who study man in a glass case. They had injected this social-scientific Negro with formaldehyde and claimed he was the new specimen of fortunate man."[3]

If Paul Niger was a bit unfair about the social scientist's valuable work, he was right on one essential point: All of Africa's past, no matter how glorious it may have been, could not solve its contemporary problems. Africa was no longer living at the time of the Askias and well-organized clans, but in a colonial society. The world around Africa had changed too. A liberated Africa was certainly not going to return to its primitive state, but was going to play a constructive role in the modern world. Paul Niger, who had been a colonial administrator, knew that technology was the instrument of European power, whether its expression was gunpowder, electricity, or machinery, and that lack of technology was the weakness of underdeveloped countries, a weakness which permitted their colonization. He therefore advised immediate commitment to those concrete transformations which alone would make African countries capable of playing the role they aspired to.

Paul Niger's friends had parallel experiences. For all of them negritude led to action. Senghor was elected a deputy from Senegal to the French assembly, and as early as 1947 he had established contact with Kwame Nkrumah, to whom Ghana owes its independence. When Jacques Rabemananjara returned to Madagascar, he too was elected by his people and actively participated in the island's revolt.[4] Apithy became a minister in Dahomey. African intellectuals were not the only ones to turn so clearly to politics. Césaire was elected deputy from Martinique, and Léon Damas soon became a deputy from French Guiana.

Alioune Diop was also, for a while, senator from Senegal, but his true bent was for more purely intellectual activity. While still a senator, he created the magazine *Présence Africaine,* an idea that gave him the reputation of being something of a dreamer. As soon as he had completed his term, Diop devoted all his time and energy to the new review.

The first issue of *Présence Africaine* appeared simultaneously in Dakar and Paris in December 1947. It soon became the principal voice of the black world in France, and today its influence extends to the whole of Africa. Among its sponsors were such important French intellectuals as Gide, Sartre, Mounier, Maydieu, and Albert Camus, as well as the ethnologists Paul Rivet, Théodore Monod, Michel Leiris, and Georges Balandier, and finally four black writers of considerable fame: Senghor

3. Paul Niger, "Les puissants," ibid., p. 30.
4. Rabemananjara was arrested shortly afterward and imprisoned until 1956.

and Césaire, of course, the American Richard Wright, and the Daho-mean Paul Hazoumé.[5]

If the names adorning this young review formed a prestigious group, the review's very simple appearance testified to its financial independence. *Présence Africaine* had nothing in common with the luxurious colonial magazines, flattering mirrors of the mother country's benevolence toward her overseas children. The poor quality of the postwar paper on which *Présence Africaine* was printed, the irregularity of its publication, the numerous typographical errors sprinkled throughout its pages—all these were indications of the financial difficulties Alioune Diop had to cope with, sometimes *in extremis* through desperate appeals for funds. African solidarity came to the rescue every time to save the work of this brother who had created so thought-provoking a publication for his brethren, this rostrum from which thinkers and writers, political men and sociologists, traditional wise men and university students attempted to "define the originality of Africa and hasten its inclusion in the modern world."[6]

This, in fact, is how Alioune Diop defined the objectives of *Présence Africaine*, specifying that the review would not owe allegiance to any philosophical or political ideology. The "African originality" it had in mind was cultural in nature and was to be demonstrated in the review by means of literary work by Africans and studies of black civilizations.

Diop pointed to the magazine's source in the group that had formed around Senghor:

The idea of it goes back to 1942–43. There we were in Paris, a number of students from overseas who—in the midst of the sufferings of a Europe questioning its very essence and the reality of its values—had gathered together to study the situation and the characteristics that defined our identity. . . . Incapable of wholly returning to our origins or of assimilating ourselves to Europe, we had the feeling we were a new race, mental half-breeds. . . . Uprooted people? We were uprooted, precisely to the extent that we had not yet thought out our position in the world, and we were floating between two societies, without recognized meaning in either one or the other, and foreigners in both of them.[7]

5. A schoolteacher who devoted himself to ethnological study of his country, and whose books, *Le pacte du sang au Dahomey* and *Doguicimi*, an ethnological novel, are greatly appreciated by scholars. [Translator's note: A second American whose name appeared, three years before she won the Pulitzer Prize, in the first issue of *Présence Africaine* was Gwendolyn Brooks. Her long poem *Ballad of Pearl Lee May* was published with a French translation on facing pages.]

6. Alioune Diop, "Niam n'goura ou les raisons d'être de *Présence Africaine*," introduction to the first issue, November–December 1947.

7. Ibid., p. 8.

But Alioune Diop differed from his predecessors. Whereas they had been preoccupied with the West Indies, he turned attention toward black Africa, seeing more and more clearly the shortcomings of Africans driven to follow the road forced upon them by history.

The tone in which he set forth his ambitions for the review was surprisingly moderate, in contrast to that of the white contributors. Diop emphasized the qualities of individual conscience and austere will that had enabled Europe to take the lead in progress. The black man, he recognized, is often content to enjoy the fruits of the present in a universe of endless marvels; he cares little for knowing and taming the world.[8] And yet, today, he no longer has a choice: "The development of a modern world allows no person nor any natural civilization to escape its grasp. . . . We are henceforth committed to an heroic phase of history. . . . We Africans need to acquire a taste for elaborating ideas and evolving a technology."[9]

Diop denounced the black African's individuality and his technical weakness. But his article treats the subject with almost exaggerated politeness and modesty. Diop not only stressed European qualities Africans urgently need acquire, but he seemed to place the world's future in the hands of Europe, "creator of the leaven of all future civilizations,"[10] adding that "it is important . . . certain deprived peoples should receive from Europe, from France especially, the necessary tools to construct this future edifice."[11] Presented as a combination of "ethical resources . . . which constitute the substance to be fertilized by Europe," the possible contribution of Africa is hardly overestimated. "Fenced in for centuries by a kind of cosmic silence—useless, in the eyes of many, to the world's evolution—reduced, according to these same persons, to a vain and bestial vitality—black peoples nevertheless continue to live according to their wisdom and a vision of life not lacking in originality. A new sensibility, a long and singular history, have endowed it with an experience which in many ways it would be profitable to make known. . . . Would it be rash to add that this experience might even enrich European civilization?"[12]

Is it possible that at this period Alioune Diop may have been a bit obsequious? In that case, he has certainly changed! What a difference of tone in the following lines, which he wrote as a preface to Aimé Césaire's *Lettre à Maurice Thorez:*[13] "Césaire's decision concerns us all:

8. Ibid., pp. 13, 14.
9. Ibid., p. 14.
10. Ibid.
11. Ibid., p. 13.
12. Ibid., p. 12.
13. Paris: Présence Africaine, 1956, p. 4. *Lettre à Maurice Thorez* was Césaire's resignation from the French Communist Party.

artists, writers, theologians, cultured men of all persuasions. He disqualifies the West as spiritual and historical advisor. He demands and affirms the occurrence of a radical change in the traditional structures of the world's cultural life." Perhaps Alioune Diop's main concern was to preserve the life of his young journal, the modesty of his introduction acting as a counterweight to the virulence of the other articles?[14] Beneath this too affable mask, do we not sense irony? Let us reread the text and note its reticence.

Diop went so far as to divide humanity today into two groups—two groups only: "one, a minority of active, productive, creative men: Europe. The other, a far greater number of overseas men. They are generally less active, producing little (or at least their productivity does not correspond to the rhythm of modern times). They are 'the white man's burden.' "[15] Then, addressing Westerners, Diop added: "But is it not precisely to your advantage to make these people exactly like you: active, productive, creative? This would certainly save you much work! No one, moreover, has the privilege of having mastered History and Progress; these are forces unleashed by the tireless activity of the European—yet which often escape his control. All the more reason why in place of a few hundreds of millions of brains which have undertaken to think, direct, and stimulate the world, assuming too the responsibility for billions of 'overseas men,' one might hope to transform these overseas men into brains and arms adapted to modern life and sharing the responsibility of thinking out and improving the condition of mankind."[16]

The irony seems flagrant. Diop said: "Is it not the height of heroism to enlighten and emancipate one's fellow man, to approach him in the very virulence of his freedom and lucidity? This seems to us the originality of Europe as seen by Africa." He added as an aside: "This certainly refers to an ideal Europe. . . ."[17]

By presenting *Présence Africaine* as a "mere window onto the world," intended to nourish the African young intellectually, thus preventing them from "suffocating and becoming sterile,"[18] by congratulating the review for "being French; for living in a French setting,"[19] Alioune Diop hoped to avoid the difficulties and interdictions which had struck

---

14. Virulence which was itself exceeded by the biting irony of the texts in *Revue des Revues*, a section at the end of the volume. In smaller print, beneath a mild title, these are the pages which most clearly show the confident and militant spirit of the magazine's editors.

15. Rudyard Kipling.

16. Alioune Diop, "Niam n'goura," p. 9.

17. Ibid., p. 11.

18. Ibid., p. 8.

19. Ibid., p. 12.

his predecessors.[20] That he did not completely avoid them we shall now show.

Diop's introduction was, at bottom, an appeal to African intellectuals to make use of all the means used by Europeans and to assert themselves. For in this modern world, Diop wrote, "any human being who does not affirm his personality is ignored. To express his particular soul, on the other hand, is to help steer public opinion and institutional leadership in more humane directions."[21]

The black who is conspicuous by his absence from the elaboration of modern cities will gradually be able to make his presence known by contributing to the re-creation of a humanism that fits the true dimensions of mankind.

For it is certain that one cannot attain authentic universality if it is formed only of European subjectivities. The world of tomorrow will be built by all men. . . .[22]

We Africans . . . must seize upon the questions now posed on an international scope and along with everyone else consider them so that one day we will be among the creators of a new order.[23]

Here Alioune Diop echoes the affirmations of Césaire's *Cahier:*

> Car il n'est point vrai que l'œuvre de l'homme est finie
> que nous n'avons rien à faire au monde
> que nous parasitons le monde
> ....
>
> Mais l'œuvre de l'homme vient seulement de commencer
> et aucune race ne possède le monopole de la beauté, de l'intelligence, de la force
> et il est place pour tous au rendez-vous de la conquête.[24]

> [For it is not true that the work of man is finished
> that there is nothing for us to do in this world
> that we are parasites on this earth
> ....
>
> but the work of man has only just begun
> and no race has a monopoly of beauty, intelligence or strength
> and there is room for everyone at the rendezvous of conquest.]

It is clear that Alioune Diop managed to spare people's feelings. Having learned from the experience of past attempts, he already gave

20. In chap. 15 above we showed how the review *Tropiques* was "sabotaged" by the French government in 1943.
21. Alioune Diop, "Niam n'goura," p. 13.
22. Ibid.
23. Ibid., p. 14.
24. Aimé Césaire, *Cahier d'un retour au pays natal,* p. 85.

evidence of those qualities of flexibility and prudence, which, in addition to his unusual tenacity, would for the first time[25] permit an authentically Negro magazine to take roots and blossom. Diop's efforts were also powerfully supported by the historical evolution of colonized peoples. *Présence Africaine* remains a committed organ that has renounced nothing of the militance of its predecessors, as the articles it has published through the years have proved.

It is true that the journal proposed no political aim. But implicitly it challenged colonization. In the literary section of the first issue, black writers denounced segregation, white American brutality,[26] and, in an ironical style, ridiculed Senegalese mulatto girls who aped the women of Paris.[27] But on the whole, the magazine's tone was reserved, and white contributors lent it strong support.

André Gide waxed ironic on the theories of Gobineau, warning that Europe's role was not merely to educate Africans but to listen to them.[28] Théodore Monod recalled the cynicism with which the West tried to justify slavery.[29] Marcel Griaule reviewed the prejudices of so-called black inferiority. In the study of African societies, he declared, "we have only reached the period of taking inventory. We are discovering the blacks as we discovered their country, foot by foot."[30] It is only by persevering that one penetrates their secret. But then what richness is discovered! Griaule was still dazzled by the Dogon cosmogony, which after fifteen years of patient study had finally been revealed to him by an elderly sage.

"Le noir est un homme" ("The black is a man") was the title Georges Balandier gave his contribution to the first issue of *Présence Africaine;* it was a caustic analysis of European and white African ideas concerning Negroes. They ranged from savage to curious animal ("If you go to Africa, you will see negroes, monkeys, and panthers," page 31), passing through metropolitan French stereotypes (the black as jazz musician, soldier, bellhop, etc.), to colonial versions of the nigger either as "evolved being" or as "missing link" ("very Darwinian, makes

25. At least in Europe and in French-language colonies. The readers of the Haitian reviews published since the independence of this island are all within West Indian territory.

26. Richard Wright, "Claire étoile du matin" (a French translation of his short story, "Bright and Morning Star," from *Uncle Tom's Children*), *Présence Africaine*, no. 1, pp. 120–35.

27. Abdoulaye Sadji, excerpt from the novel *Nini*, in ibid., pp. 89–110.

28. Andre Gide, "Avant-propos," ibid., pp. 3–6.

29. Théodore Monod, "Etapes," ibid., pp. 15–20.

30. Marcel Griaule, "L'inconnue noire," ibid., pp. 21–27.

one think of the slow progress of the species," the author remarks, page 32). In brief, rapid pictures, Balandier then describes life in African villages and the mentality of the inhabitants as he had viewed them, similar in many ways to those of French peasants.[31] After these articles denouncing Western moral prejudices, there were others emphasizing social prejudices.

Pierre Naville accomplished the latter with considerable tact: "Education, culture, the various forms of artistic life, all these are just vain words, if one does not possess the indispensable foundation: an economic and social life from which slavery, bondage, servitude, and exploitation have been banned. It is obvious therefore that it is not possible to separate intellectual culture from its social conditions."[32]

Jean-Paul Sartre's contribution went more brutally to the heart of the subject. "We are ignorant," he declared, "of the real condition of black people in Africa, and this permits us to have a clear conscience. Each time we shake hands with a black person *here*, we erase all the violence we have committed *there.*" *Here* we treat the blacks as foreigners, *there* as "natives" with whom it is shameful to fraternize. Sartre hoped *"Présence Africaine* would paint an impartial picture of the situation of black peoples in the Congo and Senegal. . . . This need not be done with anger or revolt, only with the truth. It will be enough for us to feel the scorching breath of Africa in our faces, the sour smell of poverty and oppression."[33]

Emmanuel Mounier's "Lettre à un ami africain" was written in a somewhat different tone. It "opens a dialogue . . . on the grounds of lucidity rather than on ceremony,"[34] and speaks of the dangers which threaten the young African movement, what Mounier calls its "childhood illnesses," doubtless inspired by Lenin.[35]

31. Georges Balandier, "Le noir est un homme," pp. 31–36.
32. Pierre Naville, ibid., pp. 44–46.
33. Jean-Paul Sartre, "Présence noire," ibid., pp. 28–29.
34. Emmanuel Mounier, "Lettre à un ami africain," ibid., pp. 37–43.
35. On his return from a trip to Africa, Mounier published an account of his travels in a book, *Eveil de l'Afrique noire* ("Black Africa awakens") (Paris: Seuil, 1948). Excerpts were serialized earlier in the magazine *Esprit,* July through November 1946.

Mounier's remarks and advice were both shrewd and sound. We feel compelled to point out, however, that probably because Mounier never personally experienced racism, he does not seem to understand the existence of the psychological phenomenon of racism, whose many manifestations, even in France, Frantz Fanon would analyze in 1952 in *Peau noire, masques blancs* (Paris: Seuil, 1952), translated as *Black Skin, White Masks* (New York: Grove Press, 1967). It is false to say that all whites treat blacks as they would any other socially inferior white (like certain employers in the nineteenth century who despised their workers), and thus reduce all African problems to the social level. Yet this is what Sartre did too, assimilating racial considerations with the class struggle.

On the phenomenon of racism see also Sir Alan Burns's book *Colour Prejudice* (London: George Allen & Unwin, 1948).

Mounier saw these young Africans as belonging to a generation torn between two temptations. The first, to despise the Africa which would seem to hold them back, and "more or less to embrace explicitly, the contempt of certain whites for all things African." And yet, said Mounier, an African "can no more be rid of Africa than anyone can be rid of the roots that give him life or the air he breathes." Educated Africans must therefore return to their deep and distant sources, not to gorge themselves on folklore . . . but in order to redeem the permanent values of the African heritage." The second temptation, arising from too great a sensitivity to European error, would be to "oppose white racism with a black counterracism." Cannot Europe be forgiven? Mounier asked. "Europe carried the full weight of the world in this first era of humanity. Who, under similar conditions, would not have committed as many sins?" Indeed, the author remarks, this is not a matter of race conflict but of social, economic, and moral struggle. "The white man holds all the important and most of the prestigious positions in your country: It is therefore not surprising that he alone should be the object of your criticisms and demands. But in those provocations where you see race attacking race, if the same men were placed among whites exercising the same discretionary power, they would certainly take advantage of it in the same way."

The author concluded by advising his African friends not to despise manual labor by allowing themselves to be attracted by the prestige of so-called intellectual professions; "take care not to increase the number of those 'half-skilled persons' who only live on the carcasses of words." Mounier recommended the formation of technical specialists rather than orators; he encouraged today's black elite not to isolate itself from the masses, but on the contrary to raise the masses to their level. "If there must be revolution, twentieth-century revolutions take place in the factory, the fields, the classroom, and not on the public square. . . . The form of democracy is nothing without real democracy."

20/ The Nature and Influence of *Présence Africaine*

Présence Africaine's original aim was not political but cultural. By the indirect means of culture, however, it was led to set forth the problem of colonization in all its amplitude. The magazine's white contributors themselves invited it. And when the magazine's end section ("La revue des revues") commented on articles from various French or colonial publications, here too remarks of political import inevitably occurred.

To give but a single example, *Présence Africaine* quoted two passages from the May–June 1946 issue of *La Voix du Congolais*,[1] adding a few comments, exceedingly brief but clearly revealing the editor's feelings:

How can we live under the eyes of our rulers!

. . . We must take care not to fall back to the level of the natives, to return to an apathetic animal life. We must also beware of dreams of grandeur, of becoming caricatures of civilized persons, if we do not wish to be despised and held up to ridicule by Europeans.

Simplicity and modesty are the qualifications of a civilized man. If we wish our rulers to think well of us, we must therefore remain *simple* and *modest.*

[There! Go play with your little friends.]

Some of you will be inclined to demand your rights, but above all you should accomplish your duties toward the administration and the community. A worker is entitled to his wage after he has carried out his task. You yourselves will be entitled to all the consideration of your chiefs when you have done everything to deserve it.

[Whatever the good reasons cited, all this remains painful and leaves room for thought.][2]

1. A periodical published in Leopoldville and edited by Antoine Bolamba.
2. First issue of *Présence Africaine,* p. 179.

288

As *Présence Africaine* asserted itself and increased the number of its readers, it became more sensitive to African public life. It was naturally influenced by the Negro intelligentsia and particularly by the students in Paris, who were passionately political. Nonetheless, the magazine maintained its role as the loyal witness of the always-evolving "presence" of Africa. If the demand, the insistence, on revolution at the heart of today's negritude writing, whether in poetry or fiction, did not lead to concrete action, it would have remained a mere literary theme, the writer's inauthentic expression. "Negritude today," according to Alioune Diop, "is nothing but black genius *accompanied* by the will to reveal its dignity."[3] "Its mission is to restore history to its true dimensions."[4] But how could one carry out this ambitious program and influence history today without the help of direct action?

But there is more! The desire for a *cultural* renaissance would also inevitably lead to action, because this could not be obtained, at least within the framework of French colonization, without political liberation first. Why? Because a French colonizer[5] is generally sure of his values, believes that they are universal (which is true) and that there are no others (which is less certain). He settles down in the colonies with an aggressive spirit, believing that he is distributing his knowledge and science to a backward, childish people with no other tradition but folklore, and with no culture but a "primitive" one. He wishes to raise the natives to his level, make them share *his* mentality, *his* mental schemes, *his* social habits. In short, he wishes them to be "assimilated," made "similar" to him.[6] He thus denies the original cultures and makes their authentic expression impossible. If the native who is colonized proclaims the importance of his civilization and wishes to be recognized, he sees himself compelled to reject assimilation, as well as the limits it perforce imposes, and, therefore, the new presence of the colonizer. A simple *cultural* affirmation becomes a further reason for *political* revolution, to be added to the other reasons one might have for desiring the departure of the occupier. This is why Alioune Diop claims that "cultured men in Africa can no longer hold themselves aloof from politics, which are a necessary condition for cultural renaissance."[7]

3. Alioune Diop, March 1960 lecture at the Centre International, Brussels.

4. Alioune Diop, "Le sens de ce congrès," opening speech of the Second Congress.

5. We make this reservation because, due to the fact that segregation is more common in British colonies, it is doubtful that the British, like the French, are *apostles* of their culture.

6. See Jacques Weulersse's contribution to *L'homme de couleur* entitled "La vraie solution: l'école."

7. Alioune Diop, lecture (see note 3 above).

The editors of *Présence Africaine* seemed thus to agree with the position of *Légitime Défense* that politics come first. Was this a retreat compared to the stand taken by *L'Etudiant Noir,* or was the latter mistaken in insisting on the priority of culture?

We would like to point out, along with Senghor,[8] that *Légitime Défense*'s demands were purely social and only called for the emancipation of the West Indian working class. It did not yet challenge French domination in the Islands. If the European values taught the natives were criticized, this was only in the name of surrealism and communism, values more modern but nonetheless still European. It was to spare West Indians the apprenticeship of a culture already outdated in the mother country, but not to assert the existence of Negro values as such. This was understandable for West Indians, so long cut off from their origins, incapable of imagining that these origins might be comparable in prestige to French culture. In earlier chapters, we have seen how deep cultural alienation was in the West Indies. *Légitime Défense* did not in fact demand political emancipation but demanded only that West Indians be completely integrated and henceforth considered "completely French." The resemblance to positions taken by *Présence Africaine* is therefore only apparent, due to the use of the word "political," which should be interpreted in two different ways. For *Légitime Défense* it meant internal politics, the struggle between opposing social classes. For *Présence Africaine* it meant external politics, a struggle between nations of different culture.

Légitime Défense's demands, however, already implied the recognition of the Negro as equal to the white man and the denunciation of racism, segregation, and the oppression of the black proletariat. On the other hand, if *Légitime Défense* did not strongly emphasize black culture, it nevertheless demanded that West Indians rid themselves of servile imitation and that they be allowed to express their originality within French culture. This implied a spiritual difference that was interesting to reveal. *Présence Africaine* did not reject the positions taken by *Légitime Défense* but extended and deepened a movement already outlined by its predecessors.

L'Etudiant Noir first insisted on cultural independence, apparently influenced most of all by the Africans,[9] who were closer to their black origins and still saturated with traditions whose value they knew. In the introduction to the magazine's first issue, Diop noted that the first act of these African students had been to take inventory of their assets and weigh their differences. Gradually their criticism of a Europe that was

8. See chap. 7 above.

9. Let us remember that the *Légitime Défense* team was composed entirely of West Indians.

trying to crush these worthwhile values increased. The West Indians, like Césaire and Damas,[10] who took part in these discussions, discovered the root of the originality they had guessed at and the deep reason for their feeling of discomfort within French culture. They challenged Europe's cultural predominance without, however, forgetting what *Légitime Défense* had unmasked, namely, the social oppression of which the black man is the victim. On the contrary, works like *Retour de Guyane* by Léon Damas and Senghor's first poems, *Chants d'ombre* and *Hosties noires*, went even farther in questioning European domination.

If the cultural struggle was given greater emphasis, it was because in this domain *L'Etudiant Noir*'s collaborators made the most discoveries, and perhaps because it was the one most neglected by the blacks themselves, who were more strongly motivated by the question of social equality with Europeans. It was also, no doubt, because all the editors of the magazine were writers, with a natural sensitivity to aesthetic and cultural problems, anxious to express them in a personal manner. This private artistic need did not, however, isolate them from politics. At the time, Senghor and his companions shared an idea he still defends:

> Paradoxical as this may seem, writers and artists must and do play a most important role in the struggle for decolonization. It is up to them to remind politicians that politics and administration are but one aspect of culture, and that cultural colonialism, in the shape of assimilation, is the worst of all.[11]

It was therefore assimilation above all that must be fought. *L'Etudiant Noir* had no desire to repeat the experience of Haiti, where, even after political independence, French intellectual influence remained predominant, preventing the creation of outstanding works until the day when "a man rose who said: There is a national culture in Haiti."[12]

Moreover, in the light of their discoveries, Africans clearly saw that the struggle was no longer between proletarians and bourgeois, but between blacks and whites; not between two classes, but between two cultures, and that finally the stake of this struggle was the independence of Negro nations. At that period the young men were not yet armed to make their fight on political grounds. In the meantime, they

10. We include Léon Damas among the West Indians because he finished his lycée studies in Martinique (in Césaire's class), and because in France he naturally felt closer to the West Indians than to the Africans. In reality, French Guiana is not part of the West Indies, and this is important on two counts: The Guianese do not suffer from insular psychological conditioning; but they do suffer from the presence of the penal colony in Cayenne and the prejudice it causes them abroad.

11. L. S. Senghor, *Eléments constructifs d'une civilisation d'inspiration négro-africaine*, p. 279.

12. J. S. Alexis on Dr. Jean Price-Mars during the discussions of the First Congress of Black Writers and Artists, a report of which appeared in the special issue of *Présence Africaine*, p. 69.

emphasized culture, awakening in their compatriots an awareness of their cultural difference. The criticism of European values was permitted them now, since so many Westerners had themselves begun it. After the war, as we have seen, black intellectuals engaged in direct action as soon as it was possible.

Présence Africaine took over the foundations laid by *L'Etudiant Noir:* the affirmation of African culture. Gradually, in the course of various issues of *Présence Africaine*, this culture was seen to be richer and more varied than originally imagined, and black intellectuals, becoming more keenly aware of the prejudice colonization had caused, grew even more anxious to put an end to it.

At the same time, Africa was becoming more politically minded, the possibilities of liberation were growing, and the people as a whole were beginning passionately to desire it. It was under this double pressure, both internal and external, intellectual and social, that *Présence Africaine* began to take greater interest in politics.

We come now to the orientation of its politics. It has often been said that *Présence Africaine* underwent considerable communist influence. It is true that the authors of numerous articles, particularly the young ones, without necessarily agreeing on all points with communist ideology, adopted a practical pro-Marxist attitude, either because they were attracted by certain of Karl Marx's ideas or because they were stimulated by the encouragements the Soviet Union lavished upon the still colonized countries.

Yet many other articles did not have a Marxist flavor and often expressed completely contrary ideas. The review also published articles by African seers, such as the Peuhl philosopher Hampate Ba.

The magazine's advisory board includes the names of such confirmed catholics as Léopold Senghor and Jacques Rabemananjara, rationalist humanists such as Dr. Jean Price-Mars, René Maran, and Paul Niger, well-informed ex-communists such as Richard Wright and Aimé Césaire, without forgetting the director himself, Alioune Diop, widely known as a Christian.[13]

It was therefore with good reason that Diop declared that his magazine brought together Africans of all origins and all opinions, based on their common interests. They had all understood that unity is strength. If a close collaboration of such widely different mentalities seemed surprising, Diop would reply: "Our ideological differences excite us less than they do you—because after all, we have not lived through your religious wars!"[14] In a multitude of different

13. In chap. 21 below we shall give more detailed information on the orientation of a number of black writers.
14. Alioune Diop, see note 4 above.

tones, the fundamental aim of all the intellectuals contributing to *Présence Africaine* remained the complete political and cultural emancipation of every black in Africa, the United States, or the West Indies. It was both to encourage this movement and to inform its readers about African nationalist trends that the magazine published, for example, special issues on Guinea and Ghana.

If politics occupies more space in *Présence Africaine* today than it used to, cultural matters still predominate. The review has introduced numerous black writers: Africans like Abdoulaye Sadji, Birago Diop, Jean Malonga, Bernard Dadié; black students in Paris; along with veteran authors like Mongo Beti, David Diop, Ferdinand Oyono, and especially Jacques Rabemananjara. West Indians like René Depestre and Edouard Glissant also contribute frequently.

Without limiting itself to black writers of the French language, the magazine has been interested in American Negro writers and in those from British Africa. Richard Wright and Peter Abrahams, and later Mercer Cook and Georges Lamming, were listed on the credit pages of the early issues. The absence of Spanish and Portuguese language writers is, however, regrettable. It is true that articles on Brazilian literature and special authors like (the Cuban poet) Nicolas Guillén have appeared, but apparently no black intellectual from any of the Spanish or Portuguese language countries has thus far played an active role in *Présence Africaine*.

It would be tiresome to list all the cultural domains which the review made known to its readers during its life span:* articles on traditional oral literature, on African religions and philosophies, on Haitian voodoo, on music, principally jazz, etc. Finally, the review has served as an intellectual crossroads for the confrontation of ideas, particularly on two points which seem especially interesting to us: the black intellectual's responsibility toward his people, and the existence of a national literature.

These two subjects, although broached separately by writers at the Second Congress in 1959 in Rome, were found to be closely linked. All the writers, whether West Indians or Africans, declared themselves in favor of complete liberation of their literature from Western themes and forms. They hoped African Negro authors would differentiate themselves further in order to show their national realities and the variety of their cultures to better advantage. All agreed, however, that these realities, whatever their diversity, had one important point in common that ought not to be neglected.

*Translator's note: At this writing, in 1973, *Présence Africaine* is in its twenty-sixth continuous year of publication.

There were two aspects of his national reality that a writer had to reveal, synthetized by Edouard Glissant as,

on the one hand, what can be called the essential qualities of this reality, and on the other hand, a basic demand rising from the present condition of black peoples throughout the world. In order that the relationship between the Negro novel and Negro reality may be total, the novelist must not sacrifice these basic attributes to his demands, nor should he pursue an abstract expression of these qualities, but he must recognize the demands as the real, although probably temporary, foundations of his art.[15]

Rabemananjara stressed the other fact: The black writer today is so closely bound to his people that he succeeds in bearing witness for them and representing them, simply by obeying his own inner needs. The black writer, he says,

faced with the essential mystery of life, will not merely have to settle—as all poets do—the discomfort of his own conscience. In his efforts to attain freedom, he will discover that his personal deliverance necessitates simultaneously the deliverance of his racial brothers. The tension is no longer confined to the level of a dialectical disagreement between his soul and his environment. The conflict extends beyond individual problems, and its ramifications and demands are on the scale of an entire people and include a whole portion of humanity. No one will be saved here unless everyone is saved. The poet's solidarity with his people is no freely chosen thing; it is the very foundation of his poetry and ensures its one opportunity for greatness and beauty. It is the *raison d'être* and existentialist originality of his work. In the Western world, of course, things may be different. One can easily conceive of a poetic universe constructed in the proud shape of an ivory tower, and of the Inspired one locking himself within it. . . . Yet, it is remarkable that during the period of the resistance under the rigor of foreign occupation, there was no authentic poet on the European continent who spontaneously assumed this experience of his people. At the time no one saw the solution of his own inner problems except within the global solution of his country's drama. Here again the community of destinies was not optional.[16]

René Depestre has explained in simple terms how he understood his relation to the social condition of the working class in Haiti: "It was not thrust upon me from outside" he writes, "as an order, as some catchword foreign to my deepest concerns and anxieties. It was a human tragedy for me related to the tragedy of my whole people, kept till now from the most elementary beauties of existence."[17]

With considerable clearsightedness, Rabemananjara warned poets

15. Edouard Glissant, "Le romancier noir et son peuple," *Présence Africaine*, no. 16 (October–November 1957), p. 26.

16. Jacques Rabemananjara, "Le poète noir et son peuple," *Présence Africaine*, no. 16, pp. 12–13.

17. Quoted by Rabemananjara, ibid., p. 14.

of the danger of too abstract a commitment, of the danger of loyalty to watchwords not deeply felt or thought out:

Some are more concerned with negritude than simply listening to their souls, hearing the voices . . . of superior entreaties. Poetry flows from no other source than those urgent and fleeting needs. The fact that black poetry today calls upon politics to intervene almost bodily and metaphysically, does not mean that one should fall prey to the esthetics of political poetry. This would be sheer heresy: Poetry either is or is not. If the poet remains faithful to himself, his emotions will necessarily bear the marks of political, historical, psychological or other circumstances which engendered them. Even though his behavior is caused by more sensitive and deeper emotions, it does not differ in essence from that of any other person possessed by thoughts of his people and moved by love of his country.[18]

This exchange of ideas within *Présence Africaine* bore fruit at the two international congresses, where the majority of black writers agreed on a precise and exact definition of their responsibilities.[19]

Alioune Diop's activities rapidly extended far beyond the limits of the magazine: He founded the "Editions de Présence Africaine," which published its first book, *La philosophie bantoue* by R. P. Tempels,[20] in the first six months of 1949. This was a reissue of a book published in 1945 by the Editions Lovanie in Elizabethville, whose distribution had been hindered by the local clergy. Diop had found a copy of it in Léopoldville in 1947. Since 1949, the Editions de Présence Africaine has published poetry, novels, literary criticism, commemorative biographies, as well as social, scientific, historical, and political studies.[21]

Before closing this chapter, we shall briefly consider the scope and influence of *Présence Africaine*. In France, where all black students know the magazine, there is no question they either criticize or appreciate it. It has caught on in the West Indies, Haiti, Morocco, Madagascar, and countries around France. In Africa it is read chiefly by university students in Senegal, but during the last few years it has made its way into Guinea, the Ivory Coast, Cameroon, Togo, and the former Belgian Congo.

Alioune Diop admits, however, that his magazine is little read in Africa for several reasons. Its language and intellectual level make it

18. J. Rabemananjara, ibid., p. 18.
19. See chap. 21, below.
20. R. P. Tempels, *La philosophie bantoue* (Paris: Présence Africaine, 1949).
21. We would mention as examples, the following novels: *Ville cruelle* by E. Boto (better known as Mongo Beti); *Nini* and *Maïmouna* by Abdoulaye Sadji; the collected poems *Minerai noir* by Depestre; *Lamba* and *Antsa* by J. Rabemananjara; the studies by D. Guérin *Les Antilles décolonisées*, and by Gunnar Myrdal *Théorie économique et pays sous-développés;* special editions *L'Art nègre, Le travail en Afrique noire, Les étudiants noirs parlent;* etc.

inaccessible to the uneducated masses, which still comprise 80 to 95 percent of the population. Furthermore, until 1958, the magazine was the victim of screening measures and systematic though veiled obstruction on the part of the French government: Pressure was brought to bear on booksellers to prevent them from carrying it; there were censorship and postal delays. All this explains the magazine's greater influence on black students in Europe than in Africa. Yet many of these students hold important posts when they return to their native lands, and it is significant that the rulers of the new African states are familiar with the magazine, even when, unlike Senghor and Apithy, they have not been contributors. Sékou Touré is a stepbrother and friend of Alioune Diop, who is also very close to Keita Fodeba. Finally, the former prime minister of Dahomey, M. Maga, was an ardent defender of the magazine back in 1949 when subsidies were almost refused it in Dakar.

Thus do cultural magazines and men of politics influence each other. If Sékou Touré preaches "intellectual decolonization," this is only an extension of the struggle begun in 1932 by *Légitime Défense* and successfully continued today by *Présence Africaine:* "The true political leaders of Africa . . . can only be men committed, fundamentally committed, to work against all the forms and powers that deprive African culture of its personality. They represent . . . the cultural values of their society mobilized against colonization."[22]

At the end of World War II the new African Negro literature made great strides. *Bois d'ébène* by Jacques Roumain—who had just died—was published in 1945 and met with immediate success among black students. The themes, strength, and sincerity of this Haitian poet coincided so perfectly with the Paris movement that Jacques Roumain was immediately considered one of the leaders of negritude, though in his lifetime he had never been a member of any of its groups, since his diplomatic career had kept him far from metropolitan France. In 1946, *Les armes miraculeuses* by Aimé Césaire was published. Many excerpts had already appeared in the review *Tropiques.* The collection was enriched by a major work, *Et les chiens se taisaient*, Césaire's only tragedy until then, presenting the Rebel, typical hero of every revolution.[23] Also in 1946, with *Diab'la*, the Martiniquan Joseph Zobel began a series of novels describing black peasant life. A little later Jacques

22. Sékou Touré, *Le leader politique considéré comme le représentant d'une culture*, message given at the Second Congress, p. 105.

23. Césaire is at present preparing another tragedy, *Le roi Christophe*, Negro king at the beginning of Haiti's independence. [Translator's note: *La tragédie du roi Christophe* (Paris: Présence Africaine, 1963); translated by Ralph Manheim, *The Tragedy of King Christophe* (New York: Grove, 1970).]

Roumain's excellent *Gouverneurs de la rosée* appeared, and also J. S. Alexis's *Compère General Soleil,* both novels treating the life of Haitian Negroes.

In 1947, Léon Damas published the first anthology of overseas French poets, in which the phenomenon of the New Negro movement was brilliantly contrasted with the fossilized, well-polished poems of those who still made use of recipes of the Parnassian school.

Soon afterward, the Editions Fasquelles asked Damas to edit a series of works by overseas writers. During the same year, Fasquelles published *Starkenfirst* by the West Indian René Tardon and the *Contes d'Amadou Koumba* by Birago Diop. In 1948, Corrêa published Mayotte Capécia's novel *Je suis martiniquaise* and *Soleil cou coupé* by Aimé Césaire. In Brussels, the Editions G. A. Deny published the beautiful story *Ngando* by Lomani Tchibamba, born in Brazzaville of Congolese parents. Finally came Senghor's remarkable anthology of the negritude poets, and the consecration of the young literary movement in the dazzling preface by Jean Paul Sartre.

At the same period, several rivals of *Présence Africaine* were born, like Madeleine Rousseau's review *Musée Vivant,* oriented toward Negro art, or the magazine *Tam-Tam,* through which African Catholic students were to become aware of their role in the political and cultural emancipation of their countries.

21/ Black French-Language Writers in 1960: A Survey

About forty black French-language writers command attention today. It would, of course, be premature to include all of them immediately in the literary history of our era. Several have barely begun to write, although much may be expected of them. Others, in spite of prolific production, remain minor authors. However, if we consider them as a group, the quality of their style, their diversities of genre, but above all the astonishing kinship of themes in black writings in French, compel us to recognize this work as comprising an authentic *literary movement.*

We shall attempt to outline this movement now, though our ambition does not go so far as to attempt an exhaustive study. Though it is difficult to cover the entire sweep of black writers at a glance, we can already see the main outlines of their strength. As a first step, therefore, we shall indicate the directions of the movement as clearly and as completely as possible.

It may seem surprising that these last chapters are above all devoted to the personality of black writers and the way their personalities are reflected in their literary activity. Along with Richard Wright, we are persuaded—and this is no a priori judgement but the result of long study—that "an understanding of Negro expression cannot be arrived at without constant reference to the environment which creates it."[1]

It is always interesting, of course, to know the origins of a work and the circumstances surrounding it. Where black authors are concerned, we have found this *indispensable* because their responses differ greatly from those of white Europeans, because they often refer to things about which we Europeans know little, and above all because their

1. Richard Wright, *White Man, Listen!* (Doubleday-Anchor, 1957), p. 103.

298

works are situated morally and historically in a very specific context. We therefore interviewed the writers personally, giving them a detailed questionnaire, to which they gave verbal replies.[2] Unfortunately, it was not possible to get in touch with more than twenty-five writers. A picture of the New Negro movement cannot be given here in its entirety. The literary preferences given, for example, apply only to the authors who were interviewed.

Three facts, however, will underline the interest of this first opinion polling: First, we were able to interview the leaders, those who were at the very birth of the New Negro literary movement, who now give it its tone and who have the greatest audience among university students and apprentice writers. Second, and more particularly, certain main lines show clearly even now and would doubtless be confirmed by more detailed study. When a trend seemed more or less unanimous, for example, we could be sure—in view of the importance of the authors interviewed—that it did in fact represent the opinion of the majority of black writers. Moreover, whenever possible, we referred to the works of the writers we had not been able to reach, and indicated the points on which they invalidated, confirmed, or modified the results of our inquiry. Finally, this analysis proposes also in a more general way to demonstrate the complexity of the problems which face these "Westernized elites," whose situation has been described so well by Richard Wright:

... the lonely outsiders who exist precariously on the clifflike margins of many cultures—men who are distrusted, misunderstood, maligned, criticized by Left and Right, Christian and pagan—men who carry on their frail but indefatigable shoulders the best of two worlds—and who, amidst confusion and stagnation, seek desperately for a home for their hearts: a home which, if found, could be a home for the hearts of all men.[3]

First of all, here is the questionnaire which was submitted to the writers.[4] A detailed analysis of the results might furnish material for a sociological thesis. In order not to distort our literary and historical perspective, we only give excerpts of the essentials here, particularly on what touches the heart of our subject: "commitment" in black literature in the French language.

2. The questionnaire which we give below was corrected by Mme Dorsinfang and M. Vauthier, professors at the Université Libre de Bruxelles, and completed by Professor G. Balandier, the specialist in African literatures.

3. Richard Wright's dedication to *White Man, Listen!*

4. We were not able to speak at length either to Alioune Diop or Cheik Anta Diop, but we were able to complete their replies by referring to their writings and lectures. Using the same method, we "interviewed" three other young writers: Paulin Joachim, Elolongué Epanya Yondo, and Olympe Bhêly-Quénum. They are not included in our data, but were taken into account in our analysis.

1. Name, age, nationality, place where author has lived, profession, fields of study, published works.
2. What are the reasons which originally prompted you to write? Influence of environment? A desire for escape? Aesthetic concerns? A sense of intellectual responsibility?
3. What, at that time, did you wish to create? A work of art? The personal expression of some dominant feeling (revolt, indignation, love, hate, etc.)? Did you have political or social aims? If so, what? Or did you simply wish to inform?
4. Did you deliberately choose one teacher or school? If not, do you believe you made an unconscious choice? How do you situate yourself vis-à-vis other writers? Against some? With others?
5. Has your admiration changed or not? If so, how?
6. To which writers do you feel closest today and why? To white writers? Which ones? Black writers? Which ones?
7. Which foreign system of thought has most deeply influenced you? Protestantism, Catholicism, Marxism, Rationalism, Islam, Buddhism, Personalism, Existentialism, etc.?
   a. Do you still prefer it?
   b. If not, why do you reject it?
   c. Which aspects of the system have most clearly marked you?
8. Some of these systems preach "a return to one's sources," that is, to native traditions.
   a. Do you consider this essential? If so why?
   b. In your previous works, did you personally feel the need to become more deeply aware of your traditional African culture? Have you used this culture in your work?
   c. *Before writing*, did you have the opportunity to participate in this culture? Intimately? Or, on the other hand, had you been deprived of it?
   d. When you consider this traditional culture: What are the aspects and elements of it which have penetrated you most deeply? Which of its aspects and elements do you feel are the most important and worthy of being revived today? With which aspects do you no longer agree (religious beliefs and rites, social organization and customs, etc.)?
9. What themes do you prefer to treat? Interracial problems? Description of morals and manners? Myths and religious problems? Historical themes? Personal experiences?
10. What are your principal sources of inspiration? Political events? Personal concerns and anxieties? Social problems? Traditional folklore?
11. Why did you choose this particular literary form? For reasons of efficiency? Ease?

12. What work gave you the greatest satisfaction? Why?
13. Have you changed your aims since you first began to write? Why? How?
14. Has your style changed since you began to write? Why? How?
15. What public do you wish to reach? Does the fact that you write in French limit the number of your readers or does it increase them? Do you believe that a written literature with mass distribution is possible in the African languages?
16. How do you conceive your role as a writer?
    a. As an interpreter of Negro problems, spokesman for black peoples? (Should a writer deal above all with problems of current interest to his people?)
    b. As an educator of the black masses? (Should the writer propose new problems, provoke thought, show new ways of looking at things?)
    c. As a contributor to the liberation of Negro peoples?
    d. As prompted by a desire to express yourself personally?
    e. As stemming from a wish to create something aesthetic?
17. Do you believe that your writing should be committed, militant?
    a. If so, is this because of political conditions in your country?
    b. Or because you feel it is necessary to stay in touch with the masses?
    c. In that case, do you feel such contact must be maintained, or that when conditions have changed writers will have greater freedom to choose their form?
18. If you have chosen committed writing, have you, because of this, had to:
    a. Sacrifice certain of your personal tendencies, give up certain modes of expression?
    b. Commit yourself politically, socially, culturally, etc.?
    c. Do you feel that, as far as you are concerned, in view of present conditions, literature and politics are two closely allied domains?
    d. Or, on the contrary, do you prefer your literary work to be independent?
19. As a writer, do you feel a community of interests with other writers? Of your own race? With Europeans? How?
20. What does negritude mean to you?
21. Do you believe that there is such a thing as black literature? Or merely that there are blacks writing in a number of languages (French, English, Portuguese, etc.)?
    Can a specifically "black" literature, distinct from others, exist in non-African Negro languages?

If so, does such a black literature already exist? (Who are its authors and most representative works?)

Or is this literature now being created? (What signs do you see that point to this: books, authors, movements, etc.?)

We can divide the authors interviewed into two groups: In 1960, the year of our questionnaire, thirteen were over thirty-five and nine were under that age. This is no arbitrary separation, since our investigation showed that there are differences between the two generations, which will be clear as we continue.

Nine of the writers we questioned were born in the West Indies: Aimé Césaire, Léon Damas, Frantz Fanon, Edouard Glissant, Gilbert Gratiant, René Maran, Paul Niger, Léonard Sainville, and Joseph Zobel. Only Glissant and Fanon, at the time, were under thirty-five. Eleven writers were African: F. Agblemagnon, Hampate Ba, Mongo Beti, Bernard Dadié, Alioune Diop, Cheik Anta Diop, David Diop, Ousmane Sembene, Léopold Sédar Senghor, Félix Tchicaya U Tam'si, and A. Tevoedjre. Of these, four (Dadié, Alioune Diop, Hampate Ba, and Senghor) were over thirty-five, as were the two writers from Madagascar, Rabemananjara and Ranaïvo.

Among the West Indians, all of them descendants of Negro slaves from Africa (although of mixed blood to a greater or lesser degree), six are from Martinique (Césaire, Fanon, Glissant, Gratiant, Sainville, and Zobel); Paul Niger is from Guadeloupe; and Maran and Damas are both of Guianese origin.[5] Among the Africans, Alioune Diop, David Diop, Ousmane Sembene, and Léopold Senghor are from Senegal; Cheik Anta Diop and Hampate Ba—one a Bambara, the other a Peulh —are from the former French Sudan (now Upper Volta and Mali); Tevoedjre is from Dahomey, Agblemagnon from Togo, Beti from Cameroon, Félix Tchicaya U Tam'si from Congo/Brazzaville, and Bernard Dadié from the Ivory Coast.

The Madagascans must be set apart. The dominant tribes in Madagascar are not of African origin but Indonesian and Polynesian. Ethnologists never include them among African societies. Yet we could not exclude Jacques Rabemananjara from our study. He was too intimately involved in the birth and development of *Présence Africaine* and, moreover, took as his own all the review's political and cultural ideas except that of race, even though he is black. Madagascans, even the darkest, feel less "Negro" than "Malagasy." Whether dark Melanesians or light Indonesians, they all participate in the same culture, which differs on many points from African cultures, and their insular

---

5. René Maran was born in Martinique of Guianese parents; he has, however, lived chiefly in France (see chap. 6 above). We list Damas among West Indians for reasons explained in chap. 20, note 10, above.

situation has not encouraged rapprochement with the continent.[6]

Flavien Ranaïvo does not belong to the black race. He is of the Merina people,[7] light-skinned, with dark, smooth, straight hair. His works are not therefore part of African Negro literature. Nevertheless, it seemed interesting to place him with his compatriot Jacques Rabemananjara, since he confirms that the differences one finds between Rabemananjara and other black writers are not individual differences due to the author's personality, but attributable to deeper causes which reveal the special characteristics of the Malagasy peoples.

Unfortunately we were not able to interview any Haitian authors. Four are clearly and indisputably important: Dr. Jean Price-Mars (who is over sixty), Jacques Roumain (now dead), and Jacques Stéphen Alexis and René Depestre (both under thirty-five). But readings of their work and other informed sources make it plain that these four authors can be counted with the West Indian group on all the points that interest us.

Most of the writers we are dealing with lived in their native lands from birth up to the time of their university education in France.[8] Hampate Ba and Bernard Dadié have never lived outside their native land. Others, such as René Maran,[9] Gilbert Gratiant, and David Diop, spent the greater part of their lives in Europe.

This is important. If an author has lived chiefly in the colonies, it will definitely have influenced his themes and more or less guarantees the "authenticity" of his presentation. West Indians will naturally be more "true" in speaking of their own country if they have spent many years there. We should point out that many works are to a great extent autobiographical, for example, those of Joseph Zobel, Ousmane Sembene, Edouard Glissant, Mongo Beti, Camara Laye, Ousmane Socé, Ferdinand Oyono, Paul Niger and Cheikh Kane.[10] These writers help us to understand their native milieu from the inside and also their feelings about colonization. Later, we shall examine their principal grievances against European control.

The intellectual level of the black writers interviewed is generally high: Seven are university graduates and one, the philosopher Ham-

6. As we have mentioned several times, West Indian writers feel their African origins keenly, doubtless in reaction to their socially inferior condition. In addition, due to the fact that they were brought as slaves into a country occupied by whites, their "national" feeling has not been free to develop as it did among Madagascan populations, who were already in control of their island and well organized before colonization.

7. A tribe originating in Indonesia and, according to information furnished by F. Ranaïvo, having intermarried quite extensively with Jews.

8. Tchicaya U Tam'si lived in his native country only until he was fourteen.

9. René Maran was administrator of Ubangi-Shari (see chap. 6 above).

10. This is also true of much black literature in English (*I Am Not a Free Man*, by P. Abrahams; *Black Boy*, by R. Wright, etc.).

pate Ba, completed many years of Islamic studies. We might even include in this group René Maran, who, after his baccalaureate degree, acquired on his own a much higher level of education. Two writers, Bernard Dadié and Félix Tchicaya U Tam'si, have only completed secondary school. Ousmane Sembene alone has only an elementary school education. As a stevedore in Marseilles, he was union-educated and disapproves of Parisian intellectuals, whom he considers "too bourgeois."[11]

All the university graduates have undergone cultural cross-breeding (*métissage culturel*). French is their second mother tongue, one might say. This is is especially true of the West Indians who speak French without accent and consider the Creole dialects as mere provincial idioms.[12] Educated in France, usually in the capital, they have also all been subjected to more or less similar literary and ideological influences.

As we mentioned in chapter 20, black writers are keenly aware of their responsibilities to the West and to their own peoples, and this awareness naturally affects their writing, no matter what their training. Ousmane Sembene's lower educational level may influence his style but has no clear repercussion on his ideas, which are the same as those of the other writers. Every one of the writers has a second profession: Seven are professors, eight have or have had political or union responsibilities. The others have careers in the mass media (in radio, journalism, etc.) or in scientific research. But it is worth mentioning that most of them—with the exception of those who have political or scientific responsibilities—feel that their literary role is the most important.

Let us now tackle the important issue of literary influences. This question was posed only to the *creative writers*—seventeen of the twenty-two interviewed—namely those who have literary goals, not essayists who make use of the pen as a weapon to defend certain causes (decolonization, racial demands, re-evaluation of African cultures, etc.). This, of course, does not mean that the essayists have no literary talent.[13]

11. The greater majority of black writers are also university graduates: the four Haitians mentioned above, Birago Diop and Ousmane Socé of Senegal, F. Sissoko of the Sudan (now Mali), F. Oyono (Cameroon), B. Matip (Cameroon), Camara Laye, R. Tardon, etc.

12. There seems to be a strong tendency today to reevaluate Creole. Several writers believe it capable of playing a role of literary language. The principal attempts in this direction were carried out by G. Gratiant, *Fab'compè zicaque*, poems (Fort-de-France: Editions des Horizons Caraïbes, 1958) and by Morisseau Leroy, who adapted *Antigone* in Creole.

13. Five of the writers consulted (Fanon, Alioune Diop, Ba, Agblemagnon, and Cheik Anta Diop) are not "men of letters" but "men of culture," who write in defense of certain ideas, without, however, having a particularly literary vocation. Yet they are useful in situating the other writers: Their motives, their aims, expressed with color and

By "literary influences" we mean the writers' self-declared tastes and preference for certain authors. To ascertain the real influence of these authors on the style of our writers, on the creation of their work, is a study altogether too complex to be broached here, one which would require at least as much space as the present volume. There are sometimes immediate influences, as between David Diop's poetry and Jacques Roumain's (although Diop declares he prefers Césaire), or Edouard Glissant, who seems the direct heir of his favorite poet, Saint-John Perse. Sometimes the influence is more subtle. In *Mirages de Paris*, Ousmane Socé's descriptions of dances in Paris, for example, attempts to re-create the atmosphere and movement of the magnificent dancing scenes in Claude McKay's *Banjo*. And we have seen to what extent Senghor—who makes no secret of it—has been influenced by the oral poetry of Senegal. Both Rabemananjara and Ranaïvo bear the trace of their Malagasy origins, and the inspiration for Ranaïvo's poems is drawn directly from the Madagascan *hain-tenys*.[14] These points of similarity, we repeat, should be confirmed, refined, and enriched by a more thorough study.

We thought it would be interesting to find out which authors were read by black writers: "Tell me whom you love . . ."; the old proverb is still true. To prefer a writer is to feel a certain affinity for him, and, if one is also a writer, it also reveals one's own conception of literature, its role, the problems it must tackle.

Let us classify these influences as "Western" and "Negro," since many colored writers have been influenced by the works of their black brothers. The outline given below may seem a bit academic, but we want above all to be clear.

Western Literature

French

Out of seventeen writers, fifteen keenly appreciate French poetry. The symbolists and their heirs were most often mentioned: Baudelaire four times; Mallarmé, Saint-John Perse, and Rimbaud three times; and Claudel twice. The first two writers were admired for their plastic qualities, the other three for their intense lyricism. The surrealists, mentioned only by Césaire, Damas, and Sainville (all former members of the *L'Etudiant Noir* group), did not seem to be especially appreciated by the younger generation, who, on the other hand, were not indifferent to the romantics. Several writers claimed that their poetic emotions were first aroused in high school by Victor Hugo, Lamartine, and

---

lucidity, without exaggeration or lyricism, reveal the very skeleton, the guiding principles of truly literary works, and are thus indispensable to a clear understanding of them.

14. Madagascan folk songs of a very special style, studied by Jean Paulhan in *Les hain-tenys* (Paris: NRF, 1938).

Nerval, whereas the Madagascan writers, during their student years, were more thrilled by such German romanticists as Hölderlin, Novalis, and Rilke.

The French novel has a much smaller readership. Only three black novelists (out of eight) mentioned Balzac and Zola; Flaubert and Proust were named twice, and Camus once. No mention at all was made of the writers between the two wars, Gide, Duhamel, Saint-Exupéry, Colette, or Malraux, although the two young Dahomeans mentioned Mauriac as a master.[15] As for the "new novelists," they aroused no interest except with Glissant, who described these French contemporaries of his as "very intelligent, but victims of a situation."[16]

Russian and American

It is striking to observe that in contrast to their feelings about the French novel, six writers appreciated Russian literature and singled out Dostoievski, Gogol, Chekov and Sholokhov, either for their epic inspiration or for the swarming, intense life of their characters. We should mention that they referred exclusively to pre-1917 authors. No modern Russian author was mentioned. As for American literature, it was represented by Faulkner, Hemingway, and, above all, Steinbeck.

All the writers mentioned deal with vast social problems, and this is doubtless the reason for their selection. In France, the contemporary sociological novel lacks this scope. But it is surprising that none of the black writers spoke of Malraux's *L'espoir* or *La condition humaine,* or the novels of Jules Romains, Roger Martin du Gard or Sartre. Since most of the poets and novelists that were referred to belong to revolutionary currents, it is not surprising for black writers to have found compelling resonance in their works.

Negro Literature

French

The black writers questioned had obviously read the principal works of their confreres, but we shall mention here only those authors whom they "preferred." Black poets are mentioned by twelve writers (out of seventeen). Césaire heads the list with eight votes, then Jacques Roumain (five votes), Senghor and Damas (three votes each), Rabemananjara (two votes), and Camara Laye (one). The poets, more widely read than the novelists,[17] seemed to be appreciated for their pugnacity.

15. They are Paulin Joachim and Olympe Bhêly-Quénum, both Catholic.

16. Interview with Edouard Glissant in June 1959. [Translator's note: The "new-wave" novelists are writers like Michel Butor, Alain Robbe-Grillet, Natalie Sarraute, who enjoyed great popularity in the 1950s.]

17. This can be explained by the fact that the Negro novel in French really blossomed only late in the 1950s.

Why the marked preference for Césaire, who is so difficult an author? Is it because he is recognized as the greatest by Western critics? Or because he has become the symbol of the "great Negro cry" launched by the *Cahier*? His later poetry was not as greatly appreciated. In any case, our soundings in various black student groups confirm his priority standing. Yet it seems, rather paradoxically, that Césaire is more appreciated today by young Africans than by West Indians. His most ardent fans are among the former.

Senghor, on the other hand, occupies a place unworthy of his value. It is true that his moderation ill agrees with the generally hot-headed temperament of the younger generation. It would be unusual, moreover, for them to like Césaire and Senghor at the same time. It may also be that Senghor's poetry is too deeply rooted in things Senegalese, the praise of its landscapes, history, and customs. Except for its rhythm, Senghor's verse generally evokes Senegal in particular far more than Africa in general. Nor does the rather aristocratic quality of his more recent collections of poems render them accessible to all sensibilities.

American Negro

Black American novelists were much more widely read by French-speaking writers than black American poets. The elder generation especially liked Claude McKay and Langston Hughes.[18] The young had read Richard Wright and Chester Himes and were not indifferent to their violent realism.

Traditional

A great majority of the writers (eleven out of seventeen) showed a keen interest in traditional African literature. *Chaka*, an epic novel translated from the Bantu in 1939, telling the story of the great Zulu chief's revolt, was frequently mentioned.[19] Many writers were also much interested in their local literature (tales, legends, poems). The Madagascans, especially, were anxious to link their own poetry to indigenous traditions. This was also true of the Peuhl philosopher Hampate Ba and of Bernard Dadié.

We should point out that all the black writers had been influenced by Negro literature in one or more of the three categories: traditional, American, and French. Since they had also been influenced equally by Western literature, there is good reason to speak of a cultural cross-breeding, with two exceptions, however: Bernard Dadié and Hampate Ba, who have had no French masters.[20]

18. See chap. 5 above.
19. Thomas Mofolo, *Chaka*, an epic Bantu poem written in Souto dialect. The translation was published by Editions Gallimard, Paris, 1939.
20. These two writers have always lived in Africa, where they were born.

The influence of traditional literature seems more important still if we study the works of writers whom we did not interview. Novelists and storytellers like Olympe Bhêly-Quénum, Jean Malonga, Lomani Tchibamba, Fily-Dabo Sissoko, Abdoulaye Sadji, Birago Diop, and Camara Laye, or poets like Keita Fodeba and Elolongué Epanya Yondo, draw their inspiration and even their style from African folklore. They have transcribed tales and poems of their homelands into French but in an African style.

These authors, furthermore, are certainly not "exotic" in the sense we give the word.[21] Writers who are directly connected with their traditional cultures, as they are, are usually completely bilingual, can create in both languages, and in a manner that expresses their African universe in depth. Often their work is completely devoid of polemic with very few allusions to whites. It is in this "relaxed" direction that the literary movement that has grown out of negritude seems to us to have the greatest opportunity for free development. By bringing an infinite number of themes, images, and twists of mind yet unheard in our language, it will doubtless greatly enrich the literature of the entire world.

Ideological influences were also asked about in our interviews, that is, thought systems which an author recognized as having affected him willy-nilly. It was not necessarily a question of his own choosing. Readings of the author's work confirmed in every case that these influences were real.

One notices considerable *instability* here. We believe it to be normal, considering the inner stresses that result from the acculturation process.[22] Overnight the Negro has been given two frames of reference within which he has had to place himself. His metaphysics or, less pretentiously, his customs and the sources on which they were based were wiped out because they were in conflict with civilization that he did not know and that imposed itself on him.[23]

Most of the black writers have been Christianized, but many later left the church, either to adhere to other convictions or to form some personal synthesis, usually much more complete and stable among the older writers. Occasionally the syntheses combined theories which might seem incompatible to Westerners, as for example Marxism and fetishism, Christianity and animism. When "Marxism-socialism" was mentioned we did not conclude that the writer was a member of the Communist Party, even when it was the ideology he preferred. Several of the writers called themselves Marxists or socialists but denied being

21. See discussion of "exotic" toward the end of chap. 2 above.

22. On acculturation, see Melville Herskovits's *Man and His Works: The Science of Cultural Anthropology* (New York: Knopf, 1948).

23. Frantz Fanon, *Black Skin, White Masks*, p. 110.

communists: "Black Marxists must think carefully about an African Marxism adapted to conditions in Africa," Alioune Diop has said.[24]

Most of the writers (nineteen out of twenty-two) had a Christian childhood and adolescence in their native countries. Twelve later rejected Christianity, or at least the church, whereas there is only one adult convert to the Christian faith, Alioune Diop, who was raised a Moslem.

Why this massive defection? The works of these writers explain it. Their principal reproach, both in the Caribbean and in Africa, is the collusion between missionaries and colonizers. The missionary seems to act as an auxiliary colonizer, smoothing the way for the administrator by preaching obedience and resignation.[25]

A second accusation follows closely on the first, but only where Africa is concerned. The missionary does not understand the natives; he wishes to force his own religion and morals upon them, treating the African ancestral customs and beliefs with contempt. Certainly the work of a Tempels and a Van Wing are appreciated, but their recommendations to the religious pastorate have still not sufficiently been put into practice.

The West Indians have another criticism: The religion they were taught is childish, elementary. Only one of the nine West Indians interviewed has remained Christian—Joseph Zobel. Five of them have turned to socialism and three to rationalism. All the West Indians denounce the dereliction of the local clergy. Although the African writers occasionally attack the missions very vigorously, I have never heard this criticism from them. Four Africans out of eleven, after careful thought, have remained Catholics. Others, like Mongo Beti, author of *Le pauvre Christ de Bomba,* a novel which, from beginning to end, indicts Christianity, nonetheless conclude that, all things considered, missionaries are still the least noxious of all the whites in Africa. As for the two Madagascan authors, their case is somewhat special. In Madagascar, Christianity and native cults have formed a somewhat curious but homogenous synthesis which seems to pose no problems for intellectuals.

Twelve writers have been influenced by Marxism to varying degrees, from Senghor's very flexible socialism—and he, incidentally, has remained a Christian—to Gratiant's orthodox communism. The underlying reasons are obviously social, and easy to understand when one considers the condition of the colonies, where the colonizer's interest is not the same as the native's. This antagonism fits in with the Marxist

24. Alioune Diop, conference at the Centre International, Brussels, 4 March 1960.
25. This same accusation stands out clearly from an investigation carried out by J. L. Laroche among black schoolchildren at the extramural center in Elizabethville.

scheme and explains why it has the greatest influence as an ideology.

We shall make two observations: (1) Marxism has had more appeal for the young writers (seven out of nine) than for the older ones (five out of thirteen). This corresponds to a growing interest in politics and a greater commitment to it. (2) The West Indians are more Marxist (six out of nine) than the Africans (six out of thirteen). The case of three other, Haitian, writers—J. Roumain, J. S. Alexis and R. Depestre— whom we were not able to question, confirms this. Also, Caribbean Marxists are more often members of the Communist Party, a fact rather rare among Africans. If Africans have leftist tendencies, they prefer to join corresponding parties existing in their own countries, like the Union des Populations du Cameroun (U.P.C.) in Cameroon, for example.

To explain the reasons for this state of things, we are forced to fall back upon assumptions, four of which may be equally valid: (1) West Indians are more assimilated than Africans and are not instinctively suspicious of all Western influence. Africans are much more concerned with adapting and making use of Marxism, not as a universal doctrine, but as a tool which can be improved for local needs. Senghor's position on Marxism would seem to typify this attitude. (2) Social conditions are much more stifling in the West Indies; there is the alienation of the elites, the poverty of the people, the absence of all economic or political outlets (see chapter 4 above). West Indians therefore demand more radical change than do the Africans, who wish to conserve certain social structures they appreciate. (3) A religious factor intervenes: Africans, unlike West Indians, maintain deep religious roots and are instinctively opposed to Marxist atheism. This is why Africans often only retain from socialism the economic and social method of organization.[26] (4) West Indians are an uprooted people without traditions that bind them to the earth. They have been obliged to accept assimilation, that is, to identify themselves with France, whereas Africans can remain loyal to the leaders of their country.

As to the other *ideologies* noted—rationalism, existentialism, personalism, Islamism and Buddhism—they are not as important as the first two (Christianity and Marxism-socialism) and are distributed among the twelve writers, with a slight majority in favor of the rationalism that stamped their university education.[27]

26. Among certain African intellectuals, this religious faith occasionally seemed to us rather artificial. The intellectuals seemed to emphasize this aspect of the African spirit as a contrast to Western atheism today. It was a new way to underline their difference.

27. With regard to Islam, we would point out that the writers' apparently Christian background does not reflect the social realities of certain West African countries, which occasionally are 70 percent Islamic, as in Guinea for example. In 1950, there were 6 million Moslems out of a population of 14 million in French West Africa; in the Sudan

The traditional ideologies, namely, ancestral beliefs and ideas, seem to have greater importance. Under the heading "intellectual tradition-alism" we list writers who have deliberated upon native beliefs and either entirely or in part "intellectualized" them, to such an extent that these beliefs subtly color their present ideas. Under the heading "con-crete traditionalism" we list those authors who have really lived in a native milieu and have been impregnated with native cultures, whether they have been rationalized or not.

This final group is important owing to the fact that seventeen of the writers have lived in an African world. Of the five others, David Diop and René Maran were educated in France; Paul Niger and Léon Damas grew up in the Caribbean but had a very bourgeois education, cut off from the native milieu. And Tchicaya U Tam'si, the last, came to France for secondary school and thus spent most of his youth far from his family.

Fifteen intellectuals studied their traditional values seriously, and the resultant thoughts and findings considerably modified their origi-nal ideas. One will recall the contribution of the ethnologists, taken up in chapter 8, which helped many writers to become aware of the value of Negro cultures. We are thinking particularly of Senghor, Sainville, Niger, Damas, and Alioune Diop.

In this group there are nine African and two Madagascan authors as compared to only four West Indians. This is because traditions have remained stronger and more consistent in Africa, whereas in the West Indies they are slowly disintegrating and gradually becoming part of the folklore.

The writers' study of traditional values has concentrated on three prime domains: mystical, moral, and social. Reflection on African mys-tical systems helped Alioune Diop, Senghor, Bhêly-Quénum, and Da-dié more fully to understand their Christianity. With others, it strengthened their religious feeling by giving it new color. Damas developed a belief in metempsychosis. The Madagascan writers accen-tuated their ancestor worship, and Ousmane Sembene turned to fe-tishism. Niger, Sainville, Paulin Joachim, David Diop, and Mongo Beti have given more of their attention to social and moral problems, stressing the spirit of community and solidarity and the African con-ception of sexuality: polygamy or priority of the child's rights. For Paul Niger and David Diop, we should point out, this was a purely intellec-tual, reasoned choice, since neither of them ever lived in a native society.

Of all of them we asked the following question: "Do you think that

---

3½ million Moslems out of   6½ million (according to Albert N'Goma in "L'Islam noir" in the special issue of *Présence Africaine* devoted to *Le Monde Noir*, Paris, 1950).

the African Negro culture of the future should take traditions into account?" The answers varied from "It is indispensable" to "It is desirable," with only two exceptions. Agblemagnon reacted against the general tendency to "close Africa in upon itself." "We must," he said, "have the courage to break free from certain aspects of African life which have become incompatible with the exigencies of modern life . . . no matter how attractive the past may seem." Frantz Fanon sticks closely to the Marxist scheme: When the economy changes—as will be the case in Africa—social relations will be modified, and it would be vain to want to maintain the ancient "superstructures." "Any man who wishes to explicate traditional culture," he said, "discovers that the people have already gone beyond it."

Apart from these two exceptions, the answers were generally positive. They confirmed one of the principal themes of the two congresses of black writers and artists: the originality of African Negro cultures.

In what way do the writers find the contribution of African cultures interesting?

The answers refer mainly to the artistic (fifteen positive answers) and literary (thirteen positive answers) domains: The black man has another history, other myths, different qualities of sensibility from the Westerner, and also other means of expression, which urgently need to be freed from European constraints.

Eleven writers point out the advantages of traditional social structures, emphasizing their solidarity and the community spirit. Political and economic organization, as well as religious beliefs, are now rarely defended although their quintessence is retained: democracy and mysticism.

Generally speaking, intellectuals are convinced that it is necessary to adapt, to "Africanize," the West's political and economic systems, and particularly its ideologies. The prevailing idea in both congresses was to "de-Westernize Negro cultures." We should point out, however, the ever-increasing difficulty young Negroes have seeking their origins in a changing society which is rapidly becoming Westernized.

A writer can set himself a number of *aims* of unequal importance. The two most frequently indicated by black authors are the ones we shall now consider: Are they concerned about creating something artistic? How do they conceive their intellectual responsibilities?

Every writer is anxious to write well, to present living and psychologically coherent characters, to construct his novel. But not all necessarily wish to *create*, to enrich literature with some original, personal work. As Mongo Beti admits, many young black writers were thrust into literature by circumstance. They were stimulated by political conditions as well as by the pressure of the group which had formed around *Présence Africaine.* Also, awareness of their responsibilities as intellectuals urged them to take public positions.

But if this is true for young black writers, it is less so for older writers. Among the latter, ten pure[28] writers out of twelve had always intended to write, even before beginning to do so and before committing themselves in any way or taking position on Negro problems. Césaire, Senghor, Rabemananjara, Dadié, Maran, and Ranaïvo all began to write when still in high school. Among the young writers interviewed, on the other hand, only Tchicaya U Tam'si and, more especially, Glissant feel that style and form are of major importance in their work. Others, such as David Diop, Ousmane Sembene, and Mongo Beti, had a tendency in the beginning to use their pens only to put their ideas across, in a barely acceptable style. The essential was the message; they wished to avoid, as David Diop put it, "making byproducts of the literature of France."

But vocations were awakened along the way. Mongo Beti is no longer indifferent to how he writes, and his style has grown stronger, more concise. With Bernard Dadié on the other hand, polemical poems of little consequence have taken the place of his skillful narration of folk tales.

As a general rule, the Caribbean and Madagascan writers show greater concern for literary style and form. Novels by Joseph Zobel and other authors we were not able to interview—J. S. Alexis, René Tardon, and the late Jacques Roumain—as well as the poetry of Césaire, Niger, Glissant, are more carefully written, more finished. Is this because the French language is better assimilated in the West Indies? The brilliance of exceptional Africans, such as Senghor, Birago Diop, Camara Laye, Paul Hazoumé, Tchicaya U Tam'si, and Olympe Bhêly-Quénum prevent us from leaping to conclusions, especially as the style of certain Caribbean writers such as Sainville, Mayotte Capécia, and René Depestre occasionally leaves something to be desired. The least one can say, however, is that West Indian writers always use the French language correctly. Because of a greater desire to be appreciated in France? Or because of a better educated and more demanding public in the West Indies than in Africa? At these levels a deeper grounding in the French language surely plays a part.

If negritude has awakened or stimulated some youthful literary vocations, it has sometimes misdirected others who, believing themselves limited to a literature of combat, exhaust themselves trying to write an epic poetry for which they were not made. Flavien Ranaïvo, who does not wish to be "committed," is a better advocate of native cultures than David Diop or Bernard Dadié, because he expresses his own thoughts and does not model his poems according to any set of noble, but

28. See note 13 above.

nonetheless external, requirements. The danger of any committed literature is to forget that "the tree has access to the world not from the outside, but from within itself, through its roots."[29] If the writer is too concerned about the effectiveness of the thesis he is expounding, he is in danger of no longer hearing the needs of his own feelings: He repeats slogans instead of creating. The failure of socialist realist poetry is an example of this oft-repeated error. It is possible to write good poetry of this type only when it corresponds to an intimate and personal way of seeing the world, as was the case with Jacques Roumain. This factor is always evident in the work. One need only compare *Gouverneurs de la rosée* by Roumain and *Dominique, esclave nègre* by Léonard Sainville to grasp immediately the difference between the two realist styles: The second is merely *trying* to be simple and accessible.

Another danger, almost as important, awaits the young generation: imitation. "He need only dip his pen into the ink," someone once said. For some authors this is hardly an exaggeration. Themes that have not been thoroughly thought out, that have been taken from others, with a few trimmings added, lose their life and power.[30] This is why one must strongly encourage young writers like Tchicaya U Tam'si, Jean Malonga, Abdou Anta Ka, and in certain of his poems Elolongué Epanya Yondo, who seek to depart from the beaten path and search deeply within themselves to find new themes. The novelist Olympe Bhêly-Quénum is another writer, too, who has chosen the fertile path of his ancestral resources.

A firm belief in their *responsibilities as intellectuals* is the general attitude among these black writers. Nineteen out of twenty-two feel answerable for their writings, and many were prompted to write in the first place only by this feeling. As intellectuals they feel they cannot take refuge in their privileged situation, separated from the masses, as long as their people have not obtained what they require. The only ones who stand resolutely apart from this attitude are René Maran and Gilbert Gratiant, who, along with Hampate Ba, were in 1960 the only ones over the age of fifty-five. The Madagascan, Ranaïvo, shares this view, but, as we have seen, he is not a member of the Negro race and it is therefore hardly to be expected that negritude should concern him greatly. On the other hand, it is on this point that Rabemananjara differs from his fellow countryman.

Generally this responsibility is seen in three ways.

The writer may feel obliged to *educate his people*, or else represent them, *be their spokesman*. The two roles are often thought of together.

29. René Menil, "Naissance de notre art" in *Tropiques*, no. 1 (April 1944).

30. We are particularly referring to the work of Paulin Joachim, Sylvère Alcandre, and the recent Bernard Dadié.

The artist must be an inventor of souls (Césaire).

Literature is the expression of a reality in the making. It arises out of reality, captures it, seizes that which is still in bud and helps it to mature (David Diop).

Literature must lead to thought, must be the opportunity for becoming aware of oneself, for challenging established ideas (P. Niger).

The works of other writers—J. S. Alexis, J. Price-Mars, B. Juminer, Jacques Roumain, René Depestre, F. Oyono, O. Socé, A. Sadji, and Olympe Bhêly-Quénum—all show the same feeling of responsibility, the same concern to express and educate a community. Tchicaya, Camara Laye, Birago Diop, and Jean Malonga seem more independent in this regard.

On the whole, black writers agree with the following statement made by one of them:

> Those of us who were sent to the West in order to equip ourselves have a very heavy debt to our compatriots. They expect us to bear witness for our people, to help them find their place in a quickly evolving world and, eventually, to choose a direction.[31]

The third role black writers believe they can—and must—play, is to help *free their people*. Perhaps under the double influence of African political evolution and the resolutions of the Second Congress, which insisted strongly on national independence as a condition of cultural renaissance, considerable progress has been made. Twelve writers originally thought they should take on this role; there are now seventeen. The same development, however, appears to have taken place in the three other domains, and an increased number of intellectuals, fourteen as compared to two originally, consider that these responsibilities should extend to all of them.

The "liberation of the people" through literature is rather close on certain points to education. It is not only a question of demanding political freedom and to making known to the West the aspirations of black peoples, although this is what novelists like Mongo Beti, Ousmane Sembene, Léonard Sainville, and Edouard Glissant, and poets such as Aimé Césaire, Paul Niger, Jacques Rabemananjara, David Diop, and Elolongué Epanya Yondo are trying to do. The idea is also to free the masses mentally, to make them understand what freedom is, and can be. A decolonization received without the people's understanding its significance is a bad decolonization. It is this meaning the poets wish to make clear to their people. It is true that they write in French and thus address themselves above all to a European public,

31. Joseph Ki Zerbo, "Histoire et conscience nègre," *Présence Africaine*, no. 16 (October–November 1957).

but they know that black elites read their work and transmit its contents and ideas.[32]

Our duty as men of culture, our double duty is this: to hasten decolonization now, and at this very moment to prepare a good decolonization, a decolonization without any aftereffects. . . .

It is perfectly true to say that it is generally among common people that national feeling survives in the most direct and obvious manner, in the face of strongest colonial oppression. But it is also true to say that this direct feeling must be made authentic, must be purified and propagated.[33]

There may also be a reaction against the advanced majority by these intellectuals, and against certain university students who, in Africa as in the West Indies, have assimilated the individualism of Europe. "What strikes me in most cases", said Senghor in 1953, "is their self-importance, their lack of seriousness, as if their heads were full of nothing but flightiness. Their mouths open only to make demands or to proclaim the 'rights of the elites'. . . . The elites ought to take pride in 'serving' and often be content with the 'eminent dignity of the poor.' "[34]

To synthesize the role of the elites and, therefore, of writers, as Senghor wishes, Paulin Joachim has a clear-cut formula: "The intellectual elite must devote itself to educating the masses, so that they may become capable of judging what their leaders do."

32. The events of the early 1960s in the former Belgian Congo—which has not yet produced any valid modern literature—shows the importance of the mediation of writers and their role as educators and liberators.

33. Aimé Césaire, "L'homme de culture et ses responsabilités," *Présence Africaine*, issue devoted to the Second Congress, p. 117.

34. L. S. Senghor, "Les élites de l'Union Française au service de leurs peuples," lecture delivered at Conseil de la Jeunesse de l'Union Française, Yaoundé, Cameroon, 25 August 1953.

22/ A New Generation and the Negritude Label

Since Sartre's "Orphée noir" Negro intellectuals have reacted quickly to the word "negritude," to the term, it would seem, rather than to its meaning.[1] It will be recalled that, with reason, Sartre linked negritude and neoracism, but in no way did he suggest they were one and the same. If it contained a racial nuance, something Sartre moreover felt necessary, negritude included many other positive elements, among them what he called "love," "going beyond itself," etc. Yet it is to this "accusation" of racism that blacks react so passionately. The better to deny a part, they reject the whole!

In discussing Sartre's essay, in which, they believe,[2] negritude first took shape as a theory, black students violently oppose the notion of an "antiracist racism, which seems to be the cornerstone of this theory." One might think at first that Sartre called this an antiracist racism only because he personally objected to it. Nothing of the kind. Sartre wished to help create this antiracist racism. He believed it to be an effective, the *only* effective, tool![3] Since he was addressing writers, his opinion was the same as saying:

> Blacks, sing loudly of your color, seeing fundamentally in it a sign of human value. Blacks, develop a black racism, necessarily revolutionary, because it will bring about the failure of white racism by replacing the formula, white-equals-superiority, with black-equals-superiority.[4]

This was obviously the path which was going to be chosen by numerous young poets, often without future, and in several issues of *Présence*

1. See our analysis of negritude in chap. 9.
2. *Les étudiants noirs parlent* (Paris: Présence Africaine, 1953).
3. Ibid., p. 295.
4. Ibid., p. 209.

Africaine there were worthless poems inevitably exalting "negritude."

Sartre's "Black Orpheus" seems to have been the quite unintentional cause of this passionate reaction, since the inventors of negritude (Césaire, Senghor, and Damas), as well as those who had used the term before Sartre's essay, in no way altered their position and continued to use the word with the meaning they had always given it.

Questioned today,[5] on the other hand, many young writers declare their opposition to the use of the word. For Tchicaya U Tam'si, for example, negritude implies racism and must therefore be rejected, because the only thing that counts today is national originality. Mongo Beti told us: "It is better to treat the problem in sociological than in racial terms. In any case, the situation is changing, and with the disappearance of colonial tutelage, in all probability there will be attempts by blacks to oppress blacks. It is in terms of social oppression that the situation must be seen." Agblemagnon was struck by the restrictive aspects of negritude. "This concept was necessary," he said, "but it is confining. Nor should writers be fake hunters running in someone else's smoke." Negritude can, in fact, embody key themes to be repeated by weak writers who do not dare follow a personal path but lean on political slogans to "give themselves a certain standing." As for Ousmane Sembene, he believes negritude often encourages writers to make negative and, above all, excessively passive complaints, instead of committing them to activities that are truly revolutionary.

Rabemananjara was moved by another definition of negritude in "Black Orpheus" and reacted against "some obscure essence called negritude . . . which, since a certain resounding preface, has become a source of ambiguity."[6] Sartre did in fact use the expression "essence noire" and seemed to mean by it that a black man, by his very nature, is basically different from all others. Because of his skin! To make this assertion reveals that one is unconsciously racist, Rabemananjara observes. "Negritude is explained to him [the black man] as a totality, as the very essence of his nature, and ample advantage has been taken of this confusion to convince the black man of his fundamental difference from all other human species." What the black poet really wished to do was quite the contrary, to rid his color of its imaginary stains and proclaim the "unique truth of his people":

> Beyond the color of my skin, my blood is as red as your blood,
> my flesh as red as your flesh
> and my soul is of the same essence as yours.[7]

---

5. Except where otherwise stated, the quotations are from our interviews with these writers.

6. Jacques Rabemananjara, "Le poète noir et son peuple," *Présence Africaine*, no. 16 (October–November 1957), p. 12.

7. Ibid., p. 21.

Following this, Rabemananjara rises against the claim that there is creative virtue in negritude: "It is obvious that conditions responsible for the new black poetics were in no way furnished by the influence of that notorious category, negritude.[8] In 1959, in more moderate terms, Rabemananjara protested against all notions of black "essence." Two factors, in his view, had favored the meeting and unity of blacks of all origins: First, the general contempt toward their color had engendered in all of them the same demand for dignity; second, conditions of colonial exploitation which affected all Negro peoples created a community of feeling, of suffering, and of opposition to white colonizers. "But would the Madagascan and the Dahomean," Rabemananjara writes, "have sought each other out if they had not suffered European domination? The day this state of colonization disappears, negritude will disappear all by itself."

This is an obvious restriction of Sartre, for whom negritude covered "the black man's being-in-the-world," beyond his situation of "being black in the *colonized* world." In addition, it confirms what we said at the beginning of chapter 21. Rabemananjara is not an African[9] but a Madagascan. Although black, he belongs to a different civilization, closer to the peoples of the Orient than of Africa, and he does not feel a close bond uniting him with other blacks above and beyond the present European domination.[10] He does not realize that other black peoples may feel united by the community of an ancient civilization which has left deep impressions on the entire continent and which might—after the disappearance of all white domination—enable the peoples of Africa to reinforce the ties of their common negritude. Rabemananjara is therefore right in insisting that negritude is not an *essence* separating the black man from other men, or a question of color, but a similarity of condition. He forgets, however, to include in this condition the weight of a whole common past. Instead of concluding that negritude is only transitory and bound to disappear, one ought then to conclude it will persist.[11]

To summarize, the concept of negritude has obviously changed since Sartre's study, because of the very passionate reactions it pro-

8. Ibid., p. 12.

9. He is of the Betsimisaraka race, which came from Oceania and is probably a blend of Melanesian and Polynesian (L. S. Senghor, *Anthologie*, p. 194).

10. This is confirmed by Flavien Ranaïvo, who is also a Madagascan but of Indonesian origin, and who compares negritude to racism.

11. Of course, we realize that negritude in the future will be quite different from present-day negritude. Born of three factors—racial prejudice, white domination, and a common civilization—it will see the disappearance of the first two factors, and therefore persist in a modified form, but will always endure as the mark of the black man's "being-in-the-world." See chap. 9 above.

voked. It therefore seems necessary to us to restate Césaire's present idea of it.

Starting from the "awareness of being black," which implies "the taking over of one's destiny, history, and culture," negritude becomes "the simple recognition of a fact" and "includes no racism or rejection of Europe, and no exclusivity, but on the contrary a fraternity of all men." "A greater unity between the men of the black race" does exist, however, "not because of skin, but because of a community of culture, history, and temperament." Hence "there is no need to go beyond negritude, which is a *sine qua non* condition of creative authenticity in any domain" (interview with Aimé Césaire, June 1959).

Understood thus, the concept of negritude is close to that of "cultural originality," which has today replaced it for the majority of black writers we interviewed. They were almost unanimous in preferring this new expression, which has the advantage of containing no racial nuance while emphasizing local origin. In the same way, one can speak of "the African personality" or of "de-Westernizing cultures." The resolutions of the Second Congress of Black Writers and Artists strongly insisted not only on the responsibilities of black writers toward their peoples, but also on the bonds of a common civilization:

... these considerations do not rest on ethnic or racial assumptions. They are the result of a common origin and suffering. Black peoples have borne together a series of historical misadventures which, under the special form of total colonization, involving slavery, deportation, and racism, have been imposed upon these peoples, and upon them only, in this objectively known period of history. The existence of an African Negro civilization, beyond national or regional particularities, thus appears historically justified, and reference to this civilization legitimate and enriching. This must form the basis of unity and solidarity among the various Negro peoples.[12]

We observe that to avoid being accused of racism, black writers insist on stating that their solidarity is not based on race. But, who, in fact, has shared this "community of origin and suffering" if not black peoples, and they alone? If the term negritude is therefore abandoned, everything it contained—except the racial affirmation—is maintained.

Understood in this manner, negritude would in no way impede the creation of a universal humanism shared by all Africans.

In conclusion we would like to quote two young African writers who have already gone beyond the aggressive phase of negritude to retain only its generous, positive aspect. Paulin Joachim describes it with enthusiasm: "Where are my values, I who am a racial lie? Negritude helps me to rediscover my sources, my origins, one by one, not to

12. Resolutions of the Second Congress, published in the *Présence Africaine* issue devoted to this congress, pp. 389–90.

mourn for them, but to draw upon their magnificent vitality which the world needs. Negritude is a slow-burning light from which all violence is excluded; it is a solar Pentecost, that sinks into my past in order to reawaken burnt-out suns. It is a horse I bestride, it is also the aim, the day after colonialism, when the Negro will truly be himself. It is both the path and the goal." Less lyrically, here is how Olympe Bhêly-Quénum defines negritude: "The exhuming of Negro cultural values, which have been stifled, their explication and affirmation. I hope to see negritude rid of its political context. The role of black writers is to show that negritude progresses, that it eliminates racism."

Let us now examine the principal themes the black writers address.

A majority—eighteen—speak of *colonization,* in a different way, of course, depending upon whether they are poets, novelists, or essayists. Poetry lends itself better to lyrical cries of pain and revolt (Césaire, Damas, Rabemananjara, Senghor, Niger, David Diop, and Bernard Dadié). The novel is better adapted to concrete situations, and one learns a great deal through novels about the condition of colonized natives and their psychology; colonization and the white man are exposed to a light of day never found in colonial magazines, too rarely in official reports or the exotic novels of outsiders. Finally, essayists like A. Tevoedjre, Alioune Diop, or Frantz Fanon bring weighty, scientific arguments to bear. With figures and documentation they demonstrate the great destitution and material want of the black masses, their acute frustration, the disastrous psychological effects of colonization, the complexes and alienations which result from it.

Let us briefly call attention to the aspects of *Western domination* most frequently revealed in the works of black writers. Together they form quite an indictment!

The Caribbean writers (Damas, Césaire, Sainville, Glissant, and Niger)[13] often come back to *slavery,* still an incredibly tenacious wound. But the Africans too had cause to complain of a *loss of liberty.* Through feelings of solidarity they too are interested in the ancient slavery, but rather from its historical angle; they study the archives in order to describe the slave trade, and attempt to account for Africa's decadence. For these African writers, however, slavery is never a source of literary inspiration.

Most of the writers describe with considerable force the multiple aspects of *poverty and destitution:* ever-present hunger, hard and poorly paid work, sickness and death, illiteracy, poverty of the land,[14] where peasants labor for beggarly wages, or the poverty of the cities with

13. This is also true of Haitian writers: Roumain, Depestre, Brierre, R. Bélance, and R. Tardon.

14. This is especially true of Césaire, Zobel, Glissant, J. S. Alexis, and Jacques Roumain (i.e., mainly of the West Indies).

their sad retinue of slums, unemployment, and prostitution, not forgetting the evil psychological effects of detribalization, poor adaptation to machinery, and closer contact with white masters.[15]

Colonization is rejected outright! Direct reference to its positive contributions is rare—to medical care, hygiene, education, modern techniques—although several writers such as Niger, Senghor, or Alioune Diop soften their criticism by admitting that "along with its errors and backsliding, the French presence did, historically, on the whole consitute progress."[16]

Yet even these writers share the unanimous opinion that this necessary contact with Western countries could have occurred without exploitation. They mention the example of Japan, which developed, because of economic contact with Europe and America, without brutal colonization. If the blacks readily recognize our technical superiority, they contest the use we have made of it and are opposed to European capitalism and materialism, sharing in this the reaction of many other underdeveloped lands. "It often happens that the population of an underdeveloped country has the feeling of having been . . . mistreated by the world in general or by one rich country in particular."[17]

For a European who wishes to understand the works of black writers, we would advise first of all reading a few UNESCO statistics, a book such as *Les Antilles décolonisées* by Daniel Guérin, or the voluminous report by the Bureau International du Travail, *Les problèmes du travail en Afrique noire* ("Work problems in Black Africa").[18] After this he will be less inclined to feel wounded by black accusations or to suspect their systematic indictments of exaggeration. We should like, however, to make another observation. There is no doubt that black writers show only the seamy underside of our colonial action. Doubtless this is because for too long we have been willing to show only its rosiest aspect! Some, on the other hand, like Joseph Zobel, describe colonial societies without any polemic intention and without apparent bitterness; what they show is no greater consolation to the Western conscience.

The second group of themes deals with *traditional life.* Customs, festivals, daily life, work, people, wisdom—all the aspects of native cultures, in short, are endless sources of inspiration for black authors. We have seen that most of them have lived in their native lands. Others

15. This is true of Mongo Beti, Niger, Ousmane Sembene, Tchicaya U Tam'si, Césaire, Abdoulaye Sadji, and B. Juminer.

16. L. S. Senghor, "Congrès constitutif du P.R.A." (mimeographed), p. 47.

17. Gunnar Myrdal, *Théorie économique et pays sous-développés* (Paris: Présence Africaine, 1959), p. 91.

18. Daniel Guérin, *Les Antilles décolonisées* (Paris: Présence Africaine, 1956); Bureau International du Travail, *Les problèmes du travail en Afrique noire* (Geneva, 1958).

are interested in African life, but as a European would be. This was the case of René Maran, who had a feeling of community with other blacks, having himself suffered from color prejudice. He studied their customs with considerable objectivity, though without participating in their culture. Some of the younger writers, like David Diop and Elolongué Epanya Yondo, already influenced by the "negritude movement," feel frustrated, and their works seem pained, rebellious, directed toward the future. How different the equilibrium of Senghor or Birago Diop, or of good novelists like Aké Loba and Olympe Bhêly-Quénum, who had the advantage of participating in Negro cultures, even if they had been diminished or distorted. Césaire, though he has never been to Dahomey, might thus feel comfortable in the culture of that country.[19]

Much of the flavor of the novels on rural Caribbean life, too, comes from the fact that their authors remained close to the ordinary people, their mores, beliefs, and mentalities. In the West Indies, the clearing and harvesting of the land is always a community project carried out to the sound of tom-toms. Voodoo rites, predictions, superstitions, belief in metamorphoses and in "quimboi" love potions are still an intimate part of the popular sensibility.

The novels show the obstinacy of these small, hard-working communities, their spirit of mutual aid, also their sense of humor which helps to balance lives so difficult they would be unbearable if faced on the tragic level. They tell of simple, uncomplicated loves, of men and women for whom sexuality has cosmic extensions.[20] How far the delicacy of the two scenes that follow is from the stifling eroticism of French novels today:

Ce qui court entre eux, c'est plus que la grace aiguë du désir, plus que l'ineffable et le grondement, bien plus encore que l'assurance des deux arbres qui auraient joint leurs racines sous la surface . . . oho! c'est le charroi de toute la sève, c'est le cri même de la racine, ho! c'est la geste venue du fond des ages, qu'ont parfait les ancêtres et que voici renaître.

[What flows between them is more than the sweet intensity of desire, greater than what is unutterable or looming, greater even than the certainty of two trees whose roots have intertwined beneath the surface . . . oh! It is the rising of all the sap, the very cry of their roots, the age-old motion perfected by their ancestors and born with them anew.]

Ils coulèrent dans le temps qui jusqu'à eux menait sa rivière sans crue, ils furent sur l'ocean, ils furent dans la révolte, ils connurent le goût des fruits

19. See the discussions of the First Congress of Black Writers and Artists published in *Présence Africaine*, p. 73.

20. "Fecundity and mysticism. To my mind, this is most specifically negritic" (P. Niger in *Les puissants* [Paris: Editions du Scorpion, 1958], p. 215).

de la forêt marronne, ils revinrent ensemble dans le présent presque éclairci. [21]

[They streamed through time which had brought its floodless river to them, they rode the ocean, were part of the fugitives' forests, they returned together to a present almost bright.]

Despite their incontestable kinship, African novels are nonetheless very different from those of the West Indies. We must not forget that there is a far greater distance in miles between the countries of Mongo Beti, Edouard Glissant, and Hampate Ba than between Norway, Spain, and Russia, and as great a distance emotionally. Africa is an immense continent, and if some power lines traverse it, they leave vast space for many varieties and degrees of refinement. The happy moderation of L'enfant noir[22] is a hundred leagues from the ostentation of the Dakar society described in Maïmouna,[23] which in turn derives from a very different culture than that of Le roi miraculé.[24]

If the themes of suffering and revolt are similar to the point of sounding "monochordal," as Agblemagnon[25] put it, the novels evoking traditional life and wisdom fortunately escape this defect and are fascinating in their variety. It is through the deeper investigation of their native lands that the writers differ and find a personal accent. We mentioned earlier that black writers excel at the type of tale that depicts the simple and precious aspects of traditional life, meeting up to now only with success. The wisdom, the humor of everyday, a sense of the marvelous, of myth and legend, all is recouped here, retained in its original form, and should prove of considerable interest to the curiosity of sociologists, moralists, psychologists, and artists alike. Authors such as Birago Diop, Léon Damas, and Jean Malonga deserve congratulation. In a manner sometimes too discreet to be fully appreciated, they bear witness to the ancient patrimony and nourish its most authentic art.

We would point out that the authors who attack colonization most violently are not the ones most interested in traditional life. The most careful and vivid descriptions of this life are by completely nonpolemical authors. They try to dig out, understand, and express all that is original in their societies, whose spirit and language no white writer could express as well.

21. Edouard Glissant, La lézarde (Paris: Seuil, 1958), pp. 148 and 207. Translated as The Ripening (New York: Braziller, 1959).

22. By Camara Laye (Paris: Plon, 1954). Translated The African Child (London: Collier Macmillan, 1959), and The Dark Child (New York: Farrar, Straus & Giroux, 1969).

23. By Abdoulaye Sadji (Paris: Présence Africaine, 1958).

24. By Mongo Beti (Paris: Corrêa, 1957). Translated King Lazarus (London: Muller, 1961; Heinemann Educational Books [African Writers Series], 1970).

25. Interview with Agblemagnon, June 1959.

The reason for this may be that these writers, whom we may call "traditionalist," are more deeply rooted in their ancestral cultures than their fellow writers, either because, like Hampate Ba, Paul Hazoumé, or Jean Malonga, their contact with Europe was very sparse and late, or because, like Birago Diop or Bhêly-Quénum, they had thought through their culture deeply and were able to take new root in it. These authors seem to have acquired a balance which enables them to extract greater richness from their heritage. The polemical writers, perhaps because they are more Westernized, seem frustrated and more deeply wounded. For them rebellion seems the natural outlet. They are both closer to the West and more bitterly opposed to its influence, which they consider evil. Such is the case of Césaire, Damas, David Diop, Fanon, Beti, Epanya, and others.

We only suggest this as a hypothesis, one which of course has no effect on the literary value of these writers.

One is struck however by the small role played by *personal themes* of love, death, nature, God, etc. Not that these do not frequently occur in the works of the two main schools of writers previously discussed, but we have never, for example, come across the classical love story involving two or three characters so popular in France since Madame de Lafayette. Nor are there subtle introspections like those of Proust or Sartre! Very little meditation on death or nature! In the African Negro novels or poems, the individual is part of the people and the society from which he originates. Even when he says "I" he means "we." He represents his people. He reinvests all personal emotion in a more general current. For Glissant and Rabemananjara, for example, feelings of love are always "reinvested" in the themes of freedom, love of country, or the bond with one's ancestors. Even in works that seek to defend no thesis, such as those by F.-D. Sissoko, J. Zobel, or J. Malonga, the action is never limited to the adventures of a few individuals; the principal subject is always the community, and the life of the group.[26]

Among traditional values they most appreciate, black intellectuals often single out solidarity, a sense of community. An interesting comparison could certainly be made here between ancient African culture and this aspect of literary works by black writers today.

The genres in which black writers prefer to express themselves are

26. An exception to this general rule must, however, be made for a whole series of autobiographical novels describing the tribulations of young blacks—usually students—who arrive in France. Whether well or less well analyzed, one discovers in them the efforts of naïve, uprooted blacks who attempt to penetrate and find acceptance in a white milieu, the prejudices encountered, the snubs, the disappointments, material difficulties, and loneliness. The hero fights, triumphs, or is defeated. The most successful novel of this type seems to us Aké Loba's *Kocoumbo, l'étudiant noir* (Paris: Flammarion, 1960).

poetry (thirteen poets out of seventeen writers) and novels (mentioned eleven times).

We have repeatedly indicated the marked superiority of black poetry over the novel, particularly up to the late 1940s. Since then, however, the novel has certainly caught up, and several writers—Niger, Zobel, and Bhêly-Quénum among them—declared they prefer this genre because it permits a more explicit presentation of ideas, greater nuance and emphasis.

Why did the explosion of poetry come first, and why was poetry preferred at that time? The Algerian poet, Henri Kréa,[27] speaking of *his* country's poetry, gives one possible answer. "What French poetry particularly lacks," he points out, "is a dramatic context," while Algeria is "at the smelting point." "In underdeveloped countries the imagination becomes overdeveloped, it becomes mythological." Discussing such a "dramatic context," that is, the presence of a world that one rejects and that one would wish were different, where direct action toward the transformation of reality is or seems impossible, Frantz Fanon sees poetry as "a temporary form of combativity," a verbal compensation. Poetry upsets and transforms the world intellectually, replacing it with the hope of a better world, lending the courage to endure this one.[28] The novel, a more concrete, explicit mode of action, comes only later when there is hope of real solutions.

All this is mere hypothesis, but nonetheless has elements of truth.

In any case, the black novel, which has now assumed an important place beside black poetry, is very much alive today. Much fiction, as we have said, is either autobiographical or includes a good many happenings and situations which were actually experienced by the authors or those close to him. In general, the novels are realistic, often polemical, more rarely poetic or fantastic like Glissant's *La lézarde,* or *Un piège sans fin* by Bhêly-Quénum.[29]

The folktale, on the other hand, has no controversial element at all. It makes no demands, is in no way intended to set blacks and whites in opposition to one another. Quite simply, it describes traditional life, folklore, mores, and customs, and it is in these folk narratives that one finds the most authentic impressions of Negro life. The short story would seem to be the genre par excellence of black writers, for this writer has so far not read a single one that was not successful, whether it be a West Indian story by Damas or J. S. Alexis, or an African one

27. Kréa's father was French, but he was brought up in Algeria by his Moslem mother. Author of *La révolution et la poésie sont une seule et même chose* (Paris: P. J. Oswald). The quotations are from an interview by the French daily *L'Express* of 21 July 1960.

28. As in the case of Negro spirituals, for example.

29. Paris: Stock, 1960.

by Birago Diop, Bernard Dadié, or Jean Malonga.[30]

Less personal than novels, short stories are nonetheless just as effective. They give us a better understanding of the Negro soul by showing us the wisdom and sense of humor so specific to black peoples, and describing their lives candidly and without lies.

As for the essays, these range from article and pamphlet to the more substantial kind of study. Nearly half the writers questioned (ten out of twenty-two) consider it an excellent means of making oneself clearly understood by all. For this reason the essay is favored even by poets such as Césaire (*Discours sur le colonialisme*), Senghor ("Ce que l'homme noir apporte," together with a number of his important articles on traditional cultures), or Glissant (*Soleil de la conscience*). Other essayists, like Fanon and Cheik Anta Diop, show real literary gifts.

The historical works of black writers can scarcely be considered "essays" because they have achieved too great a scope and importance. There is only one professional historian, Léonard Sainville, author of a work on Victor Schoelcher, but several others are successfully following in his wake. Aimé Césaire recently published the biography of a man he greatly admires, Toussaint Louverture. Cheik Anta Diop has written two important books: *Nations nègres et culture*[31] and *L'Afrique noire pré-coloniale*.[32] Hampate Ba has done a history of the Dogon people, and Paul Hazoumé has written about the institutions of Dahomey.

All black intellectuals are fully aware to what extent the foundations of history can help their cultural movement, and that is the reason for their passionate interest in ethnology.[33]

More than half the writers interviewed are engaged in some political or union activity parallel to their literary efforts. Six, elected by their people, have even occupied official positions. It is significant that certain of them were only elected after some cultural achievement. This was the case for Senghor, Césaire, and Damas, who were drawn into political engagement through the ideas they stood for in their writings. Not all of these writers embraced political life by personal inclination, but they were the first people to become aware of the human and political needs of their countries and to show themselves capable of asserting these needs before the West. To the extent that they pre-

30. Jean Malonga's tales, by their breadth of style and generality of appeal, are practically novels.

31. Paris: Présence Africaine, 1954.

32. Paris: Présence Africaine, 1960. Although there has been considerable discussion regarding their scientific value and the exaggeration of the opinions expressed, the works of Cheik Anta Diop created such a stir that they were considered, at that period, as inciting negritude.

33. See chap. 8 above.

sume to represent more than themselves, the fact that these writers engage in real action should not surprise us. It merely makes their artistic vocation more authentic. In his article "Le leader politique considéré comme le représentant d'une culture,"[34] Sékou Touré has an excellent perception of the close bond between the defender of a national culture—which is what these black writers seek to be—and political action.

We asked the writers: "Do you consider yourself 'committed' writers?" We admit this is rather vaguely put, covering too much and signifying too little; the term, moreover, has been far too loosely used. It is difficult nowadays to know who is "committed," to what and how. Fortunately we had at our disposal a very clear statement, thought out and elaborated by the black writers themselves:

During the present, temporary situation of the black peoples, the responsibilities (of the black writer) rest essentially on three urgent points:

(a) The writer's contribution to the development of native languages, in all countries where such development is indispensable.

(b) The true expression of his people's reality, long dimmed, distorted, or denied during the course of colonization. This expression is so necessary under present conditions that it implies on the part of the black writer or artist an *individual definition of the idea of commitment. Black writers can only participate spontaneously and completely in the general movement we have outlined. The importance of his action is immediate. How can he refuse it?*

(c) Finally and above all, [he must] contribute to the development and progress of black peoples and, particularly in those countries where the issue arises, to the struggle for their independence, since the existence of a national state will naturally encourage the flowering of a positive and fertile culture.[35]

We have already studied these three requirements: The writer, we said, could consider himself a *spokesman* ("as truly expressing the reality of his people") an *educator* ("contributing to the development and progress of black peoples") and a *liberator* of his people ("in the struggle for independence").

In this sense the majority of black writers do feel "committed," because they are aware of their responsibilities and determined to answer for them in their works—and often also in their extraliterary political action. We should not find this awareness surprising among an intellectual elite who feel observed and relied upon by the masses. For black writers, commitment is therefore the core around which his entire life is organized. In the past few years, this attitude has developed sharply, as seen by discussions on the responsibilities of black intellectuals organized in 1956 by *Présence Africaine*—discussions which

34. Message of the Second Congress in Rome published in *Présence Africaine*, pp. 104ff.

35. "Resolutions concernant la littérature," in the special issue of *Présence Africaine* devoted to the Second Congress, p. 389, italics ours.

led to the resolutions mentioned above.[36]

Here, however, an initial difficulty arises. Once committed, black writers are anxious to be effective and reach the largest public possible. In their situation, however, this public is limited to the West and the tiny French-speaking black elite. They are thus cut off from the black masses, who not only do not know French but are also illiterate.

This sets a definite limit to their activity. The writers are aware of it and try to justify themselves.

First of all, they say, underdeveloped countries are about 80 percent illiterate. Even if we were to write in a native language, our readership would still remain very small. Using an international language like French, on the other hand, permits us to reach the elite of all French colonies and thus confront the problems of our people with those of neighboring countries. It also enables us to carry out our major role as witness to the West and, in a manner understandable to the colonizer, to express the misfortunes, fears, and needs of our peoples. Some writers said that they have faith in the African future of international languages such as English and French, not because they consider these languages better as such, but because they already enable the African elites to communicate with each other. These writers believe that within twenty years blacks will be reading their books. Meanwhile, the essential has been saved: Black people know that they are championed and that their writers are working toward their liberation.

We would point out, however, that the Congress of Black Writers advocated the teaching of vernacular languages and choosing one of them as a vehicular language for all of Africa.[37]

At the end of a discussion with Edouard Glissant, Césaire concluded that the ideal is to be entirely bilingual and to be able to write in both French and a native language. Yet some authors do not seem to appreciate native languages. This is especially true of the Caribbean writers—except the Haitians—who hold that Creole is a dialect and insufficient from a literary point of view.[38]

36. See also chap. 20, p. 289, above.

37. This language would be chosen not for its present demographical scope but for the richness of its possibilities, so that it might become the base of a new Negro culture. Among the limited group of possible languages, the Language Commission of the Congress suggested: *Swahili,* which already has an important literature and is spoken in Eastern and Central Africa as far as the Congo and parts of South Africa; *Haussa,* spoken in a huge Nigerian region; *Yoruba,* spoken in the Benin territory; *Bambara* and *Mandingo,* principal languages in the Sudan; *Peuhl,* spoken sporadically in Western and Central Africa; and finally *Wolof,* the Senegalese language, which has a considerable literature and already has a scientific vocabulary.

38. On the contrary, an author such as Gilbert Gratiant—who wishes to rehabilitate Creole—obviously has greater inspiration when he writes in that language, to such an extent that his French translation of his Creole poems are more vivid, more colorful,

Another problem: contact with the popular masses. Most of the writers desire this contact, but only ten care to modify their style in order to make their ideas more comprehensible. The contradiction is only apparent, since "contact with the masses" must be seen in two ways.

Certain writers wish to be understood by the masses and therefore put themselves at their level. Zobel claims that he "never uses a word which is not part of the common people's daily vocabulary." Sainville is anxious to educate the masses, and although he is a professional historian with that aim in mind, he writes realistic novels. As for Hampate Ba, a religious teacher, it is to be expected that he should insist equally strongly on his role as educator and seek above all to be understood.

Others feel that writers must find their *inspiration in the masses*. Perhaps the extreme example is Paul Niger, who stops writing as soon as he no longer feels in spiritual contact with the people. "A writer," he says, "can create individualistic work, but his inspiration comes from the masses and their problems. A hermetic literature signifies nothing," he adds, "because even ideas difficult to grasp must be transmissible; a writer must be understood. But it is not necessary that he be understood immediately." Nor does Césaire "bother to be clearer merely to be understood more quickly." He "does not want to sacrifice anything from the literary point of view merely to bring himself within the reach of a wider public." He feels that he remains in contact with his people by understanding and expressing their problems. Finally, according to Glissant, "Whatever a writer may write or think, he does in terms of his people's destiny." That is why today's black literature is a collective literature. "It expresses a common destiny, that is to say, a common way of moving toward this destiny." Glissant too would like to be understood, but without abandoning his literary standards. "An artist must create in the form most deeply suited to his temperament; it is this way that he will have the greatest influence." To prove his contention, Glissant points to Césaire, the least accessible of black poets and yet the most read.

All the same we sense in many of the writers a marked desire to remove literature from this kind of commitment. Several found their inspiration and motivation in present-day circumstance. They consider they have a moral obligation to contribute to the liberation of their people, and, moreover, this obligation coincides with their own wishes. But today, insofar as it lies in their power to assert themselves as "writers," they hope that political circumstances will be less compel-

---

and more poetic than his poems written directly in French. In the Creole poems Gratiant reveals his true personality. See the translations published by Senghor in his *Anthologie*.

ling, and that they may now be able to break away from the rut in which their literary efforts are in danger of foundering—even if they have to give up political or extraliterary social action. A tendency to separate these two domains is therefore gradually taking shape, in order to gain greater freedom for literary expression and creation.

But this is still a wish! Glissant's reply is typical. According to him, politics and literature cannot, at the present time, be either separated or fused. A literary work can doubtless have political "significance," but a writer must refrain from politicizing when writing. Glissant regrets then that today's Negro literature should so often be a fighting literature.[39] It is also this combative aspect which struck G. Balandier, to such an extent that he somewhat neglected less aggressive works even though they were often of better quality: "Novels on African morals and manners are no longer merely educational works, but truths released with a view to rehabilitation, aiming to destroy false notions about Negroes."[40] Yet Bhêly-Quénum feels that black writers have been withdrawing from political problems since 1953 and are now attempting to make Africa better known.

Our interviews have enabled us to establish a surprising correspondence between the feelings of responsibility black writers have, the aims they propose to achieve, their concern for contact with the masses, and the themes in their work.

The intellectual milieu of France where black students met and were able to elaborate their new ideology seems to have played an important role. Most black writers are university graduates, and this seems to have a close connection with the politico-cultural manner in which they conceive their commitment. To be convinced of this it is sufficient to open *Tam-Tam*, the Catholic student journal, in which one finds the same leitmotifs, the role of the black intellectual, his responsibilities, the dreams and yearnings of black peoples, and so forth.

The old and young generations of writers meet on many themes and demands: responsibility, a desire to upgrade Negro cultures, political independence, etc. In their aims, if not their methods, the two groups differ little. This homogeneity, surprising at first glance, can be explained in many ways. First of all the second generation was formed by the first generation, either directly in the colonies (through Césaire's influence in Martinique), or in France, where the older genera-

39. Glissant criticizes *Cahier* for being "too historically situated." To use his expression, this work is "a brilliant perception of its moment," and he compares it to the *Tragiques* by Agrippa d'Aubigne. Glissant's ambition is rather to play the role of a Ronsard, "who contributed to the elaboration of the sixteenth century."

40. G. Balandier, "Littérature noire de langue française," in *Le Monde Noir,* p. 396.

tion continues to dominate the New Negro cultural life. *Présence Africaine* plays a leading role. In chapters 19 and 20 we stressed the magazine's mission as an awakener, its role as spiritual director and its influence in stimulating the literary vocations it sought.

The goals aimed for by the first generation of black writers were only partially attained and are therefore still valid for the younger. Our survey was prepared and submitted in 1959, at a time when Guinea was still the only French colony to be independent. Since then, other African states have obtained their freedom, but this does not mean that they are not still suffering from the aftereffects of colonization. If black peoples have only changed masters and still have the same regime, then they are still being exploited. Freedom does not necessarily follow independence immediately. The case of Haiti, still vegetating one hundred years after its "liberation," is a typical example. Martinique, Guiana, and Guadeloupe, as well as Algeria,[41] are at this writing still considered French *départements*.

Finally, the themes launched by Senghor, Césaire, and Damas have become "classics" of today's negritude because they reached the very depths of the Negro soul. Their echo has never ceased to resound, and the original trio has become a chorus of many voices.

---

41. The thesis which is the object of this book was submitted in January 1961, thus before Algeria obtained its independence.

VI CONCLUSIONS

23 / A Contribution to the Larger Humanism

Et si je ne sais que parler, c'est pour vous que je parlerai.
Ma bouche sera la bouche des malheurs qui n'ont point de bouche, ma voix,
la liberté de celles qui s'affaissent au cachot du désespoir. . . .

Et surtout mon corps aussi bien que mon âme, gardez-vous de vous croiser
les bras en l'attitude stérile du spectateur, car la vie n'est pas un spectacle, car
une mer de douleur n'est pas un proscenium.[1]

[And if all I know how to do is speak, it is for you that I shall speak.
My lips shall speak for miseries that have no mouth, my voice shall be the
liberty of those who languish in the dungeon of despair. . . .

And above all my body as well as my soul, beware of folding your arms in the
sterile attitude of spectator, for life is not a spectacle, for a sea of pain is not
a proscenium.]

Césaire wrote these words in 1939. Things have not changed: "The
young generation of black writers," G. Balandier has said, ". . . feel
they have not only personal vocations but also a mission."[2] Sartre had
already called them "evangelical,"[3] and the Haitian J. S. Alexis summarizes admirably:

In the present predicament . . . the mission of our creators is to sing the beauty,
tragedies, and struggles of our exploited peoples, reexamining the canons
developed by Western cultures in relation to the cultural riches of our land.[4]

This formula seems to sum up perfectly the three fundamental aims
of today's black literature: to express the drama and struggles of the

1. Aimé Césaire, *Cahier d'un retour au pays natal*, p. 43.
2. Georges Balandier, "Littérature noire de langue française," in *Le Monde Noir*.
3. J. P. Sartre, "Orphée noir," p. xv.
4. J. S. Alexis, "Ou va le roman?" in *Présence Africaine*, April–May 1957.

black peoples—but by "singing" them, with a concern for the artistic element, which, measuring its distance from "Western canons," would rely on "the cultural riches" of Negro soil!

It is in this sense that the basic element of this literature so far has been commitment. We know the word has lost value. Too often it has been an alibi for bad authors, both in France and elsewhere. Yet here it is compelling; further, it regains its full dignity. Commitment, where black writers are concerned, was the first prerequisite for the birth and flowering of this completely autonomous literary school.

How else could we characterize the attitude of Léro and his *Légitime Défense* friends when they criticized West Indian writers for ignoring black people's life and its real problems? What did they mean by an "authentic" literature, if not a literature through which black men would express their own temperament and needs, and in so doing, reveal the whole special universe of their race?

We say "in so doing", because in 1932 the black man, more than any other, was an "under-man" (*sous-homme*) by "condition," and had been for centuries, because he was black. A few students became aware of this condition, rejected it, undertook to denounce it and boldly to grasp their destiny by the horns. By this very act, they created an original literature.

Should we still be in doubt, let us ask why these writers, unlike their predecessors, arouse our interest and hold our attention. Because they proclaim new ideas with strength and passion! We feel they are inspired by a message greater than themselves, and it is the message itself that attracts us primarily. It compels us to ask anew a number of very old questions which French literature has, little by little, forgotten: What does the act of writing mean? Whose mouthpiece is the writer? For whom is he the intermediary?

In these black writers we rediscover the collective dimension of literature and the functional spirit of primitive art in which the beautiful and the useful are still combined, where ethics are not separate from aesthetics.

May the black poet be restored to his original function of bard, let it be his natural duty and right to make the powerful hear the just demands of the humble. This is an ancient lesson that the blacks of Senegal and the West Indies have undertaken to recall to our forgetful Europe.[5]

Art for art's sake does not therefore have a monopoly on perfection, and the poet who only sings for himself is no greater than the writer who seeks to represent a group. The New Negro literary movement

5. Aimé Patri, "Deux poètes noirs en langue française," in *Présence Africaine*, no. 3.

proves, on the contrary, that, carried to a high degree of depth and intensity, commitment is a lever powerful enough to rise above geographic and linguistic obstacles.

The truth is that the imperatives of our drama force us to speak Madagascan, Arabic, Wolof, and Bantu in the language of our masters. Because our language is the same, even if we do not use the same language,we manage to understand each other perfectly from Tanatave to Kingston, from Pointe-à-Pitre to Zomba.[6]

Yet at the same time, this new language is expressed in such stirring and special terms that it is singularly strengthened and arouses our interest to a far greater extent.

Because the problems of their peoples were also truly their own, by assuming them in order better to reveal them the best of the black writers discovered themselves, "remorselessly, unflinchingly" growing to maturity true to their own sap.[7] From this unique flowering, universal literature today is gathering "the succulence of fruit."

Pain and revolt are eternal themes, but blacks have revealed new ways of suffering. These ancient, suppurating afflictions, the long horror of slavery, the wounds of racism, and the racial inferiority complex had never yet been described in the French language. The fiery imprecations of Victor Hugo are quite different from the guttural cries of the immense resurrection of a continent and a race.

> Moi qui Krakatoa
> moi que tout mieux que mousson
> moi qui poitrine ouverte
> moi qui lailape
> moi qui bêle mieux que cloaque
> moi qui hors de gamme
> moi qui Zambèze ou frénétique ou rhombe ou cannibale
> ....
> Choses écartez-vous faites place entre-vous
> place à mon repos terrible qui porte en vague
> ma terrible crête de racines ancreuses
> qui cherchent où se prendre
> Choses je sonde je sonde
> moi le porte-faix je suis porte-racines
> et je pèse et je force et j'arcane
> j'omphale
> ah qui vers les harpons me ramène
> je suis très faible

6. J. Rabemananjara, "Les fondements de notre unité tirés de l'époque coloniale," in the special issue of *Présence Africaine* devoted to the Second Congress, p. 76.

7. A. Césaire, "Les pur-sang," in *Les armes miraculeuses*, p. 21.

je siffle oui je siffle des choses très anciennes
de serpents de choses caverneuses
je . . . or . . . vent . . . paix-là
et contre mon museau instable et frais
pose contre ma face érodée
ta froide face de rire défait.
Le vent hélas je l'entendrai encore
nègre nègre nègre depuis le fond
du ciel immémorial
un peu moins fort qu'aujourd'hui
mais trop fort cependant
et ce fou hurlement de chiens et de chevaux
qu'il pousse à notre poursuite toujours marronne
mais à mon tour dans l'aire implacable
à mon tour dans l'air
je me lèverai un cri et si violent
que tout entier j'éclabousserai le ciel
et par mes branches déchiquetées
et par le jet insolent de mon fût blessé et
    solonnel

  je commanderai aux îles d'exister[8]

  [I who Krakatoa
I who so much better than the monsoon
I who chest wide open
I who Laelaps
I who bleat better than the cloaca
I who beyond the limits of the scale
I who Zambezi or frenetic or rhombic or cannibal
....

Things stand back make room
room for my quiescence carrying in waves
my frightful crest of anchor roots
straining to catch hold
Things I probe I probe
I am the bearer the bearer of roots
and I ponder and I thrust and I incant
    I umbilicate
Ah what draws me back toward the barbs
    I am so frail
I whistle yes I whistle ancient things

8. A. Césaire, *Corps perdu* (Paris: Editions Fragrance, 1950); translation by Emile Snyder and Sanford Upson, "Disembodied," in the bilingual edition of Césaire's *Cadastre* (New York: Third Press, 1973). Krakatoa: volcanic isle in the East Indies, site of an immense eruption in 1883. Laelaps: from Greek mythology, the storm wind represented as a dog.

known to snakes and hollow things
I but wind enough of this
and against my cool restless muzzle
against my eroded face
place your cold face with its stifled laughter.
Alas I shall again hear the wind screaming
nigger nigger nigger from the depths
of the timeless sky
not quite so loud as today
but too loud none the less
and this crazed howling of hounds and horses
which the wind sets upon our forever run-away tracks
but I in turn will raise
a shriek so violent
that my whole being shall splatter the sky
and with my shredded branches
and with the insolent spurt of my wounded
and solemn shaft

I shall order the islands to be]

Nor had we ever before felt this "shock of being seen."[9] In the mirror the blacks hold out for us, we see the tragic miscarriage of our civilizing action. No one, thus far, had shown us such a cruel reflection of ourselves.

Washed clean at last of all the picturesque, gaudy exoticism which for so long had hidden them, West Indian and African cultures show us their true face: blunt, intense, and rhythmic as their dances and their statues. A profusion of images, names of places and objects, plants and animals, fascinating in their poetic sound and suggestive power, now swarm into our universe. Symbols too, unlike ours. The artist creates them out of his indigenous milieu—Césaire, the volcano, the sun, the island; Glissant, the river called "La Lézarde"; and Rabemananjara, the *lamba*[10]—or else they are drawn from their African cultures: the moon, scorpions, waves. One finds these African symbols in the West Indies too, occasionally distorted or with a somewhat different meaning—for example the snake, the only dangerous animal in these islands, which thus acquires, in addition to its African meaning of fecundity, an aggressiveness unknown in Africa. Other symbols too rise from Negro history: Allusions to travel are the slave trade which brought them to America; "irons" (*ferrements*) represent for Césaire the chains and leg irons of slavery, but also the bondage of colonized peoples, to which is added in the French a suggestive pun "ferments"

9. J. P. Sartre, "Orphée noir," p. ix.
10. A *lamba* is the loincloth worn by Madagascans.

(*ferments*), evoking the catalytic qualities of leaven.

Black writers thus also transmit the heritage of their verbal literature, its myths and legends. We become familiar with new forms of humor, new heroes and customs; we discover new images and unexpected comparisons which enrich the materials of poetry. What a contrast to the revisions of European translators! Birago Diop, Jean Malonga, or Keita Fodeba do not "translate" the tales told by native storytellers; they compose anew to familiar themes, and thus make true re-creations. The charm and literary interest of these tales now reside more in their form than in their subject matter.

Birago Diop modestly claims that he invents nothing, but simply translates into French the tales told by his family *griot* [bard] Amadou, the son of Koumba. Let us not be misled. Like all the good storytellers in our land, he uses an old theme to compose a new poem. And the dazzled reader easily believes it is a translation, because the narrator, skillfully combining French subtlety and fresh Wolof sobriety, knows how to bring the Negro African tale to life with its own philosophy, imagery, and rhythm.

We who have heard Amadou Koumba know that the student is as great as the master, greater perhaps, because he is a creator of life and beauty, a poet.[11]

In composing poems that are meant to be sung or recited aloud rather than read silently, certain black poets have reestablished a contact with oral literature lost to us since the medieval troubadors. Indeed, contemporary black writers have begun a possible reconciliation between art and folk literature. They have the advantage of still being linked to a tradition where the creator and his work are conceived only in relation to group understanding and feeling. Moreover, they definitely wish to be interpreters and educators of their people, and therefore desire to maintain this relationship. Perhaps these assets will permit them for a time at least to avoid the dilemma between cultural mandarinism and the sterile efforts of socialist realism.

For all these reasons we must study the Negro contribution with great interest and conclude that it enriches literature. What about the robust and hypersensitive emotivity, "porous to the breathing of the world," typical of the Negro soul and its manifestations? This emotivity transfigures the very language it uses.

This quality is noticeable in some novels by black authors, but it is especially apparent in their poetry. We have carefully analyzed Senghor's poems from this perspective and shown how they depended on a despotic rhythm, both irregular and monotonous, that responds to a greater extent to the demands of African dances and musical instruments than to the usual diction of the French language. This richness of rhythm also appears throughout Césaire's *Cahier*, and it is in fact the

11. L. S. Senghor, *Anthologie*, p. 135.

new blood brought in by Negro poetry. To be convinced of this it is sufficient to read Senghor's *Anthologie de la nouvelle poésie nègre et malgache de langue française*.[12]

Negro literature has also given our language a new dimension. This is primarily a special kind of poetic relief, most noticeable in Césaire. His language is sculpted, worked, kneaded like dough, in order to be modeled with greater success. Words are used for their very substance, for the physical and spatial sensations they produce. We find the same effort in Glissant, who tries to reproduce what he calls the "roughness" of things.

Finally, because of their participation in telluric forces, black writers have a more intimate contact with things, an intuitive and poetic understanding of nature, which they translate into fresh or brutal images: "The weakness of many men," writes Césaire, "is that they do not know how to become a stone or a tree."[13]

We do not propose to list here the many contributions of Negro literature, but it seems important to point out that, up to the present, writings in the French language from sister cultures such as the Belgian or Canadian have brought nothing very different to French literature.[14] In contrast, the cross-breeding with distant Negro African cultures often foreign to Western mentalities has already resulted in substantially modifying French literature—so substantially that we believe it less risky to speak of black literature in French than of French literature by black writers.

There now remain a few questions about the future of this literature.

We wonder first of all whether the present spectacular rallying of black writers around common themes and feelings will continue when they have left political, sociological, and racial demands behind? Will there be a break-up into a series of national literatures, more closely connected to the realities of the lands from which they spring, or will rapid development in Africa maintain enough cohesion for a kind of homogeneity to continue in spite of the many different languages the writers may use?

Will West Indian and African literatures, moreover, retain close ties when the colonial context disappears, or—as is perhaps more likely— will the Caribbean writers draw closer to South America and open themselves to a Hispano-Negro blending? The nearness of Madagas-

12. Paris: Presses Universitaires, 1948; 2d ed., 1969. [Translator's note: Senghor's anthology has never been translated, although Sartre's preface, "Orphée noir," has. Poetry of the negritude school has been collected in several more recent anthologies, however, in both bilingual and English-translation-only editions: See the bibliography for volumes by editors Collins, Jones, Kennedy, and Shapiro.]

13. A. Césaire, "Question préalable," in *Soleil cou coupé*, p. 88.

14. With a few exceptions, for example, Charles de Coster and Michel de Ghelderode.

car to the African continent might favor a relationship between Madagascan literature and that of the African group. All these movements, however, would not prevent Negro African literature from retaining common features despite the variety of local styles and languages.

But there is another series of problems requiring urgent attention, and the future of black literature in French will depend on how they are resolved.

We have explained the political and social reasons which made this literature a cry of revolt. In order to be heard, black writers had to address Europe in its own language, and to do so in no uncertain terms. Now that their demands have been heard and are in the course of being met, which direction will Negro literature take?

This literary impulse which was the result of exceptional dramatic tension, might very well fall back upon itself after attaining its aims, and the energy of black artists, temporarily mobilized by the word, might very well for a time be translated into action. Black authors would then find themselves in a situation somewhat similar to that of the Russian revolutionary writers with whom they feel such kinship. One could then fear that, following the example of their Russian elders, black writers might take the path of "efficiency" and "didacticism" to the detriment of art.

We can already see errors of this kind in certain communist poems by the Haitian exile René Depestre:

> Nous savons, O mes peuples nègres
> Que le pigment de la peau
> N'est que le bouclier
> Qui dissimule le teint sans couleur du capital.
> ....
> Nous savons qu'il n'est de race
> Que dans les yeux pourris des négriers
> Que sur la langue décomposée
> Des copains de la monnaie.[15]

> [We know, O my Negro peoples
> That the color of skin
> Is but the shield
> That hides the colorless taint of Capital.
> ....
> We know there is no race
> But in the evil eyes of slavers
> But on the distorted tongues
> Of money-changers.].

15. R. Depestre, *Traduit du grand large* (Paris: Seghers, 1952), p. 34.

Even should the great inspiration continue, it will doubtless undergo important changes.

Negro literature could abandon French for African languages exclusively, either because the writer finds them better adapted to his temperament or because he seeks closer contact with the indigenous masses. We would then see the blossoming of national works as valid as those by today's authors but reaching a more limited audience.

If black peoples choose a vernacular language, it is quite possible that black literature in French may disappear, even though at present it shows such promise. If, on the other hand, the development of education in Africa were to spread the knowledge of French throughout the black continent, we might well see French language and vernacular of African writers coexist in a common "African" or "national" literature.

Whatever may happen, today's writers must carefully review their situation. Up to now their goals were extremely clear, and the path to reach them was a single, deep furrow. They have escaped from the dilemma "either be whitened or disappear" in which the West seemed to imprison them, and have won the right to speak for themselves as they wished. They have succeeded in making themselves known as blacks and as men at the same time.

To stiffen in an attitude of revolt and antagonism would be a great mistake. If it is normal for an excess to engender its opposite—for white racism, for example, to have produced black racism—one must avoid sinking into what Frantz Fanon calls "raving Manichaeism" by merely reversing the equation good-white with bad-black. The antagonist's return to more humane behavior and brotherly language should do away with the defense mechanisms engendered by colonization. Several black intellectuals, among them the greatest, have already understood this:

I as a man of color do not have the right to hope that in the white man there will be a crystallization of guilt for the past of my race.

I as a man of color do not have the right to seek ways of trampling on the pride of my former master.

I have neither the right, nor the duty to demand reparation for the domestication of my ancestors. . . .

One day I discovered myself in the world, and I recognize for myself only one right: the right to demand human behavior from the other.

And one duty: not to renounce my liberty by my own choices.

I do not wish to be the victim of the fraud of a black world.

My life must not be devoted to drawing up the balance sheet of Negro values.

There is no white world, there are no white ethics any more than there is a white intelligence.

There are in every part of the world men who search.[16]

Isn't this the meaning of the whole New Negro cultural movement we have just studied? Once the goal is attained, must it renounce its faith?

We are men of dialogue, of the type of dialogue which mobilizes and commits the best of man to the encounter with mankind.[17]

These were Alioune Diop's words in his opening speech to the Second Congress of Black Writers and Artists. His perspective seems to us the only one capable of fully developing Negro African culture and art. Black artists have already succeeded in giving a new structure to the universe of their peoples and in "bringing order to the cultural chaos" caused by colonization.[18] They will now have to be vigilant and struggle against all forms of oppression, lies, violence that will appear in the newly independent nations! Responsibility will continue to weigh upon men of culture, and it will be their role to direct and shed light upon the rise of their people.

We Westerners look to the black artist for the creation of beauty, for expressions of the pain and joys of his people, for an exploration of the infinite riches of his long-lost patrimony, and for the sharing of all this with us, so that we in turn may be enriched. Yet we also hope he will be faithful to his ideal and help us to build the fraternity we so greatly desire.

It would be surprising for this ideal to fail, now that circumstances favor its realization. Black artists need only sincerely contemplate the words of one of their own, Aimé Césaire:

Our responsibility is that the use our peoples will make of their reconquered freedom depends to a great extent upon us. And it is this that establishes our duty as men, more deeply than our personal duties. For in the end there is one question no man of culture, whatever his nation or race can avoid, it is this: What kind of world are you preparing for us?

May this be known: In joining our effort to those for liberation of the colonized peoples, in fighting for the dignity of our peoples, for their truth and their recognition, in the end it is for the whole world we fight, to free it from tyranny, hate, and fanaticism.

Beyond the struggles of the present, manifold though they be, this is what we want, the world made young again, set in new balance, otherwise nothing

16. Frantz Fanon, *Peau noire, masques blancs*, pp. 219–20; translated as *Black Skin, White Masks* (New York: Grove, 1967), pp. 228–29.

17. Alioune Diop, opening speech of the Second Congress, in *Présence Africaine*, p. 47.

18. Aimé Césaire, "L'homme de culture et ses responsabilités," *Présence Africaine*, February-May 1959, p. 120.

will have meaning, nothing, not even victory tomorrow.

Then and then alone shall we have won and our final victory will mark the advent of a new era.

We will have helped to give a meaning, to give *its* meaning to that most sullied yet most glorious word: We shall have helped lay the foundations of a universal humanism.[19]

19. Ibid., p. 122.

APPENDIX

Problems of the Literary Critic in Africa

The Situation of Modern African Literature

To speak of the problems of literary criticism in Africa presupposes that one is well versed in the state of African literature, modern as well as traditional. It does not fall within our scope here to go into detail about the movement of "Negro awareness" (negritude), which originated at the beginning of this century in America, among the descendants of the Negro slaves imported to work the plantations. As a reminder, I shall give merely a brief outline of some of its stages.

First of all, let us briefly specify what is meant by negritude, a term that English- and French-speaking blacks have made the subject of a continuing dispute, which is, in my opinion, baseless.

I should like to point out that it was Aimé Césaire who invented this neologism, using it for the first time in his *Cahier d'un retour au pays natal*. It is therefore logical to ask Césaire himself what he means by this ambiguous term. "Negritude is the simple realization of the fact of being black, and the acceptance of this fact, of its cultural and historical consequences," is his answer. Where is the African today who can put himself against this attitude?

Of course, the concept of negritude has since been extended to include the characteristics of ancient African culture, as well as the psychological reactions of the modern black to slavery, segregation, and colonization. Sartre described negritude as "the being-in-the-world of the Negro," in other words, the manner peculiar to the Negro of understanding the universe, of feeling and defining himself and others, in short, his *Weltanschauung*.

Negritude has been confused with Negro revolt, and antiwhite aggressiveness, but this is mistaking the part for the whole. The Negro revolt is only the moment of negritude at which the black man refuses henceforth to be despised and bullied on account of his race. But negritude is, above all, that which differentiates the black African from

This essay, amended by the author in 1971, originally appeared in *Abbia*, Cameroon Cultural Review (Yaoundé), no. 8 (February–March 1965), pp. 13–28; it is printed here by permission of the author.

others, that which distinguishes his behavior, his sociopolitical structures, his history, his religions, his artistic productions, from those of other races and civilizations. It is therefore principally a cultural peculiarity, synonymous with "African originality," "African personality," "the state of being African," etc.

Negritude gave its name to the literary movement which rightly took this peculiarity into account, this cultural irreductibility of black African civilization, vindicating the black man's right to be himself, to be respected for his culture as well as in his person.

The principal literary themes that arose from this awareness and were sung for thirty years by the Negro writers are new to world literature: the slave trade and slavery, exile and the nostalgia for Africa, the thousand sufferings borne by blacks on every latitude, segregation, lynching, color prejudice, and other humiliations, not forgetting colonization and its misdeeds, forced labor, the destruction of native cultures, the inferiority complex, assimilation, etc. They comprise, in short, the Passion of the Negro world. As a necessary reaction, the writers also preached a general revolt.

During the last fifteen years before independence the negritude movement expanded these key themes in a flowering of West Indian and American as well as African poets, novelists, and essayists, both English- and French-speaking, not to mention the Portuguese-language writers, the most eminent of whom are the Angolan poets Mario de Andrade and Antonio Jacinto. Since the founding of the Society of African Culture (SAC), the *Présence Africaine* team has been spreading the ideas of negritude throughout the black world into all countries by means of subgroups, who are promoting Negro cultures. It was the SAC that organized the two big congresses of black writers and artists in 1956 and 1959, which brought together black intellectuals from the whole world, as well as the First World Festival of Negro Arts in Dakar in 1966.

On the literary level, one should note the continuing prestige of the poets in Léopold Senghor's 1947 anthology: Rabemananjara, Ranaïvo, David Diop, Birago Diop, Paul Niger, Guy Tirolien, without forgetting the old guard made up of Césaire and Damas, Jacques Roumain, J. F. Brierre, Gilbert Gratiant, and to a certain extent, René Maran and Joseph Rabearivelo.

Between 1950 and 1960 a Pleiad of novelists sprang up: Camara Laye, Mongo Beti, Ferdinand Oyono, Abdoulaye Sadji, Bernard Dadié, Aké Loba, Olympe Bhêly-Quénum, Ousmane Sembene; in the Anglo-American area, Richard Wright, Chester Himes, James Baldwin, Peter Abrahams, Ezekiel Mphahlele, Cyprian Ekwensi, Alfred Hutchinson; and, in the Caribbean region, George Lamming, Jacques Stéphen Alexis, Joseph Zobel, René Tardon, and Edouard Glissant. Meanwhile, new poets wrote on themes that have become classical; René Depestre, Georges Desportes, Paulin Joachim, Elolongué Epanya Yondo, Lamine Diakhaté. Finally one should note the very important influence of major essayists like Alioune Diop, Cheik Anta Diop, Frantz Fanon, Mamadou Dia, Sékou Touré, Padmore, Amadou Hampate Ba, Jomo Kenyatta, and Aimé Césaire.

Nineteen sixty: the world changes. It is the year of African independence. The Negro diaspora, reunited under a single banner while struggling for liberty, breaks up, once that freedom is acquired. True, the hope of pan-Africanism is not abandoned. But each independent country chooses nationalism first, before taking the risk of the great Negro unity. This is a fact even if it is temporary, and one which has cultural consequences.

Negro African literature today is seeking its way. Its themes and literary genres are decelerating, as its aims are becoming more diversified. A series of authors, who were indeed heroic tenors of the polemic literature, grew silent as soon as the goal of independence had been achieved. Some were only writers of circumstance, provoked by the situation of crisis. Others were seeking new direction.

Those who continue to be geared to politics will differ according to their country of origin and the themes they broach. While the English-speaking American, Caribbean, and South African writers sometimes carry their vindication to an extreme in isolated but all the more strident cries, the majority of African writers concentrate on internal problems of their native lands. In Mali the novels of Seydou Badian and Mamadou Gologo study the conflict of generations, the coexistence of traditional and modern societies. In Senegal, Cheikh Hamidou Kane raises the same problems to a philosophic level, as he treats the difficulty of integrating the culture of Descartes and a certain African mysticism. In his next novel Kane will treat the ups and downs of decolonization, the changes that take place, the mentalities of different social classes. With less subtlety, and in a style more "socialist-realistic," Ousmane Sembene too devotes himself to the detailed description of present African society in his recent novels *L'harmattan, Le mandat,* and *Vehi-ciosane.*

This preoccupation with the present and the objective translating of the real can be found in two genres that have flourished since independence: the theater and the short story. In Cameroon as well as in Nigeria, a theater of manners has developed, presenting on the stage, often in parody, the principal problems of African social life: alcoholism, unemployment, dowry, forced marriage, corruption of officials, conflicts between generations, conflicts between traditional chiefs and government officials and between European medicine and African witchcraft. All these themes translate the impact of two civilizations in confrontation with each other, the break with traditional culture undergone by some, the absurd and tragic situations that result from this. The same situations are sometimes treated from a political point of view, in pamphlets like Daniel Ewande's *Vive le président* and such excellent novels as *Les soleils des indépendances* by Ahmadou Kourouma. The themes are treated in varying fashion: Certain authors preach the upholding of traditions, while others are resolutely modern, thus showing clearly the hesitation before scales of opposing values which characterizes the recently decolonized African.

The most successful in the dramatic field in Cameroon are the plays of Guillaume Oyônô-Mbia, Jacques Mariel Nzouankeu, and Etienne Yanou. The same themes recur in the work of the great Nigerian Wole Soyinka and the Ruandese Saverio Naigiziki. Short stories, too, by Ousmane Sembene, Bernard Dadié, and René Philombe are quick to broach these problems of present-day life. The short story, moreover, is a genre that lends itself splendidly to the expression of the African soul. In its familiar turn of mind and relative brevity, the short story is close to the folktale, an African genre traditionally much cultivated. The short story adapts as well to sketches of daily life as to surrealist mysteries. That is why one finds it everywhere today, in the second major area that African literature is exploring, that of renewing oral traditions.

Jacques Nzouankeu and Benjamin Matip, Ibrahim Seid and Jean Malonga, Abdou Anta Ka and Camara Laye continue this vein already explored by Birago Diop, Ousmane Socé, Bernard Dadié and Lomani Tchibamba. In their short, piquant works, they re-create the fantastic and humorous world of village vigils around the fire. If the tale takes on larger proportions, it becomes an epic novel like *Soundjata* by Djibril Tamsir Niane, an epic poem or "total theater" like the *La mort de Chaka* of Seydou Badian and the *Poèmes africaines* of Keita Fodeba, or a philosophical poem like the tale of the spider in the tradition of the *mvet* Beti. At this point, theater, poetry, and song are mingled. For the writers who draw inspiration from oral literature very often do the work of adapters and even of translators, and thus combine the function of poets and ethnologists. They are in the process of recuperating for world civilization a whole invisible cultural heritage now threatened with extinction. At the same time it seems to us they are also discovering the most fertile formulae for a vigorous and original flowering of Negro African literature.

On the other hand, we are witnessing a regression of the autobiographical novel which served as a training ground for the generation before independence, as well as a retreat from anticolonialism in poetry. Here, too, one finds today either a commitment of the militant, partisan sort, or a return to traditional sources, with poets trying their hand at forms of expressions and subjects as sung in the vernacular languages. These fruitful experiments have given us, for example, the French-language poems of Ayissi, Epanya, and Charles Ngande in Cameroon. Young writers like Malik Fall, Okala Alene, Ernest Alima, Dogmo, G. Richard Dogbeh-David, and Blaise Diagne seek, on the other hand, a personal means of expression along a path in which they wish to be free from all influence.

However, we must admit that French-language Negro poetry is in a crisis. The new experiments cannot yet be compared to Nigerian or South African poetry in English, which is quite mature and already can count writers as distinguished as Christopher Okigbo, Gabriel Okara, J. P. Clark, Bloke Modisane, Denis Brutus, and other poets that we have discovered through Gerald Moore and Ulli Beier's Penguin anthology *Modern Poetry from Africa* (1963).

The only poets to achieve this level in the French-speaking area are two young men who continue the learned tradition of the first generation of the New Negro movement. I refer to the Congolese Gérald Félix Tchicaya (Tchicaya U Tam'si) and the Mauritian Edouard J. Maunick. Their poetry, which is neither political nor traditional, resolutely goes beyond racial and even nationalist problems (without ignoring them, however) to center on universal themes of love, social justice, fraternity, exile, attachment to the native country, etc. But up to now, there is no continuity between these fully developed poets and the young writers in French-speaking Africa who are still in search of their tone and their harmonies.

The State of Traditional Literature

If, as has been said, Africa is literally rotten with archaeological remains, it can be declared with even greater reason that Africa is rotten with oral literature.

Those who are even mildly interested in the question are amazed—I find no other word—when they discover the breadth, the variety, the wealth of this literary heritage that African generations have handed down to each other since antiquity. Modern essays written in English or in French appear ridiculous in comparison to these immense Negro memorials that wash down the shining gold of their poems as a rushing river carries pebbles.

It is a living, flourishing, generous literature. There are parts of Cameroon where as many as ten singers of the *mvet* may be found in each village. This country alone thus contains hundreds of bards, or *griots,* who animate the night watches or work for an aristocratic master. Their knowledge covers as vast a domain as that of the French or German Middle Ages.

It is a very complete literature with diverse genres, perfectly constituted, including epics, some of which have come down to us, like those of Soundjata, Da Monzon, or Chaka; novels of adventure like the story of Djeki na Njambe or that of Tchourouma; cosmognic narratives, the most important of them being *The Divine Pastoral* as transcribed by the Rwandan, Alexis Kagame; ritual chants of socioreligious functions; songs of mourning, of marriage, birth, harvest; songs of war or victory; cradle songs, love songs and satirical songs. So great is the humor and poetry displayed in African proverbs that even they merit a place in literature. To quote a few examples:

"He who works in the sun will eat in the shade."

"Tears are invisible in the rain."

"Your tongue is your lion; if you let it go, it will devour you."

"A patient man continues to boil a stone until he can drink its broth."

"All men belong to the tribe of the dead."

As for enigmas and riddles, Africans have raised them also to the level of literary genre; they are tournaments of metaphor on which great and small are exercised each day, during the night watches.

"He who scolds us without reason" (thunder).

"Fruits bursting in the heavens, that no one gathers" (stars).

"All the women of this village carry babes with long hair" (a field of corn).

"I did not go far and yet I left no trace" (an African pirogue).

"The seed one sows that never sprouts" (the dead).

Finally, there is the enormous reserve of folktales and fables. In Europe it is thought that Africa produces nothing but folktales, since a few volumes were collected and published very early. But if this genre is inexhaustible, it is not, in my opinion, the most original and interesting field of this literature. The folktale draws its inspiration from a foundation common to all peoples—sound common sense, which, as everyone knows, is found throughout the world. I should also mention genres still unknown in Europe, like the literature of the tom-tom, which constitutes a language all by itself, with its laws and its special scale of possibilities of expression—even, quite seriously, the song of birds interpreted in marvelously ingenious ways.

In his study for the Gallimard encyclopedia, Georges Balandier forcefully pointed out the great characteristics of traditional African literature. Today researchers like G. Calame Griaule, Eno Belingo, Mohamadou Kane, and Joseph Mufuta have published the best studies on this subject. I shall single out here only those that may baffle the European critic. First of all, due to the fact that it is *oral*, this literature is mobile, fluctuating, fragile, and, more than any other, defies analysis: I shall return to this later.

Senghor has written: "The Negro assimilates beauty, goodness, and the useful." This literature is therefore also functional, always connected with the useful, whether social, religious, or educational. This is explained by the very fact of being oral. When one composes a poem in order to *speak* it, one necessarily takes notice of the other, one composes for the other, while when one writes a poem, one can do it for oneself, to express oneself, without feeling the need to produce something to be *read*. Writing does not postulate communication. And this is capital. Indeed, considering that the epic is both tribal history and genealogy; that the cosmogonic narrative contains basic, religious myths; that mourning or marriage songs, harvest and hunting songs are prayers; that the folktale is a moral lesson, and proverbs an article of law—this literature becomes as a whole a receptacle and vehicle of culture itself, of the principal institutions on which traditional societies rest. African stories are teeming memorials transmitting both codes of wisdom and the ancestral experience.

We are confronted here with a literature all the more worthy of being saved, fixed, and studied, because it constitutes the very record of African civilization.

Another aspect interesting to the critic is that this literature is folklore in the noble sense of the term. It is made for the people and by the people. The distinction between learned and popular literature does not yet exist in traditional African society. Neither is there a small class of literary persons that produces, and a passive mass that is content with consuming, as is the case in Europe. The African bard forms an intimate part of and is inseparable from his people. Hence his work is a true projection of the universe of his people. His work is truly representative, not of himself alone but of his group, and it is in this sense that this literature is collective if not anonymous. Indeed, the names of talented *griots* become associated with such a story of which they are master raconteurs—for example, *Contes d'Amadou Koumba,* as re-told by Birago Diop. Reciprocally, to the extent that the bard faithfully interprets his people, the latter react to the literary work and intervene directly. There is nothing more astonishing than those *mvet* musical evenings when about thirty people gather in a village hut. Warmed up by a few bottles, the singer lets himself go and soon finds himself supported, questioned, accompanied by his audience to such an extent that the novel becomes a play, each spectator playing his part in it and taking a hand in the creation. These musical sessions may last up to three days.

Such freedom of communication, such spontaneity are obviously only possible in oral literature. Besides, this is oral literature's undisputed superiority over the book, a fact that has not been sufficiently emphasized.

Finally, perhaps the most striking aspect of traditional literature is the absence of distinction between prose and poetry. Or, more exactly, the two are always mingled, or alternate, in the same work. More frequently the entire work is built in the form of a poem, for the great majority of stories are sung, therefore rhymed. Why? Because literature and music are more closely linked together in Africa than elsewhere. Given the structure of the Bantu languages, which are tonal, it is not possible to compose a tune and then adapt African words to it; this would lead to the worst results. First, the words of a song have to be composed that will indicate the tones, the rhythms, around which a suitable melody can be composed. It is due to this great sensibility of the African tones and rhythms that birds or tom-toms may be said to "speak." It is due not to some mechanical code, like Morse, but to a real analogy with the language.

Literary creation in traditional Africa is therefore naturally poetic; its very rhythms are born spontaneously from the language, and its metaphors and symbols take the place of abstract concepts. It is privileged land for the poet, since an image or an association slips into the most simple expressions there. "Good-evening," in Douala, is "awindele," which means "Are you darkening indeed with the day?"

Problems of the Literary Critic in Africa

The problems of a literary critic vary, according to the literature he is dealing with—whether modern or traditional.

To appreciate the modern literature written today in Africa is, I think, possible, if not easy, for a European critic, all depending, of course, on the criteria he applies.

For poetry, this is still relatively simple, the universally recognized criteria being the image or the rhythm. Even if the images baffle us sometimes, even if the rhythms are new, we are in a position to recognize poems in which these elements exist, and those in which they are lacking.

But in French-speaking Africa today, the literary critic sometimes encounters a radically falsified conception of poetry, which is often considered by young modern writers to consist of a more or less clever arrangement of general ideas, expressed in rhymed alexandrines and disposed in the form of sonnets, ballads, odes, etc. Here, we are up against the sorry vestiges of a French romantic or Parnassian-style poetry that the Africans have inherited from an archaic and ill-adapted system of education. It is similar in many details to the West Indian situation described by the poet Etienne Léro in 1932. The literary critic, first of all, must help the Africans to break the chains that stifle their authentic inspiration. This is not always easy, so deeply rooted are the prejudices. It is a question of liberating their creative audacity, of setting right, with their aid, the very notion of what poetry is, of proposing new models to them, whether it be in contemporary French poetry, in the domain of negritude, or in their traditional poetry; to make them realize, in short, that true poetry can only blossom from the authentic roots of their personality.

In this connection, we repeat once more that English-language African poetry is far more sure, more free, and that one does not find in the former French colonies poets equal to Gabriel Okara, Christopher Okigbo, and Denis Brutus. This phenomenon is explained by a difference in colonial policy: France has practiced, to an incomparably higher degree than England, cultural assimilation and the disregard of traditional cultures.

With African prose, the critic's position is more delicate. As long as novels, short stories, and dramatic works deal with social, racial, or colonial themes, one may refer to the criteria imposed by the negritude movement. Writers like Jacques Roumain, Stéphen Alexis, Abdoulaye Sadji, Cheikh Hamidou Kane, and Mongo Beti and Ferdinand Oyono in their early novels, have left this genre with an authenticity of tone which up to now has been the surest label of quality. Consequently one may judge, without risking great error, whether a style is in keeping with the contents that it is supposed to express, or whether it does not correspond to them, as is the case with the latest novel of Oyono. *Chemin d'Europe* relates the throes of a young Cameroonian on the lookout for work and is written in the style of Alain Robbe-Grillet (a fashionable French novelist of the "New Wave" school). There is shocking distortion in the desire to apply, at any price, the patterns of thought and expressive techniques of the New French Novel to African reality. *Chemin d'Europe* could very well be the product of a French writer trying to project himself into the psychology of an African. It must in this view be considered a valid form of New Novel exoticism, just like the novels of Pierre Loti or the *Thaïs* of Anatole France. But with regard to an African, one can only judge such an attempt as an exercise in style, an imitation (or a parody), for one does not wish to do Mr. Oyono the injustice of thinking that he has fallen into the rut of what Léon Damas once so aptly described as making "tracing paper copies" of Europe, even if it is contemporary Europe. One can make an analogous criticism of Yambo Ouologuem's *Le devoir de violence*, whose European success is due to application of the most recent Western recipe—blood and sex. The Africanity of this novel is more than doubtful, as much because of its style as in the vision of the world it offers.

Dealing with novels, short stories, plays, tales of imagination, or tales describing traditional society, the European literary critic should proceed more cautiously, particularly where his own philosophical ideas, instinctive reactions, taste for the picturesque, or humanitarian ambitions are concerned. It will be indispensable for him to verify his impressions and his judgments by checking with Africans who have read and appreciated the novel according to their own criteria.

Without claiming to be exhaustive, we can begin by setting forth three criteria of almost certain value to help us judge the manuscripts people bring to us: (1) The wealth of the development and the interest of the plot. (2) The truth of the characters, that is to say, their density and their veracity, the coherence between their psychology and its expression. (Thus, I may almost certainly say that an African novel is bad if the peasants of a village speak in the style of Voltaire, and that a play is a failure if the lovers exchange confidences with the sensibility and in the language of Racine.) (3) Whether the problems dealt with are genuine ones. Novels or plays that deal in a straightforward manner with subjects such as the dowry system, the contrast between generations, superstitions, sorcery, tribal customs, marriage, parental responsibility, and the internal political problems of newly independent nations go straight to the heart of African life. Many of these are expertly done, for instance, Mongo Beti's *Mission terminée* (translated as *Mission to Kala*), Olympe Bhêly-Quénum's *Un piège sans fin,* Seydou Badian's *Sous l'orage,* and Guillaume Oyônô-Mbia's *Trois prétendants, un mari.* One must call attention in this category to the recent novels of Francis Bebey and François Evembe, the plays of Bernard Dadié and Eugène Dervain, and the latest novels of Ousmane Sembene. The works of two Nigerians, the playwright Wole Soyinka and the novelist Chinua Achebe, fall into the same category. But to determine what is genuine one must, of course, be familiar with African society. Certain novels I had enjoyed in Europe turned out to be completely false and artificial when I had an opportunity of comparing them with the state of things they purported to describe!

This preliminary clearing of the ground may be concluded with a few general observations:

1. An African writing in a European language nowadays still thinks too often of a European readership, and thus has a tendency to say only what he thinks Europeans will like. I have already mentioned the sterility this attitude produces in the field of poetry; African poems cast in the classical mold are completely uninteresting because they are merely substandard Lamartine or Victor Hugo, or, at best, inferior Verlaine.

Where prose is concerned, the result is more complex. I am not thinking at the moment of plays written in the manner of Corneille—those are always very funny, of course, but completely useless except as parodies! I am thinking of works in which the style is good but in which African problems are dealt with from the white man's point of view. For instance, in discussing problems connected with marriage, the author may be systematically hostile to polygamy and the dowry system; in the case of tribal authority, he will not have a single good word to say for the rule of the village elders. He will declare that a man who holds a diploma from the white man's school, or one who has lived in France, is invariably and on all points superior to the product of a traditional upbringing who possesses the wisdom that goes with it, the learning and experience of the ancients. Such a writer will nearly always jeer at the village sorcerer, dismiss traditional ceremonies as mere superstition, and condemn established customs as hopelessly out of date. He will take it for granted that the city dweller is superior to the villager and uphold the former as the very pattern of progress and civilization.

Such writing faithfully mirrors the distorted outlook peculiar to the French-speaking colonized person who has lost confidence in himself or his own culture. It expresses the mentality—a very prevalent one, alas—of the urbanized African, torn from his tribal environment, reduced to economic and moral instability, and convinced that his only chance of survival is to develop along European lines, yet still divided, torn between two sets of values.

Yet these ostensibly "progressive" writings reflect only part of the reality. They try to conceal the psychological cleavage. They take a position more radical than that of their authors. But a certain spurious, affected, artificial tone gives them away; they defend their views with white men's arguments, and are rather too lofty in their dismissal of traditions as only good for savages.

Once a critic has noticed this inconsistency, he should try to get in touch with the writer concerned, either directly or by inducing him to tell the truth as he sees it (even at the risk of giving European readers a shock) and to describe the problems that disturb him in their full complexity. For instance, one can urge a writer to attack abuses of the dowry system or of polygamy, not the institutions themselves, which have sound roots in African civilization. One must never, of course, try to influence the actual ideas of a writer, only to make him feel that he is entitled to put down everything he has in his mind. And his mind is never completely turned against his traditional culture.

In such cases the critic acts as a sort of cultural psychoanalyst. His task is to restore confidence to the victim suffering from an anxiety brought on by colonial education—whose most prominent characteristic (vividly described by Fanon in *Peau noire, masques blancs*) is his urge to escape from the Negro condition, a characteristic which recurs with remarkable frequency in the process of creative writing. (I must mention that I agree with Monsieur Anozie's reaction to the myth of the

African alienated by anxiety, which has been pushed to an extreme by one particular critic. It is a dangerous myth, and Anozie gives a good explanation why in his excellent work *Sociologie du roman africain,* the most lucid study of this subject yet written.)

2. The foregoing observation applies, needless to say, only to French-speaking Africans who have never participated in the negritude movement. For these ideas, transmitted through the magazine *Présence Africaine* and persons associated with it, have really succeeded in eliminating the poison of the colonial complex from most black Africans who have spent long periods in France. The work of such writers as Seydou Badian, Ousmane Sembene, Camara Laye, and Mongo Beti does not display this blemish.

But it must be remembered that nowadays the majority of young Africans with literary ambitions have never been outside their own country. Their standard of education is in many cases lower than that of the first generation, which indeed was characterized by their university background. This has two unfortunate consequences: First, these young writers are less familiar with the French language and handle it less skillfully; they make many mistakes in grammar and the use of words, and this detracts from the elegance of their style; second, they are less successful in grasping and describing the problems posed by cultural contrasts, social change, and ideological conflicts, and they discuss them with less authority.

On the other hand, these writers present situations and problems in a way that is much more specific, much closer to the world in which they are actually experienced, with its ambiguity, contradiction, even incoherence. And whenever these writers manage to shake off their inhibiting complexes, they present a much more faithful reflection of the present-day African's soul and the world in which he lives. For they have preserved what so many intellectuals lost while living abroad: a real contact with the mass of the people.

They write, moreover, in much simpler language, using a basic French which can be understood by great numbers of Africans. Their work will therefore have a circulation and an influence far beyond that of their elders, who are not widely read.

Lastly, from the point of view of form, the limitations I referred to just now are offset by an amazing inflow of images, proverbs, and idiomatic expressions, adapted or directly translated from the vernacular. This greatly enriches the literature concerned, giving it such originality, pungency, and gusto that in some cases it compares favorably with the writings of "intellectuals" on the same subjects. As an illustration of this I need only mention two plays, *Le jugement suprême,* by Benjamin Matip, a Doctor of Law and a highly esteemed writer, and *Nanga Kon,* by Stanislas Awona. The latter had an undistinguished local education; but in the poetry of its language, psychological penetration, and truth to facts his play far excels that of the brilliant jurist. It does happen that an intellectual manages to achieve the rare synthesis of fine French and an abundance of idiomatic images and expression. This is the miracle of *Diab'la*, by Joseph Zobel, or *Les soleils des indépendances*, by Ahmadou Kourouma. But miracles are so rare.

I am frequently reminded these days of something said by René Maran at the Rome Congress in 1959, which struck me at the time as paradoxical: "The real literature of negritude will be written a few years hence by peasants in the African bush who know French just well enough to write it more or less correctly."

Confronted by traditional literature, the European literary critic feels really baffled. Yet he cannot ignore it, for as I said before, it is by far the most important. Besides, its influence is continually demonstrated in modern writing, either by anecdotes concerning its heroes or allusions to its epic events, or by long-familiar forms of expression which are purely and simply carried over into French from the fund of tradition. Sooner or later, therefore, any conscientious critic feels irresistibly impelled to trace the oral literature back to its sources.

At once, however, he finds the road strewn with pitfalls. For one thing, oral literature, as such, is virtually inaccessible to the foreigner. Needless to say we can enjoy listening to a *griot* or a *mvet* singer, appreciate his mimicry, and have his tale translated for us. But to be honest, we are complete ignoramuses in the matter, and the only competent critics of such literary sessions are the Africans themselves; they alone can decide which are best among their performers.

Even when an epic poem or legend is written down in the vernacular, it remains inaccessible to most people, just like modern writing in the Yoruba, Souto, or Swahili languages. The essential is saved, however, for those who know the language can now study the work in its permanent form. Those who do not can hope that it will be translated, or even arrange to have it translated.

But when at last the work reaches us in translation or adaptation, it is still far from easy for us to form an opinion about it. We have read and enjoyed the folktales written by Birago Diop and Bernard Dadié, the epics of Soundjata, Samba Full, and Chaka, the fantastic novels of Jean Malonga and Amos Tutuola, and the interminable adventures of Akomomba. We still find ourselves in difficulty when it comes to judging them, classifying them, and deducing the laws that govern them. We tend to find everything interesting; we are perhaps too prompt with our wondering admiration, for it all seems to us to be new and original. In present circumstances, indeed, this attitude is preferable to the opposite one; for before we are able to express any worthwhile opinion about this oral literature, we must collect as much of it as we possibly can.

Meanwhile, we can assess the importance of an individual work in the light of its poetic content, the richness and scope of its episodes, and the wealth of legend it conveys (provided our ethnological knowledge is sufficient).

Another standard of judgment particularly applicable in Africa, where one of the basic characteristics of literature is its functional purpose, is that of the social implications of a work, the extent of its geographical range, and its historical importance for a particular group. For instance, the settlement of the Beti tribe in South Cameroon after the Foulbe thrust had driven them from their own lands across the Sanaga River has given rise to a number of epic poems, because the events described caused an upheaval in the life of the people and acted as a proportionate stimulus to the imagination of their poets. At this point I should say that in Africa the literary critic needs to be something of a sociologist as well, not relying solely on aesthetic criteria. We are considering a society in which all branches of culture are closely interwoven. We must not create artificial divisions, separating the mask from its religious function or the epic from its educational purpose. To do so would be to weaken the very structure of traditional African culture.

The fact remains that, as the Italian proverb points out, all translation is a betrayal; and so it is that we lose many of the elements of oral literature—its rhythm, which is an essential feature, its onomatopoeia, its songs and the accompanying dance and mime that make it a complete theatrical performance. The loss is considerable.

We also fail to grasp the meaning of much of its imagery, many of the proverbs it contains, and sometimes of whole episodes, as happens with Tutuola's *The Palm-Wine Drinkard* (Grove, 1962). We would need fuller information about the author or about his tribal traditions. Moreover, we have difficulty in appreciating certain forms of humor. Africans, for instance, will laugh heartily at scenes of cruelty or at peculiarities that we find horrifying or boring. This is a question of a different scale of values, of cultural dissimilarities.

Finally, there are some expressions which defy translation, and these are always the most characteristic and the rarest. The critic is repeatedly taken aback by finding that Africans are disappointed at the translation of some work they already know in its vernacular original.

There is, however, something that the foreign critic in Africa can accomplish. He can do his utmost to encourage the African research students who are collecting oral material and traditions. Their work is a matter of urgency, for the lapidary phrase used by the great Hampate Ba rings in our ears like a parting bell: "Whenever an old man dies, it is as though a library had been burnt to the ground."

The critic can help to arrange for tape recordings, translations,

bilingual editions, or adaptations in European languages. Once a sufficient amount of material has been assembled, it will be possible to
begin a systematic study of the various types of literature, with their
respective rules, to trace them back to their earliest versions, note
interpolations, etc.—in short, to do the same kind of work on them that
is now being done on the medieval literature of Europe. There are a
dozen versions of the *Song of Roland;* there are certainly more than that
of the legend of Akomomba.

It should not be forgotten, however, that this oral African literature,
unlike that of the Middle Ages, is contemporary. Traditional literature
does not mean ancient literature. Africa is still doing creative work in
the traditional styles, using the form of the folktale, the *chantefables,*
the *minkana,* the *minlan mimvet.* These traditional styles exist side by
side with the modern ones (lyrical poetry, comedy, short story, novel)
and they are still the most important.

So the critic must take care not to treat this literature as though it
were fossilized, arrested, finished. On the contrary, he should try to
reestimate this production, encourage its development, incite young
writers to multiply their attempts to bridge the gap between traditional
and modern literature, either by transposing certain African forms and
constructions into French or by producing his own work in the vernacular.

In conclusion, one should warn the critic against being too prompt
or too sweeping in his judgments. For no exhaustive study of traditional African literature has so far been written.

The first reason for this is the acute shortage of documents. We may,
perhaps, be in possession of a hundredth part of the heritage that can
still be heard from the lips of the *griots.* The second reason is that few
even of such documents as we do possess have real scientific value.
Too many of them are adaptations of African recitals, made with varying degrees of accuracy by schoolteachers or members of the colonial
administration for the sake of their educational interest or their quaint-
ness. They provide useful clues but do not usually merit literary study
for their own sake. What is really needed is a fresh start almost all along
the line, and actual literary studies should be preceded by thorough
philological and linguistic research. We have already said that this
literary study could not be undertaken without an ethnological and
sociological foundation. We add also that one must depart from the
habits of Cartesian analysis. If, indeed, one were to apply the criteria
of logic, noncontradiction, etc., in order to interpret an initiation
speech or even an innocent animal fable, one would greatly risk missing the meaning of the text, not being able to explain its "mistakes,"
its "useless" repetitions, its "empty" digressions. It would therefore
be more worthwhile to leave classical critical methods behind and

make use of the more scientific tools of structuralist criticism; Lévy-Strauss and Luc de Heusch have done this with Indian and African myths, Geneviève Calame Griaule with her study *The Tree Theme in West African Tales,* François Devalière in Malagasy and African mythology. These various experiments have met with such success as to prove decisive for the orientation of my own research.

If this tremendous task is to be carried to a successful conclusion, the first and most urgent need is to get together a sufficient number of literary critics and linguists who are not merely acquainted with the African languages but are themselves Africans. Literary criticism is not only a matter of technique. Intuition and sensitivity are among its indispensable instruments and guides, and we can only love whole-heartedly and respond completely to that which is of the same nature as ourselves. One cannot judge properly except from within a situation. It is usual to hold the opposite. The recent doctoral thesis of the Ivorian ethnologist Memel Foto, "The Political Institutions of the Adjou Krous," however, measures the qualitative difference that exists in a social science study when it is accomplished by a researcher who speaks of his own tribe, who has carried on an investigation in his own language, among people he has always known and who do him the honor of a confidence they would not relinquish to a foreigner. I am convinced that none but Africian critics will succeed in distilling the full essence, savor, significance, and poetry, "the succulence of the fruits" of their ancestral heritage, for the greater glory of world literature.

BIBLIOGRAPHIES

Selected Bibliography

Janet MacGaffey

Since the publication of Lilyan Kesteloot's pioneering study in 1963, the volume of literature in French by black writers has increased enormously, as has interest in it throughout the world. As a result, Mme Kesteloot's bibliography for the original edition is considerably out of date. To increase the usefulness of the English-language edition, the present bibliography was commissioned as an independent contribution to the book in the hope that, in this rapidly growing field, it would provide a useful research tool.

Lack of space has forbidden the updating of Mme Kesteloot's bibliography in its original form, which included black literature in French and in English translated into French, as well as a wide range of background material. The latter is now somewhat dated and has been omitted here, but it is of course available in the French edition. The amount of creative and critical writing now appearing in the field is so large that the new bibliography has been limited to literary material. Some ethnographic studies by the writers discussed in the text are, however, included. Most of the poetry, novels, essays, stories, and plays by the writers from Africa, and from the Caribbean and Indian Ocean areas, that are discussed or mentioned in the text are listed with existing English translations. More recent editions of some of the works discussed are included, and some other African poets have been added. The books and articles in the section on "Criticism and Commentary" include accounts of conferences and interviews with writers. Because the selections are not exhaustive, however, other relevant bibliographies and periodicals that regularly publish, review, or translate writing in French by black authors have been listed. Theses and unpublished materials are not included, and when symposiums and other collections are cited in their entirety, individual papers are not listed separately. No attempt has been made to cover works in English by black authors.

Bibliographies

Amosu, M. *A Preliminary Bibliography of Creative African Writing in the European Languages.* Ibadan, Nigeria: Institute of African Studies, University of Ibadan, 1964.

Baratte, Thérèse. *Bibliographie des auteurs africains et malgaches de langue française.* 2d ed. Paris: Office de Coopération Radiophonique, 1968.

Cameron, J. M. *Pan Africanism and Negritude: A Bibliography.* Ibadan, Nigeria: Institute of African Studies, University of Ibadan, 1964.

Jahn, Janheinz. *A Bibliography of Neo-African Literature from Africa, America and the Caribbean.* New York: Praeger, 1965.

Jahn, Janheinz, and Dressler, Claus Peter. *Bibliography of Creative African Writing.* Nendeln, Liechtenstein: Krauss-Thompson, 1971.

Mercier, R. "Bibliographie africaine et malgache." *Revue de Littérature Comparée* 37 (1963):10–31.

Páricsy, Pál. "Selected international bibliography of negritude: 1960–1969." *Studies in Black Literature* 1, no. 1 (1970):103–15.

Ramsaran, J. *New Approaches to African Literature: A Guide to Negro-African Writing and Related Studies.* Ibadan, Nigeria: Ibadan University Press, 1965.

Zell, Hans, and Silver, Hélène, eds. *A Reader's Guide to African Literature.* Annotated bibliography of French and English works. New York: Africana Publishing Corp., 1971.

Anthologies

Collins, Marie, ed. *Black Poets in French: A Collection of Caribbean and African Poets.* Totowa, N.J.: Scribner's, 1972.

Damas, Léon G., ed. *Les poètes d'expression française.* Paris: Seuil, 1947.

———. *Nouvelle somme de poésie du monde noir.* With introduction and notes. Cahier spécial (no. 57) of *Présence Africaine.* Paris, 1966.

Dathorne, O. R., and Feuser, Willfried, eds. *Africa in Prose.* Including translations from French. Baltimore, Md.: Penguin Books, 1969.

Drachler, Jacob, ed. *African Heritage: An Anthology of Black African Personality and Culture.* Poems, stories, and essays including translations from French. London: Crowell Collier and Macmillan, 1963.

Eliet, Edouard, ed. *Panorama de la littérature négro-africaine (1921–1962).* Poetry, essays, and extracts from Africa and the Caribbean. Paris: Présence Africaine, 1965.

Fitts, Dudley, ed. *Anthology of Contemporary Latin-American Poetry.* Including poems from Haiti in French with English translation. Norfolk, Conn.: New Directions, 1942.

Haiti, poètes noires. Cahier spécial (no. 12) of *Présence Africaine.* Paris, 1952.

Hughes, Langston, ed. *Poems from Black Africa.* Including translations of French poetry. Bloomington: Indiana University Press, 1963.

Jones, Edward A., ed. *Voices of Negritude.* Poems in French with English translation. Valley Forge, Pa.: Judson Press, 1971.

Justin, Andrée, ed. *Anthologie africaine des écrivains noirs d'expression française.* Stories, poems, and essays. Paris: Institut Pédagogique Africain, 1962.

Kennedy, Ellen Conroy, ed. *The Negritude Poets.* Anthology of black poetry translated from the French. New York: Viking Press, 1974.

Kesteloot, Lilyan, ed. *Anthologie négro-africaine. Panorama critique des prosateurs, poètes et dramaturges noirs du XXe siècle.* Verviers: Gérard & Co., 1967.

Lagneau, Lilyan (Kesteloot). *Neuf poètes camerounais.* Yaoundé: Editions C.L.E., 1965.

Lomax, Alan, and Abdul, Raoul, eds. *Three Thousand Years of Black Poetry.* Including twenty-six French poems in translation. New York: Dodd, Mead & Co., 1970.

Lubin, Maurice A., ed. *Poésies haïtiennes*. Rio de Janeiro: Casa do Estudante do Brasil, 1956.

Moore, Gerald, and Beier, Ulli, eds. *Modern Poetry from Africa*. With introduction and translations from the French. Baltimore, Md.: Penguin Books, 1963. Rev. ed., 1968.

Mphahlele, Ezekiel, ed. *African Writing Today*. Poems, stories, and extracts including translations from French. Baltimore, Md.: Penguin Books, 1967.

Reed, John, and Wake, Clive, eds. *A Book of African Verse*. With introduction, notes, and translations from the French. London: Heinemann Educational Books (African Writers Series), 1964.

————. *French African Verse: An Anthology of Poetry from French-Speaking Africa*. With translations. London: Heinemann Educational Books, 1972.

Reygnault, Christine, and Hughes, Langston, eds. *Anthologie africaine et malgache*. Poems, stories, and essays. Paris: Seghers, 1962.

Rutherfoord, Margaret, ed. *African Voices: An Anthology of Native African Writing*. Stories, poems, and essays including translations from French. New York: Vanguard Press, 1960.

Sainville, L., ed. *Anthologie de la littérature négro-africaine*. Paris: Présence Africaine, 1963.

Senghor, L. S., ed. *Anthologie de la nouvelle poésie nègre et malgache de langue française*. With an introduction by Jean-Paul Sartre. Paris: Presses Universitaires, 1948; 2d ed., 1969.

Shapiro, Norman R., ed. *Negritude: Black Poetry from Africa and the Caribbean*. In French with English translation. Introduction by Wilfred Cartey. New York: October House, 1970.

Shelton, Austin J., ed. *The African Assertion: A Critical Anthology of African Literature*. Including poems in French with English translations. New York: Odyssey Press, 1968.

Underwood, Edna Worthley, ed. *The Poets of Haiti, 1782–1934*. Translated into English. Portland, Maine: Mosher Press, 1934.

Wake, Clive, ed. *An Anthology of African and Malagasy Poetry in French*. With introduction and notes in English. London: Oxford University Press, 1965.

Wolitz, Seth L., ed. *Black Poetry of the French Antilles: Haiti, Martinique, Guadeloupe, Guiana*. In English translation. Berkeley: Fybate Lecture Notes, 1968.

Works

Agblemagnon, Ferdinand N'Sougan (Togo). "Du 'temps' dans la culture 'ewe.'" *Présence Africaine*, nos. 14–15 (1957), pp. 222–32.

————. "The Negro-African socio-cultural condition and the cinema." *Présence Africaine* (English edition) 27, no. 55 (1965): 34–44.

————. *Sociologie des sociétés orales d'Afrique noir: les ewe du Sud-Togo*. The Hague: Mouton, 1969.

Alexis, Jacques Stéphen (Haiti, novel). *Compère Général Soleil*. Paris: Gallimard, 1955.

———— (novel). *Les arbres musiciens*. Paris: Gallimard, 1957.

──── (novel). *L'espace d'un cillement*. Paris: Gallimard, 1959.

──── (novel). *Romancero aux étoiles*. Paris: Gallimard, 1960.

Ba, Amadou Hampate (Mali). "Culture peulhe." *Présence Africaine*, nos. 8–10 (1956), pp. 85–97.

────."Sur l'animisme." *Présence Africaine*, nos. 24–25 (1959).

Ba, Amadou Hampate, and Cardaire, Marcel (biography). *Tierno Bokar, le sage de Bandiagara*. Paris: Présence Africaine, 1957.

Badian, Seydou (Mali, play). *La mort de Chaka*. Paris: Présence Africaine, 1962. Translated by Clive Wake. *The Death of Chaka*. London: Oxford University Press, 1968.

──── (novel). *Sous l'orage*. Paris: Présence Africaine, 1963.

Bebey, Francis (Cameroon, stories, poems). *Embarras et cie*. Yaoundé: Editions C.L.E., 1968.

──── (novel). *Le fils d'Agatha Moudio*. Yaoundé: Editions C.L.E., 1968. Distributed by Africana Publishing Corp., New York. Translated by Joyce A. Hutchinson. *Agatha Moudio's Son*. London: Heinemann Educational Books, 1971.

Belance, René (Haiti, poems). *Rythme de mon cœur*. Port-au-Prince: Imprimerie Modèle, 1940.

──── (poems). *Luminaires*. Port-au-Prince: Imprimerie Morissett, 1941.

──── (poems). *Pour célébrer l'absence*. Port-au-Prince: Imprimerie Beaubrun, 1943.

──── (poems). *Survivances*. Port-au-Prince: Imprimerie de l'Etat, 1944.

──── (poems). *Epaule d'ombre*. Port-au-Prince: Imprimerie de l'Etat, 1945.

Beti, Mongo [Eza Boto] (Cameroon, novel). *Ville cruelle*. Présence africaine 16: trois écrivains noirs. Paris: Présence Africaine, 1954.

──── (novel). *Le pauvre Christ de Bomba*. Paris: Laffont, 1956. Translated by Gerald Moore. *The Poor Christ of Bomba*. London: Heinemann Educational Books (African Writers Series), 1971.

──── (novel). *Mission terminée*. Paris: Corrêa, 1957. Translated by Peter Green. *Mission Accomplished*. New York: MacMillan, 1958. Translated by Peter Green. *Mission to Kala*. London: Heinemann Educational Books (African Writers Series), 1964.

──── (novel). *Le roi miraculé*. Paris: Corrêa, 1957. Translated *King Lazarus*. London: Muller, 1961; Heinemann Educational Books (African Writers Series), 1970.

────. *Main basse sur le Cameroun: autopsie d'une décolonisation*. Cahiers libres 240–241. Paris: Maspero, 1972.

Bhêly-Quénum, Olympe (Dahomey, novel). *Un piège sans fin*. Paris: Stock, 1960.

──── (novel). *Le chant du lac*. Paris: Présence Africaine, 1965.

──── (stories). *Liaison d'un été*. Paris: SAGEREP—L'Afrique Actuelle, 1968.

Bognini, Joseph Miezan (Ivory Coast, poems). *Ce dur appel de l'espoir*. Paris: Présence Africaine, 1960.

Bolamba, Antoine-Roger (Congo Republic, poems). *Premiers essais*. Elizabethville: Editions L'Essor du Congo, 1947.

──── (poems). *Esanzo, chants pour mon pays*. Paris: Présence Africaine, 1956.

Brierre, Jean-François (Haiti, play). *Le drapeau de demain*. Port-au-Prince: Imprimerie Haïtienne, 1931.

———— (poems). *Le petit soldat.* Port-au-Prince: Imprimerie Haïtienne, 1932.

———— (poems). *Chansons secrètes.* Port-au-Prince: Imprimerie Haïtienne, 1933.

———— (novel). *Les horizons sans ciel.* Vol. 1, *Province.* Port-au-Prince: Imprimerie Deschamps, 1935.

———— (poems). *Nous garderons le dieu: en hommage du grand leader haïtien de gauche, Jacques Roumain.* Port-au-Prince: Imprimerie Deschamps, 1945.

———— (poems). *Black Soul.* Havana, Cuba: Lex, 1947.

———— (poems). *Dessalines nous parle.* Port-au-Prince: Imprimerie Deschamps, 1953.

———— (poems). *La source.* Collection du jubilé du docteur Jean Price-Mars. Buenos Aires, 1956.

———— (poems). *La nuit.* Lausanne, Switzerland: Held, 1957.

Capécia, Mayotte (Martinique, novel). *Je suis martiniquaise.* Paris: Corrêa, 1948.

———— (novel). *La négresse blanche.* Paris: Corrêa, 1950.

Césaire, Aimé (Martinique, poems). "Cahier d'un retour au pays natal," in review *Volontés,* no. 201 (Paris, 1939). *Return to My Native Land (Cahier d'un retour au pays natal).* Bilingual edition of definitive text of revised edition of 1956; English version adapted by Emile Snyder from 1947 translation by Ivan Goll and Lionel Abel. Paris: Présence Africaine, 1968. Translated by John Berger and Anna Bostock. *Return to My Native Land.* Introduction by Mazisi Kunene. Baltimore, Md.: Penguin Books, 1969.

———— (poems). *Les armes miraculeuses.* Paris: Gallimard, 1946, 1970 (Collection Poésie).

———— (poems). *Soleil cou coupé.* Paris: K Éditeur, 1948.

———— (poems). *Corps perdu. Gravures de Pablo Picasso.* Paris: Fragrance, 1950.

———— (essays). *Discours sur le colonialisme.* Paris: Réclamé, 1950; Présence Africaine, 1955. Translated by Joan Pinkham. *Discourse on Colonialism.* New York: Monthly Review Press, 1972.

———— (play). *Et les chiens se taisaient.* Paris: Présence Africaine, 1956.

————. *Lettre à Maurice Thorez.* Introduction by Alioune Diop. Paris: Présence Africaine, 1956. Translated. *Letter to Maurice Thorez.* Paris: Présence Africaine, 1957.

————. "L'homme de culture et ses responsabilités." *Présence Africaine,* February–May 1959.

———— (poems). *Ferrements.* Paris: Seuil, 1960.

———— (biography). *Toussaint Louverture; la révolution française et le problème colonial.* Paris: Club Français du Livre, 1960.

———— (poems). *Cadastre.* Paris: Seuil, 1961.

———— (play). *Le tragédie du roi Christophe.* Paris: Présence Africaine, 1963. Translated by Ralph Manheim. *The Tragedy of King Christophe.* New York: Grove Press, 1970.

————. *State of the Union.* Poems from *Les armes miraculeuses, Cadastre,* and *Ferrements.* Translated by Clayton Eshleman and Denis Kelly. Bloomington, Ind.: Caterpillar, 1966.

———— (play). *Une saison au Congo.* Paris: Seuil, 1966. Translated by Ralph Manheim. *A Season in the Congo.* New York: Grove Press, 1970.

———— (play). *Une tempête, d'apres 'La Tempête' de Shakespeare* (adapted for black theater). Collection Théâtre 22. Paris: Seuil, 1969.

Dadié, Bernard B. (Ivory Coast, poems). *Afrique debout.* Paris: Seghers, 1950.

———— (stories). *Légendes africaines*. Introduction by Alioune Diop. Paris: Seghers, 1953.

———— (stories). *Le pagne noir, contes africaines*. Paris: Présence Africaine, 1955.

———— (novel). *Climbié*. Paris: Seghers, 1956. Translated by Karen C. Chapman. London: Heinemann Educational Books, 1971.

———— (poems). *La ronde des jours*. Paris: Seghers, 1956.

———— (novel). *Un nègre à Paris*. Paris: Présence Africaine, 1959.

———— (travel). *Patron de New York*. Paris: Présence Africaine, 1964.

———— (poems). *Hommes de tous les continents*. Paris: Présence Africaine, 1967.

———— (travel). *La ville où nul ne meurt* (Rome). Paris: Présence Africaine, 1968.

———— (plays). *Sidi, maître escroc; Situation difficile; Serment d'amour*. Yaoundé: Editions C.L.E., 1969. Distributed by Africana Publishing Corp., New York.

———— (play). *Béatrice du Congo*. Paris: Présence Africaine, 1970.

———— (play). *Monsieur Thôgô-Gnini*. Paris: Présence Africaine, 1970.

———— (play). *Les voix dans le vent*. Yaoundé: Editions C.L.E., 1970.

Damas, Léon G. (Guiana, poems). *Pigments*. Paris: Guy Lévi Mano, 1937; Présence Africaine, 1962. *Pigments* suivi de *Névralgies*. Présence Africaine, 1972. "Poems from *Pigments*," translated by Ellen Conroy Kennedy, in *Black World* 21, no. 3 (January 1972): 13–28.

———— (essay). *Retour de Guyane*. Paris: J. Corti, 1938.

———— (stories). *Veillées noires*. Paris: Stock, 1943. Ottawa: Editions Leméac, 1972.

———— (poems). *Poèmes nègres sur des airs africains*. Paris: Guy Lévi Mano, 1948. Translated by Miriam Koshland and Ulli Beier. *African Songs of Love, War, Grief and Abuse*. Ibadan, Nigeria: Mbari, 1961. Distributed by Northwestern University Press.

———— (poems). *Graffiti*. Paris: Seghers, 1952.

———— (poems). *Black-Label*. Paris: Gallimard, 1956.

———— (poems). *Névralgies*. Paris: Présence Africaine, 1966.

Depestre, René (Haiti, poems). *Etincelles*. 2d ed. Port-au-Prince: Imprimerie de l'Etat, 1945.

———— (poems). *Gerbes de sang*. Port-au-Prince: Imprimerie de l'Etat, 1946.

———— (poems). *Végétations de clarté*. Introduction by Aimé Césaire. Paris: Seghers, 1951.

———— (poems). *Traduit du grand large; poème de ma patrie enchaînée*. Paris: Seghers, 1952.

————. "Un débat autour des conditions d'une poésie nationale chez les peuples noirs," *Présence Africaine*, October–November 1955.

———— (poems). *Minerai noir*. Paris: Présence Africaine, 1956.

————. *Journal d'un animal marin*. Paris: Seghers, 1965.

————. *Un arc-en-ciel pour l'occident Chrétien: poème-mystère vaudou*. Paris: Présence Africaine, 1967.

———— (verse play). *Cantate d'Octobre à la vie et á la mort du commandant Ernesto Che Guevara*. Algiers: Société Nationale d'Edition et de Diffusion, 1969.

Dervain, Eugène (Cameroon, plays). *La reine scélérate; la langue et le scorpion*. Yaoundé: Editions C.L.E., 1968.

———— (play). *Abra Pokou*. Theatre (new plays published in serial formation). Yaoundé: Editions C.L.E., n.d.

Diakhaté, Lamine (Senegal, poems). *La joie d'un continent.* Alès, Sardinia: Imprimerie Benoît, 1954.

———— (play). *Sarzan; adaption théâtrale d'un conte de Birago Diop.* Traits d'Union, no. 7 (Dakar, March–April 1955).

———— (poems). *Primordiale du sixième jour.* Paris: Présence Africaine, 1963.

————. "The acculturation process in Negro Africa and its relations with negritude." *Présence Africaine* (English edition) 28, no. 56 (1965):68–81.

———— (poems). *Temps de mémoire.* Paris: Présence Africaine, 1967.

————. "Valeurs de la négritude et convergence." *Présence Africaine,* no. 68 (1968), pp. 149–52.

Diop, Alioune (Senegal). "Niam n'goura ou les raisons d'être de *Présence Africaine.*" Introduction to the first issue, November–December 1947.

————. *Diversité et unité de l'Afrique noire.* Lyon, XXXVe session des Semaines Sociales de France. Paris: Editions Gabalda, 1948.

————. "Colonialisme et nationalisme culturel." *Présence Africaine,* no. 4 (1955), pp. 5–15.

————. "Political and cultural solidarity in Africa." *Présence Africaine* (English edition) 13, no. 41 (1962):65–71.

————. "Remarks on African personality and negritude." With comments by E. Mphahlele, Ben Enwonwu, and T. O. Oruwariye; followed by discussion. In *Pan Africanism Reconsidered,* edited by the American Society of African Culture, pp. 337–57. Berkeley and Los Angeles: University of California Press, 1962.

Diop, Birago (Senegal, stories). *Les contes d'Amadou Koumba.* Paris: Fasquelle, 1947. Translated by Dorothy Blair. *Tales of Amadou Koumba.* London: Oxford University Press, 1966.

———— (stories). *Les nouveaux contes d'Amadou Koumba.* Preface by L. S. Senghor. Paris: Présence Africaine, 1958.

———— (poems). *Leurres et lueurs.* Paris: Présence Africaine, 1960.

———— (stories). *Contes et lavanes.* Paris: Présence Africaine, 1963.

———— (stories). *Contes choisis.* London: Oxford University Press, 1967.

Diop, Cheik Anta (Senegal). *Nations nègres et culture.* Paris: Présence Africaine, 1954.

————. *L'unité culturelle de l'Afrique noire.* Paris: Présence Africaine, 1959. Translated *The Cultural Unity of Negro Africa.* Paris: Présence Africaine, 1970.

————. *L'Afrique noire pré-coloniale.* Paris: Présence Africaine, 1960.

Diop, David (Senegal). "Contribution au débat sur la poésie nationale." *Présence Africaine,* no. 6 (1956), pp. 113–15.

———— (poems). *Coups de Pilon.* Paris: Présence Africaine, 1956.

————. "Ten Poems." In French and English; new translations by Paulette J. Trout and Ellen Conroy Kennedy. *Journal of the New African Literature and the Arts,* no. 5/6 (Spring and Fall 1968), pp. 28–49.

Dogbeh-David, G. Richard (Dahomey, poems). *Les eaux du mono.* Vire, Calvados, France: Société Lec-Vire, 1963.

———— (poem). *Rives mortelles.* Porto Novo, India: Editions Silva, 1964.

———— (poems). *Cap liberté.* Yaoundé: Editions C.L.E., 1969.

Epanya Yondo, Elolongué (Cameroon, poems). *Kamerun! Kamerun!* Paris: Présence Africaine, 1960.

Evembe, François-Borgia Marie (Cameroon, novel). *Sur la terre passant.* Paris: Présence Africaine, 1966.

Fall, Malik (Senegal, poems). *Reliefs.* Introduction by L. S. Senghor. Paris: Présence Africaine, 1964.

———— (novel). *La plaie.* Paris: A. Michel, 1967.

Fanon, Frantz (Martinique, essays). *Peau noire, masques blancs.* Paris: Seuil, 1952. Translated by Charles Lam Markmann. *Black Skin, White Masks.* New York: Grove Press, 1967.

———— (essays). *L'an V de la révolution algérienne.* Rev. ed. Paris: Maspero, 1959. Translated by Haakon Chevalier. *Studies in a Dying Colonialism.* New York: Monthly Review Press, 1965. Translated by Haakon Chevalier. *A Dying Colonialism.* New York: Grove Press, 1967.

———— (essays). *Les damnés de la terre.* Paris: Maspero, 1961. Translated by Constance Farrington. *The Wretched of the Earth.* New York: Grove Press, 1965.

———— (essays). *Pour la révolution africaine.* Cahiers libres 53–54. Paris: Maspero, 1964. Translated by Haakon Chevalier. *Toward the African Revolution.* New York: Grove Press, 1966.

Fodeba, Keita (Guinea, poems). *Poèmes africaines.* Paris: Seghers, 1950.

———— (poems). *Le maître d'école, suivi de minuit.* Paris: Seghers, 1952.

———— (poems, stories). *Aube africaine.* Paris: Seghers, 1965.

Glissant, Edouard (Martinique, poems). *Un champ d'îles.* Paris: Editions Instance, 1953.

———— (poems). *La terre inquiète.* Paris: Editions du Dragon, 1955.

———— (poems). *Les Indes; poème de l'une et l'autre terre.* Paris: Falaize, 1956.

———— (essays). *Soleil de la conscience.* Paris: Falaize, 1956.

———— (novel). *La lézarde.* Paris: Seuil, 1958. Translated by Frances Frenaye. *The Ripening.* New York: G. Braziller, 1959.

———— (poems). *Le sel noir.* Paris: Seuil, 1960.

———— (play). *Monsieur Toussaint.* Paris: Seuil, 1961.

———— (poems). *Le sang rivé.* Paris: Présence Africaine, 1961.

———— (essay). *L'intention poétique.* Paris: Seuil, 1969.

Gologo, Mamadou (Mali, poems). *Mon cœur est un volcan.* Moscow: Editions en Langues Etrangères, 1961.

———— (autobiographical novel). *Le rescapé de l'Ethylos.* Paris: Présence Africaine, 1963.

Gratiant, Gilbert (Martinique, poems). *Poèmes en vers faux.* Paris: "La Caravelle," 1931.

———— (poems). *Cinq poèmes martiniquais en créole.* Hauteville, Ain, France: N.p., 1935.

———— (poems). *An moué.* Fort-de-France, Martinique: Imprimerie Populaire, 1950.

———— (poems). *Fab' compè zicaque* (poèmes en créole). Fort-de-France: Imprimerie Courrier des Antilles, 1950; Editions des Horizons Caraïbes, 1958.

————. "D'une poésie martiniquaise, dite nationale." *Présence Africaine,* December–January 1956.

———— (poems and essay). *Une fille majeure. Credo des sang-mêlé (ou: Je veux chanter la France).* Paris: Editions L. Soulanges, 1961.

———— (poems). *Sel et sargasses; poésies lyriques de France et des Antilles.* Paris: Le Livre Ouvert, [1963].

Hazoumé, Paul (Dahomey, essay). *Le pacte du sang au Dahomey.* Paris: Institut d'Ethnologie, 1937.

———— (novel). *Doguicimi.* Paris: Larose, 1938.

Joachim, Paulin (Dahomey, poems). *Un nègre raconte.* Paris: Editions des Poètes, 1954.

———— (poems). *Anti-grâce.* Paris: Présence Africaine, 1967.

Juminer, Bertène (Guiana, novel). *Les bâtards.* Introduction by Aimé Césaire. Paris: Présence Africaine, 1961.

———— (novel). *Au seuil d'un nouveau cri.* Paris: Présence Africaine, 1963.

————. *La revanche de Bozambo.* Paris: Présence Africaine, 1968.

Ka, Abdou Anta (Senegal, play). *La fille des dieux; légende dramatique.* Traits d'Union, no. 10 (Dakar, 1955).

Kane, Cheikh Hamidou (Senegal, novel). *L'aventure ambiguë.* Paris: Julliard, 1962. Translated by Katherine Woods. *Ambiguous Adventure.* New York: Walker, 1963; Collier, 1969.

Kanie, Anoma (Ivory Coast, poems). *Les eaux du comoé.* Paris: Editions du Miroir, 1951.

Khaly, Nene (Guinea, poems). *Lagunes.* La Courneuve, France: Edition de l'Académie Populaire de Littérature et Poésie, 1956.

Koné, Maurice (Ivory Coast, poems). *La guirlande des verbes.* Paris: Grassin, 1961.

———— (poems). *Au bout du petit matin.* Bordeaux: Germain, 1962.

———— (novel). *Le jeune homme de Bouaké.* Paris: Grassin, 1963.

———— (poems). *Au seuil du crépuscule.* Rodez, France: Subervie, 1965.

Kourouma, Ahmadou (Ivory Coast, novel). *Les soleils des indépendances.* Presses de l'Université de Montréal, 1968; Paris: Seuil, 1970.

Laye, Camara (Guinea, autobiography). *L'enfant noir.* Paris: Plon, 1954. Translated by James Kirkup. *The African Child.* London: Collier Macmillan (Fontana Books), 1959. Translated by James Kirkup. *The Dark Child.* New York: Farrar, Straus & Giroux, 1969.

———— (novel). *Le regard du roi.* Paris: Plon, 1955. Translated by James Kirkup. *The Radiance of the King.* New York: Macmillan, 1971.

———— (novel). *Dramouss.* Paris: Plon, 1966. Translated by James Kirkup. *A Dream of Africa.* New York: Macmillan, 1971.

Loba, Aké (Ivory Coast, novel). *Kocoumbo: l'étudiant noir.* Paris: Flammarion, 1960.

———— (novel). *Les fils de Kouretcha.* Nivelles, Belgium: Editions de la Francité, 1970.

Malonga, Jean (Congo Republic, novel). *Cœur d'Aryenne.* Présence africaine 16: trois écrivains noirs. Paris: Présence Africaine, 1954.

———— (story). *La légende de m'pfoumou ma Mazono.* Paris: Editions Africaines, 1954.

Maran, René (Martinique, poems). *La maison de bonheur.* Paris: Editions du Beffroi, 1909.

———— (poems). *La vie intérieure.* Paris: Editions du Beffroi, 1912.

———— (novel). *Batouala—véritable roman nègre*. Paris: A. Michel, 1921. Translated by Adele Szold Seltzer. New York: Seltzer, 1922. Translated by Alvah C. Bessie. New York: Limited Editions Club, 1932. Translated by Barbara Beck and Alexandre Mboukou. *Batouala: A True Black Novel*. Washington, D.C.: Black Orpheus Press, 1972.

———— (poems). *Le visage calme; stances*. Paris: Editions du Monde Nouveau, 1922.

———— (stories). *Le petit roi de chimérie*. Paris: A. Michel, 1924.

———— (novel). *Djouma, chien de brousse*. Paris: A. Michel, 1927.

———— (novel). *Le cœur serré*. Paris: A. Michel, 1931.

———— (novel). *Le livre de la brousse*. Paris: A. Michel, 1934.

———— (poems). *Les belles images*. Bordeaux: Delmas, 1935.

———— (novel). *Bêtes de la brousse*. Paris: A. Michel, 1941.

———— (stories). *Mbala, l'éléphant*. Paris: Editions Arc-en-Ciel, 1943.

———— (stories). *Peines de cœur*. Paris: S.P.L.E., 1944.

———— (novel). *Un homme pareil aux autres*. Paris: Editions Arc-en-Ciel, 1947.

———— (novel). *Bacouya, le cynocéphale*. Paris: A. Michel, 1953.

———— (poems). *Le livre de souvenir*. Paris: Présence Africaine, 1958.

Matip, Benjamin (Cameroon, novel). *Afrique, nous t'ignorons!* Paris: Lacoste, 1956.

———— (stories). *A la belle étoile: contes et nouvelles d'Afrique*. Paris: Présence Africaine, 1962.

———— (play). "Le jugement suprême" (act III, scene III). *Abbia*, no. 2 (1963), pp. 64–66.

————. *Afrique, ma patrie*. Yaoundé: Editions Peuple Africain, n.d.

Maunick, Edouard J. (Mauritius, poems). *Ces oiseaux du sang*. Mauritius: Regent Press, 1954.

———— (poems). *Les manèges de la mer*. Paris: Présence Africaine, 1964.

———— (poems). *Mascaret ou le livre de la mer et de la mort*. Paris: Présence Africaine, 1966.

———— (poem). *Fusillez-moi*. Paris: Présence Africaine, 1970.

Niane, Djibril Tamsir (Mali, novel). *Soundjata ou l'épopée mandingue*. Paris: Présence Africaine, 1966. Translated by G. D. Pickett. *Soundiata; An Epic of Old Mali*. London: Longmans Green & Co., 1965.

Niger, Paul (Guadeloupe, poems). *Initiation*. Paris: Seghers, 1954.

———— (novel). *Les puissants*. Paris: Editions du Scorpion, 1958.

———— (novel). *Les grenouilles du Mont Kimbo*. Ecrivains noirs du monde. Lausanne, Switzerland: Editions de la Cité, 1964.

Nokan, Charles (Ivory Coast, novel with poems). *Le soleil noir point*. Paris: Présence Africaine, 1959.

———— (novel with poems). *Violent était le vent*. Paris: Présence Africaine, 1966.

———— (play). *Les malheurs de Tchakô*. Honfleur and Paris: P. J. Oswald, 1968.

————. *Abraha Pokou; ou une grande africaine* (play). Suivi de *La voix grave d'óphimoi* (poem). Honfleur: P. J. Oswald, 1970.

Nyunai, Jean-Paul (Cameroon, poems). *La nuit de ma vie*. Paris: Debresse, 1961.

———— (poems). *Piments sang. Poèmes 1953*. Paris: Debresse, 1963.

———— (poems). *Chansons pour Ngo-lima*. Poètes de notre temps, 314. Monte Carlo: Regain, 1964.

Nzouankeu, Jacques Mariel (Cameroon, play). "L'agent spécial." *Abbia*, no. 5 (1964), pp. 146–65; no. 7, pp. 160–68.

———— (stories). *Le souffle des ancêtres.* Yaoundé: Editions C.L.E., 1965.

Ouologuem, Yambo (Mali, novel). *Le devoir de violence.* Paris: Seuil, 1968. Translated by Ralph Manheim. *Bound to Violence.* New York: Harcourt Brace Jovanovich, 1971.

————. *Lettre à la France nègre.* Paris: Nalis, 1968.

Ousmane, Sembene (Senegal, novel). *Le docker noir.* Paris: Editions Debresse, 1956.

———— (novel). *O pays, mon beau peuple!* Paris: Amoit-Dumont, 1957.

———— (novel). *Les bouts de bois de Dieu.* Paris: Livre Contemporain, 1960. Translated by Francis Price. *God's Bits of Wood.* New York: Doubleday, 1962, 1970; London: Heinemann Educational Books (African Writers Series), 1970.

———— (stories). *Voltaique.* Paris: Présence Africaine, 1962.

———— (novel). *L'harmattan.* Paris: Présence Africaine, 1964.

———— (novellas). *"Vehi-ciosane ou Blanche-genèse" et "Le mandat."* Paris: Présence Africaine, 1965.

Oyono, Ferdinand (Cameroon, novel). *Une vie de boy.* Paris: Julliard, 1956. Translated by John Reed. *Houseboy.* London: Heinemann Educational Books (African Writers Series), 1969. Translated by John Reed. *Boy!* New York: Macmillan, 1970.

———— (novel). *Le vieux nègre et la médaille.* Paris: Julliard, 1956. Translated by John Reed. *The Old Man and the Medal.* London: Heinemann Educational Books (African Writers Series), 1970. New York: Macmillan, 1971.

———— (novel). *Chemin d'Europe.* Paris: Julliard, 1961.

Oyônô-Mbia, Guillaume (Cameroon, play). *Trois prétendants, un mari.* Yaoundé: Editions C.L.E., 1964. Translated in *"Three Suitors: One Husband" and "Until Further Notice."* London: Methuen, 1968.

———— (stories). *Chroniques de Mvoutessi.* Vols. 1, 2, and 3. Yaoundé: Editions C.L.E., 1971.

Philombe, René (Cameroon, stories). *La passerelle divine.* Yaoundé: Association des Poètes et Ecrivains Camerounais, 1959.

———— (autobiographical stories). *Lettres de ma cambuse.* Yaoundé: Editions Abbia avec la collaboration de C.L.E., 1964; Editions C.L.E., 1970.

———— (novel). *Sola, ma chérie.* Yaoundé: Editions Abbia avec la collaboration de C.L.E., 1966; Editions C.L.E., 1969.

———— (novel). *Un sorcier blanc à Zangali.* Yaoundé: Editions C.L.E., 1969.

———— (stories). *Histoires queue-de-chat.* Yaoundé: Editions C.L.E., 1971.

Price-Mars, Jean (Haiti, ethnographic essay). *Ainsi parla l'oncle.* Compiègne, France: Bibliothèque Haïtienne, 1928.

————. "Survivances africaines et dynamisme de la culture noire outre-Atlantique." *Présence Africaine,* June–November 1956.

———— (essay). *De Saint-Domingue à Haïti.* Essay on culture, the arts, and literature. Paris: Présence Africaine, 1959.

————. *Silhouettes de nègres et de négrophiles.* Paris: Présence Africaine, 1960.

Rabearivelo, Jean-Joseph (Malagasy Republic, poems). *La coupe de cendres.* Tananarive, Malagasy Republic: Pitot de la Beaujardière, 1924.

———— (poems). *Sylves*. Tananarive: Imprimerie de l'Imerina, 1927.

———— (poems). *Volumes*. Tananarive: Imprimerie de l'Imerina, 1928.

———— (poems). *Poèmes: Presque-songes, Traduit de la nuit.* Tananarive: Amis de Rabearivelo, Imprimerie Officielle, 1960. First editions 1934 and 1935.

———— (play). *Imaitsoanala, fille d'oiseau.* Tananarive: Imprimerie Officielle, 1935.

———— (poems). *Chants pour Abéone*. Tananarive: Liva, 1959.

————. *Twenty-four Poems*. Translated by Gerald Moore and Ulli Beier. Ibadan, Nigeria: Mbari, 1962. Distributed by Northwestern University Press.

Rabemananjara, Jacques (Malagasy Republic, poems). *Aux confins de la nuit, sur les marches du soir*. Paris: Editions Ophrys, 1942.

———— (play). *Les dieux malgaches*. Paris: Editions Ophrys, 1947.

———— (poems). *Antsa*. Paris: Présence Africaine, 1956.

———— (poem). *Lamba*. Paris: Présence Africaine, 1956.

———— (poems). *Rites millénaires*. Paris: Seghers, 1956.

———— (play). *Les boutriers de l'aurore*. Paris: Présence Africaine, 1957.

———— (essays). *Nationalisme et problèmes malgaches*. Paris: Présence Africaine, 1958.

———— (poems). *Antidote*. Paris: Présence Africaine, 1961.

———— (play). *Agapes des dieux—Tritriva*. Paris: Présence Africaine, 1962.

Ranaïvo, Flavien (Malagasy Republic, poems). *L'ombre et le vent*. Tananarive: Imprimerie Officielle, 1947.

———— (poems). *Mes chansons de toujours*. Paris: Privately published by the author, 1955.

———— (poems). *Le retour au bercail*. Tananarive: Imprimerie Nationale, 1962.

————. "Poésie malgache: les 'Hain-Teny.' " *Culture Française* 15 (1966):23–25.

Roumain, Jacques (Haiti, stories). *La proie et l'ombre*. Port-au-Prince: Editions "La Presse," 1930.

———— (novel). *Les fantoches*. Port-au-Prince: Imprimerie de l'Etat, 1931.

———— (novel). *La montagne ensorcelée*. Port-au-Prince: Imprimerie E. Chassaing, 1931.

———— (novel). *Gouverneurs de la rosée*. Port-au-Prince: Imprimerie de l'Etat, 1944. Translated by Langston Hughes and Mercer Cook. *Masters of the Dew*. New York: Reynal and Hitchcock, 1947; Collier Macmillan, 1971.

———— (poems). *Bois d'ébène*. Port-au-Prince: Imprimerie Deschamps, 1945. Translated by Sidney Shapiro. *Ebony Wood*. New York: Interworld Press, 1972.

Sadji, Abdoulaye (Senegal, novel). *Nini, mulâtresse du Sénégal*. Présence africaine 16: trois écrivains noirs. Paris: Présence Africaine, 1954.

———— (novel). *Maïmouna*. Paris: Présence Africaine, 1958.

———— (story). *Tounka*. Paris: Présence Africaine, 1965.

Sainville, Léonard (Martinique, biography). *Victor Schoelcher, 1804–1893*. Paris: Fasquelle, 1950.

———— (novel). *Dominique, esclave nègre*. Paris: Fasquelle, 1951.

———— (novel). *Au fond du bourg*. Lausanne, Switzerland: Editions de la Cité, 1964.

Seid, Joseph Brahim (Tchad, stories). *Au Tchad sous les étoiles*. Paris: Présence Africaine, 1962.

———— (autobiographical story). *Un enfant du Tchad.* Dossiers littéraires de l'Afrique actuelle. Paris: SAGEREP—L'Afrique Actuelle, 1967.

Sembene, Ousmane. Also known as Sembene Ousmane. See entry.

Sengat-Kuo, François (Cameroon, poems). *Fleurs de latérite.* Poètes de notre temps 89. Monte Carlo: Editions Regain, 1954. Reissued with *Heures rouges.* Yaoundé: Editions C.L.E., 1971.

———— (poems). *Colliers de Cauris.* Suivi d'une étude de Thomas Melone. Paris: Présence Africaine, 1970.

Senghor, Léopold Sédar (Senegal). "Ce que l'homme noir apporte." In *L'homme de couleur.* Paris: Plon, 1939.

———— (poems). *Chants d'ombre.* Paris: Seuil, 1945. Reissued *Chants d'ombre suivis de hosties noires.* Paris: Seuil, 1956.

———— (poems). *Hosties noires.* Paris: Seuil, 1948.

———— (poems). *Chants pour Naëtt.* Paris: Seghers, 1949.

————. *"L'apport de la poésie nègre."* In *Temoignages sur la poésie du demi-siècle.* Brussels: Maison du Poète, 1953.

————. *"Langage et poésie négro-africaine."* In *Poésie et langage.* Brussels: Maison du Poète, 1954.

————. "Suite du débat autour des conditions d'une poésie nationale chez les peuples noirs; réponse." *Présence Africaine,* no. 5 (1955–56), pp. 79–83.

————. "African-Negro aesthetics." *Diogenes,* no. 16 (1956), p. 33.

————. "L'esprit de la civilisation ou les lois de la culture négro-africaine." *Présence Africaine,* nos. 8, 9, 10 (1956), pp. 51–65.

———— (poems). *Ethiopiques.* Paris: Seuil, 1956.

————. "Eléments constructifs d'une civilisation d'inspiration négro-africaine." *Présence Africaine,* no. 24–25 (1959), pp. 249–79.

———— (poems). *Nocturnes.* Paris: Seuil, 1962. Translated by John Reed and Clive Wake. Introduction by Paulette J. Trout. New York: Third Press, 1971.

————. "On Negrohood: Psychology of the African-Negro." *Diogenes,* no. 37 (1962), p. 2.

————. "Latinité et négritude." *Présence Africaine,* no. 52 (1964), pp. 5–13.

———— (articles and lectures). *Liberté 1. Négritude et humanisme.* Paris: Seuil, 1964.

———— (essays). *On African Socialism.* Translated and introduced by Mercer Cook. New York: Praeger, 1964.

————. *Poèmes* ("Chants d'ombre," "Hosties noires," "Ethiopiques," "Nocturnes," and others). Paris: Seuil, 1964.

————. *Selected Poems.* Translated and introduced by John Reed and Clive Wake. New York: Atheneum, 1964.

————. *Prose and Poetry.* Edited and translated by John Reed and Clive Wake. London: Oxford University Press, 1965.

———— (poetry, addresses, lectures, essays). *The Mission of the Poet.* Art and Civilisation Series 1. Port of Spain, Trinidad: University of the West Indies Extra Mural Department, 1966.

————. "Négritude et arabisme. La dialectique négro-arabe." *Présence Africaine,* no. 61 (1967), pp. 94–102. Translated in *Afro-Asian Writings* 1 (1968): 20–25.

———— (address). "De la négritude." In *Anthologie des écrivains congolais,* pp.

12–24. Kinshasa, Zaïre; S.N.E.C., Ministère de la Culture, 1969.

———. *Liberté 2. Nation et voie africaine du socialisme.* Paris: Seuil, 1971.

———. "Problématique de la négritude." *Présence Africaine,* no. 78 (1971), pp. 3–26.

Sissoko, Fily-Dabo (Mali, poems). *Crayons et portraits.* Mulhouse, France: Imprimerie Union, 1953.

——— (poems). *Harmakhis; poèmes du terroir africain.* Paris: Editions La Tour du Guet, 1956.

——— (novel). *La passion de Djeiné.* Paris: Editions La Tour du Guet, 1956.

——— (novel). *La savane rouge.* Avignon: Presses Universelles, 1962.

——— (poems). *Poèmes de l'Afrique noire. Feux de brousse, Harmakhis, Fleurs et chardons.* Paris: Debresse, 1963.

Socé, Ousmane (Senegal, novel). *Karim, roman sénégalais.* Paris: Editions F. Sorlot, 1935; Nouvelles Editions Latines, 1948.

——— (novel). *Mirages de Paris.* Paris: Nouvelles Editions Latines, 1937. Reissued with *Rythmes du khalam* (poems), 1955.

——— (stories). *Contes et légendes d'Afrique noire.* Paris: Nouvelles Editions Latines, 1962.

——— (poems). *Rythmes du khalam.* Paris: Nouvelles Editions Latines, 1963.

Tardon, René (Haiti, novel). *Starkenfirst.* Paris: Fasquelle, 1947.

Tati-Loutard, Jean-Baptiste (Congo Republic, poems). *Poèmes de la mer.* Yaoundé: Editions C.L.E., 1968.

——— (poems). *Les racines congolaises.* Honfleur, France: P. J. Oswald, 1968.

Tchibamba, Lomani P. (Congo Republic, novel). *Ngando.* Brussels: G. A. Deny, 1948.

Tevoedjre, A. (Dahomey). *L'Afrique révoltée.* Paris: Présence Africaine, 1958.

Tirolien, Guy (Guadeloupe, poems). *Balles d'or.* Paris: Présence Africaine, 1960.

Traoré, Mamadou (Guinea, poems) [pseud., Ray Autra; also known as Amadou Traoré]. *Mamadou Traoré—Ray Autra: Vers la liberté.* Peking, China: Librairie du Nouveau Monde, 1961.

U Tam'si, Tchicaya (Congo Republic, poems). *Le mauvais sang.* Paris: Caractères, 1955. *Le mauvais sang, suivi de Feu de brousse et A triche-coeur.* Paris: P. J. Oswald, 1970.

——— (poems). *Feu de brousse.* Paris: Caractères, 1957. Translated by Sangodare Akanji. *Brush Fire.* Ibadan, Nigeria: Mbari, 1964. Distributed by Northwestern University Press.

——— (poems). *A triche-coeur.* Paris: Caractères, 1958; P. J. Oswald, 1960.

——— (poems). *Epitomé.* Introduction by L. S. Senghor. Tunis, Tunisia: Société Nationale d'Edition et de Diffusion, 1962.

——— (poems). *Le ventre.* Paris: Présence Africaine, 1965.

——— (stories). *Légendes africaines.* Paris: Seghers, 1968.

——— (poems). *"Arc musical"* and *"Epitomé."* Introduction by Claire Créa. Paris: P. J. Oswald, 1970.

———. *Selected Poems.* Translated and introduced by Gerald Moore. London: Heinemann Educational Books (African Writers Series), 1970. Distributed by Humanities Press, New York.

———. "Engagement et tradition." *L'Afrique Littéraire et Artistique* 3 (1970): 46–47.

Zobel, Joseph (Martinique, novel). *Diab'la.* Paris: Nouvelles Editions Latines, 1946.

––––– (novel). *La rue Cases-Nègres.* Paris: Editions J.Froissart, 1950.

––––– (stories). *Le soleil partagé.* Paris: Présence Africaine, 1964.

––––– (poems). *Incantation pour un retour au pays natal.* N.p.: 1965.

Criticism and Commentary

Abanda Ndengue, Jean-Marie. *De la négritude au négrisme: essais polyphoniques.* Yaoundé: Editions C.L.E.; New York: Africana Publishing Corp, 1970.

Actes du colloque sur la littérature africaine d'expression française, Dakar, 26–29 mars 1963. Publications de la Faculté des Lettres et Sciences Humaines. Langues et Littératures 14. Dakar, Senegal: l'Université, 1965.

Africa Seen by American Negro Scholars. Paris: Présence Africaine, 1958, 2d ed., 1963. Distributed by American Society of African Culture, New York.

Aguessy, Honorat. "La phase de la négritude." *Présence Africaine,* no. 80 (1971), pp. 33–49.

Allen, Samuel W. "La négritude et ses rapports avec le noir américain." *Présence Africaine,* no. 27–28 (1959), pp. 16–26.

––––––. "Negritude: Agreement and disagreement." In *Pan-Africanism Reconsidered.* Berkeley: University of California Press for American Society of African Culture, 1962.

Anozie, Sunday O. *Sociologie du roman africain: réalisme, structure et détermination dans le roman moderne ouest-africain.* Paris: Aubier-Montaigne, 1970.

Antoine, Jacques. "From Toussaint L'Ouverture to Jacques Roumain." In *An Introduction to Haiti,* edited by Mercer Cook. Washington D.C.: Pan-American Union, 1951.

Badday, Moncef S. "Ahmadou Kourouma, écrivain africain." *L'Afrique Littéraire et Artistique* 10 (1970): 2–8.

Baldwin, James. "Princes and powers." Essay in *Nobody Knows My Name.* New York: Dial, 1961.

Bastide, Roger. "Variations on negritude." *Présence Africaine* (English edition) 8, no. 36 (1961):83–91.

Beier, Ulli. "The theme of the ancestors in Senghor's poetry." *Black Orpheus* 5 (1959):15–17.

––––––. "The novel in the French Cameroons." *Black Orpheus* 2 (1958):42–52.

––––––, ed. *Introduction to African Literature: An anthology of Critical Writings from "Black Orpheus."* Evanston, Ill.: Northwestern University Press, 1967.

Benoit, Jean. "Tchikaya U Tam'si, poète du Congo-Brazzaville: celui qui conte le pays." *L'Afrique Littéraire et Artistique* 8 (1969):28–30.

Berrian, Albert, and Long, Richard, eds. *Negritude: Essays and Studies.* Hampton, Va.: Hampton Institute Press, 1967.

Blair, Dorothy S. "Negritude: I." *Contrast* (Capetown) 1, no. 2 (1961):38–48.

––––––. "Negritude: II." *Contrast* 1, no. 3 (1961):38–49.

––––––. "Whither negritude?" *The Classic* (Johannesburg) 2, no. 2 (1966):5–10.

Boucquey-de Schutter, Eliane. *Jacques Rabemananjara.* Poètes d'Aujourd'hui 112. Paris: Seghers, 1964.

Boudry, Robert. *J.-J. Rabearivelo et la mort.* Paris: Présence Africaine, 1958.

Brench, A. C. *The Novelists' Inheritance in French Africa.* London: Oxford University Press, 1967.

———. *Writing in French from Senegal to Cameroon.* London: Oxford University Press, 1967.

———. "Camara Laye: Idealist and mystic." *African Literature Today,* no. 2 (1969), pp. 11–31.

Cartey, Wilfred. *Whispers from a Continent: The Literature of Contemporary Black Africa.* New York: Random House, 1969.

———. *Black Images.* New York: Teachers College Press, 1970.

———. *Palaver: Modern African Writing.* Camden, N.Y.: Thomas Nelson, 1970.

Chapman, Abraham. "The black aesthetic and the African continuum." *Pan-African Journal* 4, no. 4 (1971):397–406.

Colin, Roland. *Littérature africaine d'hier et de demain.* Paris: A.D.E.C., 1965.

Colloque: fonction et signification de l'art nègre dans la vie du peuple et pour le peuple. Contributions of the Festival Conference in Dakar, 1966. Paris: Présence Africaine, 1967.

"La conférence de Bandoeng." *Présence Africaine,* August–September 1955.

"Le 1er congrès international des écrivains et artistes noirs." *Présence Africaine,* nos. 8, 9, 10 (June–November 1956).

"Deuxième congrès des écrivains et artistes noirs," vol. 1: L'unité des cultures négro-africaines. *Présence Africaine,* nos. 24–25 (February–May 1959).

"Contributions au 1er congrès des écrivains et artistes noirs." *Présence Africaine,* no. hors-serie, 14, 15 (June–September 1957).

Cook, Mercer. *Five French Negro Authors.* Washington, D.C.: Associated Publishers, 1943.

———. "Trends in recent Haitian literature." *Journal of Negro History* 32 (April 1947):220–31.

———. "The poetry of Léon Damas." *African Forum* 2, no. 4 (Spring 1967): 129–32.

———. "African voices of protest." In *The Militant Black Writer in Africa and the United States,* by Mercer Cook and Stephen E. Henderson. Madison: University of Wisconsin Press, 1969.

Cornevin, Robert. "Bernard Dadié: seigneur des lettres ivoiriennes." *Culture Française* 19, no. 3 (1970):3–7.

Corzani, Jack. "Guadeloupe et Martinique: la difficile voie de la négritude et de l'antillanité." *Présence Africaine,* no. 76 (1970), pp. 16–42.

Coulthard, G. R. *Race and Color in Caribbean Literature.* London: Oxford University Press, 1962.

Damas, Léon G. "Price-Mars, the father of Haitianism." *Présence Africaine* (English edition), 4–5, nos. 32–33, (1960):204–18.

Davidson, Basil. "Alioune's Africa." To Alioune Diop on 20th anniversary of *Présence Africaine. West Africa* 6 (January 1968):14.

Debré, François. "Douce et triste: la poésie malgache." *L'Afrique Littéraire et Artistique* 3 (1969): 3–9.

de Leusse, Hubert. *Léopold Sédar Senghor, l'africain.* Paris: Hatier, 1967.

Depestre, René. "Jean Price-Mars et le mythe de l'orphée noir ou les aventures de la négritude." *L'Homme et la Société* 7 (1968):171–81.

Desanti, Dominique. "Le conflit des cultures et 'L'aventure ambiguë.' " *African*

Arts/Arts d'Afrique 1, no. 4 (1968):60–61, 106, 109–10.

Diakhaté, Lamine. "The myth in Senegalese folk poetry" (and its presence in the work of L. S. Senghor and Birago Diop). *Présence Africaine* (English edition) 11, no. 39 (1961):13–31.

Donat, Claude. "Bernard Binlin Dadié." *L'Afrique Littéraire et Artistique* 5 (1969):16–21.

Dorsinville, Roger. "Jean Price-Mars." *L'Afrique Littéraire et Artistique* 4 (1969): 58–61.

Dubuis, Olivier. *L'Afrique reconnue: panorama de la littérature négro-africaine.* Kinshasa, Zaïre: Editions L.E.C.O., 1969.

Durozoi, Gérard. "Importance et signification de la statuaire traditionelle dans la poésie de L. S. Senghor." *L'Afrique Littéraire et Artistique* 8 (1969):41–45.

Eboussi, E. " 'L'aventure ambiguë' by Cheikh Hamidou Kane." *Abbia* no. 6 (1964), pp. 207–13.

Edwards, Paul, and Ramchaud, Kenneth. "An African sentimentalist: Camara Laye's *The African Child.*" *African Literature Today*, no. 4 (1970), pp. 37–53.

Esprit Créateur (Lawrence, Kansas) 10, no. 3 (1970). Issue devoted to African literature in French.

Etienne, Gérard Vergniaud. *Essai sur la négritude.* Port-au-Prince: Imprimerie Panorama, 1963.

Etudes Littéraires (Quebec, Canada) 6, no. 1 (April 1973). Issue devoted to Aimé Césaire.

Feuser, Willfried. "Negritude—the third phase." *The New African* 5, no. 3 (1966):63–64.

Flather, Newell. "Negritude: Words and deeds—impressions of the Dakar Festival." *Africa Report* 11, no. 5 (May 1966):57–60.

Fraisse, André. "René Maran et les traditions africaines." *L'Afrique Littéraire et Artistique* 11 (1970):48–52.

Franklin, Albert. "La négritude: réalité ou mystification? Réflexions sur 'Orphée noir.' " In *Les étudiants noirs parlent*, pp. 287–303. Cahier spécial (no. 14) of *Présence Africaine.* Paris, 1953.

Gaillard, Roger. *L'univers romanesque de Jacques Roumain.* Port-au-Prince: Imprimerie Deschamps, 1965.

Gérard, Albert. "Historical origins and literary destiny of negritude." *Diogenes*, no. 48 (1964), pp. 14–37.

———. "Stèle pour un poète malgache." (J.-J. Rabearivelo) *Académie Royale des Sciences d'Outre-Mer, Bulletin des Séances* 2 (1968):181–89.

Gleason, Judith Illsley. *This Africa: Novels by West Africans in English and French.* Evanston, Ill.: Northwestern University Press, 1965.

———. "An introduction to the poetry of Aimé Césaire." *Negro Digest* 19, no. 3 (1970):12–19, 64–65.

Godin, Jean-Cléo. "Les soleils des indépendances." *Etudes Françaises* 4 (1968): 208–15.

"The great battle of negritude, Algiers '69." (issue on Algiers Festival 1969). *Journal of the New African Literature and the Arts*, no. 7–8 (1969), pp. 58–89.

Grunebaum, G. E. von. *French African Literature: Some Cultural Implications.* The Hague: Mouton, 1964.

Guberina, Petar. "Structure de la poésie noire d'expression française." *Présence*

Africaine, no. 5 (December 1955–January 1956), pp. 52–78.

Guibert, Armand. *Léopold Sédar Senghor*. Poètes d'Aujourd'hui 82. Paris: Seghers, 1962.

———. *Léopold Sédar Senghor, l'homme et l'œuvre*. Paris: Présence Africaine, 1962.

Hoffman, F. "French Negro poetry." *Yale French Studies* 21 (1958):60–71.

"Hommage à Jacques Stéphen Alexis." *Europe*, no. 501 (January 1971), pp. 1–80.

Hommage à René Maran (essays). Paris: Présence Africaine, 1965.

Ilboudo, G. "Modern literature in French-speaking Africa" (an article translated from the French which first appeared in *Afrique Nouvelle*). *Ibadan* 19 (1964):28–31.

Irele, Abiola. "A defence of negritude: A propos of Black Orpheus by Jean-Paul Sartre." *Transition* 3, no. 13 (1964):9–11.

———. "Negritude and black cultural nationalism." *Journal of Modern African Studies* 3, no. 3 (1965):321–48.

———. "Negritude—literature and ideology." *Journal of Modern African Studies* 3, no. 4 (1965):499–526.

———. "Post-colonial negritude: The political plays of Aimé Césaire." *West Africa* 27 (January 1968):100–1.

Ita, J.M. "A propos" (on Léon Damas's *Black-Label*). *African Arts/Arts d'Afrique* 3, no. 2 (1970): 84–87.

Jahn, Janheinz. "Aimé Césaire." *Black Orpheus* 2 (1958):32–36.

———. *Muntu: The New African Culture*. Dusseldorf, 1958. Translated from German by Marjorie Green. New York: Grove, 1961.

———. "Camara Laye—an interpretation." *Black Orpheus* 6 (1959):35–38.

———. *Neo-African Literature: A History of Black Writing*. Translated from German by Oliver Coburn and Ursula Lehrburger. New York: Grove, 1968.

James, Emile. "Sembene Ousmane: 'Je n'utilise pas de vedettes: ça coûte trop cher" (interview). *Jeune Afrique* 28 (July 1969):40–41.

James-Sarreau, P. "Le poème de l'anhistorique" (on "L'intention poetique" by Edouard Glissant). *Présence Africaine*, no. 74 (1970), pp. 210–16.

Jeanpierre, W. A. "Negritude, its development and significance." *Présence Africaine* (English edition) 11, no. 39 (1961):32–49.

Joachim, Paulin. "African literature: French-speaking Africa." *Africa Report* 8, no. 3 (1963):11–12.

———. "French-speaking Africa's poètes-militants." In *A Handbook of African Affairs*, edited by H. Kitchen. New York: Praeger, 1964.

Jones, E. A. "Contemporary French Negro poets." *Phylon* 12 (1951):20–28.

Juin, Hubert. *Aimé Césaire, poète noir*. Paris: Présence Africaine, 1956.

Kane, Mohamadou. *Les contes d'Amadou Koumba, du conte traditionnel au conte moderne d'expression française*. Publications de la Faculté des Lettres et Sciences Humaines. Langues et Littératures 16. Dakar, Senegal: l'Université, 1968.

Kennedy, Ellen Conroy. "*Les écrivains noirs de langue française*, by Lilyan Kesteloot." *Comparative Literature Studies* (University of Maryland) 3, no. 4 (December 1966):472–75.

———. "A literary postscript on the Dakar Festival." *African Forum* 3, no. 1 (Summer 1967):54–58.

————. "Aimé Césaire: Interview with an architect of negritude." *Negro Digest* 17 (May 1968):53–61.

————. "Léon Damas: *Pigments* and the Colonized Personality." *Black World* 21, no. 3 (January 1972):4–12.

Kennedy, Ellen, and Trout, Paulette J. "The roots of negritude." *Africa Report* 2, no. 5 (May 1966):61–62.

Kesteloot, Lilyan. *Aimé Césaire.* Poètes d'Aujourd'hui 85. Paris: Seghers, 1962.

————. *Négritude et situation coloniale.* Yaoundé: Editions C.L.E., 1968. Translated by Alexandre Mboukou. *Intellectual Origins of the African Revolution.* Washington, D.C.: Black Orpheus Press, 1972.

Koshland, Miriam. "The poetry of Madagascar." *Africa South* 4 (1960):114–19.

————. "Development of the literary idiom in Haiti." *Black Orpheus* 7 (1961): 46–56.

Lagneau, L. (Kesteloot). "The negritude of L. S. Senghor." *Présence Africaine* (English edition) 11, no. 39 (1961):124–39.

Larson, Charles R. "Laye's unfulfilled African dream." *Books Abroad* 33 (1969):209–11.

————. *The Emergence of African Fiction.* Bloomington: Indiana University Press, 1971.

Lindfors, Bernth. "Anti-negritude in Algiers." *Africa Today* 17, no. 1 (1970): 5–7.

Long, Richard A. "Negritude." *Negro Digest* 18, no. 7 (1969):11–15, 57–59.

Makouta-Mboukou, Jean Pierre. *Introduction à la littérature noire.* Yaoundé: Editions C.L.E., 1970.

Makward, Edris. "Tchikaya U Tam'si interviewed." *Cultural Events in Africa* 60 (1969):i–iv.

Mara, P. " 'Déracialiser' la négritude." *Jeune Afrique* 12 (May 1970):58–60.

Markovitz, Irving Leonard. *Léopold Sédar Senghor and the Politics of Negritude.* New York: Atheneum, 1969.

Marteau, P. "On Aimé Césaire's 'Cadastre.' " *Présence Africaine* (English edition) 9, no. 37 (1961):45–55.

Mbelelo Ya Mpiku, J. "From one mystification to another: 'Négritude' and 'négraille' in 'Le devoir de violence.' " *Review of National Literatures* 2, no. 2 (1971):124–47.

Melone, Thomas. *De la négritude dans la littérature négro-africaine.* Paris: Présence Africaine, 1962.

————. "The theme of negritude and its literary problems." *Présence Africaine* (English edition) 20, no. 48 (1963):166–81.

————. "New voices of African poetry in French." *African Forum* 1, no. 4 (1966):65–74.

————. "Mongo Beti, l'homme et le destin." *Présence Africaine*, no. 70 (1969), pp. 120–36.

————. "Mongo Beti et la terre camerounaise." *Annales de la Faculté des Lettres et Sciences Humaines* (Yaoundé) 1, no. 1 (1969): 87–118.

Mercier, Roger. *Les écrivains négro-africains d'expression française.* Tendances no. 37, Vie culturelle 58. Paris: "Tendances," 1965.

————. "Un conteur d'Afrique noire: Birago Diop." *Etudes Françaises* 4 (1968): 119–49.

———. "L'imagination dans la poésie de Léopold Sédar Senghor." *Literature East and West* 12 (1968):35–55.

Mercier, Roger, and Battestini, Monique and Simon. Série Littérature Africaine (Classiques du Monde). Paris: Fernand Nathan. Booklets of selected writings with biographical and critical notes on the following authors: no. 1, *Cheikh Hamidou Kane, écrivain sénégalais,* 1964; no. 2, *Camara Laye, écrivain guinéen,* 1964; no. 3, *Léopold Sédar Senghor, poète sénégalais,* 1964; no. 4, *Olympe Bhêly-Quénum, écrivain dahoméen,* 1964; no. 5, *Mongo Beti, écrivain camerounais,* 1964; no. 6, *Birago Diop, écrivain sénégalais,* 1964; no. 7, *Bernard Dadié, écrivain ivorien,* 1964; no. 8, *Ferdinand Oyono, écrivain camerounais,* 1964; no. 9, *Aimé Césaire, écrivain martiniquais,* 1967; no. 10, *Seydou Badian, écrivain malien* (Simon and Monique Battestini only), 1968.

Mezu, S. Okechukwu. *Léopold Sédar Senghor et la défense et illustration de la civilisation noire.* Paris: Didier, 1968.

———. "Yambo Ouologuem interviewed." *Cultural Events in Africa* 61 (1969): i–iv.

Milcent, Ernest, and Sordet, Monique. *Léopold Sédar Senghor et la naissance de l'Afrique moderne.* Paris: Seghers, 1969.

Mohome, Paulus M. "Negritude: Evaluation and elaboration." *Présence Africaine,* no. 68 (1968), pp. 122–40.

Moore, Gerald. *Seven African Writers.* London: Oxford University Press, 1962; reprinted with extended bibliography, 1966.

———. "Ferdinand Oyono and the colonial tragicomedy." *Présence Africaine* (English edition) 18, no. 46 (1963):61–73.

———. "Towards realism in French African writing." *Journal of Modern African Studies* 1, no. 1 (1963):61–73.

———, ed. *African Literature and the Universities.* Ibadan, Nigeria: University Press for the Congress for Cultural Freedom, 1965.

———. "Literary protest in French-speaking Africa." In *Protest and Power in Black Africa,* edited by Robert Rotberg and Ali Mazrui. New York: Oxford University Press, 1970.

———. "The debate on existence in African literature." *Présence Africaine,* no. 81 (1972), pp. 18–48.

Mounikou, Mathieu. "Jean Malonga, écrivain congolais." *Présence Africaine,* no. 73 (1970), pp. 172–88.

Mphahlele, Ezekiel. *The African Image.* New York: Praeger, 1962.

Mpondo, Simon. "David Mandessi Diop: An assessment." *Présence Africaine,* no. 75 (1970), pp. 97–107.

Ngande, C. "Cameroon poetry." *Abbia* no. 2 (1963), pp. 136–37.

Obenga, Théophile. "Methode et conception historiques de Cheik Anta Diop." *Présence Africaine,* no. 74 (1970), pp. 3–28.

Oddon, Marcel. "Les tragédies de la décolonisation: Aimé Césaire et Edouard Glissant." In *Le théâtre moderne II: depuis la deuxième guerre mondiale,* edited by Jean Jacquot. Paris: Editions du Centre National de la Recherche Scientifique, 1967.

Pageard, Robert. *Littérature négro-africaine: le mouvement contemporain dans l'Afrique noire d'expression française.* Paris: Livre Africain, 1966.

Palmer, Eustace. "Mongo Beti's *Mission to Kala:* An interpretation." *African Literature Today,* no. 3 (1969), pp. 27–43.

――――. *An Introduction to the African Novel.* New York: Africana Publishing Corp., 1972.

Patient, S. "Sur les voies d'une poésie guyanaise." *Présence Africaine,* June–July 1958.

Paulhan, Jean. *Les hain-tenys.* Paris: Gallimard, 1939.

Pieterse, Cosmo. "G. Oyônô Mbia, Camerounian playwright, interviewed." *Cultural Events in Africa* 55 (1969):i–iv.

Pieterse, Cosmo, and Munro, Donald, eds. *Protest and Conflict in African Literature.* New York: Africana Publishing Corp., 1969.

Piquion, René. *Négritude.* Port-au-Prince: Imprimerie de l'Etat, 1961.

――――. *Les 'Trois Grands' de la négritude.* Port-au-Prince: Imprimerie Deschamps, 1964.

――――. *Manuel de négritude.* Port-au-Prince: Imprimerie Deschamps, 1966.

Quillateau, C. *Bernard Binlin Dadié.* Paris: Présence Africaine, 1967.

Ravelonansy, G. *J. Rabemananjara.* Textes commentés. Série Littérature Malgache 3 (Classiques du Monde). Paris: Fernand Nathan, 1970.

Razafintsambaina, G. "Tribute to Rabearivelo." *Présence Africaine* (English edition) 8, no. 36 (1961):120–26.

Sainville, Léonard. "Le roman et ses responsabilités." *Présence Africaine* nos. 27–28 (1959):37–50.

Sartre, Jean-Paul. "Orphée noir." In *Anthologie de la nouvelle poésie nègre et malgache de langue française.* Edited by L. S. Senghor. Paris: Presses Universitaires, 1948. Translated by John MacCombie. "Black Orpheus." *Massachusetts Review* 6, no. 1 (1964–65):13.

Scheub, Harold. "Symbolism in Camara Laye's *Le regard du roi.*" *Ba Shiru* (University of Wisconsin), Spring 1970, pp. 24–36.

――――. "Soukeîna and Isabelle—Senghor and the West." In *Africa and the West: Intellectual Responses to European Culture,* edited by Philip Curtin. Madison: University of Wisconsin Press, 1972.

Schipper de Leeuw, Mineke. "Noirs et blancs dans l'œuvre d'Aimé Césaire." *Présence Africaine,* no. 72 (1969), pp. 124–47.

"Second session of the International Congress of Africanists, Dakar, 11–20 December 1967." *Présence Africaine,* no. 67 (1968), pp. 201–33.

Sellin, Eric. "Aimé Césaire and the legacy of surrealism." *Kentucky Romance Quarterly,* Supplement 13 (1967):71–79.

――――. "Alienation in the novels of Camara Laye." *Pan-African Journal* 4, no. 4 (1971):455–72.

Senghor, L. S. "Flavien Ranaivo, poète malgache." *Présence Africaine,* no. 2 (1948), pp. 333–36.

Senghor, L. S. *et al.* "Procès à la négritude." *L'Afrique Littéraire et Artistique* 7 (1969):14–29.

"Senghor relance la négritude" (conference in Cameroon). *Jeune Afrique* 23 (1970):54–56.

Shelton, Austin J. "The black mystique: Reactionary extremes in 'negritude.' " *African Affairs* 63, no. 251 (1964):115–28.

Simon, Erica. "Negritude and cultural problems of contemporary Africa." *Présence Africaine* (English edition) 19, no. 47 (1963):122–46.

Skurnik, W. A. E. Letter to the editor (on negritude, followed by "Editor's note" by Joseph O. O. Okpaku). *Journal of the New African Literature and the Arts*, no. 2 (1966), pp. 6–9.

Snyder, Emile. "The problem of negritude in modern French poetry." *Comparative Literature Studies*, Special Advance Issue (1963), pp. 101–13.

"Something *new* out of Africa?" (on Ouologuem's *Le devoir de violence*). *Times Literary Supplement*, no. 3,662 (May 5, 1972), p. 525.

Soyinka, Wole. "And after the narcissist?" *African Forum* 1, no. 4 (1966):53–64.

"Speaking to Senghor" (interview). *West Africa* 10 (October 1970):1181–82.

Theobalds, T. "La littérature engagée et l'écrivain antillais." *Présence Africaine* nos. 27–28 (1959):27–36.

Thomas, Louis Vincent. *Les idéologies négro-africaines d'aujourd'hui.* Publications de la Faculté des Lettres et Sciences Humaines. Philosophie et Sciences Sociales 1. Dakar, Senegal: l'Université, 1965.

———. "Senghor and negritude." *Présence Africaine* (English edition) 26, no. 54 (1965):102–33.

Towa, Marcien. "Aimé Césaire, prophète de la revolution des peuples noirs." *Abbia*, no. 21 (1969), pp. 49–57.

———. " 'Les pur-sang' (négritude Césairienne et surréalisme)." *Abbia*, no. 23 (1969), pp. 71–82.

———. *Léopold Sédar Senghor: négritude ou servitude.* Yaoundé: Editions C.L.E., 1971.

Traoré, Bakary. *Le théâtre négro-africain et ses fonctions sociales.* Paris: Présence Africaine, 1958. Translated by Dapo Adelugba. *The Black African Theatre and Its Social Functions.* Nigeria: Ibadan University Press, 1972.

Trouillot, Henock. *L'itinéraire d'Aimé Césaire.* Port-au-Prince: Imprimerie des Antilles, 1968.

Trout, Paulette. "Recent developments in French African literature." *Journal of the New African Literature and the Arts*, no. 4 (1967), pp. 16–17.

Trout, Paulette, and Kennedy, Ellen. "David Diop: Negritude's angry young man." *Journal of the New African Literature and the Arts*, no. 5/6 (Spring and Fall 1968), pp. 76–78.

Valette, Jean. *Flavien Ranaïvo.* Poèmes commentés. Série Littérature Malgache 2. (Classiques du Monde). Paris: Fernand Nathan, 1968.

Valette, Paul. *J.-J. Rabearivelo.* Poèmes commentés. Série Littérature Malgache 1 (Classiques du Monde). Paris: Fernand Nathan, 1967.

Wake, Clive. "Cultural conflict in the writings of Senghor and Mongo Beti." *Books Abroad* 37 (1963):156–57.

———. "The personal and the public: African poetry in French." *Review of National Literatures* 2, no. 2 (1971):104–23.

Wake, Clive, and Reed, John. "Modern Malagasy literature in French." *Books Abroad* 38 (1964):14–19.

Wauthier, Claude. *The Literature and Thought of Modern Africa: A Survey.* Translated from the French by Shirley Kay. New York: Praeger, 1967.

Williams, Sandra. "La renaissance de la tragédie dans l'œuvre dramatique d'Aimé Césaire." *Présence Africaine*, no. 76 (1970), pp. 63–81.

Periodicals

Abbia: Cameroon Cultural Review, B.P. 808, Yaoundé, Cameroon. Published by the Minister of National Education. Appears irregularly, several issues a year. Articles in English and French.

African Arts / Arts d'Afrique: Published by African Studies Center, University of California, Los Angeles. Four issues a year, one primarily devoted to literature. Articles in English and French.

African Forum (1965–68): Published by American Society of African Culture, 401 Broadway, New York, 10013. Quarterly review, several issues devoted primarily to literature.

African Literature Today: Editor Eldred Jones, Heinemann Educational Books, 48 Charles St., London W.1. Formerly two issues yearly, now annual hardcover edition. Critical and interpretive articles.

L'Afrique Actuelle: Published by Olympe Bhêly-Quénum, 23, rue Barbet-de-Jouy, Paris 2e. Monthly, bilingual.

L'Afrique Littéraire et Artistique: Published by Société africaine d'édition, 32, rue de l'Echiquier, Paris 10e. Bimonthly. Creative work and criticism.

Black Orpheus: Editor Abiola Irele, Mbari Publications, Ibadan, Nigeria. African and Afro-American literature.

Black World (formerly *Negro Digest*): Editor Hoyt Fuller, Johnson Publications, Chicago, Illinois. Monthly.

Jeune Afrique: Published by a group of North Africans, 51, Avenue des Ternes, Paris 17e. Weekly.

Journal of the New African Literature and the Arts: Editor Joseph Okpaku, P.O. Box 4392, Stanford University, Stanford, California. Biannual. Literature and criticism in English and French.

Légitime Défense: Single issue only, Paris, June 1932.

Présence Africaine: Cultural Review of the Negro World: Editor Alioune Diop, 25 bis, rue des Ecoles, Paris 5e. Quarterly. A French language journal which for a time printed separate English and French editions of each issue, now has articles in French and English.

Présence Francophone: Published by the University of Sherbrooke, Sherbrooke, Quebec. Biannual. All French literatures. Started in 1970.

Research in African Literature: Editor Bernth Lindfors, African and Afro-American Research Institute, University of Texas, Austin. Biannual.

La Revue du Monde Noir (1931–32). Edited by Dr. Léo Sajous and Mlle Paulette Nardal. Editions de la revue mondiale, 45, rue Jacob, Paris 6e. Six issues appeared. Articles were printed in French and English in double columns. Copies may be found in the Moorland-Spingarn Research Center, Howard University Library, Washington, D.C.

Tropiques: Cultural review. Fort-de-France, Martinique. Nos. 1–9, April 1941–October 1943.

Supplementary Bibliography of Black Literature in French, 1974–1990

David Westley

Bibliographies

Baratte-Eno-Belinga, Thérèse et al. *Bibliographie des auteurs africains de langue française*. Paris: F. Nathan, 1979.

Bjornson, Richard. *A Bibliography of Cameroonian Literature*. Austin: University of Texas Press, 1986.

Déjeux, Jean. *Dictionnaire des auteurs maghrebins de langue française*. Paris: Karthala, 1984.

Hale, Thomas Albert. *Les écrits d'Aimé Césaire: bibliographie commentée*. Montréal: Presses de l'Université de Montréal, 1978.

Kom, Ambroise, ed. *Dictionnaire des oeuvres littéraires négro-africaines de langue française: des origines à 1978*. Sherbrooke, Quebec: Naaman, 1983.

Mekkawi, Mohamed. *African and Caribbean Literature in French: Guide to Research and Documentation*. Washington, D.C.: Howard University Libraries, 1989.

Merand, Patrick and Dabla, Sewanou. *Guide de littérature africaine (de langage français)*. Paris: L'Harmattan, 1979.

Michael, Colette Verger. *Negritude: An Annotated Bibliography*. West Cornwall, CT: Locust Hill Press, 1988.

Philombre, René. *Le livre camerounais et ses auteurs: une contribution à l'histoire littéraire du Cameroun avec notice bio-bibliographique*. Yaoundé: Editions Sémences Africaines, 1977.

Saint-Andre-Utudjian, Elaine. *A Bibliography of West African Life and Literature*. Waltham, MA: African Studies Association, 1977.

Zell, Hans. *A New Reader's Guide to African Literature*. 2d ed. New York: Africana Publishing, 1983.

Anthologies

Anon. *Anthologie de la littérature gabonaise*. Québec: Beauchemin, 1978.

Anon. *Littératures de langue française hors de France: anthologie didactique*. Paris: Federation Internationale des Professeurs de Français, 1976?

Anon. *Le Sénégal écrit: anthologie de la littérature sénégalaise contemporaine*. Tubingen: Horst Erdmann Verlag, 1975.

Chevrier, Jacques, ed. *Anthologie africaine*. Paris: Hatier, 1981.

Condé, Maryse. *La Poésie antillaise*. Paris: Nathan, 1977,

Corzani, Jack. *La Littérature des antilles-guyane françaises*. Six vols. Fort-de-France: Librairie Desormeaux, 1978.

Dogbe, Yves-Emmanuel. *Anthologie de la poésie togolaise*. Lomé: Akpagnon, 1980.

Kayo, Patrice. *Anthologie de la poésie camerounaise*. Yaoundé: Le Flameau, 1977.

Kennedy, Ellen Conroy, ed. *The Negritude Poets: An Anthology of Translations from the French*. New York: Viking, 1975; Thunder's Mouth, 1990.

Mamonsono, Léopold P. *La nouvelle génération de poètes congolais; anthologie de la jeune poésie congolaise*. Brazzaville: Hêros dans l'Ombre, 1978.

Masegabio, Nzanzu Mabele ma Diko. *Le Zaire écrit: anthologie de la poésie zairoise en langue française*. Kinshasa: Dombi Diffusion, 1977.

Ministère de l'Education et des Affaires Culturelles de l'Ile Maurice. *Mauritius Anthology of Literature in the African Context*, 1977. Prose, poetry, drama, most in French, some in English.

Mudimbe, V.Y. *Poésie vivante*, 2 vols. Kinshasa: Mont Noir, 1972.

Ndiaye, Papa G. *Manuel de littéraire africaine*. Paris: Présence Africaine, 1978.

Rombaut, Marc. *La nouvelle poésie négro-africaine d'expression française: anthologie*. Paris: Seghers, 1976.

Rancourt, Jacques. *Poètes et poèmes contemporains: Afriqué-Antilles*. Paris: St. Germaine, 1981.

Senghor, Léopold Sédar. *Anthologie de la nouvelle poésie nègre et malgache de langue française, précédée de Orphée Noir par Jean Paul Sartre*. 4th ed. Paris: Presses Universitaires de France, 1977.

Tati-Loutard, Jean Baptiste. *Anthologie de la littérature congolaise d'expression française*. Yaoundé: CLE, 1977.

Waters, Harold A. *Black Theater in French: A Guide*. Sherbrooke: Editions Naaman, 1978.

Works

Abega, Sévérin Cécile. *Les Bimanes: sept nouvelles due village et du quartier*. Dakar: Nouvelles Editions Africaine, 1982.

―――――. *Entre terre et ciel*. Nouvelles Editions Africaine/EDICEF, 1987.

Almeida, Fernando d'(Benin, poems). *Au seuil de l'exil*. Paris: P.J. Oswald, 1976.

Bâ, Amadou Hampaté (Mali, novel). *The Fortunes of Wangrin*. Translation of *l'Etrange destin de Wangrin* by Aina Pavollini Taylor with an introduction by Abiola Irele. Ibadan: New Horn Press, 1987.

―――――― (oral tradition). *Njeddo Dewal: mère de la calamité: conte initiatique peul*. Abidjan: Les nouvelles éditions africaine, 1985.

Bâ, Mariama (Senegal, novel). *So Long a Letter*. Translation of *Si longue lettre* (1980) by Modupe Bode-Thomas. Ibadan: New Horn, 1981.

Badian, Seydou (Mali, novel). *Le Sang des masques*. Paris: Robert Laffont, 1976.

―――――― (novel). *Noces Sacrées: les Dieux de Kouroulamini*. Paris: Présence Africaine, 1977.

Bandaman, Maurice (Côte d'Ivoire, stories). *Une femme pour une médaille: nouvelles*. Abidjan: CNOU/CEDA, 1987.

Bebey, Françis (Cameroon, novel). *The Ashanti Doll*. Translation of *La poupée ashanti* (1873) by Joyce Hutchinson. London: Rex Collings, 1977.

———— (poems). *Nouvelle saison des fruits*. Dakar: Nouvelles Editions Africaine, 1980.

———— (stories in verse). *Concert pour un vieux masque*. Paris: La Harmattan, 1980.

Beti, Mongo (Cameroon, novel). *Perpetua and the Habit of Unhappiness*. Translation of *Perpétue ou l'habitude du malheur* (1974) by John Reed and Clive Wake. London: HEB, 1978 (AWS 181).

————. *Remember Reuben*. Translation of *Remember Reuben* (sic) (1974) by Gerald Moore. London: HEB, 1980 (AWS 214).

————. *La ruine presque cocasse d'un polichinelle*. Paris: Peuples Noirs, 1979.

Bhély-Quenem, Olympé (Benin, novel). *L'Unité*. Paris: Présence Africaine, 1979.

———— (novel). *Snares Without Ending*. Translation of *Un piège sans fin* (1960) by Dorothy Blair. Washington, D.C.: Three Continents, 1981.

———— (stories). *Les mille haches*. Paris: Hatier, 1981.

Césaire, Aimé (Martinique). "An Introduction to American Negro Poetry." Translation from *Tropiques*, the 1940s literary magazine of Martinique, and with an introduction by Ellen Conroy Kennedy; also "Aimé Césaire on Sterling Brown," *The Black Collegian*, April/May, 1981, pp. 143–45.

————. *Moi laminaire—poèmes*. Paris: Seuil, 1982.

————. *The Collected Poetry*. Translated by Clayton Eshleman and Annette Smith. Berkeley: University of California Press, 1983.

————. *Non-Vicious Circle: Twenty Poems of Aimé Césaire*. Translated by Gregson Davis. Stanford: Stanford University Press, 1984.

————. *Lost Body*. Translation of *Corps perdu* (1950) by Clayton Eshleman and Annette Smith. New York: G. Braziller, 1986.

————. "Césaire Welcomes Senghor to Martinique." Translated by Ellen Conroy Kennedy, *Delos*, 4, (1988): 76–79 (illustrated w/photos).

————. "Cahier d'un retour au pays natal." Passages from the *Cahier* presented bilingually with "Notes on a Return to the Native Land." Translated by Ellen Conroy Kennedy, *Delos*, 4, (1988): 82–93, glossary and acknowledgements, 102–3.

Dadié, Bernard Binlin (Côte d'Ivoire, play). *Papassidi, maître-esroc: comédie*. Dakar: Nouvelles Editions Africaine, 1975.

————. *Opinions d'un nègre: aphorisms, 1934–1946*. Dakar: Club Afrique Loisirs, 1979.

———— (play). *Commandant Taureault et ses nègres*. Abidjan: CEDA, 1980.

———— (play). *Les voix dans le vent: (tragédie)*. Abidjan: Nouvelles Editions Africaine, 1982.

————. *The City Where No One Dies*. Translation of *La ville où nul ne meurt* (1968) by Janis Mayes. Description of Rome. 1986.

Depestre, René (Haiti, poems). *Poète à Cuba*. Paris: Pierre Jean Oswald, 1976.

———— (poems). *En état de poésie*. N.p. Editeurs Français Réunis, 1980.

Diabaté, Massa Makan (Mali, epic). *L'aigle et l'épervier ou la geste de Sunjata*. Paris: Pierre Jean Oswald, 1975.

———— (novel). *Le lieutenant de Kouta*. Paris: Hatier, 1979.

———— (novel). *Le coiffeur de Kouta*. Paris: Hatier, 1980.

————. *Comme un piqûre de guepe*. Paris: Présence Africaine, 1981.

Diop, Birago (Sénégal, autobiography). *La plume raboutée: mémoires I*. Paris: Présence Africaine, 1978.

———— (play). *L'os de Mor Lam*. Dakar: Nouvelles Editions Africaine, 1976.

———— (stories). *Contes d'Awa*. Dakar: Nouvelles Editions Africaine, 1977.

Dogbe, Yves-Emmanuel (Togo, poems). *Le Devin Amor*. N.p. 1982.

———— (poems). *Morne soliloque*. Paris: Editions Akpagnon, 1982.

Glissant, Edouard (Martinique). *The Ripening*. Translation of *La lézarde* (1958) by Michael Dash. London: Heinemann, 1985.

————. *Caribbean Discourse: Selected Essays*. Ed. A. J. Arnold and Kandioura Drame. Translation of *Discours antillais* and introduction by J. Michael Dash. London: Heinemann Educational Books, 1989.

Hazoumé, Paul (Benin, novel). *Doguicimi*. Paris: G.P. Maisonneuve et Larose, 1978. (Originally published 1935).

Kourouma, Amadou (Côte d'Ivoire). *Les Soleils des Indépendances*. Paris: Seuil, 1970, (Presses Univ. Montréal, 1968).

Lopes, Henri (Congo, novel). *La nouvelle romance*. Yaoundé: Editions CLE, 1976.

———— (novel). *The Laughing Cry: An African Cock and Bull Story*. Translation of *Pleurer-rire* by Gerald Moore. New York: Readers International, 1987.

————. *Tribaliks: Contemporary Congolese Stories*. Translation of *Tribaliques* (1971) by Andrea Leskes. London: Heinemann, 1987.

Ndao, Cheik Aliou (Sénégal, stories). *Le Marabout de la sécheresse: nouvelles*. Dakar: Nouvelles Editions Africaine, 1979.

————. *Excellence, vos épouses!* Nouvelles Editions Africaine, 1983.

————. *Du Sang pour un trône ou Gouye Ndiouli un dimanche*. Paris: L'Harmattan, 1983.

————. *Un bouquet d'épines pour elle*. Paris: Présence Africaine, 1988.

Niane, Djibril Tamsir (Guinea, stories). *Méry: nouvelles*. Dakar: Nouvelles Editions Africaine, 1975.

———— (plays). *Sikasso ou la dernière citadelle suivi de Chaka*. Paris: P.J. Oswald, 1976.

Ousmane, Sembene (Senegal, novel). *Xala*. Translated by Clive Wake. London: Heinemann Educational Books, 1976 (African Writers Series 175).

———— (novel). *Le dernier de l'empire*. Paris: L'Harmattan, 1979.

————. *Le Mandat, précédé de Vehi Ciosane*. Paris: Présence Africaine, 1979.

———— (novel). *L'Harmattan I: Référendum*. Paris: Présence Africaine, 1984.

———— (novel). *Black Docker*. Translation of *Le Docker noir* by Ros Schwarz. London: Heinemann, 1987.

————. *Nüwam suivi de Taaw*. Paris: Présence Africaine, 1987.

Philombe, René. *Choc anti choc: romans en poèmes: écrits de prison, 1961*. Yaoundé: Editions Sémences Africaines, 1978.

————. *Tales from Cameroon*. Translated by Richard Bjornson. Washington. D.C.: Three Continents, 1984.

Pliya, Jean (Bénin, stories). *Le Chimpanzé amoureux: Nouvelles*. Paris: Saint-Paul, 1977.

————. *La fille têtue*. Nouvelles Editions Africaine, 1982.

————. *Les Tresseurs de corde*. Paris: Hatier/CEDA, 1987.

Rabéarivelo, Jean Joseph (Malagasy). *Translations From the Night: Selected Poems of Jean-Joseph Rabéarivelo*. Translated by John Reed and Clive Wake, 1975.

Sassine, Williams (Guinée). *Wirriyamu*. Paris: Présence Africaine, 1976.

———. *Le Jeune homme de sable*. Paris: Présence Africaine, 1979.

———. *Le Zéheros n'est pas n'importe qui*. Paris: Présence Africaine, 1985.

Senghor, Léopold Sédar. *Poèmes*. Paris: Seuil, 1974.

———. *Selected Poems/Poésies choisies*. Translated by Craig Williamson. Bilingual edition. London: Rex Collings, 1976.

———. *Elégies majeures suivi de Dialogue sur la poésie francophone*. Paris: Seuil, 1979.

———. "Chant pour signare" and "Song for Signatare," "A l'appel de la race de Saba" (extract) and "The Call of the Race of Saba," "Le Retour de l'Enfant Prodigue (fin)" and "Return of the Prodigal Son (conclusion)," "Chant de l'inité" and "Song of the Initiate," four poems presented bilingually and translated by Ellen Conroy Kennedy, in *Delos*, 4 (1988).

Tadjo, Véronique (Côte d'Ivoire). *Latérite*. Paris: Hatier/ACCT: Abidjan: CEDA/CEDAF, 1984.

———. *A Vol d'oiseau*. Paris: Nathan, 1986.

Tansi, Sony Labou (Congo, novel). *La vie et demie*. Paris: Seuil, 1979.

——— (novel). *L'état honteux*. Paris: Seuil, 1981.

——— (plays). *La parenthèse de sang*: suivi de *Je soussigné cardiaque*. Paris: Hatier, 1981.

——— (novel). *Les sept solitudes de Lorsa Lopez*. Paris: Seuil, 1985.

——— (play). *Parentheses of Blood*. Translation of *Parenthèse de sang* (1981) by Lorraine Alexander Veach. New York: Ubu Repertory Theater Publications, 1985.

——— (novel). *The Antipeople*. Translation of *Anti-peuple* by J.A. Underwood. London: M. Boyars, 1988.

——— (novel). *Les yeux du volcan*. Paris: Seuil, 1988.

Tchicaya, Tam'si U. (Congo, novel). *The Madman and the Medusa*. Translation of *Méduses, ou Les orties de mer* (1982) by Sonja Haussmann Smith and William Jay Smith. Charlottesville: University Press of Virginia, 1989.

——— (stories). *La Main sèche: nouvelles*. Paris: Laffont, 1980.

———. *Les Méduses ou Les orties de mer*. Paris: Albin Michel, 1982.

———. *Les Phalènes*. Paris: Albin Michel, 1984.

———. *Ces fruits si doux de l'arbre à pain*. Paris: Seghers, 1987.

Zadi, Bernard Zaourou (Côte d'Ivoire). *Fer de lance*. Paris: Oswald/Diff. L'Harmattan, 1975.

———. *Césarienne* suivi de *Aube prochaine* et *Chants du souvenir*. Paris: CEDA, 1984.

———. *La Tignasse* suivi de *Kitamandjo* Paris: CEDA, 1984.

Criticism and Commentary

Anise, Ladun. "The African Redefined: The Problems of Collective Black Identity," *Issue* IV, 4(1974): 26–32.

Arnold, James A. *Modernism and Negritude: The Poetry and Poetics of Aimé Césaire.* Cambridge: Harvard University Press, 1981.

Battestini, Simon P.X. "Le Président Mobutu: complémentaire entre négritude et authenticité." *Bingo* 288 (1977): 57.

Bekombo, Manga. "Idéologies et langages: Le problème de l'identité nègre." *Négritude: Traditions et développement.* Brussels: Editions Complexes, 1978, pp. 27–38.

Béti, Mongo. "Identité et tradition," *Négritude: Traditions et développement.* Brussels: Editions Complexes, 1978, pp. 9–26.

Blair, Dorothy S. "L. S. Senghor, poète bicontinental: La Présence francaise dans l'oeuvre de l'apôtre de la négritude." *L'Information littéraire* 28 (1976): 160–69.

———. *Senegalese Literature: A Critical History.* Boston: Twayne, 1984.

Blérard, Philippe Alain. "La Négritude et le problème colonial (1932–1946)" *Révue algérienne scientifique, juridique, économique et politique* 15,1 (1979): 95–135.

Bouygues, Claude. "Négrisme, négritude, et après . . . analyse-entretien avec René Depestre." *Contemporary French Civilization* 10,1 (1986): 78–98.

Carrilho, Maria. "La Négritude: Dalla letteratura la potere." *La Critica sociologica* 29(1974): 169–74.

Chalendar, Pierrette and Gérard Chalendar. "Les Chemins de la négritude." *Esprit* 2 (1978): 75–89.

Chappelle, Yvonne Reed. "The Negritude Process." *Black World* 24 (1974–1975): 72–76.

Chenet, Gérard. "La Négritude à l'ère symbiotique." *Ethiopiques* 10 (1977): 81–95.

Chikwendu, E.E. "The Relevance of Negritude to Senegalese Development." *Umoja: A Scholarly Journal of Black Studies* 1,3 (1977) 43–58.

Cismaru, Alfred. "Negritude in Selected Works of Aimé Césaire." *Renascence* 26 (1974): 105–11.

Climo, Martha Louise. "L. S. Senghor's Imagery: An Expression of His Negritude." *Hommage à Léopold Sédar Senghor: Homme de culture.* Paris: Présence Africaine, 1976, pp. 241–77.

Condé, Maryse. *Cahier d'un retour au pays natal. Césaire: Analyse Critique.* Paris: Hatier, 1978.

———. "Propos sur l'identité culturelle." *Négritude: Traditions et developpement.* Brussels: Editions Complexes, 1978, pp. 77–84.

Dailly, Christopher. "Léon Damas et la Négro-Renaissance." *Présence africaine* 112 (1979): 163–80.

Damas, Léon. "La Négritude en question." *Jeune afrique* 532 (1971): 57–59, 61, 63, 65.

Depestre, René. *Bonjour et adieu à la négritude.* Paris: Editions Robert Laffont, 1980.

Dieng, Amady Aly. "Négritude et civilisations." *Hegel, Marx, Engels et les problèmes de l'afrique noire.* Dakar: Sankore, 1978, pp. 105–8.

Dogbé, Yves-Emmanuel. *Négritude, culture, et civilisation. Essai sur la finalité des faits sociaux.* Le Mée-sur-Seine: Akpagnon, 1980.

Fabre, Michel. "René Maran, the New Negro and Négritude." *Phylon* 36, 3 (1975): 340–51.

Feuser, Willfried. "Afro-American Literature and Negritude." *Comparative Literature* 28 (1976): 289–308.

———. "Léon Damas: A Critical Exploration." *Hommage à Léon-Gontron Damas*. Paris: Présence Africaine, 1979, pp. 401–23.

Filostrat, Christian. "La Négritude et la 'Conscience raciale et révolution sociale' d'Aimé Césaire." *Présence francophone* 21 (1980): 119–30.

Gassama, Makhily. "Léopold Sédar Senghor et la Négritude." *Ecriture française dans le monde* 2, 3–4 (1980): 15–20.

Gonzales-Cruz, Luis F. "Nature and the Black Reality in Three Caribbean Poets: A New Look at the Concept of Negritude." *Perspectives on Contemporary Literature* 5 (1979): 138–45.

Hale, Thomas. *Scribe, Griot and Novelist: Narrative Interpreters of the Songhay Empire*. Gainesville: University of Florida Press, 1990.

Hoffman, Léon-François. "L'Etranger dans le roman haitien." *L'Esprit créateur* 17, 2 (1977): 83–102.

Hommage à Léon-Gontran Damas. Paris: Présence Africaine, 1978.

Irele, Abiola. "Negritude—Philosophy of African Being." *Nigeria Magazine* 122 (1977): 1–13.

Kennedy, Ellen Conroy. "Léon Damas: A Reminiscence" in *Léon Gontran Damas 1912–1978: Founder of Negritude: A Memorial Casebook*, ed. Daniel L. Racine. Washington, D.C.: University Press of America, 1979.

———. "Césaire and Senghor: When 'Parallel Lives' Converged." *Delos*, 4 (1988). College Park, Maryland: The Center for World Literature.

———. "The Poet-Statesman of Senegal," a review of *Black, French and African: A Life of Léopold Sédar Senghor* by Janet G. Vaillant, The Washington *Post*, 11 November 1990, pp. 1 and 14.

Kesteloot, Lilyan (oral tradition). *L'Eclat de l'étoile. Récit initiatique peul*. With Alpha Sow Hampate and Christiane Seydou. Paris: Colin, 1974.

——— (oral tradition). *La Prise de dionkoli: Episode de l'épopée bambara*. Performed by Sissoko Kabine. Edited by Gerard Dumestre with J.B. Traore. Paris: Colin, 1975.

———. "La Négritude et son expression littéraire" in *L'Encyclopédie larousse*. Paris, 1975.

———. "Problématique de la littérature orale (avec un exemple sur un mythe de Ngor)." *Afrique littéraire* 54–55 (1977).

——— (oral tradition). *Le Mythe et l'histoire dans la fondation de l'empire de Ségou*. Bulletin IFAN, 1978. Bilingual text.

———. *Aimé Césaire*. Paris: Séghers, 1979.

———. *Le mythe et l'histoire dans la formation de l'empire de Ségou* avec un récit de Tairou Bembera transcrit par Mamadou Boidié Diarra. Dakar: IFAN 1980, pp. 578–618.

———. *Comprende le Cahier d'un Rétour au pays natal d'Aimé Césaire*. Issy les Moulineaux: *Classiques africaines*, 1982.

———. *Comprendre les poèmes de Léopold Sédar Senghor*. Issy les Moulineaux: *Classiques africaines*, 1986.

————. *Contes et mythes du Sénégal.* Paris: IFAN, 1987.

————. "Les Epopées de l'afrique de l'ouest" in *Dictionnaire des poétiques* Paris: Flammarion, 1988.

————. "L'Epopée." *Dictionnaire des littératures comparées.* Limoge: Université de Bordeaux, 1988.

————. "Senghor, Negritude and Francophonie on the Threshhold of the Twenty-first Century." *Research in African Literatures* 21, 3 (Fall 1990): 51–57.

Kesteloot, Lilyan and Ellen C. Kennedy. "Negritude and Its American Sources." *Boston University Journal* 22, 11 (1974): 54–56.

Kesterloot, Lilyan; Barbey, Christian and Ndongo, Siré Mamadou. *Tyamaba, Mythe Peul, et ses rapports avec le rite, l'histoire et la géographie.* Notes Africaines, Université de Dakar, Institut Fondamental d'Afrique Noire. Nos. 185–186, 1985.

Knight, Vere W. "Negritude and the Isms." *Black Images* 3, 1 (1974): 3–20.

Knipp, Thomas R. "Negritude and Negation: The Poetry of Tchicaya U Tam'si." *Books Abroad* 48 (1974): 511–14.

Lindfors, Bernth. "Negritude and After: Responses to Colonialism and Independence in African Literatures." *Problems in National Literary Identity and the Writer as Social Critic.* Whitestone, NY: Council on National Literatures, 1980, pp. 29–37.

Logan, Paul E. "Leo Frobenius and Negritude." *Negro Historical Bulletin* 41 (1978): 794–96.

Lubin, Maurice A. "Les Débuts de la négritude en haiti." *Mélànge*, special issue of *Présence africaine* (1976): 284–308.

————. "David Diop et la génération de la négritude" in *David Diop: Temoignages—etudes.* Paris: Présence Africaine, 1979, pp. 108–11.

Luvai, A.I. "Negritude: A Redefinition." *Busara* 6, 11 (1974):79–90.

Madubuike, Ihechukwu. "What Negritude is Not: A Comment." *Renaissance* 2, 4 (1975), 27–29.

Mazrui, Ali A. "Negritude, the Talmudic Tradition and the Intellectual Performance of Blacks and Jews." *Hommage à Léopold Sédar Senghor.* Paris: Présence Africaine, 1976, pp. 300–26.

Metellus, Jean. "Identité et idéologies." *Négritude: Traditions et développement.* Brussels: Editions Complexes. 1978, pp. 63–75.

Miller, Christopher C. *Theories of Africans: Francophone Literature and Anthropology in Africa.* Chicago: University of Chicago Press, 1990.

Musanji, Ngalasso Mwatha. "Pour un humanisme de la francophonie? Réfléxion critique sur un discours de Senghor." *Présence francophone* 17 (1978): 69–78.

Ngal, Mbwila Mpaang. *Aimé Césaire. Un Homme à la recherche d'une patrie.* Dakar: Nouvelles Editions Africaine, 1975.

Ntonfo, André. "Jalons pour une autonomie de la littérature antillaise." *Présence francophone* 22 (1981): 141–56.

Palacios, Arnoldo. "Mondes et sangs en fusion: Négritude et latinité." *Hommage à Léopold Sédar Senghor: Homme de culture.* Paris: Présence Africaine, 1976, pp. 350–57.

Paratore, Éttore. "Négritude et culture classique dans la pensée de Senghor." *Ethiopiques* 14 (1978): 59–63.

Rácine, Daniel L. *Léon-Gontran Damas. 1912–1978: Founder of Negritude. A Memorial Casebook.* Washington, D.C.: University Press of America, 1979.

———. *Léon-Gontran Damas: L'Homme et l'oeuvre approchés.* Paris: Présence Africaine, 1983.

———. "A Profile of Léon-Gontran Damas." *Negro Historical Bulletin* 42 (1979): 61–63.

———. "Tribute." *Research in African Literatures* 10 (1979): 90–94.

Scharfman, Ronnie Leah. *Engagements and the Language of the Subject in the Poetry of Aimé Césaire.* Gainesville: University of Florida Press, 1987.

Senghor, Léopold Sédar. "Authenticité et négritude." *Zaire-Afrique* 102 (1976): 81–87.

———. *The Foundations of "Africanité" or "Négritude" and "Arabité."* Translation By Mercer Cook. Paris: Présence Africaine, 1971.

———. *Parôles.* Dakar: Nouvelles Editions Africaine, 1975.

———. "Poètes du Sénégal" *Poésie-1* 131 (1986): 8–128.

———. *Liberté 3: Négritude et civilisation de l'universel.* Paris: Seuil, 1977.

———. "Négritude et américanisme ou Let America Be America." *Ethiopiques* 4 (1975): 56–63.

Songolo, Aliko. *Aimé Césaire: Une poétique de la découverte.* Paris: L'Harmattan, 1985.

Souffrant, Claude. "L'Eclatement de la négritude sous le choc du développement." *Hommage à Léopold Sédar Senghor* Paris: Présence Africaine, 1976, pp. 374–93.

Steins, Martin. "Négritude: Un second souffle?" *Cultures et développement* 12, 1 (1980): 3–43.

Thomas, Louis-Vincent. "De l'oralité à l'écriture: Le Cas négro-africain." *Négritude: Traditions et développement.* Brussels: Editions Complexes, 1978, pp. 119–50.

Tito, Yisuku Gafudzi. *La Négritude et les tendances de la poésie contemporaine au zaire.* Kinshasa: Grue, 1977.

Tomich, Dale. "The Dialect of Colonialism and Culture: The Origins of the Negritude of Aimé Césaire." *Review of National Literatures* 2, 3 (1979): 351–85.

Trouillot, Henock. "Deux concepts de négritude en haiti." *Présence francophone* 12 (1976): 183–88.

Vaillant, Janet G. *Black, French and African: A Life of Léopold Sédar Senghor.* Cambridge: Harvard University Press, 1990.

Vantibah, Monsengo. "Négritude et situation actuelle." *Zaire* 391 (8 February 1976): 42–44.

Walker, Keith Louis. *La Cohésion de l'oeuvre césairienne.* Tubingen: G. Narr, 1979.

Wanjala, Chris L. "African Response to Negritude and Pan-Africanism." *Busara* 6, 1 (1974): 39–42.

Wylie, Hal. "Negritude and Beyond: The Quest for Identity and Meaning." *Interdisciplinary Dimensions of African Literature.* Edited by Kofi Anyodoho et al. Washington, D.C., Three Continents Press, 1985.

Zadi, Bernard Zaourou. *Césaire entre deux cultures: Problèmes théorétiques de la littérature négro-africaine d' aujourdui.* Abidjan: Nouvelles Editions Africaine, 1978.

INDEX

Index

403